Managing and Designing Online Courses in Ubiquitous Learning Environments

Gürhan Durak
Balıkesir University, Turkey

Serkan Çankaya
İzmir Democracy University, Turkey

A volume in the Advances in Mobile and Distance Learning (AMDL) Book Series

Published in the United States of America by
	IGI Global
	Information Science Reference (an imprint of IGI Global)
	701 E. Chocolate Avenue
	Hershey PA, USA 17033
	Tel: 717-533-8845
	Fax: 717-533-8661
	E-mail: cust@igi-global.com
	Web site: http://www.igi-global.com

Copyright © 2020 by IGI Global. All rights reserved. No part of this publication may be reproduced, stored or distributed in any form or by any means, electronic or mechanical, including photocopying, without written permission from the publisher. Product or company names used in this set are for identification purposes only. Inclusion of the names of the products or companies does not indicate a claim of ownership by IGI Global of the trademark or registered trademark.
	Library of Congress Cataloging-in-Publication Data

Names: Durak, Gurhan, 1984- author. | Cankaya, Serkan, 1979- author.
Title: Managing and designing online courses in ubiquitous learning
   environments / Gurhan Durak and Serkan Cankaya, Editors.
Description: Hershey, PA : Information Science Reference, [2020] | Summary:
   "This book examines the effective construction of ubiquitous learning
   environments and projections for the future of managing and designing
   ubiquitous learning environments"-- Provided by publisher.
Identifiers: LCCN 2019009421 | ISBN 9781522597797 (hardcover) | ISBN
   9781522597803 (paperback) | ISBN 9781522597810 (ebook)
Subjects: LCSH: Instructional systems--Design. | Distance education. |
   Classroom environment. | Ubiquitous computing.
Classification: LCC LB1028.38 .M26 2020 | DDC 371.3--dc23
LC record available at https://lccn.loc.gov/2019009421

This book is published in the IGI Global book series Advances in Mobile and Distance Learning (AMDL) (ISSN: 2327-1892; eISSN: 2327-1906)

British Cataloguing in Publication Data
A Cataloguing in Publication record for this book is available from the British Library.

All work contributed to this book is new, previously-unpublished material. The views expressed in this book are those of the authors, but not necessarily of the publisher.

For electronic access to this publication, please contact: eresources@igi-global.com.

Advances in Mobile and Distance Learning (AMDL) Book Series

Patricia Ordóñez de Pablos
Universidad de Oviedo, Spain

ISSN:2327-1892
EISSN:2327-1906

Mission

Private and public institutions have made great strides in the fields of mobile and distance learning in recent years, providing greater learning opportunities outside of a traditional classroom setting. While the online learning revolution has allowed for greater learning opportunities, it has also presented numerous challenges for students and educators alike. As research advances, online educational settings can continue to develop and advance the technologies available for learners of all ages.

The **Advances in Mobile and Distance Learning** (AMDL) Book Series publishes research encompassing a variety of topics related to all facets of mobile and distance learning. This series aims to be an essential resource for the timeliest research to help advance the development of new educational technologies and pedagogy for use in online classrooms.

Coverage

- Educational Presentation and Delivery
- Location-Based Integration
- Economics of Distance and M-Learning
- Online Collaborative Learning
- Student-Teacher Interaction
- Course Design
- Online Class Management
- Cloud Computing in Schools
- Managing Sustainable Learning
- Globalization

IGI Global is currently accepting manuscripts for publication within this series. To submit a proposal for a volume in this series, please contact our Acquisition Editors at Acquisitions@igi-global.com or visit: http://www.igi-global.com/publish/.

The Advances in Mobile and Distance Learning (AMDL) Book Series (ISSN 2327-1892) is published by IGI Global, 701 E. Chocolate Avenue, Hershey, PA 17033-1240, USA, www.igi-global.com. This series is composed of titles available for purchase individually; each title is edited to be contextually exclusive from any other title within the series. For pricing and ordering information please visit http://www.igi-global.com/book-series/advances-mobile-distance-learning/37162. Postmaster: Send all address changes to above address. ©© 2020 IGI Global. All rights, including translation in other languages reserved by the publisher. No part of this series may be reproduced or used in any form or by any means – graphics, electronic, or mechanical, including photocopying, recording, taping, or information and retrieval systems – without written permission from the publisher, except for non commercial, educational use, including classroom teaching purposes. The views expressed in this series are those of the authors, but not necessarily of IGI Global.

Titles in this Series

For a list of additional titles in this series, please visit: www.igi-global.com/book-series

Advancing Mobile Learning in Contemporary Educational Spaces
Dominic Mentor (Columbia University, USA)
Information Science Reference • ©2019 • 394pp • H/C (ISBN: 9781522593515) • US $195.00

Student Support Toward Self-Directed Learning in Open and Distributed Environments
Micheal M. van Wyk (University of South Africa, South Africa)
Information Science Reference • ©2019 • 321pp • H/C (ISBN: 9781522593164) • US $195.00

Administrative Leadership in Open and Distance Learning Programs
Koksal Buyuk (Anadolu University, Turkey) Serpil Kocdar (Anadolu University, Turkey) and Aras Bozkurt (Anadolu University, Turkey)
Information Science Reference • ©2018 • 378pp • H/C (ISBN: 9781522526452) • US $195.00

Empowering Learners With Mobile Open-Access Learning Initiatives
Michael Mills (University of Central Arkansas, USA) and Donna Wake (University of Central Arkansas, USA)
Information Science Reference • ©2017 • 357pp • H/C (ISBN: 9781522521228) • US $190.00

Handbook of Research on Mobile Devices and Applications in Higher Education Settings
Laura Briz-Ponce (University of Salamanca, Spain) Juan Antonio Juanes-Méndez (University of Salamanca, Spain) and Francisco José García-Peñalvo (University of Salamanca, Spain)
Information Science Reference • ©2016 • 608pp • H/C (ISBN: 9781522502562) • US $300.00

Handbook of Research on Mobile Learning in Contemporary Classrooms
Dominic Mentor (Teachers College, Columbia University, USA)
Information Science Reference • ©2016 • 475pp • H/C (ISBN: 9781522502517) • US $300.00

Mobile and Blended Learning Innovations for Improved Learning Outcomes
David Parsons (The Mind Lab by Unitec, New Zealand)
Information Science Reference • ©2016 • 366pp • H/C (ISBN: 9781522503590) • US $185.00

Integrating Touch-Enabled and Mobile Devices into Contemporary Mathematics Education
Maria Meletiou-Mavrotheris (European University Cyprus, Cyprus) Katerina Mavrou (European University Cyprus, Cyprus) and Efi Paparistodemou (Cyprus Pedagogical Institute, Cyprus)
Information Science Reference • ©2015 • 341pp • H/C (ISBN: 9781466687141) • US $190.00

701 East Chocolate Avenue, Hershey, PA 17033, USA
Tel: 717-533-8845 x100 • Fax: 717-533-8661
E-Mail: cust@igi-global.com • www.igi-global.com

Table of Contents

Preface xv

Acknowledgment xix

Chapter 1
Online Learning Support in a Ubiquitous Learning Environment 1
    Ramashego Shila Mphahlele, University of South Africa, South Africa

Chapter 2
A Specified Ubiquitous Learning Design for Seamless Learning 19
    Ibrahim Emin Deryal, Ministry of National Education (MoNE), Turkey
    Veysel Demirer, Suleyman Demirel University, Turkey

Chapter 3
Supporting Digital Information Literacy in the Age of Open Access: Considerations for Online
Course Design 52
    Sarah Felber, University of Maryland Global Campus, USA
    Pascal Roubides, University of Maryland Global Campus, USA

Chapter 4
Learning Communities: Theory and Practice of Leveraging Social Media for Learning 72
    Heather Robinson, University of North Texas, USA
    Whitney Kilgore, University of North Texas, USA
    Aras Bozkurt, Anadolu University, Turkey & University of South Africa, South Africa

Chapter 5
Enhancing Personal Professional Development Through Technology Integration: The Need for
Ubiquitous Learning 92
    Özden Şahin İzmirli, Çanakkale Onsekiz Mart University, Turkey
    Gökhan Çalışkan, Çanakkale Onsekiz Mart University, Turkey

Chapter 6
Seamless Learning Design Criteria in the Context of Open and Distance Learning 106
    Erkan Yetik, Eskişehir Osmangazi University, Turkey
    Nilgun Ozdamar, Anadolu University, Turkey
    Aras Bozkurt, Anadolu University, Turkey & University of South Africa, South Africa

Chapter 7
Supporting Learners with Special Needs in Open and Distance Learning.. 128
    Hakan Genc, Anadolu University, Turkey
    Serpil Kocdar, Anadolu University, Turkey

Chapter 8
The Contribution of Information Communication Technologies in Online Career Counseling:
Case Study of an Online Community Within Higher Education 152
    Nikolaos Mouratoglou, Aristotle University of Thessaloniki, Greece
    George K. Zarifis, Aristotle University of Thessaloniki, Greece

Chapter 9
Ubiquitous Learning for New Generation Learners' Expectations... 176
    Tarık Kişla, Ege University, Turkey
    Bahar Karaoğlan, Ege University, Turkey

Chapter 10
Considering Social Presence in the Designing of Ubiquitous Learning Environments 201
    Serkan İzmirli, Çanakkale Onsekiz Mart University, Turkey

Chapter 11
From Ubiquitous to Ubiquitous Blended Learning Environments 215
    Alev Ateş-Çobanoğlu, Ege University, Turkey

Chapter 12
The Challenges and Opportunities of Partnership in Establishing Online Postgraduate
Provision 233
    Faye Taylor, Nottingham Trent University, UK

Chapter 13
A Framework for Developing Open Distance E-Learning Curriculum for Library and Information
Science (LIS) Programme in Eswatini.. 244
    Vusi W. Tsabedze, University of South Africa, South Africa

Chapter 14
The Usability of Mobile Devices in Distance Learning 262
    Fırat Sarsar, Ege University, Turkey
    Tarık Kişla, Ege University, Turkey
    Melih Karasu, Ege University, Turkey
    Yüksel Deniz Arıkan, Ege University, Turkey
    Murat Kılıç, Ege University, Turkey

Chapter 15
Ubiquitous Learning and Heutagogy in Teacher Education 279
    Beril Ceylan, Ege University, Turkey

Chapter 16
Transition From E-Learning to U-Learning: Basic Characteristics, Media, and Researches 296
    Alaattin Parlakkılıç, Ufuk University, Turkey

Compilation of References 311

About the Contributors 349

Index 354

Detailed Table of Contents

Preface xv

Acknowledgment xix

Chapter 1
Online Learning Support in a Ubiquitous Learning Environment 1
    Ramashego Shila Mphahlele, University of South Africa, South Africa

The ubiquitous learning environment (ULE) is both an ontological and epistemological problem. For most scholars, ULE provides an interoperable, pervasive, and seamless learning architecture to connect, integrate, and share three major dimensions of learning resources: learning collaborators, learning contents, and learning services. Furthermore, ULE is described as an educational paradigm that mainly uses technology for curriculum delivery. Through reflection and exploration, this chapter argues that online learning support has a symbiotic relationship with ULE because the student, at some point, should move beyond the "text" level into concepts and conceptual organization schemes (ontologies). In line with this viewpoint, this chapter problematizes the gap created by real-world and digital-world resources—and argues that online learning support for teaching and learning processes have not yet emulated ULE as an important pedagogical resource.

Chapter 2
A Specified Ubiquitous Learning Design for Seamless Learning 19
    Ibrahim Emin Deryal, Ministry of National Education (MoNE), Turkey
    Veysel Demirer, Suleyman Demirel University, Turkey

Seamless learning and ubiquitous learning are nested concepts and they may be confused notions without elaborating definitions and implications. In this chapter, seamless learning is handled deeply, and ubiquitous computing and ubiquitous learning concepts are explained. Seamless learning is explained through the definition stated by Kuh and implications carried out by numerous researchers who conducted many studies in the field. Each implication and study are analyzed and elaborated carefully in order to propose an efficient seamless learning management system. In addition to those analyses, after explaining ubiquitous computing and ubiquitous learning concepts, MOOCs are mentioned in order to give a well applied ubiquitous learning system. Finally depending on seamless learning fundamentals (stated by authors) an efficient seamless learning management system is proposed.

Chapter 3
Supporting Digital Information Literacy in the Age of Open Access: Considerations for Online Course Design 52
    Sarah Felber, University of Maryland Global Campus, USA
    Pascal Roubides, University of Maryland Global Campus, USA

In this chapter, the authors aim to inform the audience about the issues pertaining to access to educational resources, with a focus on open access; how to access such sources; ways of integrating principles of information literacy into the entire educational experience; and the potential of open access sources in providing much needed, affordable information literacy to all knowledge seekers, especially in academic endeavors. The issue of information literacy and open access is defined and explored, with a bias toward practical implementation and impact in the academic setting, culminating in hands-on recommendations for academic professionals.

Chapter 4
Learning Communities: Theory and Practice of Leveraging Social Media for Learning 72
    Heather Robinson, University of North Texas, USA
    Whitney Kilgore, University of North Texas, USA
    Aras Bozkurt, Anadolu University, Turkey & University of South Africa, South Africa

The purpose of this chapter is to present the similarities and differences of three learning communities: communities of practice (CoPs), professional learning communities (PLCs), and professional learning networks (PLNs). For this purpose, researchers adopted a qualitative phenomenological approach and interviews with three connected educators and content area experts were conducted regarding their views, perceptions, and experiences of the various learning communities and how technology (specifically Twitter) is used as part of their learning in an open community. Additionally, the interviews helped explain the current practices in community development and support, the evolution from a lurker to a contributor to a community leader, and the evolution from a community to a network.

Chapter 5
Enhancing Personal Professional Development Through Technology Integration: The Need for Ubiquitous Learning 92
    Özden Şahin İzmirli, Çanakkale Onsekiz Mart University, Turkey
    Gökhan Çalışkan, Çanakkale Onsekiz Mart University, Turkey

In this chapter, personal professional development trainings, which need to include ubiquitous learning environments, are discussed. First of all, professional development is explained. Then, the authors discussed factors affecting the efficiency of professional development activities and how they can incorporate new technologies into professional development activities to meet the needs of adult learners. After that, based on the definition of ubiquitous learning, ways of using technology in terms of meeting adult needs with professional development are examined. Finally, the process that was evaluated within the framework of technology integration is presented to readers.

Chapter 6
Seamless Learning Design Criteria in the Context of Open and Distance Learning 106
    Erkan Yetik, Eskişehir Osmangazi University, Turkey
    Nilgun Ozdamar, Anadolu University, Turkey
    Aras Bozkurt, Anadolu University, Turkey & University of South Africa, South Africa

Seamless learning is a form of learning whereby, regardless of location, the learning process, as it relates to learning needs and readiness, can continue through the aid of technology. Seamless learning environments are spaces that can be accessed independent of time and place through mobile or stationary devices, and that are equipped with technologies capable of meeting learning needs. With the advancements in technology, seamless learning environments are becoming increasingly popular. In this regard, the design of environments that are suitable for seamless learning in open and distance learning (ODL) fields is of critical importance. This study aimed to determine the criteria for the design of seamless learning environments in the context of ODL. In line with this aim, the Delphi technique, a qualitative research approach, was used. A total of 47 criteria under 10 different themes were identified in the study.

Chapter 7
Supporting Learners with Special Needs in Open and Distance Learning... 128
    Hakan Genc, Anadolu University, Turkey
    Serpil Kocdar, Anadolu University, Turkey

Open and distance learning (ODL) systems provide learners with a flexible learning environment independent of time and place. However, the advantage of this flexibility may turn out a disadvantage if the learners do not find a solution to problems they may face before, during, and after the learning process. In eliminating this disadvantage, learner support services play an important role. The quality of support services has a direct impact on learner retention and academic success. Especially, for the learners with special needs, the quality of support services has a particular importance. Within this context, in this chapter, the authors address accommodations for learners with special needs in ODL. First, this chapter focuses on support services in ODL, then learners with special needs in ODL and what accommodations learners with special needs require according to their disability type. Finally, the authors exemplify the accommodations for learners with special needs in ODL institutions and offer recommendations.

Chapter 8
The Contribution of Information Communication Technologies in Online Career Counseling:
Case Study of an Online Community Within Higher Education 152
    Nikolaos Mouratoglou, Aristotle University of Thessaloniki, Greece
    George K. Zarifis, Aristotle University of Thessaloniki, Greece

Information communication technologies have undoubtedly affected the discipline of career counselling. Nevertheless, online career counselling remains a rather limited practice in Greece; therefore, the chapter attempts to contribute to the wider dialogue that has been addressed so far, by focusing on the design, implementation, and assessment of an online career counselling program for higher education students and graduates. The purpose of the study is to present the main parameters related to participants' learning experience, such as motivation, barriers to participation, as well as adopted strategies for overcoming these barriers during the online program. The researchers conducted 15 semi-structured interviews to collect data for summative assessment. The analysis of the data indicates that prior acknowledgement of learners' motivation, educator/career counsellor's role, the learning environment, the methods utilized, and the teaching material can maximize the effectiveness of equivalent programs, due to the fulfillment of their needs, goals, and expectations.

Chapter 9
Ubiquitous Learning for New Generation Learners' Expectations 176
Tarık Kişla, Ege University, Turkey
Bahar Karaoğlan, Ege University, Turkey

It cannot be denied that environmental influence has a great effect on the characteristics of individuals: reason why people can be profiled with their generation. Generation is a collection of lifespans which fall into a time duration when major changes have occurred. The last decades are labeled as information and technology era where the world is witnessing great changes in lifestyles that go in parallel with the speed of evolving digital technology. Young people born after 2000 are categorized as "Generation Z," who are born into a world of IT technology and are independent, social individuals competent in using technology and mostly interested in technology-driven/enabled events and devices. Due to this fact, portable/wearable smart devices may be used to offer new opportunities for delivering education tailored according to situational needs and preferences of these people. In this chapter, after touching distinctive characteristics of the generations, concepts regarding ubiquitous learning and how it aligns with the aspirations and values of Generation Z are highlighted.

Chapter 10
Considering Social Presence in the Designing of Ubiquitous Learning Environments 201
Serkan İzmirli, Çanakkale Onsekiz Mart University, Turkey

Ubiquitous learning is an emerging research area in which learning occurs at the right time, in the right place, with the help of various technologies. Since ubiquitous learning helps to improve learning, motivation, and creativity, effective ubiquitous learning environments should be designed. Theories, models, and strategies should be considered to design these environments. One of these models is the community of inquiry approach, which has three elements: social presence, teaching presence, and cognitive presence. In this study, social presence is selected as a focus. In this context, the purpose of the study is to present techniques for establishing social presence in ubiquitous learning environments. In line with this purpose, first, ubiquitous learning and social presence are explained. Then, techniques to establish social presence in ubiquitous learning environments are expressed. Following on, a sample ubiquitous learning environment (a ubiquitous history museum) is designed and presented, considering social presence as a specific element.

Chapter 11
From Ubiquitous to Ubiquitous Blended Learning Environments 215
Alev Ateş-Çobanoğlu, Ege University, Turkey

As advances in information and communication technology increasingly transform learning and teaching; blended learning and ubiquitous learning concepts have gained attention and become pervasive in 21st century. With the help of recent advances in mobile learning, wireless networks, RFID tags, a new model of blended learning—ubiquitous blended learning—that takes advantage of increasing ubiquity of online devices in online phase of blended learning is considered to gain attention in designing online courses. In this chapter, the author presents a picture of ubiquitous and blended learning studies while focusing on the results of ubiquitous learning and suggesting a rationale for such designs. The author defines ubiquitous blended learning as an instructional design approach that integrates ubiquitous technologies involved on-line and/or virtual learning with face-to-face learning by decreasing seat-time in class and increasing outdoor learning activities to facilitate learning from not just the teacher but from peer to peer and on-line learning communities as well.

Chapter 12
The Challenges and Opportunities of Partnership in Establishing Online Postgraduate Provision 233
Faye Taylor, Nottingham Trent University, UK

This chapter shares some of the 'lessons learned' from the author's perspective of adopting a higher education services provider as partner for the design, development, and delivery of online postgraduate provision. Ultimately, partnering with a higher education services provider for the development of online learning offers distinct benefits in terms of marketing support, project management, and instructional design but the key to ensuring the partnership works effectively and impacts positively upon student experience, is to ensure a clear delineation of roles and responsibilities from the outset, avoid unnecessary shifts in personnel, and have a system of monitoring and control in place from the university's perspective to ensure that roles and responsibilities within the partnership are being upheld.

Chapter 13
A Framework for Developing Open Distance E-Learning Curriculum for Library and Information Science (LIS) Programme in Eswatini.. 244
Vusi W. Tsabedze, University of South Africa, South Africa

The dependency by foreign countries institutions such as South Africa, Botswana, and Namibia for library and information science (LIS) training and development of staff members, to acquire higher education, has become expensive and complex for Eswatini government to handle. The expensive nature and complex situation of sending employees out of the country for training has paralysed most of the organisation due to their absence from operations in the office. This study therefore seeks to investigate, developing open distance e-learning curriculum for LIS programme in Eswatini. The University of Eswatini (UNESWA), which is one among other institution of higher learning in the country, does not offer any programme in LIS. Considering this situation in Eswatini, this chapter proposes a framework for developing the ODeL curriculum for LIS. Such a programme could be offered through the UNESWA to accommodate students within and outside the country. Thus, ensuring Eswatini becomes a player in LIS space within the African continent.

Chapter 14
The Usability of Mobile Devices in Distance Learning 262
    Fırat Sarsar, Ege University, Turkey
    Tarık Kişla, Ege University, Turkey
    Melih Karasu, Ege University, Turkey
    Yüksel Deniz Arıkan, Ege University, Turkey
    Murat Kılıç, Ege University, Turkey

Thanks to technological developments, distance education helped new techniques and strategies to emerge in the instruction field. However, these developments may cause problems about integration of the interaction between students and instructors. Communication is seen as one of the biggest problems. Instructors' online communications and their attitudes towards this process affect quality of teaching and learning processes. Other factors affecting this process are learning environment and its effective use. This study is designed to incorporate a mixed method with the aim of reflecting instructors' experiences about different communication techniques and learning environments. In scope of this research, the researchers planned a four-week process using the communication that the researchers have been establishing with Ege University Faculty of Education's instructors. The researchers will use different mobile devices and feedback methods for the process.

Chapter 15
Ubiquitous Learning and Heutagogy in Teacher Education 279
    Beril Ceylan, Ege University, Turkey

The learning and teaching horizon is changing nowadays. Learner-centered learning is preferable to teacher-centered learning. Teachers and learners prefer mobility and flexibility in education. Ubiquitous learning provides the flexibility and connection with mobility. Due to advantages of technology use, ubiquitous learning is preferred for individual and public learning. Heutagogy emphasizes the capability of learners' self-regulation process. Heutagogical learning occurs at two levels. The first level is competencies. The second level is deeper learning. In heutagogy, learners design their learning situation in a non-linear learning approach in a flexible way. In this chapter, heutagogy and ubiquitous learning connection will be discussed in the light of literature in the context of education and teacher education. A heutagogical ubiquitous learning interaction will be offered.

Chapter 16
Transition From E-Learning to U-Learning: Basic Characteristics, Media, and Researches 296
    Alaattin Parlakkılıç, Ufuk University, Turkey

E-learning systems have increased the prevalence of information and computer technologies in education. U-learning is a modern teaching system based on the use of computer technologies (ubiquitous computing technology) everywhere in the environment of existing wired, wireless, mobile, and sensor systems. The interaction between information, object/device, and user/learner/student is formed at any time, anywhere, and form in the communication environment called u-environment. In u-learning, the presence of information in objects (embeded) and mobility is the highest. Training services are among mobile systems and sensors that can move independently in the environment. The status of the learners is followed due to the characteristics of the server systems and objects. Researches on u-learning are ongoing. Especially u-learning system theory and application methods are being investigated. Most of the researches are about u-learning applications rather than u-learning framework. This chapter focuses on basic features, media, and research in the transition from e-learning to u-learning.

Compilation of References 311

About the Contributors 349

Index 354

Preface

In the market there are a lot of new jobs which did not exist ten years ego. Hence the market needs new skills from the employees continuously. To deal with this change, an effective lifelog learning is necessary (Jung, 2014). As a result of this need and the technological developments, especially in mobile technologies, the importance of Ubiquitous Learning Environments (ULE) have increased. ULE is the environment where the learners can choose the way, the time, and the context in which they prefer to learn (Sharples, 2000). For an effective ULE, the environment which can be accessed anytime, anywhere, by any means like handheld devices, wearable devices, computers, should be designed and managed well by taking example of the experiences in literature.

ULE is an integrated environment that contains educational institutions, learners, parents, tools etc. (Zhang, Zhang, & Liu, 2013). It can be said that ULE is basically based on individual self-directed learning. So, it should meet the preferences of different learners that some learners may prefer individualized learning and some other learners may prefer collaborative learning. In the design of ULE, pedagogy and learning theories should be taken into consideration. In a study, it was stated that the knowledge about learner's profile and needs; the context; the educational paradigm or model and the technological qualifications are the basic four aspects in the design of ULEs (Saccol et al., 2009).

Because of the support of different contexts, ULEs are called as context-aware (Kalaivani & Sivakumar, 2017; Piovesan, Passerino, & Medina, 2012; Saccol et al., 2009). Environment, device and user are tree important components for context-aware ULEs and should be taken into consideration in the design of ULEs. Environment is the surrounding conditions of the learner like temperature, air conditioning, cleanness, noise, etc. Device context is the learners' preferred devices to connect to the ULE. User context is the learning preferences of learners. In other words, ULE is supposed to satisfy the needs of learmers in the presence of mobility. Hence ULEs should be developed as flexible, adaptable and intelligent (Kalaivani & Sivakumar, 2017). On the other hands, Shotsberger and Vetter (2000) stated that ULEs should have the features of ubiquity, self-directed learning, mobility, interactivity, personalization (context customization), accessibility, and portability. In an another study, Saccol et al. (2009) proposed a design framework for ULE in which they considered four aspects of ULE: learner's profiles and needs, contextual elements (physical, temporal, social), educational paradigm, the possibilities and limitations of mobile and wireless Technologies with the basic design principles in mind.

Consequently, understanding the different perspectives of ubiquitous learning will empower education administrators and professionals, educators, researchers, course designers who are interested with ubiquitous learning. Managing and Designing Online Courses in Ubiquitous Learning Environments is a vital reference source that will help institutions to offer ubiquitous learning environments. This reference source boasts 16 chapters that were carefully selected through a robust double-blind peer review. Brief descriptions of each of the chapters can be found in the following paragraphs:

In Chapter 1, "Online Learning Support in a Ubiquitous Learning Environment," the author Dr. Ramashego Shila Mphahlele from The University of South Africa, South Africa, argues that online learning support has a symbiotic relationship with ULE because the student, at some point, should move beyond the "text" level into concepts and conceptual organization schemes (ontologies). In line with this viewpoint, the chapter problematizes the gap created by real-world and digital-world resources and argues that online learning support for teaching and learning processes have not yet emulated ULE as an important pedagogical resource.

In Chapter 2, "A Specified Ubiquitous Learning Design for Seamless Learning," the authors İbrahim Emin Deryal from National Ministry of Education, Turkey and Dr. Veysel Demirer from Süleyman Demirel University, Turkey, propose a specified ubiquitous learning design for seamless learning. They discuss seamless learning fundamentals for designing utilizable seamless learning environments. As a result, they state that Seamless Learning Fundamentals can be considered as a trigger force of all studies on establishing a ubiquitous learning system serving seamless learning environments.

In Chapter 3, "Supporting Digital Information Literacy in the Age of Open Access: Considerations for Online Course Design," the authors Dr. Sarah Felber and Dr. Pascal Roubides from The University of Maryland University College, United States, provide discussion for online course designers on preparing learners for high levels of digital information literacy. The chapter includes trends in open access publishing of which online course designers should be aware; discusses of the role of libraries in helping learners obtain open access materials; and proposes the use of the Association of College & Research Libraries' Framework for Information Literacy for Higher Education as a lens for understanding what concepts are important to learners when working with open access materials.

In Chapter 4, "Learning Communities: Theory and Practice of Leveraging Social Media for Learning," the authors Dr. Heather Robinson and Dr. Whitney Kilgore from The University of North Texas, United States and Dr. Aras Bozkurt from Anadolu University & The University of South Africa, provide clear definitions of three types of learning communities: Communities of Practice, Professional Learning Communities, and Professional Learning Networks. This includes descriptions of their key characteristics, practices, and underlying theory, which are also synthesized in the review of literature. The authors also clarify how and why learning networks are formed, the characteristics of these networks, and the role technologies play in a learning community.

In Chapter 5, "Enhancing Personal Professional Development Through the Technology Integration: The Need for Ubiquitous Learning," the authors Dr. Özden Şahin İzmirli and Gökhan Çalışkan from Çanakkale Onsekiz Mart University, Turkey, discuss the personal professional development trainings which need to include ubiquitous learning environments. The chapter examines the ways of using technology in terms of meeting adult needs with professional development based on the definition of Ubiquitous Learning.

In Chapter 6, "Seamless Learning Design Criteria in the Context of Open and Distance Learning," the authors Erkan Yetik from Eskisehir Osmangazi University, Turkey, Dr. Nilgun Ozdamar from Anadolu University, Turkey and Aras Bozkurt from Anadolu University & University of South Africa, aim to determine the criteria for the design of seamless learning environments in the context of open and distance learning. They identified a total of 47 criteria under 10 different themes by utilizing the Delphi technique.

Preface

In Chapter 7, "Supporting Learners With Special Needs in Open and Distance Learning," the authors Hakan Genç and Dr. Serpil Koçdar from Anadolu University, Turkey, address accommodations for learners with special needs in open distance learning (ODL). First, the chapter focuses on support services in ODL then, learners with special needs in ODL and what accommodations learners with special needs require according to their disability type. Finally, the authors exemplify the accommodations for learners with special needs in ODL institutions and offer recommendations.

In Chapter 8, "The Contribution of Information Communication Technologies in Online Career Counseling: Case Study of an Online Community Within Higher Education," the authors Nikolaos Mouratoglou and Dr. George K. Zarifis from Aristotle University of Thessaloniki, Greece, present the main parameters related to participants' learning experience, such as motivation, barriers to participation, as well as adopted strategies for overcoming these barriers during the online career counselling program for Higher Education students and graduates. They state that prior acknowledgement of learners' motivation, educator/career counsellor's role, the learning environment, the methods utilized, and the teaching material can maximize the effectiveness of equivalent programs, due to the fulfillment of their needs, goals and expectations.

In Chapter 9, "Ubiquitous Learning for New Generation Learners' Expectations," the authors Dr. Tarık Kışla and Dr. Bahar Karaoğlan from Ege University, Turkey, explains the distinctive characteristics of the generations, and show how the general characteristics of generation z is aligned with the ubiquitous educational features enabled by IT, based on a qualitative analysis of the thoughts of the generation on ubiquitous learning.

In Chapter 10, "Considering Social Presence in the Designing of Ubiquitous Learning Environments", the author, Serkan İzmirli from Çanakkale Onsekiz Mart University, Turkey, presents techniques for establishing social presence in ubiquitous learning environments. Then he designs and presents a sample ubiquitous learning environment (a ubiquitous history museum) considering social presence as a specific element.

In Chapter 11, "From Ubiquitous to Ubiquitous Blended Learning Environments," the author Dr. Alev Ateş-Çobanoğlu from Ege University, Turkey, defines Ubiquitous Blended Learning (U-blended learning) as an instructional design approach which integrates ubiquitous technologies involved online and/or virtual learning with face-to-face learning by decreasing seat-time in class and increasing outdoor learning activities to facilitate learning from not just the teacher but from peer to peer and on-line learning communities as well. According to the author, U-blended designs aim to integrate in and outside class learning experiences meaningfully for reaching the goals of instruction.

In Chapter 12, "The Challenges and Opportunities of Partnership in Establishing Online Postgraduate Provision," the author Dr. Faye Taylor from Nottingham Business School, Nottingham Trent University, England, shares her perspective, of adopting a Higher Education Services provider as partner for the design, development and delivery of online postgraduate provision. She states that the partnership may be beneficial in terms of marketing support, project management and instructional design, if certain conditions are set like ensuring a clear delineation of roles and responsibilities, avoiding unnecessary shifts in personnel and having a system of monitoring and control.

In Chapter 13, "A framework for Developing Open Distance E-Learning Curriculum for Library and Information Science (LIS) Programme in Eswatini," the author Dr. Vusi Tsabedze from The University of South Africa, South Africa, proposes a framework for developing the open distance e-learning curriculum for the Library and Information Science (LIS) programme. He argues that a LIS programme offered through the University of Eswatini by utilizing the proposed framework could make the Eswatini a player in LIS space within the African continent.

In Chapter 14, "The Usability of Mobile Devices in Distance Learning," the authors Dr. Fırat Sarsar, Dr. Tarık Kışla, Melih Karasu, Dr. Yüksel Deniz Arıkan and Murat Kılıç from Ege University, Turkey, aim of reflecting instructors' experiences about different communication techniques and learning environments. As a result, they found that screen sizes are a decisive and significant feature for mobile devices to be used in distance education. In addition, touch screen pen use, keyboard use, camera opening problems, ergonomic problems, internet and quota problems are the other factors affecting the distance education process.

In Chapter 15, "Ubiquitous Learning and Heutagogy in Teacher Education," the author Beril Ceylan from Ege University, Turkey, discusses heutagogy and the ubiquitous learning connection with literature in the context of education and teacher education. The chapter shows that the characteristics of both heutagogy and ubiquitous learning are similar, and both these structures emphasize individualism and accessibility.

In Chapter 16, "Transition From E-Learning to U-Learning: Basic Characteristics, Media, and Researches," the author Alaattin Parlakkılıç from Ufuk University, Turkey, focuses on basic features, media and research in the transition from e-learning to u-learning. The chapter presents the basic characteristics and advantages of u-learning, proposes a framework and reveals the current trends in u-learning.

REFERENCES

Jung, H.-J. (2014). Ubiquitous Learning: Determinants Impacting Learners' Satisfaction and Performance With Smartphones. *Language Learning & Technology*, *18*(3), 97–119. doi:10.21614/chirurgia.111.5.379

Kalaivani, R., & Sivakumar, R. (2017). A Survey on context-aware ubiquitous learning systems. *International Journal of Control Theory and Applications*, *10*(23), 111–124.

Piovesan, S. D., Passerino, L. M., & Medina, R. D. (2012). U-ALS : A Ubiquitous Learning Environment. In *IADIS International Conference on Cognition and Exploratory Learning in Digital Age (CELDA 2012)* (pp. 197–204). Academic Press.

Saccol, A. Z., Reinhard, N., Kich, M., Barbosa, J. L. V., Schlemmer, E., & Hahn, R. (2009). A framework for the design of ubiquitous learning applications. *Proceedings of the 42nd Annual Hawaii International Conference on System Sciences, HICSS*, 1–10. 10.1109/HICSS.2009.13

Sharples, M. (2000). The design of personal mobile technologies for lifelong learning. *Computers & Education*, *34*(3-4), 177–193. doi:10.1016/S0360-1315(99)00044-5

Shotsberger, P. G., & Vetter, R. (2000). The Handheld Web: How Mobile Wireless Technologies Will Change Web-based Instruction and Training. *Educational Technology*, *40*(5), 49–52. doi:10.2307/44428613

Zhang, J., Zhang, L., & Liu, B. (2013). A Design of Ubiquitous Learning Environment with the Support of Pervasive Computing. *Applied Mechanics and Materials*, *397–400*, 2483–2486. doi:10.4028/www.scientific.net/AMM.397-400.2483

Acknowledgment

We received high quality submissions from global researchers interested in this subject area. All submitted chapters to this book underwent a robust double-blind peer review process in order to achieve the highest level of quality and accuracy. We are thankful to all of our reviewers for providing their expertise and their rigorous and unbiased assessment of the chapters assigned to them.

We would also like to convey our gratitude to Maria Rohde, Assistant Development Editor, for assisting us with editorial activities related to this publication. Additionally, we would like to thank the IGI Global Sales and Marketing Department for their support in promoting this publication.

Thank you to everyone who has contributed to this publication.

Gürhan Durak
Balıkesir University, Turkey

Serkan Çankaya
İzmir Democracy University, Turkey

Chapter 1
Online Learning Support in a Ubiquitous Learning Environment

Ramashego Shila Mphahlele

https://orcid.org/0000-0002-9917-7089

University of South Africa, South Africa

ABSTRACT

The ubiquitous learning environment (ULE) is both an ontological and epistemological problem. For most scholars, ULE provides an interoperable, pervasive, and seamless learning architecture to connect, integrate, and share three major dimensions of learning resources: learning collaborators, learning contents, and learning services. Furthermore, ULE is described as an educational paradigm that mainly uses technology for curriculum delivery. Through reflection and exploration, this chapter argues that online learning support has a symbiotic relationship with ULE because the student, at some point, should move beyond the "text" level into concepts and conceptual organization schemes (ontologies). In line with this viewpoint, this chapter problematizes the gap created by real-world and digital-world resources—and argues that online learning support for teaching and learning processes have not yet emulated ULE as an important pedagogical resource.

DOI: 10.4018/978-1-5225-9779-7.ch001

INTRODUCTION

The Ubiquitous Learning Environment (ULE) has become a central issue for curriculum delivery in the 21st century and remains most instrumental in the digital world. Notwithstanding the fact that ULE enables learning at any time and place, it is a pre-condition for the student to be familiar with languages like Hypertext Markup Language revision 5 (HTML5), Structured Query Language (SQL), Resource Description Framework (RDF), and Web Ontology Language (OWL), to name a few. Furthermore, the student at some point should move beyond the 'text' level into concepts and conceptual organization schemes (ontologies). Once the student has moved into the conceptual processing realm (Artificial Intelligence), very important and exciting functionalities like knowledge inference (reasoning) can then be provided—functionalities which will mark a true technological turning point in the student's learning (Mikelloydtech, 2013).

Against this background, it can be argued that ULE places varying demands on delivery and feedback methods and relies on different levels of knowledge and skills. That being the case, this chapter aims to

1. Delineate the importance of planning online learning support when managing and designing online courses in the ULE;
2. Explore the prominence of online learning support in the ULE; and
3. Reflect on the symbiotic relationship between online learning support and ULE in order to close the gap created by real-world and digital-world resources.

BACKGROUND

The ULE is described by Calimag, Miguel, Conde, and Aquino (2014: 119) as "being any setting wherein students can become totally immersed in the learning process". Researchers with a similar view include Chin and Chen (2013), who consider ULE as being a complementary teaching technique that reduces both time and location constraints within the learning environment. Previous studies (such as Jones & Jo, 2004; Calimag et al., 2014) have considered ULE as being a new hope for the future of education. Nevertheless, as new technologies have evolved—and as more ubiquitous forms of technology have emerged—the need for online learning support has become evident in order to achieve core capabilities of ULE. There are six core capabilities of ULE (as described by Kwon, 2011):

1. Cognitive capability,
2. Relational capability,
3. Emotional capability,
4. Adaptability,
5. Technology literacy, and
6. Effective learning ability.

The aforementioned capabilities can be realized, provided the following identified challenges can be addressed:

- Gaining and retaining the motivation of the students (Calimag et al., 2014);
- Identifying when and how technologies are best deployed, including the appropriate matching of devices with students and learning outcomes in the effective design of learning activities (Agarwal & Nath, 2011); and
- Limited access for marginalized communities in the African continent (Letseka, Letseka, & Pitsoe, 2018).

This section has demonstrated that in the ULE, some students may need to balance different capabilities mentioned above. For example, balancing cognitive capability with technology literacy, will improve the limitations of students' (created by barriers which are discussed in the next section) cognitive capabilities such as memory, thinking and problem solving capabilities, and to transfer some of the low level tasks such as calculations, storage and information retrieval to the computer.

The following section explores the barriers to students' ubiquitous learning and the importance of planning online learning support when managing and designing online courses in the ULE is outlined. The chapter further presents the prominence of online learning support in the ULE followed by the different types of online learning support in the ULE. It has commonly been assumed that most of the students in the ULE breeze through the online learning programs on their own. However, it was later shown by several researchers (such as Hwang, Yang, Tsai, & Yang, 2009; K.-Y.; Chin & Chen, 2013) that there are those students who require ongoing assistance throughout the entire ubiquitous learning experience. With that in mind, it is worth noting that regardless of the students' learning style in the ULE, they should always have access to online learning support. It is now necessary to present some of the barriers to students' ubiquitous learning.

BARRIERS TO STUDENTS' UBIQUITOUS LEARNING

Much of the current literature on ULE pays particular attention to what the ULE can offer to students—such as its ability to improve collaborative learning, accessibility, and other fundamental concepts in education. Despite the fact that the students can participate and grow with the lifestyle challenges or personal issues in the ULE, there are some barriers to learning that require proper learning support. Muilenburg and Berge (2005) gave a comprehensive review on the underlying constructs that comprise barriers to students' ubiquitous learning. The focus of their review was on the following eight factors:

1. Administrative issues,
2. Social interaction,
3. Academic skills,
4. Technical skills,
5. Learner motivation,
6. Time and support for studies,
7. Cost and access to the Internet, and
8. Technical problems.

Administrative Issues

The findings from Muilenburg and Berge's (2005) study revealed that students in the ULE perceive barriers emanating from administrative issues as: course materials not always being delivered on time, a lack of sufficient academic advisors online, and a lack of timely feedback from the instructor. In a different study, (Alhassan, 2016) found out that students were concerned about the lack of rules regulating how to use the mobile phone text messages, especially in the ULE. Some of the students' barriers to ubiquitous learning were found to be encountered due to administration policies, budgets, or online program development. To specify some of the specific factors relating to the aforementioned factors, as highlighted by Ebritchi, Lipschuetz, and Santiague (2017), these include a lack of online learning support; a lack of incentive when designing the online program; and instructors who demonstrate unwillingness to design and implement an online courses.

Against this backdrop, it is worth noting that students who are affected by the administrative issues might have poor performance due to a lack of support. The instructors seem not committed when designing and implementing the online courses (which is affected by a lack of incentive) could lead to poorly developed programs—ones which do not address the relevant outcomes or needs of the students.

Social Interactions

There is some evidence to suggest that some of the students' barriers to ubiquitous learning are caused by a lack of student online collaboration, the lack of social context cues, or their being afraid of feeling isolated in online courses. With regard to social interactions, it is a widely held view that when students in the ULE experience boredom, and eventually drop-out. It is the responsibility of the program designers to create relevant and relatable ubiquitous learning experiences that solve real-world challenges. In addition, develop personal learning paths that allow ubiquitous students to be flexible in their learning activities. It should also be noted that online boredom may be prevented by recognizing different learning styles of the students (such as visual, audio and kinesthetic) when designing the online learning material.

The research conducted by Nir-Gal (2002) discovered that there are students who finds it difficult to learn in an environment without a social framework, and that there are those who are not inclined toward group learning. Nir-Gal also alluded to the student's sense of isolation on the Net, while others can be overwhelmed by the sheer magnitude of material and tremendous diversity of content on the Internet. On the other hand, Kebritchi et al. (2017) depicted that students may have inappropriate expectations (such as expecting instant feedback on their online comments and assignments) or may appear rude and demanding in their emails. Furthermore, some students were reported to be struggling with identification and adopting learning styles and skills required to participate in the ULE. Different learning styles required to participate in the ULE are explained in the following section of students' experiences of learning through the ULE.

Academic Skills

The research study by Muilenburg and Berge (2005) also found that lack of academic skills in areas such as writing, reading, or communication were perceived barriers to online learning. This chapter outlines these academic skills as students' barriers to ubiquitous learning.

Writing

It is believed that much of professional communication is done in writing. For the students in the ULE, the inability to write might make it difficult to seek out information, explore subjects in-depth, and gain a deeper understanding of the world around them. It is likely that students with writing difficulties won't be able to express their knowledge to their tutors/peers or to the people who are making the big decisions in their studies or careers. In the ULE, students need to be able to express themselves in writing for effective communication with the tutors and peers. Since students are studying towards their future careers, there is a proverb that says: "The inability to write makes for a stillborn career."

Reading

It is a widely held view that engaged reading leads to engaged learning. Learning in the ULE requires of the students to engage with the learning material mainly through reading. If the students experience difficulties in reading effectively, they run a risk of failing to grasp important concepts and, ultimately, fail to meet educational milestones. There is some evidence such as the study conducted by Aliponga (2013) to suggest that ability to read increases concentration and discipline which are fundamental requirements for successful learning in the ULE. Reading skills allow students to learn with ease. When they cannot read well, they become discouraged and frustrated.

Communication

Communicating online requires computer-mediated communication systems such as computer conferencing systems, audio recording software, email, and video recording devices, to name a few. The students' inability to use the aforementioned systems in the ULE might drop out or feel the sense of isolation. It should be noted that the goal of online communications is the same as the goal in face-to-face communications: to bond; to share information; to be heard; and to be understood. There is a possibility that poor online communication can discourages a sense of community in the ULE and will make the learning experience more difficult for students. The ability to communicate clearly and effectively forms the foundation of modern life. The online course designers and managers should make the point that learning materials are designed in such a way that effective communication is encouraged to foster a sense of community within the ULE and to promote support and a good learning experience.

Technical Skills

There is some literature such as Hysong (2008) that recognizes the importance of technical skills such as knowing how to use email, upload files, and navigate and search the web, when learning through the ULE. Muilenburg and Berge (2005) attest that a lack of technical skills—such as those related to fearing new tools for online learning; having a lack of software skills; or being unfamiliar with online learning technical tools—creates barriers to ubiquitous learning. The barriers that are encountered as a result of lack of technical skills are, among others, the inability to comment within a discussion forum, to upload an assignment file, to display hidden toolbars, and to insert images. Students experiencing barriers to ubiquitous learning as a result of a lack of technical skills are viewed as not having digital competence[1], as they will be lagging behind. According to Welsh Government (2016) digital competence is the set of skills, knowledge and attitudes that enable the confident, creative and critical use of technologies and systems.

Motivation

Previous research findings (from studies such as Hartnett, George, & Zealand, 2011; and Muilenburg & Berge, 2005) have revealed that poor motivation has a detrimental effect on online courses because some of the dropout rates in the ULE are attributed to it. Muilenburg and Berge (2005) further maintained that signs of lack of motivation in the ULE are procrastination and choosing easier aspects of an assignment to complete. It has conclusively been shown that students in the ULE are mostly motivated when they are the ones in control of the situation—for example, when they are given the opportunity to be autonomous.

Time and Support for Studies

It is now well established from a variety of studies such as Fry, H., Ketteridge, S., and Marshall (2015) and Dunlosky, Rawson, Marsh, Nathan, and Willingham (2013) that studying through the ULE gives students "the maximum possible control over the time and pace" of their learning. It should, however, be noted that some of the students opting to learn through ULE are adults with jobs and families as well as certain public responsibilities, which certainly affects their learning process. That being the case, it is safe to conclude that students with that background would require support from family, friends, or people in the workplace/employer. Lack of such support might result in the difficulty to manage the study time, which would cause barriers to their online learning. Pozdnyakova and Pozdnyakov (2017) reflected on the European Union framework which was studied in Latvia and recognized that work and family commitments were considered as being one of the main barriers that prevent adult students from participating in educational activities.

Cost and Access to the Internet

According to the Internet Society (2017) internet has immense potential to improve the quality of education, which is one of the pillars of sustainable development. The Sustainable Development Goal (SDG) 9: Industry, Innovation and Infrastructure ascertains that the world is becoming ever more interconnected and prosperous due to the internet (Ono, Iida, & Yamazaki, 2017). However, there is an inconsistency with this argument, because it is reported that about four billion people in the developing countries have not yet accessed the internet. In some areas where the internet is accessible, it is too expensive for students to use frequently The study conducted by Muilenburg and Berge (2005) also revealed that students find the internet very expensive for them, while some raised a concern regarding having limited access to the internet. The most interesting finding about barriers to ubiquitous leaning in the Muilenburg and Berge's study was the students' fear for the loss of privacy, confidence, or property rights when studying through the ULE. Against this background, it is worth concluding that the cost, limitedness, and slow internet connections may make accessing course materials in the ULE frustrating.

Technical Problems

Very often in the ULE, there are compatibility issues with operating systems, browsers or smartphones. This adds to the frustrations of the students, because their learning experience is disrupted. As a result, they might (or probably will) abandon the course. This statement can be aligned with Gillett-Swan's (2017) reflections on the challenges in the online space where technical problems are viewed as being limitations to the learning process. It can be seen from the aforementioned variables that technical assistance is required in the ULE to reduce the students' barriers to ubiquitous learning. Having discussed the students' barriers to the ubiquitous learning, it appears that different students might have various experiences in the ULE. What follows is an account of students' experiences of learning through the ULE from different contexts.

STUDENTS' EXPERIENCES OF LEARNING THROUGH THE ULE

This section presents some review of studies which identified some gaps created by real-world and digital-world resources in the ULE. Chiou, Tseng, Hwang, and Heller (2010) cautioned that in order to situate students in a real-world learning environment (a term which refers to direct experiences that take place within the context of practice), it is important to place the students in a series of learning activities that combine both a real-world environment and ULE. As the nature of ULE was explained in the introduction, Agarwal and Nath (2011) corroborate that learning material in the ULE is not semantically related to the physical environment. To give an example: Students who are learning through ULE may feel the urge to learn everywhere they can find some time such as while waiting in a doctor's waiting room or at the airport. They further advised that students will not only learn by means of desktop and mobile PCs but also by means of a set of diverse local and mobile devices based on ubiquitous technology.

The study conducted by Hwang, Yang, Tsai, and Yang (2009) theorized that it is almost impossible for the students to learn complex science experiments that involve problem-solving skills in the ULE without observing and practicing in the real world. They proposed an online learning support which is adaptive and which is able to sense the students' personal and environmental contexts. Taking into account the findings from Hwang et al. (2009)'s study, it is worth noting that online learning support is required to improve the performance of training complex problem-solving skills in the real world.

Similarly, Chiou et al. (2010) have analyzed the students' own and environmental-related parameters for the ULE. They found out that there are a number of students experiencing navigation problems in the ULE, especially in a very large learning area, such as a national park or a palace museum. Some of their recommendations include the development of the ULE that provides students with real-world experiences and knowledge. Agarwal and Nath (2011) shared the same sentiments and attest that supporting students in the ULE can be of great help.

The study conducted by K. Y. Chin, Lee, and Chen (2018) displayed a possibility of bridging the divide between real-world and digital world resources. They explored the use of interactive ubiquitous learning system to enhance students' authentic learning experiences in a cultural heritage course. For K. Y. Chin et al (2018), authentic learning activities include the use of role-playing exercises, problem-based activities, and participation in virtual communities of practice. They also view authentic learning activities as part of real-world complex problems and solutions. The digital resources (interactive ubiquitous learning system) yielded positive results for students in the liberal arts education. The most striking result from this study was that the interactive ubiquitous learning system increased students' motivation and overall interest in learning the course content. That led to the increase in students' performance without discrimination regarding the cognitive-style students identified with.

From the students' experiences gathered, one can uncover the unique situations students might find themselves in the ULE. It should be noted that the students' experiences in the ULE discussed in this chapter are not exhaustive. Only a few were selected for the purpose of this chapter and to exhibit a need for an online learning support in the ULE. Thus far, the chapter has argued that students in the ULE require some online learning support in one way or another. Nevertheless, the section that follows goes on to consider the importance of planning the online learning support when managing and designing the online courses in the ULE.

THE IMPORTANCE OF PLANNING ONLINE LEARNING SUPPORT WHEN MANAGING AND DESIGNING ONLINE COURSES IN THE ULE

Before discussing the importance of planning the online learning support when managing and designing the online courses in the ULE, it is necessary to explain the reasons for the development of online courses. Some reasons why online courses were developed, as put forward by (Calimag et al., 2014) among others, include distance learning. The term *distance learning* according to Srichanyachon (2014) has been applied to many instructional methods such as an interactive DVD-ROM instead of a simple textbook, videotaped lectures, and audiotapes with lessons sent through the mail. In contrast, Gerber (2013) describe distance learning as a correspondence learning that takes place off campus with limited channels to break the students' barriers to learning. Gerber advocates for Open Distance Learning (ODL), which she views as being learning that is open and accessible to everyone regardless of age, race, economic position, class, disability, and criminality.

Notwithstanding the fact that ODL is viewed as a flexible tool that caters to the diverse needs of students, some researchers such as Ngubane-Mokiwa and Letseka (2015) saw a need to shift from ODL to Open Distance and e-Learning (ODEL) in order to optimally support the students by modern electronic technologies and other digital facilities. Although this chapter focuses on the online learning support in the ULE, this journey of distance learning need to be highlighted—because most students in the ODEL institutions learn through the ULE.

This chapter emphasizes that for the ODEL students to cope in the ULE, it is imperative to a that the presence of the teacher is inbuilt in the material and in the activity as recommended by Agarwal and Nath (2011). The questions that one should ask are:

1. To what extend can the students learn in this increasingly informal and opportunistic mode?
2. How can one keep the students motivated enough to not only complete the online courses created, but also to actually enjoy learning the skills and knowledge that is set before them?
3. What should be done to help the students beyond the formal delivery of content and development of skills?

Online Learning Support in a Ubiquitous Learning Environment

To answer these three questions, one should look at the difference between traditional classroom learning and ubiquitous learning—because previously, the ULE students have been learning through traditional classroom learning. Traditional classroom learning requires one to be at a specific place and time for teaching and learning to take place. By contrast, ubiquitous learning requires one to set aside some time to study and time to go through the lessons on one's own. This requires discipline and a real understanding about how to wisely use one's time throughout the day. It is quite clear that there are crucial differences between the ULE and traditional classroom learning. Nevertheless, some researchers such as Egbert (2009) advise that ULE should support content standards and learning goals in the same ways that the traditional classroom does.

Fry, Ketteridge, and Marshall (2009), who hold to a view similar to that of Egbert, base their argument on the fact that students learn in different learning styles which they classified as follows:

- Activists are students who learn by doing and responding most positively to learning situations that offer challenges. They like to brainstorm, and they're open to group discussions and problem-solving sessions.
- Reflectors are students who learn best by watching people and thinking about what is happening. They respond most positively to structured learning activities where they are provided with time to observe, reflect, and think; and where they are allowed to work in a detailed manner.
- Theorists are students who seek to understand the theory behind the action; and they respond well to a logical, rational structure and clear aims. They enjoy following models (and reading up on facts) to better engage in the learning process.
- Pragmatists are students who experiment with theories, ideas, and techniques and who take the time to think about how what they've done relates to reality. They respond most positively to practically based, immediately relevant learning activities—which allow scope for practice and the use of theory

Things to Consider When Planning the Online Learning Support in the ULE

Planning for the online support may reduce the limitations in the access which might decrease the environment usage by the students. Piovesan, Passerino, and Medina (2012) ascertain that not considering the different students' net contexts in the ULE can reflect in the resistance to, or even in the abandonment of, using the environment, which can also negatively affect the course. This chapter argues that learning in the ULE can sometimes be lonely, severe, and difficult—especially if the learning material does not match the diversity of the students. Barbosa, Barbosa, and Rabello (2016) demonstrated that the ULE serve the needs of students to achieve continuous integration between technology and the environment. Given this background, it is sound to recommend that the diversity of students needs to be considered when planning an online learning support for students in the UEL.

Secondly, guided by Agarwal and Nath (2011)'s views, it is vital to also consider the following:

1. The deployment of the technologies;
2. The appropriateness of the devices with students and learning outcomes; and
3. The frequency of access to learning materials.

Reflecting on these views, it is worth recommending that students' age, culture, socioeconomic background, personal interests, experience, and level of education—especially the level of mastery of the technological tools—should also be taken into account. Lastly, as maintained by Benson and Morgan (2013), one should take into account the compatibility of the ULE materials and the security of the data.

In summary, it has been shown from this section that planning the online learning support will assist in designing activities which provide opportunities for personalized learning in the ULE. For example, lecturers or course designers or ODEL practitioners will be able to base their online learning support on the cultural/geographical contexts of student and on their frequency of access to learning materials. In the section that follows, the importance of reflecting on students' experience in order to provide relevant online learning support is illustrated.

THE PROMINENCE OF ONLINE SUPPORT IN THE ULE

The debate about the ULE has gained fresh eminence with many arguing that without online learning support, students who are not self-reliant might not take the online learning seriously. More recently, literature that considers the prominence of online learning support in the ULE has emerged from the researchers such as Barbosa et al. (2016) and Piovesan et al. (2012). Barbosa et al. (2016) detected that the "user interface could be improved, including the use of techniques such as affective computing". They argue that online learning support could enhance the experience of interaction between students (given the different characteristics of individual students and the fact that they learn in different learning styles). Piovesan et al. (2012) affirmed that the ULE should be made adequate to the students by considering the uniqueness of the learning environment. In this chapter making the ULE adequate is viewed as providing the necessary and relevant online learning support.

Apart from the fact that ULE is dynamic, online learning support can provide the possibility of personalizing the environment for each student. It could also be argued that the online learning support serve as the student's accompaniment process in the ULE context. Drawing from Piovesan et al. (2012)'s views, this chapter maintains that online learning support serves as enablement and adaptive process focusing on the specific student's reality. In the same vein, Egbert (2009) theorized that the students in the ULE could participate in other ubiquitous learning activities including communicating with external experts, accessing remote resources, mentoring and tutoring students at other sites, and working in projects where students collaborate with external peers or other audiences.

Against the background of students' barriers to ubiquitous learning, the experiences of students learning through the ULE and the importance of the online learning supporting it could be noted that supporting students in the ULE cannot be made "one size fits all." As a result, the section below presents a few types of online learning support that were employed in different contexts of the ULE.

DIFFERENT TYPES OF ONLINE LEARNING SUPPORT IN THE ULE

There is evidence from researchers (such as K.-Y. Chin & Chen, 2013; and Zahrani, 2010) that online learning support plays a crucial role in enhancing learning in the ULE. This evidence also suggests that online learning support can be offered for different aspects in different levels of learning. In this section, several types of online learning support are discussed; and they are summed up in Table 2 to illustrate their benefits and challenges in the ULE.

A Mobile Learning Support System

A Mobile Learning Support System (MLSS) for ULE is in the form of GPS and 2D-code barcodes technologies that have been used to enable students to organize information by interacting with their environment. As explained in K.-Y. Chin and Chen's (2013) study, this online learning support is effective in the sense that when students are supported through MLSS, there is no need to input text; they just scan 2D barcode tags and gain immediate access to various online materials. Apart from that, the low technical barrier of reading 2D barcode tags makes it possible for students to incorporate these tags into their real-world learning environment to make learning in the ULE easy and accessible.

Radio Frequency Identification

Another online learning support one which is in the form of wireless communication that incorporates the use of electromagnetic or Electrostatic Technology Integrated (ETI) with Radio Frequency Identification (RFID)—was used to enhance teaching and learning activities in the ULE. This learning support was implemented with consideration of potential vulnerabilities in mind—vulnerabilities which, according to (Zahrani, 2010), are not limited to identity theft and network sabotage. For Zahrani, the possibilities were considered, because there is a likelihood of there being an unwilling exchange of information and the potential for academic dishonesty across the network. Despite the few challenges illustrated in Table 1, Zahrani (2010) found out that this form of online learning support has the potential to optimize and maximize effectiveness and efficiency in the ULE.

Mobile-Assisted Language Learning

Most of the previous studies, including those discussed in this chapter, established the importance and benefits of the ULE in different fields of learning. However, it is essential to highlight that there are some barriers experienced by students as suggested by (Alhassan, 2016). Some of the barriers were identified by (Cui and Bull, 2005; Tan and Liu, 2004) respectively, in relation to English language learning. Cui and Bull's (2005) study revealed that students who are English as a foreign language speakers tend to experience difficulties with the use of tense and articles during their learning activities; whereas Tan and Liu's (2004) study was about providing students with online learning support in order to increase their interest in learning English. This section could be linked with the question asked in the fourth section of this chapter as follows: "What should be done to help the students, beyond the formal delivery of content and development of skills?"

Table 1. MALL activities on different mobile devices

Device	Activity	Medium	Learning
Mobile phone	SMS Administration SMS vocabulary SMS quiz Email Video clip Coaching Media board	Text Text Text Text Video Audio material/text/graphics	Tutor-learner Learner-tutor
Mobile phone and interactive TV	Informal language learning through SMS/WAP/iTV	iTV Text	iTV–learner
Handheld Computer (IPad/Tablet)	Grammar drills Synchronous chat Reading poems Listening to poems	Text Text Text Listening material	Web–learner Tutor–learner Learner–tutor Web–learner
MP3 player	Listening to songs Listening to podcasts Listening to native speakers of English Listening to feedback on work Recording work	Audio material	Web–learner Learner–web-learner

Source: (Kukulska-Hulme & Shield, 2007)

Table 2. Benefits and challenges of different Online Learning Support in the ULE

	Benefits	Challenges
MLSS for ULE	• Combining real-world and digital-world resources • Interpretation and organization of personal knowledge • Can overcome the difficulties of mobile learning that exist in traditional text input methods • Can allow students to gain knowledge through interactions with their environment • Automatically share or summarize the key information for students • A suitable cooperative function for students to team up with peers	• Cannot run on many computer-assisted ULE programs • Challenges in text typing and editing capabilities
RFID	• Increased accessibility for real-time chats between students and teachers • Provide flexibility and accessibility to programs such as ODEL • Some applications include real-world functions • Provide the students with a variety of superior services through the integration of an effective ULE. • Improves user-friendliness across some services.	• Vulnerability to intrusion • High-budget program development
MALL	• Available through numerous devices • Implemented to aid English learning • Can significantly increase students' interest in learning English • Peer-assisted learning system for collaborative, early English First Language, reading • Enhance vocabulary ability • Enables the access of mobile content and YouTube videos.	• Cannot be applied widely to train students in listening to and speaking a language.

To address the barriers experienced in the learning of English in the ULE, Kim, Ruecker, and Kim (2017) suggested Mobile-Assisted Language Learning (MALL) to keep up with students' desires to study anywhere and anytime. For Kim et al. (2017) MALL can also be used to ignite a passion for ULE experiences among students while improving their contextual language learning experiences. There are a variety of activities related to language learning that can be supported by MALL—activities such as (though not limited to) vocabulary, reading, writing, reading comprehension, listening, speaking, describing a picture or a scene, and roleplaying situations. Table 1 illustrates how MALL can be used to support students' different language activities.

Table 1 shows various learning activities that can be done with different devices which can be used within the ULE. The table also indicates types of media which can be used to deliver the activity to students: text, audio, or iTV. Drawing from the "anytime; anyplace" ULE principle of learning, Kukulska-Hulme and Shield (2007) theorize that MALL is an online learning support that is cost-effective and which is worth consideration not only for language activities. With that in mind, it is worth summing up the benefits and challenges of the three types of online learning support discussed in this chapter.

It could be seen from Table 2 that the benefits of providing online learning support are higher than the challenges identified. The most common benefit in the three types of online learning support is enabling access to students. While it is clear that the challenges are different in the three types of online learning support, the author wish to highlight one of the challenges identified for supporting students with MLSS. It is evident from Table 2 that when supporting students with MLSS, one may run the risk of having limited computer memory and restricted broadband transmission of PDAs prevent this online learning support from running many computer-assisted ubiquitous learning programs. In addition, when K.-Y. Chin and Chen (2013) piloted, the use of MLSS on mobile phones the small touchscreen interface posed a major challenge in terms of text typing and editing capabilities.

SOLUTIONS AND RECOMMENDATIONS

This chapter has identified and described students' barriers to ubiquitous learning. It has affirmed that there are more complex issues to consider when managing and designing online courses in the ULE. The chapter also depicted that most ULE is viewed as an opportunity to learn from anywhere, at any time, for anyone. It may, however, be noted that the ULE, like any other learning environment, requires a means of being as inclusive as students would need. It appears from the description of students' barriers to ubiquitous learning that one of the barriers emanates from the students' inappropriate expectations. This chapter recommends that the managers and designers of online courses in the ULE should clearly communicate their course rules and policies at the beginning of the course so as to minimize the barriers resulting from the inappropriate expectations indicated in this chapter.

The other important note to the managers and designers of the online courses in the ULE is to recognize and support the nature of students' participation inclusively. The students' participation should not be judged by the quantity or length of their online postings (Kebritchi et al., 2017). The section on the experiences of students in the ULE exhibited there being a need to include online learning support when managing and designing online courses in the ULE. Although the studies reviewed in the section on the experiences of students in the ULE were taken from different contexts, proved the significance of the importance of supporting the students in the ULE. That brought to light the importance of planning such support, due to the uniqueness of the students' barriers to ubiquitous learning.

The most striking finding from the types of online learning support was the increased motivation of students who were supported through the interactive ubiquitous learning system. That being the case, this chapter suggests that students' motivations (consideration of the different types of motivation) should be regarded as being an important ingredient for the initial engagement as well as for retention in ULE. Hartnett (2016) declared that motivation play an important role in determining whether a student persists in a course. Online learning support is recommended in this chapter for all students involved in the ULE for ease of access, flexibility, and motivation to complete the online courses. By supporting students in the ULE through providing online learning support, will be contributing towards the delivery of quality education—particularly for the poor and underserved.

FUTURE RESEARCH DIRECTIONS

It was shown in the section on students' experiences of learning in the ULE that more and more institutions of higher learning are encouraging programs or online courses that are suitable for the ULE, with the aim of reducing costs for students and of expanding recruitment in the face of rising competition. This calls for an extensive research to explore the institutions' readiness in ensuring appropriate systems to promote online courses and relevant online learning support for the students.

Another future research direction should include the full execution of an empirical study designed to explore and determine the effects of online learning support in the ULE. The study should include the role of online learning support in enhancing students' performance in the ULE.

CONCLUSION

This chapter has attempted to characterize online learning support as being an instrument that can close the gap in the ULE (addressing barriers to ubiquitous learning) created by real-world and digital-world resources. It has reflected on the students' barriers to ubiquitous learning and has unpacked the reasons why online learning support should be planned alongside the managing and designing of the online courses in the ULE. Drawing from the challenges and benefits of the different types of online learning support in the ULE, this chapter pronounces that online learning support has the potential to make the ULE a most accessible and inclusive learning environment. It is also worth noting that online learning support in the ULE has the important role of students' learning and, ultimately, in assisting them to realize their final outcome of their educational achievement. It is the view of the author that providing students who are learning through the ULE with online learning support will reduce the drop-out rate and increase access and participation.

REFERENCES

Agarwal, S., & Nath, A. (2011). Some Challenges in Designing and Implementing Learning Material for Ubiquitous E-learning Environment. *Journal of Global Research in Computer Science Journal of Global Research in Computer Science, 2*(2), 29–32.

Alhassan, R. (2016). Mobile Learning as a Method of Ubiquitous Learning: Students' Attitudes, Readiness, and Possible Barriers to Implementation in Higher Education. *Journal of Education and Learning, 5*(1), 176–189. doi:10.5539/jel.v5n1p176

Aliponga, J. (2013). Reading Journal : Its Benefits for Extensive Reading. *International Journal of Humanities and Social Science, 3*(12), 73–80.

Barbosa, J., Barbosa, D., & Rabello, S. (2016). A collaborative model for ubiquitous learning environments. *International Journal on E-Learning: Corporate, Government, Healthcare, and Higher Education, 15*(1), 5–25.

Benson, V., & Morgan, S. (2013). Student Experience and Ubiquitous Learning in Higher Education: Impact of Wireless and Cloud Applications. *Creative Education, 04*(08), 1–5. doi:10.4236/ce.2013.48A001

Calimag, J. N. V., Miguel, P. A. G., Conde, R. S., & Aquino, L. B. (2014). Ubiquitous Learning Environment Using Android Mobile Application. *International Journal of Research in Engineering & Technology, 2*(2), 119–128. Retrieved from http://oaji.net/articles/2014/489-1393936203.pdf

Chin, K.-Y., & Chen, Y.-L. (2013). A Mobile Learning Support System for Ubiquitous Learning Environments. *Procedia: Social and Behavioral Sciences, 73*, 14–21. doi:10.1016/j.sbspro.2013.02.013

Chin, K. Y., Lee, K. F., & Chen, Y. L. (2018). Using an interactive ubiquitous learning system to enhance authentic learning experiences in a cultural heritage course. *Interactive Learning Environments, 26*(4), 444–459. doi:10.1080/10494820.2017.1341939

Chiou, C. K., Tseng, J. C. R., Hwang, G. J., & Heller, S. (2010). An adaptive navigation support system for conducting context-aware ubiquitous learning in museums. *Computers & Education, 55*(2), 834–845. doi:10.1016/j.compedu.2010.03.015

Cui, Y., & Bull, S. (2005). Context and learner modelling for the mobile foreign language learner. *System, 33*(2), 353–367. doi:10.1016/j.system.2004.12.008

Dunlosky, J., Rawson, K. A., Marsh, E. J., Nathan, M. J., & Willingham, D. T. (2013). Improving Students ' Learning With Effective Learning Techniques : Promising Directions From Cognitive and Educational Psychology. *Psychological Science in the Public Image, 14*(1), 4–58. doi:10.1177/1529100612453266 PMID:26173288

Egbert, J. (2009). *Supporting Learning with Technology: Essentials of Classroom Practice*. Upper Saddle River, NJ: Pearson Merrill Prentice Hall.

Fry, H., Ketteridge, S., & Marshall, S. (2009). Understanding student learning. In H. Fry, S. Ketteridge, & S. Marshall (Eds.), *A Handbook for Teaching and Learning in the Higher Education: Enhancing Academic Practice (3rd ed.)*. New York: Routledge.

Fry, H., Ketteridge, S., & Marshall, S. (2015). A Handbook for Teaching and Learning in Higher Education (4th ed.). Academic Press.

Gerber, L. (2013). *What is the difference between Open Distance Learning and Distance Learning*. Pretoria: University of South Africa. Retrieved from https://www.careersportal.co.za/education/universities/what-is-the-difference-between-open-distance-learning-and-distance-learning

Gillett-Swan, J. (2017). The Challenges of Online Learning Supporting and Engaging the Isolated Learner. *Journal of Learning Design*, *10*(1), 20–30. doi:10.5204/jld.v9i3.293

Hartnett, M. (2016). *Motivation in Online Education*. Singapore: Springer; doi:10.1007/978-981-10-0700-2

Hartnett, M., George, A. S., & Zealand, N. (2011). Examining Motivation in Online Distance Learning Environments : Complex, Multifaceted, and Situation-Dependent. *International Review of Research in Open and Distance Learning*, *12*(6), 20–38. doi:10.19173/irrodl.v12i6.1030

Hwang, G. J., Yang, T. C., Tsai, C. C., & Yang, S. J. H. (2009). A context-aware ubiquitous learning environment for conducting complex science experiments. *Computers & Education*, *53*(2), 402–413. doi:10.1016/j.compedu.2009.02.016

Hysong, S. J. (2008). The role of technical skill in perceptions of managerial performance. *Journal of Management Development*, *27*(3), 275–290. doi:10.1108/02621710810858605

Ilomäki, L., Kantosalo, A., & Lakkala, M. (2011). *What is digital competence? 2. Digital competence is an evolving concept*. Retrieved from https://tuhat.helsinki.fi/portal/files/48681684/Ilom_ki_etal_2011_What_is_digital_competence.pdf

Internet Society. (2017). *Internet Access and education: Key considerations for policy makers*. Retrieved from https://cdn.prod.internetsociety.org/wp-content/uploads/2017/11/Internet-Access-Education_2017120.pdf

Jones, V., & Jo, J. H. (2004). Ubiquitous learning environment: An adaptive teaching system using ubiquitous technology [Ambiente de aprendizaje ubicuo: Un sistema de enseñanza adaptativa utilizando tecnología ubicua]. *Beyond the Comfort Zone: Proceedings of the 21st ASCILITE Conference*, 468–474.

Kebritchi, M., Lipschuetz, A., & Santiague, L. (2017). Issues and Challenges for Teaching Successful Online Courses in Higher Education. *Journal of Educational Technology Systems*, *46*(1), 4–29. doi:10.1177/0047239516661713

Kim, D., Ruecker, D., & Kim, D.-J. (2017). Mobile Assisted Language Learning Experiences. *International Journal of Mobile and Blended Learning*, *9*(1), 49–66. doi:10.4018/IJMBL.2017010104

Kukulska-Hulme, A., & Shield, L. (2007). An overview of Mobile Assisted Language Learning: Can mobile devices support collaborative practice in speaking and listening. *EuroCALL, 2007*, 1–20. doi:10.1017/S0958344008000335

Kwon, S. (2011). Technical, educational issues and challenges in ubiquitous learning. In *2011 International Conference on Pattern Analysis and Intelligent Robotics (ICPAIR 2011). Putrajaya, Malaysia, 20110628* (p. 183). IEEE. 10.1109/ICPAIR.2011.5976940

Letseka, M., Letseka, M., & Pitsoe, V. (2018). The challenges of e-Learning in South Africa. In M. Sinecen (Ed.), *Trends in e-Learning*. London: IntechOpen. doi:10.5772/intechopen.74843

Mikelloydtech. (2013). *Internet of Learning-Things*. Retrieved from https://clwb.org/2013/06/10/what-is-ubiquitous-learning/

Muilenburg, L. Y., & Berge, Z. L. (2005). Students Barriers to Online Learning: A factor analytic study. *Distance Education, 26*(1), 29–48. doi:10.1080/01587910500081269

Ngubane-Mokiwa, S., & Letseka, M. (2015). *Shift from Open Distance Learning to Open Distance e-Learning*. Academic Press.

Nir-Gal, O. (2002). Distance Learning: The Role of the Teacher in a Virtual Learning Environment. *Ma'of u-Ma'aseh, 8*, 23–50.

Ono, T., Iida, K., & Yamazaki, S. (2017). Achieving sustainable development goals (SDGs) through ICT services. *Fujitsu Scientific and Technical Journal, 53*(6), 17–22.

Piovesan, S. D., Passerino, L. M., & Medina, R. D. (2012). U-ALS : A Ubiquitous Learning Environment. *IADIS International Conference on Cognition and Exploratory Learning in Digital Age (CELDA 2012)*, 197–204.

Pozdnyakova, O., & Pozdnyakov, A. (2017). Adult Students' Problems in the Distance Learning. Procedia Engineering, 178, 243–248. doi:10.1016/j.proeng.2017.01.105

Srichanyachon, N. (2014). The barriers and needs of online learners. *Turkish Online Journal of Distance Education, 15*(3), 50–59. doi:10.17718/tojde.08799

Tan, T.-H., & Liu, T.-Y. (2004). The MObile-Based Interactive Learning Environment (MOBILE) and A Case Study for Assisting Elementary School English Learning 2. The MObile-Based Interactive Learning. In *Proceedings of the IEEE* (pp. 4–8). IEEE.

Welsh Government. (2016). *Digital Competence Framework*. Cathays Park. Retrieved from http://learning.gov.wales/docs/learningwales/publications/160831-dcf-guidance-en-v2.pdf

Zahrani, M. S. (2010). The benefits and potential of innovative ubiquitous learning environments to enhance higher education infrastructure and student experiences in Saudi Arabia. *Journal of Applied Sciences (Faisalabad), 10*(20), 2358–2368. doi:10.3923/jas.2010.2358.2368

KEY TERMS AND DEFINITIONS

Artificial Intelligence: The ability of a computer to perform tasks normally requiring human intelligence, such as, speech recognition and translation between languages.

Digital World: The articulation of the dominance of the use of technology in the modern-day society.

Learning Styles: The way a learner or students acquire knowledge and skills during the teaching activities.

Mobile-Assisted Language Learning: An online learning support that uses smartphones and other mobile technologies in language learning.

Open Distance and e-Learning: A distance learning where the academic community uses technology to achieve the learning outcomes.

Pedagogical Resource: Resources used to enhance the teaching and learning activities.

Radio Frequency Identification: The process whereby electromagnetic fields are used to automatically identify and track tags attached to objects.

Traditional Classroom: A classroom which do not cater for innovation and creativity because its main resource is a teacher.

ENDNOTE

[1] Digital incompetence was the term introduced in 2011 by Ilomäki, Kantosalo, & Lakkala (2011) as the concept describing technology-related skills not limited to confident and critical usage of the full range of digital technologies for information, communication and basic problem-solving in all aspects of life.

Chapter 2
A Specified Ubiquitous Learning Design for Seamless Learning

Ibrahim Emin Deryal
https://orcid.org/0000-0002-3231-1271
Ministry of National Education (MoNE), Turkey

Veysel Demirer
Suleyman Demirel University, Turkey

ABSTRACT

Seamless learning and ubiquitous learning are nested concepts and they may be confused notions without elaborating definitions and implications. In this chapter, seamless learning is handled deeply, and ubiquitous computing and ubiquitous learning concepts are explained. Seamless learning is explained through the definition stated by Kuh and implications carried out by numerous researchers who conducted many studies in the field. Each implication and study are analyzed and elaborated carefully in order to propose an efficient seamless learning management system. In addition to those analyses, after explaining ubiquitous computing and ubiquitous learning concepts, MOOCs are mentioned in order to give a well applied ubiquitous learning system. Finally depending on seamless learning fundamentals (stated by authors) an efficient seamless learning management system is proposed.

DOI: 10.4018/978-1-5225-9779-7.ch002

INTRODUCTION

Each learning approach and learning management system possess their own philosophical ground and accumulation of knowledge through a wide or specific chronological and practical channel. With this respect, ubiquitous learning, MOOCs or proposed Seamless Learning Management System (proposed in this chapter) are not distinguished from any other learning systems or approaches. This is the most basic idea why it is substantially significant to set a rigor starting point of the process before alluding to MOOCs, ubiquitous learning or Seamless Learning System (SLMS). At this point, seamless learning fundamentals can be accepted as the first milestone of SLMS empowered by ubiquitous computing or ubiquitous learning. In essence, it is inevitable to annotate seamless learning with philosophy, fundamentals, implementations and outcomes.

The term "seamless" was discoursed by American College Personnel Association (John C. Calhoun, 1996) in order to emphasize the value of in and out of class activities for the students' enhancing their knowledge and academic success. In addition to this, the detailed definition of seamless learning is elucidated by Kuh (1996) as;

The word seamless suggests that what was once believed to be separate, distinct parts (e.g., in-class and out-of-class, academic and non-academic; curricular and co-curricular, or on-campus and off-campus experiences) are now of one piece, bound together so as to appear whole or continuous. In seamless learning environments, students are encouraged to take advantage of learning resources that exist both inside and outside of the classroom... students are asked to use their life experiences to make meaning of material introduced in classes... (p.136)

BACKGROUND

A Philosophical Perspective on Seamless Learning

As Michael W. Galbraith (2017) stated, any instructional and learning route should be prompted by a solid philosophical approach of education to facilitate placing headstones of instructional design and to draw outlines in order to make choices. As many, seamless learning has its philosophical foundations. By the projection of seamless learning, life itself is a significant learning environment. Learning occurs at any chronological and locational point of human's life. Thence, the act of learning should be handled like any other vital activities like feeding, inhaling, sleeping etc. with one critical difference. Seamless learning does not mean that learners have to be educed in every second of their lives while they are available (Wong & Looi, 2011). The problem is, at this point, how to seize upon the valuable time interval at the right place with respect to learners' readiness for gaining information and knowledge. Learners should benefit from learning environment "anytime" and "anywhere" they desire. The terms "anywhere" and "anytime" should not be shuffled with "everywhere" and "every time" (Wong & Looi, 2011).That is why learning environments should provide learners knowledge at "any" learnable moment. For instance a plant consumes water best when it most needs. In other words, the efficacy of learning

A Specified Ubiquitous Learning Design for Seamless Learning

Figure 1. Seamless learning diagram (Wong, 2012)
Source: Wong, 2012

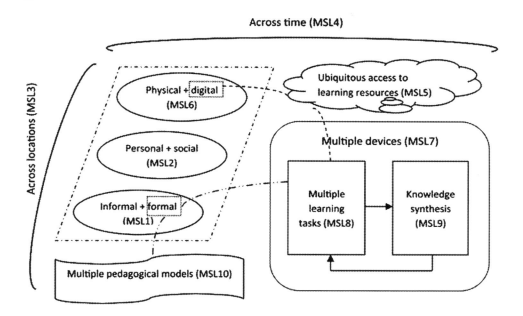

activities reaches the top point when instruction required mostly. Thus, the learning environment should facilitate learners to perform tasks when they are most ready and triggered or needed. That means it is not possible to set strict lines of learning experiences and instruction formally. In essence learning is not a performance constrained by walls and roof, and a well-planned schedule; it is an ongoing process as long as learner breathes.

Fundamentals of Seamless Learning

Seamless learning is an approach, and an accumulation of formative learning perspectives. Thus, allowing us to create seamless learning environments, it consists of associations of particular cornerstones. In general "Mobile Seamless Learning" (MSL) is being much more mentioned by the excessive evolution of the mobile and wireless technology. This situation drives us to put forward general terms from MSL features list of Wong and Looi (2011) to be able to state the fundamentals of seamless learning.

- *(MSL1) Encompassing formal and informal learning;*
- *(MSL2) Encompassing personalized and social learning;*
- *(MSL3) Across time;*
- *(MSL4) Across locations;*
- *(MSL5) Ubiquitous knowledge access (a combination of context-aware learning, augmented reality learning, and ubiquitous Internet access);*

- *(MSL6) Encompassing physical and digital worlds;*
- *(MSL7) Combined use of multiple device types (including "stable" technologies such as desktop computers, interactive whiteboards);*
- *(MSL8) Seamless switching between multiple learning tasks (such as data collection + analysis + communication).*
- *(MSL9) Knowledge synthesis (a combination of prior + new knowledge, multiple levels of thinking skills, and multi-disciplinary learning);*
- *(MSL10) Encompassing multiple pedagogical or learning activity models*

In order to visualize the 10 dimensions of MSL list of Wong and Looi a diagram (Wong, 2012) is placed below.

Seamless Learning Fundamentals (SLF) based on Wong and Looi's (2011) features list lies under following lines:

- **SLF1:** Seamless learning environments should establish a healthy conjunction of formal and informal learning activities and frameworks.
- **SLF 2:** Seamless learning environments should assist both individual tasks and cooperative learning power of social interactions.
- **SLF 3:** Seamless learning environments should provide "anytime" learning opportunities in order seamless learners to use their learnable moments effectively.
- **SLF 4:** Seamless learning environments should provide "anywhere" learning opportunities to facilitate seamless learners' performances by eliminating locational restrictions.
- **SLF 5:** Seamless learning environments should enhance attainability of knowledge that makes feasible learning tasks in context.
- **SLF 6:** Seamless learning environments should encapsulate hands on experiences and real life experiences in addition to blessings of improving digital world.
- **SLF 7:** Seamless learning environments should utilize every kind of tools without any discrimination (the emphasis must be here how the tool serves the purpose).
- **SLF 8:** Seamless learning environments should furnish smooth transitions from one different learning task to another.
- **SLF 9:** Seamless learning environments should combine learners' skills already they had and their developing ones, prior knowledge and newly assimilated and different contexts of fields.
- **SLF 10:** Seamless learning environments should be structured in the light of different pedagogical approaches and various instructional designs.

SLF list draws a humble outline for not only mobile but also all kinds of seamless learning environments. It is vital for designing any learning design to have a solid fundamental ground in order to set productive activities and efficient implementations. The SLF list which interpreted from MSL list may be helpful designing utilizable seamless learning environments anticipating desired outcomes.

MAIN FOCUS OF THE CHAPTER

Seamless Learning on Practice

Through the definition of seamless learning and SFL1, seamless learning implications should contain both formal and informal learning activities. At this point it is really important to touch the definitions of formal and informal learning. Commonly, formal learning defined as the learning occurs in planned and structured vertical instructional systems, on the other hand informal learning occurs with student-initiated, unintended and unplanned (including incidental learning) activities. There is confusion here that, in the formal learning systems it is possible informal learning to be carried out, or vice versa. So, it is crucial to separate both formal learning and "formal learning settings" and informal learning and "informal learning settings" (Looi et al., 2010). So it is possible, even more common, learners to perform informal learning in planned and structured learning systems. Seamless learning designs should smooth the lines between formal and informal learning settings in order to help learners to achieve learning goals in both ways, formal and informal learning, in both systems, formal and informal learning systems.

While the school schedule is on duty, it is critical that learners' having associated with formal instructional context. Furthermore, enhancing the quality of the instruction, classroom activities may be the first engagement of the learners. As seen on the table (Figure 2) of seamless learning activities (Seow et al., 2008) "Challenge – Articulating the problem" activity is a classroom activity and the first one. Moreover, introducing the learners with the context require a substantial guidance which should be provided by a mentor or an expert. However, in class activities cannot be restricted just being trigger of the process. Formal instruction is critical for each checkpoint of the continuum for the seamless learning designs of implications. Though the indispensable value of formal instruction, in order to mention any seamless learning implication, the key point of the design is having smooth transition between formal instructions and informal learning. Having a second look at the table of seamless activities

Experience (Field Activity) is a well-prepared out-class task. The nob of the seamless learning implications is not just carrying on both in and out class activities, also establishing a perfect smooth passing through each other is the most noteworthy aspect of instructional design. As a matter of fact, separating formal and informal learning is a meaningless venture. According to Hodkinson et al. (2003) formal and informal learning are strongly connected and nested. By looking from this perspective it is inevitable to position the informal learning both in class and out of class environment. Furthermore, seamless transition is inextricably linked feature to the aggregate continuum of the seamless learning implications.

Figure 2. Example of seamless learning activities (Seow et al., 2008)
Source: Seow et al., 2008

Activity	Day	Location	Description
Challenge – Articulating the problem	1	Classroom	The teacher gave a short introduction to the problem of having too much garbage. Students created KWL* tables and shared with each other about their learning objectives (1 hour)
Experience – Field Activity	5	Supermarket and Fast Food Restaurant with wireless network	Three activities that students performed at a supermarket: 1. Study different sizes and materials for packaging and take photos of the products; 2. Observe how many plastic bags are dispensed at the checkout counters within five minutes; 3. Interview customers about their attitudes and practices of 3Rs; (2 hours) Students uploaded their data collected during the field trip at a fast food

With respect to SLF 2, another crucial aspect of seamless learning implications is that they provide individualized learning opportunities as many as cooperative learning ones. Learners always have got different instructional needs, motivations, readiness and capabilities. Individualized instruction is a set of implementations which includes appropriate learning strategies fulfilling individuals' particular academic needs. It also provides specialized motivational sources in order to keep learners on instructional performance. Individualized instruction environments also have flexibility of contents which can be modified so that learners do not have to adapt to the content but instructional environments fit to learners' readiness. Furthermore, any well-prepared learning system should be learner centered versus being content centered. Another advantage of individualized learning systems is conferring personal speed of progress. Each needs its own specific time of comprehension. So, any flexible learning environment must service by regarding those requirements. However, seamless learning environments do not rely on just individualized learning activities, also provide cooperative learning opportunities. Because of humans being social creatures, as each part of our life requires qualified interaction with others, also while performing learning activities we highly need social interplay. That is why cooperative learning has enormous importance for instructional activities established in learning strategies. Learners share their knowledge, idea and experiences naturally through a cooperative learning process. Furthermore learners encourage other participants of learning environments taking advantage of their lore and exploring new information. Cooperative learning provides numerous other contributions to seamless learning environments, like any other instructional environments. However it is not possible to handle all of the advantages of cooperative learning, so that we will allude to the most important ones with respect to seamless learning. Social interaction may be the first feature to mention because of learners needs for being a member of the learning community. Social interaction also furnishes gaining knowledge from others and learning from other learners' experiences. Seamless learning forums and communities also facilitate learning by teaching, which is accepted as one of the most effective way of keeping information in mind. As learning by teaching, learning by deliberation is a powerful tool for not just keeping in mind but also obtaining higher levels of comprehension like analysis, synthesis and evaluation. The happiness of sharing knowledge is another significant cooperative learning feature which is additionally a good example of intrinsic motivation for seamless learners. Learners' communities which are parts of the seamless learning systems yield individual attribution to community that make individuals feel a valuable member of the society what is also an important motivation source. Scaffolding is another crucial aspect of cooperative learning. Seamless learning society members help each other with learning processes. When a learner has difficulty about understanding any issue, there will be many helpers to support the learner with a problematic issue.

As mentioned in SLF 3 time aspect of seamless learning is vital for seamless learning environments. Especially "any time" protocol is highly significant by utilizing any learnable moments of learners. A learner should be both mentally and motivationally ready in order to perform learning activities. When a learner catches the moment, the moment has to be parlayed, so that the learning activity will be extremely effective. Well-structured seamless learning environments are designed to serve at "any time" the learners' being ready. Thanks to developing information technologies, today we all can reach information anytime we desire. Here a general example; what would you do when you are curious about something? Is not the first thing that comes to mind the relatively new verb to *google it*? Yes it is a fact that most of us use the internet in order to get information anytime we need or want. As information technology is a part of our daily life, it is also an important part of seamless learning environments providing us information anytime. So, with respect to seamless learning environments "anytime" aspect, an instructional design should be enhanced by new information technology tools.

According to SLF 4 an important contribution of developing information technologies to our lives is, with respect to seamless learning, they serve us "anywhere" we are and need information. At this point, mostly mobile technology facilitates "anywhere" learning opportunities. When we need any information about anything the first things we cling is our smartphones. Mobilization of the information technology provides us significant flexibility to be free of space gaining knowledge. However, when mentioned mobility the spotlight should not just be on information technology. Projected by seamless learning understanding, each item of a learning environment should be mobile. Especially the learner should perform learning tasks anywhere life is going on. Instructional design of a seamless learning environment should bring about a different lifestyle which the learner has a perspective that any space in the world contains learning chances. For instance, a field trip to nature in addition to science class activities should offer real-life experiences about the topic the learner exposed in the class. In fact when learning design includes such out of class activities in time learners will gain another point of view to nature which they will see nature as an important source of knowledge. The desired outcome of seamless learning environments is that learner's seeing each point of life as a learning opportunity. Furthermore, the understanding that a learning environment is built under a roof with four walls and the learners are bound to one door to enter being in learning activity is reasonably old-fashioned. Every inch of earth has the capacity of being a valuable learning opportunity source. Seamless learning philosophy deals with using those inches in order to serve instructional activities at "anywhere" the learners are ready to perform. According to this philosophy, seamless learning environments are configured to be mobile both physically and digitally purposing to save learners from being locked up behind walls.

We alluded to formal and informal learning opportunities in seamless learning environments before. Additionally both individualized and cooperative learning facilities were mentioned too. By those contexts seamless learning structures should provide *attainability (SFL 5) of knowledge in both formal and informal, teacher-student, expert-student, and student-student interactions*. Seamless learning environments' being liberated from time and space is also another crucial aspect of making learning activities ubiquitous. Although the accessibility of information is prevailing as a result of developing technology, sharing personal experiences and knowledge is completely something else. Carefully planned and structured learning systems should be used aiming to bring students, teachers and experts together to furnish sharing both knowledge and experiences. Seamless learning designs provide a strong continuity between formal and informal learning. It is commonly accepted that both formal and informal learning types have their advantages, and they both are different sources of knowledge. Skipping any source of information will be a huge misfortune.

Even though digital tools have great contributions to seamless learning designs, hands-on activities and real-life experiences should not be separated from learning activities (SFL 6). Hands-on activities offer different types of real-life experiences. By having a look at Bloom's Taxonomy synthesis or creating are high levels of learning. By providing learners different hands on activities it will be possible that the learners will get the chance to create artifacts. As a result of any learning environment including hands-on activities and real-life experiences, a high level of learning may occur. Especially for science educations real-life experiences helps learners to build knowledge by linking academic information with their observations or incidental learning. For example, according to Wu (2003), while learner built knowledge about chemical concepts they may link information with their life experiences. At this point real-life experiences and hands-on activities may be considered as both source of information and a complementary of knowledge. In seamless learning designs, outdoor activities are considered as supportive power of in-class activities as formal learning. As seen on "Case Study 2: The MLE science curriculum" (Wong, 2013b) contains both indoor and outdoor activities, and those activities are so nested that each out of school performance has an effect on each in-class activities. The learning performance never stops and all activities support following ones. The word seamless embodies here literally, the boundaries of the formal and informal learning almost invisible. For instance, students take photos while performing field trips about the topic given in class and they share their work with other students in the class. With this project both nature and school are handled as knowledge sources, and each environment has a complementary role on other. The meaning of the word seamless has a great effect on the transaction between physical and digital world too. Seamless learning environments may include a great integration of information and communication technology. Used technology also may provide digital information and should be an essential tool for physical activities. A good example of using information and communication technology in order to support real-life experiences is seen in the conducted study by Looi et al. (2010) Developed seamless learning design is comprised a mobile device with "a digital camera, wireless capability, Internet browser and text input function". They also developed a software application which is named as learning 3Rs (reduce, reuse and recycle) in order for the learners to follow specific tasks. Using specified information technology it is aimed to support students' experiential learning activities with the blessing of digital technology. The software developed by the researchers contains 5 steps in a cycle as "Challenge, Experience, Reflecting, Planning and Applying" "Challenge" step seems to be formal because of being an in-class activity, however the performance expected from student is not restricted by school walls. There is almost no line between in class and out of class activities. In addition to this, students are anticipated to put forward their existing experiences and knowledge. Furthermore, by the step "Experience" the students are exposed to a new real-life experience with the task given which meant to be performed on the field. Additionally they need to use their digital device to complete a given task. Students are also employed to share, "Reflecting", their real life experiences in an online portal by using the digital devices they are given. It is quite obvious that in a well-established seamless learning design both real-life experiences and the digital world are nested properly. "Planning" step is consisted of tasks which require utilizing their obtained knowledge for real life problems. Although this step seems to require cognitive performance, again real-life experiences and hands-on activities have a significant effect on the tasks given. The last step "Applying" is completely about how to carry out hands-on activities about relevant topic 3Rs.

7th fundamental of seamless learning is about which tools should be used for seamless learning designs. There is no restriction on choosing tools for establishing any seamless environment, but the instruments to be taken advantage of must serve the purposes. From a single notebook with a pen to high tech tablet using cloud technology all kind of tools can be considered as a significant tool for seamless learning

A Specified Ubiquitous Learning Design for Seamless Learning

Figure 3. Learning 3Rs software interface screen (Looi et al., 2010)
Source: Looi et al., 2010

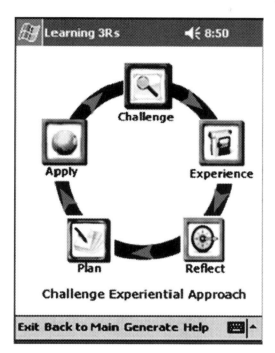

designs. For instance, in context of a science class, after in class activity a field trip to nature may be planned, while on the field trip, learners can use microscope and can take notes about their experiences to their notebook and also they can take photos with their tablets or phones, in cloud account they can categorize their photos and share with other learners and instructor. Even more, specified software can be developed in order for learners to use for a specific task. Again here we have to mention "Project 3Rs" conducted by Looi et al.(2010). The software was developed in order the learners to perform different tasks about "Learning 3Rs" facilitates and supports learning activity, in other words, the software serves the purpose. A screen of the software is placed below.

The core and the hue of seamless learning are having indefinite transitions of learning tasks. This feature of seamless learning gives the name "seamless" to learning environments. The aim is to link formal and informal, individual and social, physical and digital learnings together. The reason for linking formal and informal learning is that the seamless learning intends to evaluate all learning opportunities. In order to increase the quality of learning informal environment should be established and utilized in addition to the formal environment. Therefore in seamless learning designs, out of class tasks bonded to in class tasks have great importance. For instance in an experimental study conducted by Hwang Wu and Ke (2011), before a field study students were allowed to develop initial concept maps in class, after in-class task, students asked to perform an out of class activity. While field study was going on, students were asked to refine their concept maps depending on their field study. When the students were refined

Figure 4. Field study photo of a seamless learning implication (Hwang et al., 2011)
Source: Hwang et al., 2011

their concept maps the learning management system software provided a simultaneous evaluation of the work done by the students, which is generally expected as an in-class activity. With a careful look, it is easy to see the compounding of the different learning tasks. Another project named "SCROLL (System for Capturing and Reminding Of Learning Log)"(Ogata et al., 2011) should be analyzed with respect to seamless learning. "SCROLL" provides learners many learning opportunities, two of them are "ULL recorder" and "ULL finder." "ULL recorder" allows the learner to record and share what the learner has learned and "ULL finders" allows the learner what the learner learned before and other learners shared. When those two properties of "SCROLL" examined, it is obvious that both individual (recording knowledge) and social learning (sharing knowledge and reaching knowledge shared by others) opportunities are furnished. Seamless learning designs are great platforms for implementation of technology-enhanced learning (TEL), which is supporting learning activities with the blessing of developing the technology. This feature of seamless learning facilitates to combine physical learning and digital learning. A significant example of TEL with respect to seamless learning is shown with the study conducted by Hwang et al. (2011). That experimental study shows that, supporting real-life learning with mobile learning has positive effect on the students learning. The first step of study includes learning how to use mobile devices and the concept maps. Then, they were expected to build their concept maps by using PCs about butterfly ecology depending on what they have learned before. The second step of study includes a field trip supported by mobile devices. Based on their field experiments the learners were expected to refine their concept maps about the ecology of butterflies by using their mobile devices. A photo of the field study is below.

As seen on the photo, physical and digital learning are perfectly combined. In addition, mobility aspect is not only about mobile devices or technology, but also about mobility of the learners and learning activities.

A Specified Ubiquitous Learning Design for Seamless Learning

The study conducted by Hwang et al. (2011) establish a great connection with what have already learned and what is to learn (SFL9) in addition to smooth transition of physical and digital learning, which is another highly important and indispensable feature to allow learners to combine the skills they already had and developing skills, likewise putting together prior knowledge and newly assimilated, different contexts of learning field. As a first activity, the participants of the study conducted by Hwang, et al. (2011) took an instruction about the ecology of the butterflies in class. With this in-class activity, it is intended to set a base knowledge. After the in class activity the students were allowed to perform a field activity. They were told to explore the ecology of butterflies in real life of the butterflies. With those two steps of the study, a connection was established between what have learned (instruction about the ecology of the butterflies in the class) and what is to learn (the learning through observation of the real lives of the butterflies with the field activity). Another study which should be analyzed with respect to setting links between existing information and new knowledge was conducted by Wong and Looi (2010). One of the two case studies is about "a lesson on six English prepositions." A lesson design which includes extra technology-enhanced learning in addition to present lesson activities was developed to support students' learning by using mobile devices. The participants of the study were asked to take photos related to the prepositions which were already learned in the class. After taking photos the students were encouraged to share their photos with other students. The second step of the learning design is a substantial contribution to the knowledge already gained in class. It is possible to see that there is a good connection between what have learned (the class activity about the six English prepositions) and what is to learn (the technology enhanced learning activity which facilitates real life experiences about the topic was learned before).

Seamless learning is a new holistic approach to how the learner learns. Different pedagogical approached and various instructional designs provide an important point of view to seamless learning. More than one pedagogical approach should be embraced in seamless learning environments. In order to elaborate on this fundamental of seamless learning, it is required to ask some questions about the learning process of the learners. Do they learn socially or individually? Do they learn formally or in informal settings? Is there any specific time interval for learning process? Is any specific physical environment required in order for the learning to occur? Are the learners able to perform learning tasks by themselves or is any specific mentor required in order them to perform? Should the learners be provided digitally or should they be allowed to have real-life experiences? Seamless learning answers all of the questions the same. The answer is "both." The learners learn both socially and individually and seamless learning environments should offer both social and individual learning tasks. The learners learn in both formal and informal settings, so seamless learning should wipe off the boundary between formal and informal learning. With respect to seamless learning, learning does not require any specific time interval or any specific physical environment; learning occurs anytime and anywhere. In seamless learning environments the learners should be allowed to perform the learning tasks by themselves and they a teacher or mentor should be provided to them in case they need any support with their learning tasks. Again in seamless learning environments both digital and real-life experiences should be furnished.

As a result seamless learning does not handle learning in only one pedagogical approach. All blessings of the theories and studies about learning and how learning occurs with the learner should be evaluated and utilized while designing a seamless learning environment.

Ubiquitous Learning

Ubiquitous computing was a foresight of an environment which could be integrated with portable and wireless technology (Weiser, 1993). Today, it is not an idea or foresight as a result of developing wireless technology and improving portable power units (Lyytinen & Yoo, 2002), ubiquitous computing is so common that almost each human lives with a computer in pocket or hand. In order to build a solid understanding of ubiquitous learning, it is needed to articulate ubiquitous computing. Ubiquitous computing is a new phenomenon that includes mobility of information and communication technology like smartphones, palm computers, tablets and other portable computing units with wireless communication (Sakamura & Koshizuka, 2005) and ubiquitous computing is a new paradigm of technology which comprises all those ubiquitous information and communication devices in everyday life. Ubiquitous learning utilizes those digital, portable devices, physical environment integrated with wireless technology, common elements of mobile technology and wireless information and communication technology in order to transmit knowledge and information to the learner at anytime and anywhere needed (Cárdenas-Robledo & Peña-Ayala, 2018). According to Sakamura and Koshizuka the definition is that "ubiquitous learning, in which we learn anything at anytime and anywhere utilizing ubiquitous computing technology and infrastructure." However, Yahya et al. (2010) have a different point of view about the definition of ubiquitous learning with respect to content, time and space features, which is "U-learning is a learning paradigm which takes place in a ubiquitous computing environment that enables learning the right thing at the right place and time in the right way".

Where is Ubiquitous Learning in Seamless Learning?

According to the definition, it is obvious that ubiquitous learning is related to knowledge, time and space by utilizing the blessings of ubiquitous computing. Having a look at SLF3, SLF4 and SLF5 it is possible to see the direct connection between seamless learning and ubiquitous learning. SLF3 indicates the time aspect of an instructional environment. It is claimed that learning should be independent of any specific time. It is mentioned that seamless learning environments should provide learning activities anytime needed. Ubiquitous learning definition by Yahya et al. (2010) it is articulated that "ubiquitous computing environment" should facilitate learning at the "right time." Seamless learning and ubiquitous learning establish a direct connection through two statements "anytime needed" and "at the right time." Another connection between ubiquitous learning and seamless learning is about space. SLF4 claims that a learning environment should serve anywhere needed. Again having another look at the definition of the ubiquitous learning with respect to space element, "ubiquitous computing environment" should provide learning "at the right place", a strong connection between ubiquitous learning and seamless learning draws the attention through with another two statements which are "anywhere needed" and "at the right space." The third connection between ubiquitous learning and seamless learning is about information, content and knowledge. SFL5 claims that "learning environments should enhance attainability of knowledge that makes feasible learning tasks in context" (In this chapter). Furthermore, the definition of ubiquitous learning given by Yahya et al. (2010) alludes to "the right thing" about a learning environment. The third connection between ubiquitous learning and seamless learning depends on other two statements which are "the right thing" and "attainability of knowledge that makes feasible learning tasks in context." With all those three connections, ubiquitous learning could be placed into seamless learning environments effectively. At first look, ubiquitous learning seems to be depending on just ubiquitous computing devices and supporting seamless learning by the power of those devices. However, ubiquitous learning is not just about hardware or ubiquitous devices empowered by wireless, RFID, GPS technology etc. It is also about establishing learning environments by designing and developing applications and web sites which to be used on ubiquitous computing devices. In practice there are numerous learning environments designed and developed to be used on pocket PCs and other portable devices. With respect to ubiquitous learning environments, MOOCs can be considered as the most important one of all designs.

MOOCs as Tools of Ubiquitous Learning

In order to understand MOOCs it is needed to look deeply into Open Educational Resources (OER). A Turkish thinker Yunus Emre said that "the things you are sharing belong to you, not the things you gather" and substantially all knowledge about education, science and technology we have today are an accumulation of shared knowledge and information by scientist, philosophers, educators an etc. who devoted their lives to humankind for ages (Kurşun, 2016). OER movement has the similar philosophy with Turkish thinker Yunus Emre. MIT OpenCourseWare (OCW) should be considered as the pioneer of the OER movement which has two missions, one is to deliver all educational contents of MIT courses online to the educators, students and all members of the learning community in the world, another one is to enlarge the accessibility and influence of MIT OCW and notion of opencourseware. OER movement is also based on the Universal Declaration of Human Rights' declaration about educational rights of humans which is,

"Everyone has the right to education. Education shall be free, at least in the elementary and fundamental stages. Elementary education shall be compulsory. Technical and professional education shall be made generally available and higher education shall be equally accessible to all on the basis of merit." (Nations, 1948).

OER movement is mostly related to the sentence, "Technical and professional education shall be made generally available and higher education shall be equally accessible to all on the basis of merit." of the Universal Declaration of Human Rights. OpenCourseWares can be considered as the first action of the OER movement, which is supported by Massachusetts Institute of Technology (MIT), the Open University, Johns Hopkins, Kyoto University, Notre Dame, and Korea University (Caswell et al., 2014). As seen the OER movement aims to build a huge accumulation of academic knowledge and information and let educators, students and any other individuals who have the purpose learning in order to improve themselves through different fields access the right content whenever and wherever they need. MOOCs are a great example of OER tools providing the right content supported by readings, presentations, instructional videos, images and student-student and student-expert interactions, at the right time(whenever the learners need) and at the right space (wherever the learners need). However, MOOCs are released after a while the OER movement initiated.

Although New York Times announced 2012 "The Year of the MOOC" (LAURA PAPPANO, 2012), Massive Open Online Courses (MOOCs) have been evolving since 2008, aiming to both maintain more learning occasions and to enlarge opportunities of knowledge acquisitions (Gaebel, 2013). MOOCs serve to an infinite number of learners. That is why the word "Massive" is used to name the system. They are all "Open" learning environments including text, images, presentations, videos and expert interactions. Another characteristic of MOOCs is them being "Online" which provides ubiquitous access to the content. The latter feature of MOOCs is about the content structure which MOOCs are well structured "Courses". When a learner enrolled any course on a MOOC, well prepared and rendered course content welcomes the learner.

In 2008 the first time the locution, MOOC, emerged and mentioned by Stephen Downes and George Siemens depending on "'connectivist' distributed peer learning model" and until 2012 some professors from Stanford University prepared instructional videos and delivered them by using open online technology (Baturay, 2015). That is why the New York Times named the year 2012 as "The Year of the MOOC" (2012). After that, in 2012 Coursera was released to the global community by two professors, Daphne Koller and Andrew Ng, from Stanford University Computer Science (Coursera, 2013). They wished to share their "knowledge and skills" with all members of the global community. The reason under the idea of sharing such qualified contents is profoundly critical. The thought is that all people in the world who are trying to learn something and improve themselves through their career or personal evolution should be able to access the right content whenever and wherever they need. If more learning opportunities are provided to the global community, the knowledge of the world will be able to rise substantially. That is because well-rendered knowledge should be released ubiquitously. This is the main idea under the movement of MOOCs. Since then, numerous MOOC sites have been established which are (Shah, 2017):

- Coursera / United States
- edX / United States
- FutureLearn / United Kingdom
- XuetangX / China
- Udacity / United States
- Kadenze / United States
- Canvas Network / United States
- Stanford Languita / United States
- Miríada X / Spain
- MéxicoX
- France Université Numérique (FUN)
- EduOpen / Italy
- ThaiMOOC / Thailand
- Federica.eu / Italy
- SWAYAM / India
- NPTEL / India
- CNMOOC / China
- Chinese MOOCS / China

- University of China MOOC — icourse163.org / China
- ewant — Education you want / Taiwan
- Edraak (Arabic) / Jordan
- European Multiple MOOC Aggregator (EMMA)
- Zhihuishu / China
- OpenHPI / Germany
- gacco / Japan
- Fisdom / Japan
- OpenLearning / Japan
- JMOOC / Japan
- Open Education (openedu.ru) / Russia
- Open Education (openedu.tw) / Taiwan
- K-MOOC / Korea
- IndonesiaX
- Prometheus / Ukraine
- And more…

Characteristics of MOOCs

Participants and Partners

MOOCs are "Massive" learning systems. All members of the world's learner community are invited to MOOCs' learning chateau. Anyone in the world is welcome to sign up a MOOC site and enroll any course needed. Here a list of MOOC user numbers (Shah, 2018);

- Coursera: 30 million users
- edX: 14 million users
- XuetangX: 9.3 million users
- Udacity: 8 million users
- FutureLearn: 7.1 million users

The list above shows just top five MOOCs according to their registered users. There are more than those 68, 4 million MOOC users in the world. The question should not be "How many people use MOOCs in the world?" it should be "Why do so many people use MOOCs?" Both questions have the same answer which is the qualification of the partners of the MOOCs. Almost all partners of the all MOOCs have great experience in education and developing instructional materials. Here the partner list of top two MOOCs according to their registered members.

Coursera:

- The University of North Carolina at Chapel Hill
- Sberbank Corporate University
- VITO

- CentraleSupélec
- IE Business School
- University of Virginia
- The George Washington University
- Yandex
- Eindhoven University of Technology
- Johns Hopkins University
- Palo Alto Networks
- Icahn School of Medicine at Mount Sinai
- The University of Chicago
- Università Bocconi
- The Pennsylvania State University
- Sciences Po
- National Research Nuclear University MEPhI
- Unity
- Google
- Moscow State Institute of International Relations (MGIMO)
- University of California, Irvine
- Universidade Estadual de Campinas
- California Institute of the Arts
- The World Bank Group
- The Museum of Modern Art
- The Hong Kong University of Science and Technology
- University of Cape Town
- Nanyang Technological University, Singapore
- University of Manchester
- EIT Digital
- University of California, San Francisco
- American Museum of Natural History
- Rice University
- Arizona State University
- University of California, Santa Cruz
- Universidade de São Paulo
- ESSEC Business School
- HubSpot Academy
- Carnegie Mellon University
- (ISC)^2
- University of Minnesota
- Exploratorium
- University of Leeds
- Saint Petersburg State University

A Specified Ubiquitous Learning Design for Seamless Learning

- Stanford University
- BCG
- Princeton University
- LearnQuest
- Universitat de Barcelona
- University of Michigan
- Amazon Web Services
- The Chinese University of Hong Kong
- The University of Hong Kong
- Duke University
- New York University Tandon School of Engineering
- Hebrew University of Jerusalem
- National Geographic Society
- The State University of New York
- Insper
- Moscow Institute of Physics and Technology
- Universidad de Chile
- EIT RawMaterials
- Emory University
- University of Kentucky
- Macquarie University
- The University of Edinburgh
- Yale University
- Case Western Reserve University
- University System of Georgia
- Utrecht University
- National Taiwan University
- Universidad Nacional Autónoma de México
- University of Illinois at Urbana-Champaign
- ESCP Europe
- ESADE Business and Law School
- Peter the Great St. Petersburg Polytechnic University
- École Polytechnique
- Northwestern University
- VMware
- Commonwealth Education Trust
- Brightline Initiative
- Politecnico di Milano
- Ludwig-Maximilians-Universität München (LMU)
- Autodesk
- University of Pennsylvania

- Pontificia Universidad Católica de Chile
- Shanghai Jiao Tong University
- Georgia Institute of Technology
- University of Alberta
- Berklee College of Music
- Universidad Austral
- Northeastern University
- The University of Tokyo
- University of Maryland, College Park
- Technion - Israel Institute of Technology
- H2O
- University of Western Australia
- Fundação Lemann
- Nanjing University
- École normale supérieure
- National University of Singapore
- PwC
- The University of Sydney
- Yeshiva University
- Tel Aviv University
- IESE Business School
- University of London
- Copenhagen Business School
- The Linux Foundation
- Rutgers the State University of New Jersey
- Universiteit Leiden
- Fundação Instituto de Administração
- University of Pittsburgh
- École Polytechnique Fédérale de Lausanne
- Indian School of Business
- Fudan University
- Google AR & VR
- Caltech
- ConsenSys Academy
- Vanderbilt University
- Relay Graduate School of Education
- Tufts University
- Institut Mines-Télécom
- Match Teacher Residency
- Koç University
- Novosibirsk State University

A Specified Ubiquitous Learning Design for Seamless Learning

- New Teacher Center
- National Research University Higher School of Economics
- Peking University
- École des Ponts ParisTech
- University of Lausanne
- Wesleyan University
- Google Cloud
- Instituto Tecnológico de Aeronáutica
- University of Arizona
- Technical University of Denmark (DTU)
- University of Florida
- Imperial College London
- Yonsei University
- Universitat Autònoma de Barcelona
- Intel
- Erasmus University Rotterdam
- University of California San Diego
- Atlassian
- Tecnológico de Monterrey
- IBM
- Columbia University
- Goldman Sachs
- University of Science and Technology of China
- McMaster University
- University of Houston System
- West Virginia University
- Cisco
- Lund University
- University of Copenhagen
- The University of Melbourne
- Technische Universität München (TUM)
- University of Washington
- University of California, Davis
- University of Zurich
- University of New Mexico
- JetBrains
- emlyon business school
- University of Amsterdam
- High Tech High Graduate School of Education
- Sapienza University of Rome
- deeplearning.ai

- University of Colorado Boulder
- HEC Paris
- MongoDB Inc.
- University of Colorado System
- Xi'an Jiaotong University
- Korea Advanced Institute of Science and Technology
- Michigan State University
- Association of International Certified Professional Accountants
- University of Geneva
- University of Toronto
- Oxfam
- UNSW Sydney (The University of New South Wales)
- Curtis Institute of Music
- University of Rochester
- Pohang University of Science and Technology
- Universidad de los Andes
- University of Nebraska
- National Research Tomsk State University

(Coursera, 2019)
edX

- Massachusetts Institute of Technology
- Harvard University
- University of California, Berkeley
- The University of Texas System
- Australian National University
- Boston University
- Georgetown University
- The Hong Kong Polytechnic University
- RWTH Aachen University
- Sorbonne Université
- Delft University of Technology (TU Delft)
- University of Adelaide
- University of British Columbia
- The University of Queensland
- University System of Maryland
- Arizona State University
- Berklee College of Music
- Brown University
- Caltech

A Specified Ubiquitous Learning Design for Seamless Learning

- Columbia University
- Cornell University
- Dartmouth College
- Davidson College
- École polytechnique fédérale de Lausanne
- ETH Zurich
- The Georgia Institute of Technology
- The Hong Kong University of Science and Technology
- IITBombay
- Imperial College London
- KIx: Karolinska Institutet
- Kyoto University
- KU Leuven University
- McGill
- Peking University
- Princeton University
- Rice University
- Seoul National University
- Technische Universität München
- Tsinghua University
- Université catholique de Louvain
- The University of California, San Diego
- University of Chicago
- The University of Edinburgh
- University of Hong Kong
- The University of Michigan
- University of Notre Dame
- University of Oxford
- University of Pennsylvania
- The University of Tokyo
- University of Toronto
- The University of Iceland
- University of Washington
- Wellesley College

(edX, 2014)

The massive list of valuable partners of Coursera and edx should be enough to explain why millions of users register to the MOOCs and enroll courses provided by those partners.

A Specified Ubiquitous Learning Design for Seamless Learning

Figure 5. Coursera web page screenshot (Coursera, 2018a)
Source: Coursera, 2018

Figure 6. Coursera web page screenshot (Coursera, 2018b)
Source: Coursera, 2018

Figure 7. Coursera web page screenshot (Coursera, 2018b)
Source: Coursera, 2018

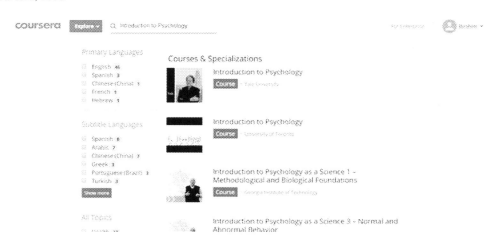

Figure 8. Coursera web page Introduction to Psychology course screenshot (Joordens, 2019)
Source: Joordens, 2019

Figure 9. Coursera web page Introduction to Psychology course screenshot (Joordens, 2019)
Source: Joordens, 2019

Open Content

Another significant characteristic of MOOCs is that all of the content provided by individual and institution partners are open to anyone who wants to enroll in any specific course. Users need to have a computer, tablet PC or even a smartphone and an internet connection in order to take any interested established course. Coursera has 645 English, 33 French, 10 Spanish, 8 Portuguese, 3 Chinese, 3 Russian, 2 German, 2 Japanese and 1 Turkish courses. It seems like most of the courses offered by Coursera in English; however, those courses are supported by subtitles for other languages (Coursera, 2018b). On the other hand edX has 1927 English, 204 Spanish, 66 Chinese-Mandarin, 51 French, 40 Italian, 5 Japanese, 5 Russian, 3 Dutch, 3 Korean, 3 Portuguese, 3 Turkish, 2 German, 1 Arabic, 1 Chinese-Simplified, 1 Hindi and 1 Hungarian courses (edX, 2019). In addition to Coursera and edX, other MOOC sites also offer numerous courses under numerous topics.

A Specified Ubiquitous Learning Design for Seamless Learning

Figure 10. Coursera web page Introduction to Psychology course screenshot (Joordens, 2019)
Source: Joordens, 2019

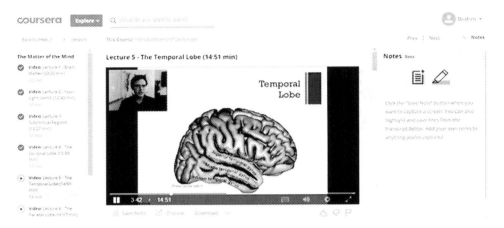

Figure 11. Coursera web page Introduction to Psychology course screenshot (Joordens, 2019)
Source: Joordens, 2019

Online

All contents delivered by MOOCs and their partners are online readings, images, presentations, videos and other instructional materials. Any motivated learner can find any course about any issue just by using a ubiquitous computing device with internet connection.

Well Planned and Structured Courses

As seen above almost all of the partners of the MOOCs are significantly experienced in higher education and instructional materials. Contents developed by those partners are also well planned and structured instructions. This characteristic of MOOCs can be considered as the most important one. If MOOCs

A Specified Ubiquitous Learning Design for Seamless Learning

Figure 12. Coursera web page Introduction to Psychology course screenshot (Joordens, 2019)
Source: Joordens, 2019

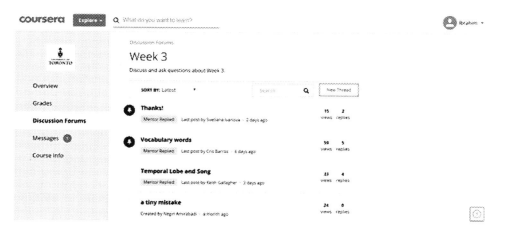

did not provide qualified instructions it was impossible to answer the question World Wide Web already provides any kind of information, why should we use MOOCs in order to gain knowledge and information? When a learner enrolls any course in a MOOC well organized, step by step instruction welcomes him/her. The course does not just include videos or readings, all kind of instructional materials are placed one by one according to the progress of the content. Even more, for some courses there is a timeline in order to plan learner's instruction schedule.

How Does a MOOC Work?

MOOCs do not only provide free well-structured courses, but they also facilitate learner-expert and learner-learner interactions at anytime and anywhere the learner need or wish. With respect to seamless learning MOOCs serve several seamless learning fundamentals which are *Seamless learning environments should assist both individual tasks and cooperative learning power of social interactions* (SLF2), *Seamless learning environments should provide "anytime" learning opportunities in order seamless learners to use their learnable moments effectively* (SLF3), *Seamless learning environments should provide "anywhere" learning opportunities to facilitate seamless learners' performances by eliminating locational restrictions* (SLF4), *Seamless learning environments should enhance the attainability of knowledge that makes feasible learning tasks in context* (SLF5). In addition, ubiquitous computing has a great role on the expanse of MOOCs in terms of production, establishment and user access. First of all in order to serve, MOOCs need a base system which can provide a related course to the learners.

Latter, partners of the MOOC sites, two MOOC sites' partners were listed before, offers their instruction to the learners with all materials through this MOOC system. In general, those MOOCs' systems are web based systems and they also have applications for smartphones and tablet PCs which shows that ubiquitous computing serves to the MOOCs and MOOCs users well. When a MOOC application on a ubiquitous computing device like smartphone or tablet PC is started or MOOC web page on a PC or laptop is opened a user-friendly interface welcomes the learners. For example, a screenshot of Coursera is placed below.

The learner can search the title which s/he needs to or wants to gain knowledge and information about it. Depending on to OER movement philosophy, courses on the MOOCs are free to access. The learner needs to sign up and login to the MOOC site and then s/he is ready to learn from the bests. After logging in to MOOC, a learner's page greets the learners.

At this page, the learner can see his/her ongoing courses and find more instructions offered by the partners of the MOOC. The learners are welcome to start any course released by the partners through the MOOC. When the learner searches the topic which s/he wants to learn about, a list of the instructions are listed with the name of the partner offered the course. In addition, the learner can filter the search results by the language, subtitle or related topic of the courses.

After listing by desired filters, the learner clicks on the course and general information of the course is given on the first page of the course.

The learner enrolls the course and s/he wants and ready to start a well-designed and structured instruction with a well-planned course schedule. At this point, if the learner wants to get a certificate s/he may need to pay a certificate fee, however if s/he wants to gain knowledge and information about the topic chosen by her/him, there is no fee required the instruction with all materials is completely free. Weekly progress and instructor's note may be shown after starting the course. Those features of the course are needed to offer a well-planned instruction.

The instructions of the course offered by the partners of MOOC include different type of course materials as readings, presentations, videos, questions and guides of the instructors. Furthermore, those materials are produced by the best institutions and instructors on the field of the related topic which is desired to learn.

The learner is free to download the materials used in the instruction in order to study the topic whenever s/he needs or wishes. Utilizing learnable moments of the learner is important.

MOOCs provide individual learning in addition to social learning with discussion forums. With these forums both student-student and student-expert interactions are guaranteed. With respect to seamless learning MOOCs systems seem to serve *SLF 2: Seamless learning environments should assist both individual tasks and cooperative learning power of social interaction;* furthermore, MOOCs establish a qualified connection between learner and expert. MOOCs systems by setting good interactions between instructors and learners serve another powerful pedagogical approach which can be named as "guidance of the instructor" or "scaffolding" which is also another significant seamless learning fundamental, *SLF 10: Seamless learning environments should be structured in the light of different pedagogical approaches and various instructional designs.*

In addition to all features of the MOOCs, the learners are free to get instruction again and again even after finishing the course. All members of the learning world are welcome to enroll in any course which they want to access well designed and well provided instructions.

As seen MOOCs facilitate to access any knowledge and information desired, the right thing, with the blessing of great partners of the MOOCs and ubiquitous computing devices at any time anywhere the learners need. Having another look at the definition of ubiquitous learning which is given by Yahya, et al. (Yahya et al., 2010) which is "U-learning is a learning paradigm which takes place in a ubiquitous computing environment that enables learning the right thing at the right place and time in the right way", MOOCs can be considered as great tools of ubiquitous learning. Furthermore, theoretically from

Figure 13. Example of Seamless Learning Activities table (Seow et al., 2008)
Source: Seow et al., 2008

Activity	Day	Location	Description
Challenge – Articulating the problem	1	Classroom	The teacher gave a short introduction to the problem of having too much garbage. Students created KWL* tables and shared with each other about their learning objectives (1 hour)
Experience – Field Activity	5	Supermarket and Fast Food Restaurant with wireless network	Three activities that students performed at a supermarket: 1. Study different sizes and materials for packaging and take photos of the products; 2. Observe how many plastic bags are dispensed at the checkout counters within five minutes; 3. Interview customers about their attitudes and practices of 3Rs; (2 hours) Students uploaded their data collected during the field trip at a fast food restaurant using the wireless network (10 minutes)
Reflecting and Planning - Post Field Activity 1	7	Computer Lab	Student provided feedbacks to each other's data collected and posed questions to environmental experts (1 hour)
Applying - Post Field Activity 2	14	Classroom	Student groups presented to the whole class about how their groups have designed artifacts for promoting 3Rs ideas and getting feedback from the class (1.5 hours)

K = What I know, W = What I want to know, L = What I learned

the point of seamless learning MOOCs serve well according to seamless learning fundamentals about the content, the time and the space issues. Also, MOOCs can be counted as great systems with respect to facilitating both individual and social learning in addition to providing accessibility of knowledge and information. Although there are many other learning management systems, so far there is not any learning management system which can serve any seamless learning environment or design. Researchers who are studying seamless learning had to design and develop their seamless learning management systems for their special purposes (Hwang et al., 2011; Looi et al., 2010; Wong, 2013a; Wong, 2013b).

SOLUTIONS AND RECOMMENDATIONS

A Specified Ubiquitous Learning Design for Seamless Learning

Think about a learning management system which provides formal and informal learning settings supporting in an out class activities. Furthermore that learning management system furnishes social learning by discussion forums in addition to well-prepared individualized learning contents. By developing mobile devices applications integrated with the main learning management system anytime and anywhere learning activities can be provided through that seamless learning management system structure. Within the seamless learning management system (SLMS) the delivery of instruction can be designed and developed depending on some specific standards, in order to make sure the quality of the learning.

Proposed Structure of SLMS

At first, the SLMS should have a general theme aiming to serve any instructor and any learner in the world. There are some other examples of such systems like MOOCs and Moodle. Institutions and individuals should be able to join the system as a partner or participant. As seen with MOOCs system, qualified and well-known institutions should feed the SLMS with a well-designed and structured instructional framework. The SLMS should contain two systems, one is the instructor's management system, and the other is learner's interface (the interface can be considered as a ubiquitous computing device application). Latter, the structure of the instructional framework should be designed and developed depending on seamless learning fundamentals stated in this chapter. On the SLMS the instructor should start a course and add activities, and then the learners are welcome to join to the SLMS and enroll the course included seamless learning activities. While adding the activities the instructor should be able to specify each of them as in or out of class activity (SLF1), social or individualized learning task or both, (SLF2) or requiring digital learning or real-life experiences (SLF6). The learner should be able to share their findings related to the tasks and their work with other learners. The SLMS may serve a cloud system in order to let the learners share their work. Within that cloud system, other learners should be able to articulate their thoughts about the work or findings shared and any learner should be able to ask questions to the owner about the findings or work shared through SLMS. For each activity, the instructor should be able to state which kind of tools (pen, notebook etc.) or devices (camera, tablet PC, smartphone, etc.) to be used in order the learner to perform the task (SLF7). The learner should be guided by clear instructions while performing the learning task. The learner should be able to perform tasks at "anytime" and "anywhere" needed or desired by using any kind of ubiquitous computing devices (SLF3 and SLF4). Furthermore, the learners should be able to ubiquitously be connected to the instructor and the learner should be able to access internet and other learners through the combination of ubiquitous computing device and the SLMS, so that instructor guide and attainability of knowledge will be guaranteed anytime and anywhere the learner needed (SLF5). And each learning task should be so supportive and connected to the next one that there should not be any separator line between any two tasks. In other words, the transition between learning activities should be as seamless as possible (SLF8). In addition, the activities should be carefully planned so that those activities should *combine learners' skills already they had and their developing ones, prior knowledge and newly assimilated* and constructed knowledge (SLF9). At last, the activities or the learning tasks should be designed and structured depending on *different pedagogical approaches and various instructional designs* (SLF10). A good example of seamless activities table is shown above.

FUTURE RESEARCH DIRECTIONS

That kind of a learning management system is open to study, design and develop in order to serve any institution or instructor wants to apply seamless learning to their curriculum. The proposed structure of SLMS could be a start point of designing and developing a ubiquitous learning system for any instructor or institution which desires to apply seamless learning into their curriculum. With a well-designed and structured learning managements system, ubiquitous computing and ubiquitous learning would be utilized in order to empower and universalize seamless learning. For any institution which considers designing and developing an SLMS, the seamless learning fundamentals and the proposed structure of SLMS would be significantly helpful. However, more researches and studies are needed in order to state an efficient model of SLMS, because seamless learning requires different features and implications from a learning management system which are not fulfilled by existing learning managements systems.

CONCLUSION

Seamless learning is about utilizing all opportunities aiming to improve teaching and learning. It is about combining informal learning (out of class activities) with formal learning (in class activities). It lets the learners support their individual learning with social sources. It also provides learning opportunities at any learnable moments (anytime) of the learners in addition to furnishing learning activities "anywhere" needed. Furthermore, seamless learning suggests that the learners should be able to access information and knowledge ubiquitously and effectively and they should have the right to reach instructors and experts anytime and anywhere they need. In a seamless learning environment the learners should be exposed to both digital and physical experiences in order to structure their knowledge and improve their understandings. All activities planned in a seamless learning environment should designed in a way that there should not be any distinctive line between in-class and out of class activities, individual and social learning, digital and physical experiences. Also, seamless learning designs should provide an effective constructive learning by offering learning tasks which support earlier experiences and knowledge. The last and the most important feature of seamless learning environments is planning and designing all learning tasks and activities in the light of different pedagogical approaches in order to offer a qualified learning system.

On the other hand, ubiquitous learning is about utilizing all ubiquitous computing components in order to improve learning. In spite of different definitions of seamless learning and ubiquitous learning they are nested terms in applications. Ubiquitous learning can be considered as the most important supportive power of seamless learning. Different ubiquitous learning systems like MOOCs should be analyzed in order to increase the effect of ubiquitous learning on seamless learning environments. Furthermore, ubiquitous computing and ubiquitous learning should be evaluated as empowering forces of seamless learning designs.

However, creating a seamless learning environment for a specific topic requires so much work. Teachers are the most responsible members of learning for this process and planning a seamless learning environment requires a good level of digital skills. Integration of technology in education plays very important role for this part of seamless learning and proposed seamless learning systems. Teachers should gain digital skills and they should have more experience with digital world in order to plan and run a seamless learning process about any specific topic. This can be considered as the first and the most important problem with seamless learning environments. However, by sharing seamless learning plans and instructions about running the seamless learning environment through a specified seamless learning system may eliminate the human source problem. Other teachers can use seamless learning plans prepared by others and they may take other teachers seamless learning processes as examples of applying seamless learning in their schools. In addition to human source problem of seamless learning there is a financial problem too. Seamless learning includes ubiquitous learning and ubiquitous learning requires ubiquitous computing. Most of the ubiquitous computing devices seem to be very expensive for many countries and members of learning club. With this respect, seamless learning increases the need of finance for education.

Despite of the human and finance source problems, as a result, a ubiquitous learning system should be designed and developed in order to generalize seamless learning implications. As mentioned before MOOCs are great example of universalizing a learning management system around the world. Despite of existing learning management systems like Moodle or others, any learning management system cannot fulfill the requirements of seamless learning environments. All implications conducted by researchers were realized by designing and developing specified ubiquitous learning systems. However, a generalized ubiquitous learning system could be established in order to serve any instructor or institution which plan to apply seamless learning into their instructional process. Seamless Learning Fundamentals stated in this chapter can be considered as a trigger force of all studies on establishing a ubiquitous learning system serving seamless learning environments.

REFERENCES

Baturay, M. H. (2015). An overview of the world of MOOCs. *Procedia: Social and Behavioral Sciences, 174*, 427–433. doi:10.1016/j.sbspro.2015.01.685

Calhoun, J. C. (1996). *The student learning imperative: implications for student affairs.* Washington, D.C.: American College Personnel Association. Retrieved from http://www.housing.berkeley.edu/student/ACPA_student_learning_imperative.pdf

Cárdenas-Robledo, L. A., & Peña-Ayala, A. (2018). Ubiquitous learning: A systematic review. *Telematics and Informatics, 35*(5), 1097–1132. doi:10.1016/j.tele.2018.01.009

Caswell, T., Henson, S., Jensen, M., & Wiley, D. (2014). February – 2008 Open Educational Resources : Enabling universal education. *International Review of Research in Open and Distance Learning, 9*(1), 1–7.

Coursera. (2013). *Coursera blog.* Retrieved from http://coursera.tumblr.com/post/42486198362/five-courses-receive-college-credit

Coursera. (2018a). *Coursera | Online Courses Credentials by Top Educators.* Retrieved from https://www.coursera.org/

Coursera. (2018b). *Free courses.* Retrieved from https://www.coursera.org/courses?languages=en&query=free+courses

Coursera. (2019). *Partners | Coursera.* Retrieved from https://www.coursera.org/about/partners

edX. (2014). *Schools and partners.* Retrieved from https://www.edx.org/schools-partners

edX. (2019). *edX Courses | View all online courses on edX.org.* Retrieved from https://www.edx.org/course

Gaebel, M. (2013). *MOOCs – Massive Open Online Courses.* Retrieved from http://www.leru.org/files/meetings/A3_EUA_Occasional_papers_MOOCs.pdf%5Cnhttp://www.leru.org/index.php/private/communities/vice-rectors-for-learning-and-teaching/

Galbraith, M. W. (2017). Philosophy and the instructional process. *Adult Learning, 11*(2), 11–13. doi:10.1177/104515959901100204

Hodkinson, P., Colley, H., & Malcolm, J. (2003). The interrelationships between informal and formal learning. *Journal of Workplace Learning, 15*(7/8), 313–318. doi:10.1108/13665620310504783

Hwang, G.-J., Wu, P.-H., & Ke, H.-R. (2011). An interactive concept map approach to supporting mobile learning activities for natural science courses. *Computers & Education, 57*(4), 2272–2280. doi:10.1016/j.compedu.2011.06.011

Joordens, S. (2019). *Introduction to Psychology - Home | Coursera.* Retrieved from https://www.coursera.org/learn/introduction-psych/home/welcome

Kuh, G. D. (1996). Guiding principles for creating seamless learning environments for undergraduates. *Journal of College Student Development, 37*(2), 135–148.

Kurşun, E. (2016). Açık eğitim kaynaklari. In *Öğretim Teknolojilerinin Temelleri Teoriler, Araştırmalar* (pp. 667–682). Eğilimler.

Looi, C., & Peter, S. (2010). Leveraging mobile technology for sustainable seamless learning: A research agenda. *British Journal of Educational Technology*, *41*(2), 154–169. doi:10.1111/j.1467-8535.2008.00912.x

Lyytinen, K., & Yoo, Y. (2002). Research Commentary: Issues and challenges in ubiquitous computing. *Communications of the ACM*, *45*(12), 62–65.

Nations, U. (1948). Universal Decleration. *Human Rights (Chicago, Ill.)*.

Ogata, H., Li, M., Hou, B., Uosaki, N., El-bishouty, M. M., & Yano, Y. (2011). SCROLL: Supporting to share and reuse ubiquitous learning log in the context of language learning. *Research and Practice in Technology Enhanced Learning*, *6*(2), 69–82. Retrieved from http://apsce.net/RPTEL/RPTEL2011JulIssue-Article1_pp69-82.pdf

Pappano, L. (2012). Massive open online courses are multiplying at a rapid pace. *The New York Times*. Retrieved from https://www.nytimes.com/2012/11/04/education/edlife/massive-open-online-courses-are-multiplying-at-a-rapid-pace.html

Sakamura, K., & Koshizuka, N. (2005). Ubiquitous computing technologies for ubiquitous learning. In *Proceedings - IEEE International Workshop on Wireless and Mobile Technologies in Education, WMTE 2005* (Vol. 2005, pp. 11–18). IEEE. 10.1109/WMTE.2005.67

Seow, P., Hui, Z. B., Hyo-jeong, S., Chee-kit, L., Wenli, C., & Seow, P. Chen, W. (2008). Towards a framework for seamless learning environments 3Rs – A Primary Environment Education Project. *8th International Conference of the Learning Sciences (ICLS)*, *2*, 327–334.

Shah, D. (2017). *Massive list of MOOC providers around the world*. Retrieved from https://www.class-central.com/report/mooc-providers-list/

Shah, D. (2018). *A product at every price: A review of MOOC stats and trends in 2017*. Retrieved from https://www.class-central.com/report/moocs-stats-and-trends-2017/

Weiser, M. (1993). *Ubiquitous computing*. Computer.

Wong, L.-H. (2012). A learner-centric view of mobile seamless learning. *British Journal of Educational Technology*, *43*(1), E19–E23. doi:10.1111/j.1467-8535.2011.01245.x

Wong, L. H. (2013a). Analysis of students' after-school mobile-assisted artifact creation processes in a seamless language learning environment. *Journal of Educational Technology & Society*, *16*(2), 198–211.

Wong, L. H. (2013b). Enculturating self-directed learners through a facilitated seamless learning process framework. *Technology, Pedagogy and Education*, *22*(3), 319–338. doi:10.1080/1475939X.2013.778447

Wong, L. H., & Looi, C. K. (2010). Vocabulary learning by mobile-assisted authentic content creation and social meaning-making: Two case studies. *Journal of Computer Assisted Learning*, *26*(5), 421–433. doi:10.1111/j.1365-2729.2010.00357.x

Wong, L. H., & Looi, C. K. (2011). What seams do we remove in mobile-assisted seamless learning? A critical review of the literature. *Computers & Education, 57*(4), 2364–2381. doi:10.1016/j.compedu.2011.06.007

Wu, H. K. (2003). Linking the microscopic view of chemistry to real-life experiences: Intertextuality in a high-school science classroom. *Science education, 87*(6), 868–891. doi:10.1002ce.10090

Yahya, S., Ahmad, E. A., & Jalil, K. A. (2010). The definition and characteristics of ubiquitous learning: A discussion [La definición y características del aprendizaje ubicuo: Un debate]. *International Journal of Education and Development Using Information and Communication Technology, 6*(1), 117–127.

KEY TERMS AND DEFINITIONS

Formal Settings: Scheduled a planned in-class activities.

Informal Settings: Scheduled a planned out of class activities.

MOOCs: Massive open online courses, a learning system that provides open and well-structured online contents to the learners.

Seamless Learning: A new approach of implementation of learning which provides seamless transition between different learning tasks.

Seamless Learning Management System: A proposed learning management system specified for seamless learning.

Ubiquitous Computing: The digital technology including all kinds of portable digital devices and software applications for those devices.

Ubiquitous Learning: A type of learning which is enhanced by ubiquitous computing.

Chapter 3
Supporting Digital Information Literacy in the Age of Open Access:
Considerations for Online Course Design

Sarah Felber
University of Maryland Global Campus, USA

Pascal Roubides
University of Maryland Global Campus, USA

ABSTRACT

In this chapter, the authors aim to inform the audience about the issues pertaining to access to educational resources, with a focus on open access; how to access such sources; ways of integrating principles of information literacy into the entire educational experience; and the potential of open access sources in providing much needed, affordable information literacy to all knowledge seekers, especially in academic endeavors. The issue of information literacy and open access is defined and explored, with a bias toward practical implementation and impact in the academic setting, culminating in hands-on recommendations for academic professionals.

DOI: 10.4018/978-1-5225-9779-7.ch003

Supporting Digital Information Literacy in the Age of Open Access

INTRODUCTION

Advances in technology have brought about a plethora of benefits in many fields of human endeavor, including in education and learning. Following the trend to infuse more technology in educational settings, educational research has shifted its focus from previously dominant philosophies (behaviorism and cognitivism) to more encompassing ideology (constructivism and connectivism) that promotes the use of technology in creating widely accessible and socially inclusive ubiquitous learning experiences. Based on such changes in the perceptions of how learning takes place, and how content necessary for learning can or should be accessed, different pathways for designing and delivering information have emerged.

With the advent of online platforms specifically created for managing and sharing knowledge and information in the new era, the expected increase in using connected networks for delivering and accessing information has been ongoing for almost two decades. Along with that new paradigm, shifts in the way content is designed and delivered as well as theories supporting these ideas have been constant. Moving rapidly from e-learning to m-learning to ubiquitous learning, both content and access to it seem to have become, in some ways, a hindrance to achieving information literacy in an otherwise digitally connected world.

Regardless of any technologies or their benefits to learning, creating content and enabling prospective learners' access to it has and shall always remain a necessity. Content for the most part has been the mainstay of large commercial publishing companies, and costs of educational and scholarly materials have been on the rise for several decades. Education costs in the United States, for instance, have had a multi-fold increase against the rate of inflation since the early 1980s (Roubides, 2018). New approaches in the development and dissemination of educational and scholarly content have been the goal of new movements, such as the open educational resources (OER) and open access scholarship movements, which contribute to a ubiquitous learning environment by allowing more people access to content without limitations in time and space.

Promotion of and interest in open content, whether in the form of open access scholarship, which is usually funded by public institutions, hence taxpayer money, or in the form of OER, which can be used to develop formal or informal, academic and non-academic learning experiences, have been growing in recent years. While teaching and learning issues surrounding OER have been garnering increased attention (see, e.g. Colvard, Watson, & Park, 2018; Lawrence & Lester, 2018; Winitsky-Stephens & Pickavance, 2018), the spotlight being shined on open access of scholarship (henceforth, *open access*) has often focused on economic viability (see, e.g. Frankland & Ray, 2017; Jack, 2017) and on the perspectives of the producers of such scholarship (see, e.g. Rowley, Johnson, Sbaffi, Frass, & Devine, 2017; Watson, 2018) with little attention given to the impact on learners as consumers of information products.

This chapter will discuss considerations for online course designers who seek to assist learners in meeting the digital information literacy demands created by open access. Online course designers in this context may include anyone who works alone or as part of an online course design team, from instructional designers to subject matter experts or instructors. The chapter includes trends in open access publishing of which online course designers should be aware; discusses of the role of libraries in helping learners obtain open access materials; and proposes the use of the Association of College & Research Libraries' Framework for Information Literacy for Higher Education as a lens for understanding what concepts are important to learners when working with open access materials. The chapter culminates in a summary of recommendations for course designers.

DIGITAL INFORMATION LITERACY AND OPEN ACCESS: AN OVERVIEW

Generally speaking, information literacy may be one of the most pressing issues of modern societies in the quest to nurture an informed and educated populace. The rapid expansion of the Internet's reach and coverage has been a boon for the availability of information—but also, unfortunately, for the availability of misinformation. Though educators have long recognized the importance of information literacy, public attention on this issue in the United States reached fever pitch during and after the 2016 presidential election, when accusations of "fake news" took the spotlight.

Since the introduction of the concept of information literacy half a century ago, instruction in this area has become increasingly important at all levels of the educational spectrum. Defined as the ability to locate, evaluate, and use appropriate information for a given purpose, information literacy may be expressly taught in academic writing courses as well as in other subject areas, as learners are guided to evaluate sources for authority, reliability, and relevance. In formal post-secondary learning in particular, part of this instruction is often focused on articles found in academic journals, sources to which learners may have had little to no prior exposure, but that are held up as a higher standard of being able to provide credible, in-depth information.

As consumers of information increasingly find that information—including scholarly sources—in electronic form, the term *digital literacy* has often been used when discussing the skills and abilities needed to navigate information created, stored, and accessed digitally. Given competing views of the relationship between information literacy and digital literacy (Cordell, 2013; Jarson, 2015), in this chapter, the term *digital information literacy* is used to refer to information literacy skills for a digitally connected world.

Facilitated by the affordances of digital technologies, the open access movement has arisen largely in response to the concern voiced by many in academia about handing over control of their intellectual work to for-profit enterprises (Maternowsky, 2009) and the view of knowledge as a public good (Verschraegen & Schiltz, 2007). The cost of such sources of information and knowledge from commercial publishers has been growing at a rate far exceeding the general rate of inflation, and despite early expectations, digitization has not eased the financial burden (Wenzler, 2017). A recent survey of the costs of academic journals showed that journals in many disciplines had average annual journal subscription prices of over $2000 (Bosch & Henderson, 2016). At these prices, libraries are forced to limit their collections, and even a single subscription is out of reach for many individual knowledge seekers.

The public funding of scholarly work further strengthens arguments for open access (Kimbraugh & Gasaway, 2016). In many cases, the public must buy from commercial publishers the same research that its own tax contributions have funded through grants and salaries at public institutions. As concern for the cost and fairness of access grows, so does interest in publishing scholarly work through open-access venues. Increasingly, funding agencies require that research output they fund be published in open access venues.

The term *open access* refers to the ability of the public to freely access and use materials. The influential Budapest Open Access Initiative (2002) defines open access as

free availability on the public internet, permitting any users to read, download, copy, distribute, print, search, or link to the full texts of these articles, crawl them for indexing, pass them as data to software, or use them for any other lawful purpose, without financial, legal, or technical barriers other than those inseparable from gaining access to the internet itself. (para. 3)

Their definition alludes to the affordances of internet technology to make materials accessible, and it requires the granting of permission for a broad range of uses, thereby distinguishing open access from a model that simply makes material available on public library shelves. Though the free nature of open access materials generally receives the most attention, an interesting aspect of the definition is that it relies on users' ability to reuse open access materials, an issue that will be revisited later in this chapter.

It is important to note, as well, that various types of materials can be open. Though the term *open access* on its own is generally reserved for research output, like journal articles and monographs, OERs are also becoming more popular and important in the instructional design and delivery of academic courses, especially in the online environment. These resources include textbooks, lesson plans, media, software, and even full academic courses. Also of interest is the growth of serious academic dialogue on blogs and social networks. Once viewed as being of little worth for academics and research, these venues are now entering the academic and scholarly conversation, amid the climate of online openness. The work of distance education researcher Tony Bates provides a nice example of both OERs and scholarly conversation via blogging. During the process of writing his open textbook, *Teaching in a Digital Age*, Bates (2015) posted chapter drafts on his blog (http://www.tonybates.ca/), generating public conversation among the very scholars whose work his book covered, as well as other blog visitors. Though this chapter focuses primarily on scholarly publication, similar questions can be raised about awareness, discovery, and appropriate use of OERs, blogs, and the various other open materials that are bursting onto the scene.

The proliferation of open-access scholarly materials is clearly a step in the right direction for making high-quality sources of information available to and usable by all, for ubiquitous learning experiences, but it also places increased demands on learners for digital information literacy. Open access means that knowledge seekers have more places to look for sources and additional issues to consider when evaluating sources. Learners must be guided in the identification and evaluation of sources, as selecting appropriate sources will be crucial both within and beyond the virtual classroom. Yet learning professionals may, themselves, be in the process of navigating the rapidly changing landscapes of open access and digital information literacy. Accordingly, the next section describes trends in open access publishing of which online course designers should be aware.

SCHOLARLY SOURCES GOING OPEN

At the most fundamental level, online course designers who wish to help learners make use of scholarly sources must know where to find them. Open access is bringing changes to the nature of this task, making scholarly sources more ubiquitous; this section describes these changes.

The 21st century has seen online overtake print as the primary way to access scholarly sources (Marks & Janke, 2012; Prabha, 2007). The digitization of resources has many advantages, among them the ability of users to access resources at any time and any place, and of multiple users to access a resource simultaneously. But digitization may also present a barrier to access, in that print materials on library shelves tend to be publicly available, whereas digital materials accessed through library databases tend to be password protected, to protect the financial interests of publishers. Accessing scholarly journals without the support of a library is also not a viable option for most; despite early speculation that digitization would reduce costs, that result has not been obtained (Marks & Janke, 2012). Digitization without openness, therefore, is limited in its ability to provide content to anyone, anywhere, at any time.

Traditional information literacy instruction may, in fact, reinforce the idea that scholarly content is not fully available to all. This instruction may rightly stress the importance of scholarly journal articles based on the qualifications of their authors, the degree of reliability supported by the peer review process, their depth of information, and their ability to bring learners into the scholarly conversation of a field. Part of this instruction often includes a sharp distinction between scholarly articles sourced through a library database, and websites or items found on the "free web." Items on the free web, learners are taught, have to be more carefully examined to determine their degree of authority, reliability, and coverage. In essence, the message is that the "best" sources are not likely to be free.

There has been pushback against this tendency for instructors to emphasize categorization of sources by where and how they are published, even independent of the open access movement. Wiebe (2012) expresses frustration as a librarian working with students who are given assignments with requirements for certain types of sources in certain numbers (e.g. at least two scholarly journal articles, no more than one website, mix of print and online sources). Wiebe argues that this "checklist" approach stifles the critical thinking required to assess sources based on their individual merits and appropriateness for a particular assignment and topic.

The open access movement, while making scholarship more universally available, also makes learners' task of identifying appropriate scholarly sources more challenging by changing much of what used to be true about where to find scholarly work. To be sure, many articles are still published in traditional commercial journals (also called toll-access journals) and accessed through library databases or, for a fee, on journal websites. Increasingly however, scholars, unhappy with ceding their intellectual property rights to publishers, are turning to other models and publishing in other venues. Scholarly sources can be found in more places than ever before.

Self-Archive, Green, Gold, Platinum

One option for making scholarly work open access is to publish in a toll-access journal, but self-archive the work, making it available to the public for free. This method, called green open access, requires that the copyright agreement with the journal publisher allow for self-archiving. Authors may self-archive in a variety of ways. These can include depositing works in institutional repositories, created by institutions to house the work of their academic communities, or in disciplinary repositories, created by scholars or organizations within a discipline for the same purpose. Authors may also choose to place their work on personal websites or social networking sites like academia.edu or ResearchGate.

A second alternative to toll-access journals is gold-access publishing. In the gold-access model, journals publish works that are freely accessible to the public. The cost of publishing in gold open access journals may be covered by article processing fees charged to the author, who can sometimes pass on expenses to their employing or grant-funding institutions (Solomon & Björk, 2012). Some journals publish only open-access articles, while others take a hybrid approach, giving authors the choice of toll access publishing or open access publishing for a fee.

Platinum open access is now sometimes being recognized as a different publishing model from gold open access. In this view, the term "gold open access" refers only to journals with author processing charges for open access, while "platinum open access" is used for journals that are completely open access without author processing charges (Beall, 2012). Funding for platinum open access journals may come from a sponsoring foundation or agency.

Peer Review

A key feature signaling reliability of scholarly work is peer review, making it important to understand the role of peer review in open access publishing. Typically, institutional and disciplinary repositories have no peer review requirements; work archived there may include pre-prints or post-prints of journal articles that have undergone the peer review process, or they may be unreviewed (although new models in open peer review are emerging—see Pandelis et al., 2017). The same goes, of course, for articles posted on personal websites and social networking sites. Open access journals typically incorporate peer review, but the character of the peer review process can vary widely (Wicherts, 2016); readers unfamiliar with a particular journal should be prepared to investigate its publishing standards.

Of particular concern are the so-called "pay-to-publish" journals. Though many open access journals charge article processing fees to cover publishing expenses, the term "pay-to-publish" is generally reserved for journals with predatory practices. These journals have low standards of quality, making publishing decisions based on receipt of a fee. They may have the appearance of a peer review process, but this process is either non-existent or not of the rigor that one would expect from a well-respected journal (Harzing, & Adler, 2016). It can be difficult to identify a pay-to-publish or predatory journal, but some authors, including Harzing and Adler (2016) and Shamseer, et al. (2017) have put forth criteria for consideration.

Awareness

Those involved in the course design process certainly cannot help guide learners in an understanding of open access unless they are aware of it themselves. A number of studies have found limited awareness of open access publishing on the part of college and university faculty, though there is variation from one location or discipline to another, and overall awareness seems to be increasing. In a 2007 University of California survey, almost two thirds of faculty respondents reported that they were unaware of, or had little knowledge about, open access journals (University of California, 2007). Several years later, in a study of business faculty, Hahn and Wyatt (2014) found that nearly 50% were unaware of open access journals in their fields. The type of institution can play a role as well. Kocken and Wical (2013) report on their survey of faculty at a small liberal arts university, in which over 50% were unaware of open access journals in their fields, and in fact, over 20% did not have even a basic understanding of what open access was. More encouragingly, in a study of Texas A&M University faculty across disciplines, Yang and Li (2015) found that 88% of faculty were aware of an open access journal in their field. Xia's (2010) meta-analysis determined that, overall, faculty awareness of open access has been increasing since the mid-1990s and was expected to continue increasing.

Instructional designers and librarians involved in course design may wish to explore open access resources with faculty and subject matter experts, as the availability of open access resources and awareness level of team members cannot be taken for granted.

Course designers' awareness is the first step in helping learners build information literacy as open access grows. In addition, online libraries play a very important role in helping learners work with the variety of sources that are available. The role of libraries is the subject of the next section.

THE ROLE OF LIBRARIES WHEN SCHOLARLY SOURCES GO OPEN

Online course designers should consider what role their institutional library might play in supporting learners' use of open access materials and development of digital information literacy. Given that a major role of libraries in the toll-access model is to arrange for the purchase of materials and supply them to users, one might ask whether the open access movement could, at some point, contribute to the obsolescence of libraries. At this point, that appears unlikely. Open access, in fact, presents new and interesting challenges in information management, and online libraries especially have a strong role to play in helping online instructors and learners identify and obtain appropriate resources. These components involved in bringing to users the materials they need have been called discovery, "the process of finding things on a topic," and fulfillment, "the process of acquiring things that have been discovered" (Fons, 2016). Martin (2010) calls libraries' efforts to help with the discovery and fulfillment of open access materials "a value-added service for patrons." Though perhaps the aforementioned "patrons" (library users) could get to these materials on their own, libraries can make the process faster and easier, while also providing education on working with open access sources.

There are various discovery methods that individuals try on their own when looking for information on a given topic. For many learners, the most common tool—and maybe even the only tool—used is the Google search engine (Connaway, White, Lanclos, & Le Cornu, 2013; Marks & Janke, 2012). When open access materials are discovered in this way, the discovery process can sometimes lead seamlessly to fulfillment, without the intervention of a library. But evaluation and selection of sources remain an important part of what the user must accomplish, and libraries have a role to play here.

Although Google is often an effective discovery tool, appearance of a source in Google search results depends upon a variety of factors. Google helps this process along through its indexation of scholarly material in Google Scholar, and through guidance for improving the likelihood that open access materials will appear in search results (Google Scholar, n.d.), but if open access databases are not in compliance with the guidelines, it may be more difficult for users to find open access materials via Google search. Libraries can provide another avenue for discovering these items by identifying good sources of open access materials and including them among the resources learners can find through the online library portal. There are multiple ways that this can occur. Many of the databases to which libraries subscribe, such as ScienceDirect, index some journals that have moved to an open access model. Libraries can also link to open access collections like PubMed Central. In addition, libraries can elect to facilitate search of open access databases through aggregators like EBSCO Discovery Service, which allow interested readers or researchers to search across multiple databases at once. Overall, assisting in discovery of open access materials is a challenge for libraries, which employ a variety of strategies. In the future, more consistent use of metadata on open access materials could help libraries with this task (Bonn, 2015; Bulock, Hosburgh, & Mann, 2015).

Discovery and fulfillment of open access resources is often one integrated process, but this is not always the case. Sometimes users discover citation information only, and still need to figure out how to access the resource. With open access materials being found in so many different locations, including journal websites, institutional and disciplinary repositories, personal websites, and social networking sites, fulfillment can be a challenge. Though all readers can access these materials (given access to the internet), not all have the ability or inclination to locate them.

Libraries' use of link resolvers has been one way to address the problem of fulfillment. Link resolvers are tools that take as input certain information about a source and use that information to match a target URL, which may change over time (Younghusband, 2005). Libraries can include databases of open access materials among those targeted by their link resolvers, thereby easing the task of fulfillment for their users.

One especially notable use of link resolvers is with Google Scholar, which combines the ease of a Google search with a focus on scholarly sources. By using a link resolver integrated with Google Scholar, libraries can help interested readers or researchers to quickly retrieve sources found through Google scholar, whether open access or non-open library holdings.

Libraries also assist with fulfillment by offering interlibrary loan (ILL) services. Through ILL, libraries obtain and deliver materials that are not in their own holdings. Libraries have been observing a contraction in ILL requests in recent years, a change due, in part, to the growth of open access (McGrath, 2015). However, so far ILL remains relevant and is even used in connection with open access. McGrath (2014) responds to the idea that the expansion of open access will lead to the death of ILL, listing a number or reasons that ILL will survive. One reason is that green open access publishing often involves an embargo period, a waiting period between publication and the author's ability to self-archive. If the journal in question is not in the library's holdings, then ILL requests to access articles during the embargo period can be made. Citing Bennett (2012), McGrath observes that libraries may even choose not to subscribe to certain green open access journals, instead preferring to rely on ILL during the embargo period, after which those interested can be referred to the self-archived copy of an article. Another reason McGrath gives for the use of ILL with open access materials is that users may have difficulty finding what they are looking for. Baich (2015) echoes this point, arguing that users are willing to forego the speed of locating open access materials themselves for the ease and convenience of making ILL requests. She found that borrowing requests for open access materials at a large public university increased every year from 2010 to 2013.

While learners may consult libraries for assistance, they can also be expected to do much of their searching on their own. It is especially important that they develop the ability to do so in preparation for lifelong learning experiences that may occur without institutional support. Course designers may find value in using the Framework for Information Literacy for Higher Education as a lens for examining the digital information literacy concepts that will be important for learners to master and take with them beyond their formal education.

OPEN ACCESS THROUGH THE LENS OF THE ACRL FRAMEWORK

In 2015, the Association of College & Research Libraries (ACRL) introduced its Framework for Information Literacy for Higher Education, replacing its previous guidance from the year 2000. The new framework focuses on integrating principles of information literacy into the entire educational experience, with the learner's critical thinking and inquiry as prominent aspects of the framework.

For course designers seeking to develop learners' digital information literacy, the framework can provide a guide to the concepts that will be important for learners in working with open access materials. They can thus help learners prepare to develop the related dispositions and engage in the related practices in lifelong ubiquitous learning experiences. The framework is presented as six frames, each including a core concept along with related knowledge practices and dispositions, with four having clear relevance to working with open access materials.

Authority is Constructed and Contextual

This frame discusses the importance of understanding what leads to the recognition of authority within a given domain. Connections can be found between open access and several of the knowledge practices in this frame:

- Learners should "use research tools and indicators of authority to determine the credibility of sources, understanding the elements that might temper this credibility" (ACRL, 2015, p. 4). When searching a library database, it is often possible for a learner to limit search results to scholarly journal articles. Open access materials, however, are often located and accessed outside of library databases, requiring other means to determine authority and credibility.
- Learners should "recognize that authoritative content may be packaged formally or informally and may include sources of all media types" (ACRL, 2015, p. 4). This practice suggests a questioning of the very system by which academia traditionally measures the value of scholarly work. Open access represents just one way in which authors can step outside the conventional expectations of scholarship. Learners may be encouraged to consider whether and how the dominant publishing model lends value to scholarly material. (For related discussion, see Beilin, 2015.)
- Learners should "understand the increasingly social nature of the information ecosystem where authorities actively connect with one another and sources develop over time" (ACRL, 2015, p. 4). The climate of openness has encouraged ongoing and public idea exchange and knowledge construction among scholars, for example as in blogs, as previously discussed. Learners should recognize that conversations among experts may be encountered on the open web, and recognize the relationship between these conversations and peer-reviewed, published work.

The issue of developing sources over time leads directly to the next core concept of the framework.

Information Creation as a Process

This second frame relates to the understanding that sources are created through varying processes, and that some processes may be better aligned with particular information needs than others. Two knowledge practices stand out as particularly relevant to open access:

- Learners should "articulate the traditional and emerging processes of information creation and dissemination in a particular discipline" (ACRL, 2015, p. 5). Open access is a driving force in new processes for creating and disseminating information.
- Learners should "recognize the implications of information formats that contain static or dynamic information" (ACRL, 2015, p. 5). Whereas traditionally published articles are static, some types of open access materials are dynamic in their content or availability. For example, authors may post papers online before publication, remove them during the peer review process, and later put up post-prints in an open access format.

Information Has Value

The connection here to open access is that it is precisely because of the value of information that access to it is important. It can be difficult to discern the value of various information sources when there is so much, and such varied, freely available information. Several of the knowledge practices in this frame have clear connections with open access:

- Learners should "understand that intellectual property is a legal and social construct that varies by culture" (ACRL, 2015, p. 6). Publishing practices are central to the question of who controls access to and use of information resources.
- Learners should "articulate the purpose and distinguishing characteristics of copyright, fair use, open access, and the public domain" (ACRL, 2015, p. 6). This is the one direct mention of open access in the framework. The ACRL recognizes that open access is a significant part of the information landscape and that learners should be aware of its existence and features.
- Learners should "recognize issues of access or lack of access to information sources" (ACRL, 2015, p. 6). When attending a school that has a library with access to full text databases and interlibrary loan services, learners have privileged access to scholarly information. By recognizing this, they can learn the value and importance of open access.

Searching as Strategic Exploration

The idea here is that learners must develop the skills to find the information they need – using a process of discovery to find sources on a topic and to explore beyond their initial ideas on a topic. This last portion of the ACRL framework breaks the discovery process into component skills, and connections are evident between several of these skills and open access:

- Learners should "match information needs and search strategies to appropriate search tools" (ACRL, 2015, p. 9). As we've seen, open access has the effect of broadening the range of search tools for scholarly materials. While library databases have long been recognized as a preferred tool for this purpose, the increase in open access has brought with it increased usefulness for alternate strategies, including use of Google Scholar and other search engines.
- Learners should "understand how information systems (i.e., collections of recorded information) are organized in order to access relevant information" (ACRL, 2015, p. 9). Lower-level learners can first be introduced to the idea of articles published in journals and indexed in databases, as well as open access articles collected in various online repositories. As learners move into more advanced studies, they become familiar with the particular journals, databases, and repositories crucial to their fields of study.
- Learners should "use different types of searching language (e.g., controlled vocabulary, keywords, natural language) appropriately" (ACRL, 2015, p. 9). Learners are most likely accustomed to using something akin to natural language search when using Google, and they are taught specialized search techniques, such as keywords and Boolean operators, when searching library databases. To maximize their success in locating open access sources via Google Scholar and other open search tools, they may need to apply many of the same specialized search techniques used with library databases.

So far, the focus has been on how learners locate, evaluate, and understand information, but learners are also users and emerging creators of information. Thus, questions of copyright and reuse are important, and these are issues that are deeply intertwined with open access. All widely used definitions of open access, including that of the Budapest Open Access Initiative (2002), specify that a strict definition of open access requires materials not only to be freely accessible, but also to be freely available for copying and reuse. Many authors license their open access materials with Creative Commons or other licenses that guarantee reuse, but the presence or absence of reuse restrictions is not always so clear. Some authors may release their work without specifying whether reuse restrictions apply, and some publishers claiming to offer open access do, in fact, place restrictions on reuse (Hrynaszkiewicz & Cockerill, 2012). Though it may be difficult to guide learners through this issue, exploring the ambiguities of reuse together with learners is one way of bringing them into the fold of current scholarly conversation.

SUMMARY OF RECOMMENDATIONS FOR COURSE DESIGNERS

This section summarizes recommendations for the design of online course designers that support digital information literacy with consideration for open access.

Join Forces With the Library

Course designers should maintain a relationship with their institution's library and understand the library's approach to helping users work with open access materials. An institutional library offers crucial support, not only for learners, but for course designers as well. Librarians are typically more than willing to work with course designers on their own understanding of resources and on developing ways to work with learners. Course designers can use this list of questions as a starting point for developing and maintaining a productive relationship with the library:

- Is there a library liaison for my department, and if so, who is it?
- In what ways does the library work with learners to promote (digital) information literacy? Is there a library course for learners? Does my institution use embedded librarians? Are there online tutorials to help learners find and evaluate sources?
- In what ways does the library work with course designers and instructors to promote (digital) information literacy? Are there workshops available?
- How does the library support users in finding open access materials? Are open access databases searchable through the online library portal?

Stay Informed

As discussed above, awareness of open access, though increasing, remains variable. It is important for course designers to cultivate their own awareness of issues surrounding open access, both general and discipline-specific.

Course designers and other academic personnel can cultivate their own awareness of open access by following higher education media sources like *Inside Higher Ed* (https://www.insidehighered.com) and *The Chronicle of Higher Education* (http://www.chronicle.com), each of which publishes frequent news and commentary about open access and other pertinent issues. They can also participate in workshops and webinars offered by their institutions' libraries or by outside organizations.

In addition to maintaining general knowledge about open access, course designers can also build the knowledge and awareness they share with learners by keeping abreast of publishing trends and attitudes toward open access in the disciplines for which they design courses. The role and perception of open access can vary widely from one discipline to another; understanding the climate for open access in one's discipline is part of expertise in the discipline's knowledge practices. The examples below briefly illustrate some of the diversity that is found in the open access landscapes of various disciplines:

Chemistry

Many science fields have been leaders in open access, but chemistry has somewhat lagged behind other fields like biology and physics in this regard (Wilson & Humphrey, 2017). Chemistry publications come with some of the highest subscription costs (Bosch & Henderson, 2016), making open access particularly important. In addition, agencies funding research may require open access. For example, the National Institutes of Health (NIH) Public Access Policy of 2008 specifies open access requirements for federally funded research (Pence & Losoff, 2011), and the Bill & Melinda Gates Foundation has strict open access requirements for its funded research (Bill & Melinda Gates Foundation, 2017). Recent years have seen several chemistry journals move to open access models; while some of these show promise as well-respected publications, reputation and impact factor of open access journals in comparison to traditional toll access journals remains a concern (Wilson & Humphrey, 2017).

Linguistics

The field of linguistics has experienced a forceful move into open access publishing during the 21st century. Grassroots efforts by linguists have strongly supported open access publishing, and prominent journals and organizations have taken corresponding action. The professional organization Linguistic Society of America (LSA) has made changes to its publishing practices, introducing a new platinum open access journal and meeting green open access standards for its other publications (LSA, 2013). In another notable move, the editorial board of the journal *Lingua* resigned en masse after a disagreement with the publisher, Elsevier, about open access policies (Wexler, 2015). This is an interesting situation because Elsevier was running *Lingua* as a hybrid open access journal with article processing fees (APCs) charged to authors. Linguists are less likely to have access to funding that covers APCs than authors in the hard sciences, making Elsevier's open access option out of reach for many. After their resignation, the former editorial board of Lingua went on to found a new platinum open access journal, *Glossa*. The commitment of these editors to open access has led to the exploration of alternative funding mechanisms so that high-quality research can be freely disseminated and used without cost to authors.

Business

As noted earlier, Hahn and Wyatt reported in 2014 that nearly 50% of business faculty were unaware of open access journals in their disciplines. Of those who were aware of open access journals, many did not want to publish in those venues, citing their lack of prestige (Hahn & Wyatt, 2014). This situation highlights one of the major issues in open access that every discipline has to address to some degree: The value of open access publishing is dependent upon the willingness of scholars to participate in an open access system, while scholars' willingness depends upon the perceived value of open access publishing. It is not surprising, then, that movement towards open access can sometimes be slow and difficult, as it depends on a shift of the ethos of a field.

Encourage Critical Thinking About Sources

The new information landscape demands a redoubling of efforts to guide learners in evaluating sources found both with and without the assistance of library tools.

Georgas (2015) found that, when asked to find any source on a topic, undergraduates are more likely to come up with a high-quality scholarly source using a library search tool than using Google. However, with more specific direction to find a scholarly article, there is a smaller gap in the quality of what they find using the two search tools (Georgas, 2015). Learners should therefore be supported in searching for and evaluating sources on the open web, with emphasis on the type of source that is most appropriate for the task at hand.

This kind of guidance has to go beyond surface characteristics of sources like publication types and domain names. For example, we have seen that blogs, though they have sometimes been dismissed wholesale as unreliable sources, are now emerging as a relevant part of scholarly conversation. It is now even possible to find blog posts being referenced in peer-reviewed scholarly literature. (For instance, see Prinsloo and Slade (2014), who refer to a post from Audrey Watters's blog "Hack Education.") At the same time, what appears to be a legitimate journal article could be published by a predatory journal without an effective peer review process. Teaching learners ways to critically evaluate all of their sources is more important now than ever.

Learners may have been taught at some point that certain domain names indicate reliable sources. They may believe, for example, that .edu, .gov, and .org indicate good sources and .com indicates a poor source. This is another area where learners can be prompted to deepen their critical thinking about sources, considering the authorship of sources, regardless of their internet domains, and the biases and other limitations that may influence sources.

There are many online sources that course designers can use to develop creative lessons on evaluating Internet-based sources. One of these, which is suitable for instruction at lower educational levels but that could also be used at the college/university level, is "The Pacific Northwest Tree Octopus" (http://zapatopi.net/treeoctopus), a site about a completely fictitious endangered species, complete with a Frequently Asked Questions page and links to media and information about other (non-fictitious) animals of interest. More generally, designers can seek out online sources that tie in with the subject matter of their course being developed and create lessons that help learners critically evaluate and contrast various sources on a topic.

CONCLUSION

Open access, while broadening the availability of scholarly sources, also increases the complexity of digital information literacy.

In a toll access model, scholarly sources are most commonly accessed through academic libraries, and for learners early in their academic careers, discovering the resources available through a school library can be a revelation. Through library instruction and use, learners develop the ability to home in on high-quality academic sources more easily, compared to an internet search, which is often their initially preferred method of finding sources.

With the introduction and growth of open access, library services and instruction continue to be important since, as discussed, libraries have various ways of directing users to open access sources. However, learning to evaluate information and sources, whether they are accessed with or without the use of library tools, is even more fundamental to every learner's overall development as an information consumer functioning in increasingly ubiquitous learning environments.

The increase in open access means that more high-quality scholarly materials are available online to the public. With that availability comes the need to recognize scholarly information and to understand when it is useful. This is just one part of the puzzle of digital information literacy, which requires that individuals develop a well-rounded understanding of the various types of information they may encounter online. Reinforcement of digital information literacy lessons across disciplines will help learners to prepare for higher level academic work that they might choose to pursue and to practice their information literacy skills in a variety of contexts, with the goal of transferring those skills to other areas of their lives.

REFERENCES

Association of College & Research Libraries (ACRL). (2015). *Framework for information literacy for higher education*. Retrieved from http://www.ala.org/acrl/standards/ilframework

Baich, T. (2015). Open access: Help or hindrance to resource sharing? *Interlending & Document Supply, 43*(2), 68–75. doi:10.1108/ILDS-01-2015-0003

Bates, A. W. (2015). *Teaching in a Digital Age*. BC Open Textbooks. Retrieved from https://opentextbc.ca/teachinginadigitalage/

Beall, J. (2012). *Predatory publishers and opportunities for scholarly societies*. Retrieved from http://eprints.rclis.org/18044/

Beilin, I. (2015). Beyond the threshold: Conformity, resistance, and the ACRL Information Literacy Framework for Higher Education. *In the Library with the Lead Pipe*. Retrieved from http://www.inthelibrarywiththeleadpipe.org/2015/beyond-the-threshold-conformity-resistance-and-the-aclr-information-literacy-framework-for-higher-education/

Bennett, L. (2012). *The potential effect of making journals free after a six-month embargo: A report for the Association of Learned, Professional and Society Publishers [ALPSP] and The Publishers Association*. Retrieved from https://www.recolecta.fecyt.es/sites/default/files/contenido/documentos/ALPSP-PApotentialresultsofsixmonthembargofv.pdf

Bill & Melinda Gates Foundation. (2017). *Bill & Melinda Gates Foundation open access policy*. Retrieved from http://www.gatesfoundation.org/How-We-Work/General-Information/Open-Access-Policy

Bonn, M. (2015). Maximizing the benefits of open access: Strategies for enhancing the discovery of open access content. *College & Research Libraries News, 76*(9), 491–494. doi:10.5860/crln.76.9.9381

Bosch, S., & Henderson, K. (2016). Fracking the ecosystem: Periodicals price survey 2016. *Library Journal, 141*(7), 32–38. Retrieved from http://lj.libraryjournal.com/2016/04/publishing/fracking-the-ecosystem-periodicals-price-survey-2016/#_

Budapest Open Access Initiative. (2002). Retrieved from http://www.budapestopenaccessinitiative.org/read

Bulock, C., Hosburgh, N., & Mann, S. (2015). OA in the library collection: The challenges of identifying and maintaining open access resources. *The Serials Librarian, 68*(1-4), 79–86. doi:10.1080/0361526X.2015.1023690

Colvard, N. B., Watson, C. E., & Park, H. (2018). The impact of open educational resources on various student success metrics. *International Journal on Teaching and Learning in Higher Education, 30*(2), 262–276. Retrieved from http://www.isetl.org/ijtlhe/

Connaway, L. S., White, D., Lanclos, D., & Le Cornu, A. (2014). Visitors and residents: What motivates engagement with the digital information environment? *Information Research, 18*(1). Retrieved from http://www.informationr.net/ir/18-1/paper556.html#.WNKwysDyu00

Fons, T. (2016). Improving web visibility: Into the hands of readers. *Library Technology Reports, 52*(5).

Frankland, J., & Ray, M. A. (2017). Traditional versus open access scholarly publishing: An economic perspective. *Journal of Scholarly Publishing, 49*(1), 5–25. doi:10.3138/jsp.49.1.5

Georgas, H. (2015). Google vs. the library (part III): Assessing the quality of sources found by undergraduates. *Libraries & The Academy, 15*(1), 131–161. doi:10.1353/pla.2015.0012

Google Scholar. (n.d.). *Inclusion guidelines for webmasters*. Retrieved from https://scholar.google.com/intl/en/scholar/inclusion.html

Hahn, S. E., & Wyatt, A. (2014). Business faculty's attitudes: Open access, disciplinary repositories, and institutional repositories. *Journal of Business & Finance Librarianship, 19*(2), 93–113. doi:10.1080/08963568.2014.883875

Harzing, A., & Adler, N. J. (2016). Disseminating knowledge: From potential to reality– New open-access journals collide with convention. *Academy of Management Learning & Education, 15*(1), 140–156. doi:10.5465/amle.2013.0373

Hrynaszkiewicz, I., & Cockerill, M. J. (2012). Open by default: A proposed copyright license and waiver agreement for open access research and data in peer-reviewed journals. *BMC Research Notes, 5*(1), 494–505. doi:10.1186/1756-0500-5-494 PMID:22958225

Jack, J. (2017). Free-to-publish, free-to-read, or both? Cost, equality of access, and integrity in science publishing. *Journal of the Association for Information Science and Technology, 68*(6), 1584–1589. doi:10.1002/asi.23757

Kimbrough, J. L., & Gasaway, L. N. (2016). Publication of government-funded research, open access, and the public interest. *Vanderbilt Journal of Entertainment & Technology Law, 18*(2), 267–302. Retrieved from http://www.jetlaw.org/wp-content/uploads/2016/03/KimbroughGasaway_SPE_7-FINAL.pdf

Kocken, G. J., & Wical, S. H. (2013). "I've never heard of it before": Awareness of open access at a small liberal arts university. *Behavioral & Social Sciences Librarian, 32*(3), 140–154. doi:10.1080/01639269.2013.817876

Lawrence, C. N., & Lester, J. A. (2018). Evaluating the effectiveness of adopting open educational resources in an introductory American Government course. *Journal of Political Science Education, 14*(4), 555–566. doi:10.1080/15512169.2017.1422739

Linguistic Society of America (LSA). (2013). *Changes to LSA publications (2013)*. Retrieved from http://www.linguisticsociety.org/content/update-status-lsa-publications

Marks, J., & Janke, R. (2009). The future of academic publishing: A view from the top. *Journal of Library Administration, 49*(4), 439–458. doi:10.1080/01930820902832579

Martin, R. A. (2010). Finding free and open access resources: A value-added service for patrons. *Journal of Interlibrary Loan. Document Delivery & Electronic Reserves*, *20*(3), 189–200. doi:10.1080/1072303X.2010.491022

Maternowsky, K. (2009). *Who profits from for-profit journals?* Retrieved from Inside Higher Ed website: https://www.insidehighered.com/news/2009/06/12/journals

McGrath, M. (2014). Viewpoint: Open access–a nail in the coffin of ILL? *Interlending & Document Supply*, *42*(4), 196–198. doi:10.1108/ILDS-07-2014-0035

McGrath, M. (2015). A review of changes in the delivery of information to users. *The Bottom Line (New York, N.Y.)*, *28*(1/2), 70–76. doi:10.1108/BL-12-2014-0031

Murphy, A. (2012). Benchmarking OER use and assessment in higher education. *29th Annual Conference of the Australasian Society for Computers in Learning in Tertiary Education*, (1), 675–677.

Pandelis, P., Agnes, P., Isabel, B., Carles, S., Nardine, O., Concha, M., & Emilio, L. (2017). OPRM: Challenges to including open peer review in open access repositories. *Code4lib Journal*, (35). Retrieved from http://journal.code4lib.org/articles/12171

Pence, H. E., & Losoff, B. (2011). Going beyond the textbook: The need to integrate open access primary literature into the chemistry curriculum. *Chemistry Central Journal*, *5*(1), 18–21. doi:10.1186/1752-153X-5-18 PMID:21470429

Prabha, C. (2007). Shifting from print to electronic journals in ARL university libraries. *Serials Review*, *33*(1), 4–13. doi:10.1080/00987913.2007.10765086

Prinsloo, P., & Slade, S. (2014). Educational triage in open distance learning: Walking a moral tightrope. *International Review of Research in Open and Distributed Learning*, *15*(4). doi:10.19173/irrodl.v15i4.1881

Roubides, P. (2018). Emergent technologies shaping instructional design. In *Innovative Applications of Online Pedagogy and Course Design* (pp. 1–24). IGI Global. doi:10.4018/978-1-5225-5466-0.ch001

Rowley, J., Johnson, F., Sbaffi, L., Frass, W., & Devine, E. (2017). Academics' behaviors and attitudes towards open access publishing in scholarly journals. *Journal of the Association for Information Science and Technology*, *68*(5), 1201–1211. doi:10.1002/asi.23710

Shamseer, L., Moher, D., Maduekwe, O., Turner, L., Barbour, V., Burch, R., ... Shea, B. J. (2017). Potential predatory and legitimate biomedical journals: Can you tell the difference? A cross-sectional comparison. *BMC Medicine*, *15*(28), 1–14. doi:10.118612916-017-0785-9 PMID:28298236

Solomon, D. J., & Björk, B. (2012). Publication fees in open access publishing: Sources of funding and factors influencing choice of journal. *Journal of the American Society for Information Science and Technology*, *63*(1), 98–107. doi:10.1002/asi.21660

University of California Office of Scholarly Communication and the California Digital Library eScholarship Program. (2007). *Faculty attitudes and behaviors regarding scholarly communication: Survey findings from the University of California.* Retrieved from http://osc.universityofcalifornia.edu/2007/08/report-onfaculty-attitudes-and-behaviors-regarding-scholarly-communication/

Verschraegen, G., & Schiltz, M. (2007). Knowledge as a global public good: The role and importance of open access. *Societies Without Borders, 2*(2), 157–174. doi:10.1163/187219107X203540

Watson, J. (2018). The new world of republishing in open access: A view from the author's side. *Journal of Scholarly Publishing, 49*(2), 231–247. doi:10.3138/jsp.49.2.231

Wenzler, J. (2017). Scholarly communication and the dilemma of collective action: Why academic journals cost too much. *College & Research Libraries, 78*(2), 183–200. doi:10.5860/crl.78.2.183

Wexler, E. (2015). What a mass exodus at a linguistics journal means for scholarly publishing. *The Chronicle of Higher Education.* Retrieved from http://www.chronicle.com/article/What-a-Mass-Exodus-at-a/234066

Wicherts, J. M. (2016). Peer review quality and transparency of the peer review process in open access and subscription journals. *PLoS One, 11*(1), 1–19. doi:10.1371/journal.pone.0147913 PMID:26824759

Wiebe, T. (2012). Books and websites, e-journals or print: If the source fits, use it. *College & Undergraduate Libraries, 19*(1), 108–113. doi:10.1080/10691316.2012.652554

Wilson, E. K., & Humphrey, J. (2017). Successfully transitioning the world's largest chemistry subscription journal to a gold open access publication. Insights. *The UKSG Journal, 30*(1), 38–46. doi:10.1629/uksg.343

Winitzky-Stephens, J. R., & Pickavance, J. (2017). Open educational resources and student course outcomes: A multilevel analysis. *The International Review of Research in Open and Distributed Learning, 18*(4). doi:10.19173/irrodl.v18i4.3118

Xia, J. (2010). A longitudinal study of scholars' attitudes and behaviors toward open-access journal publishing. *Journal of the American Society for Information Science and Technology, 61*(3), 615–624. doi:10.1002/asi.21283

Yang, Z. Y., & Li, Y. (2015). University faculty awareness and attitudes towards open access publishing and the institutional repository: A case study. *Journal of Librarianship and Scholarly Communication, 3*(1), 1–29. doi:10.7710/2162-3309.1210

Younghusband, D. (2005). Electronic journals and link resolver implementation. *Serials, 18*(1), 64–69. Retrieved from http://serials.uksg.org/articles/abstract/10.1629/1864/

ADDITIONAL READING

Bravender, P., McClure, H., & Schaub, G. (Eds.). (2015). *Teaching information literacy threshold concepts: Lesson plans for librarians*. Chicago: Association of College and Research Libraries.

Hebrang Grgic, I. (2016). Information literacy and open access in Croatian academic libraries. *Library Review, 65*(4–5), 255–266. doi:10.1108/LR-01-2016-0009

Jagman, H., & Swanson, T. A. (Eds.). (2015). *Not just where to click: Teaching students how to think about information*. Chicago: Association of College and Research Libraries.

Johnson, M., Buhler, A. G., & Gonzalez, S. R. (2013). Communicating with future scholars: Lesson plans to engage undergraduate science students with open access in a semester-long course. In S. Davis-Kahl & M. K. Hensley (Eds.), *Common ground at the nexus of information literacy and scholarly communication* (pp. 153–180). Chicago: Association of College and Research Libraries; Retrieved from https://digitalcommons.iwu.edu/bookshelf/36/

May, C. (2010). Openness in academic publication: The question of trust, authority and reliability. *Prometheus, 28*(1), 91–94. doi:10.1080/08109021003676417

Tenopir, C., Levine, K., Allard, S., Christian, L., Volentine, R., Boehm, R., ... Watkinson, A. (2016). Trustworthiness and authority of scholarly information in a digital age: Results of an international questionnaire. *Journal of the Association for Information Science and Technology, 67*(10), 2344–2361. doi:10.1002/asi.23598

Zhao, L. (2014). Riding the wave of open access: Providing library research support for scholarly publishing literacy. *Australian Academic and Research Libraries, 45*(1), 3–18. doi:10.1080/00048623.2014.882873

Zuccala, A. (2010). Open access and civic scientific information literacy. *Information Research, 15*(1). Retrieved from https://eric.ed.gov/?id=EJ881439

KEY TERMS AND DEFINITIONS

ACRL Framework: Document adopted in 2016 by the Association of College and Research Libraries. Contains six "frames," each composed of an essential information literacy concept and associated practices and dispositions.

Course Designer: Anyone involved, individually as part of a team, in planning the aims, organization, and approaches of a course. For the purposes of this chapter, also includes course development activities such as selecting course materials and creating lessons and assessments.

Digital Information Literacy: The ability to locate, evaluate, and use information that has been created, stored, or accessed digitally.

Discovery: The process of finding resources on a given topic. May be separate from fulfillment.

Fulfillment: The retrieval or acquisition of discovered resources.

Open Access: The quality of being digitally available for free use, storage, and reuse. Often applied to scholarly works freely accessed online, but not fully available for reuse or adaptation.

Repository: An online location for storing and disseminating content. Repositories are often disciplinary or institutional.

Scholarly Sources: Materials, typically peer reviewed, written by experts for an academic audience.

Chapter 4
Learning Communities:
Theory and Practice of Leveraging Social Media for Learning

Heather Robinson
University of North Texas, USA

Whitney Kilgore
University of North Texas, USA

Aras Bozkurt
https://orcid.org/0000-0002-4520-642X
Anadolu University, Turkey & University of South Africa, South Africa

ABSTRACT

The purpose of this chapter is to present the similarities and differences of three learning communities: communities of practice (CoPs), professional learning communities (PLCs), and professional learning networks (PLNs). For this purpose, researchers adopted a qualitative phenomenological approach and interviews with three connected educators and content area experts were conducted regarding their views, perceptions, and experiences of the various learning communities and how technology (specifically Twitter) is used as part of their learning in an open community. Additionally, the interviews helped explain the current practices in community development and support, the evolution from a lurker to a contributor to a community leader, and the evolution from a community to a network.

DOI: 10.4018/978-1-5225-9779-7.ch004

INTRODUCTION

Since the early 1990s, considerable attention has been dedicated to the topic of informal learning in communities. There is a significant amount of literature associated with Professional Learning Communities (PLCs) and Communities of Practice (CoPs). As ubiquitous technologies have afforded new methods for informal learning to occur, they have been accompanied by the rise of Professional Learning Networks (PLNs) by the end of the 20th century and beginning of 21st century (Brown & Duguid, 1991; Dufour & Eaker, 1998; Hord, 1997; Saint-Onge & Wallace, 2003; Siemens, 2005; Wenger, McDermott & Snyder, 2002). Generally, individuals develop such communities, groups, and networks with a shared endeavor or interest (Dufour & Eaker, 1998; Wenger et al., 2002). In this context, individuals belong to one or more communities through work, schools, home and/or hobbies, and members of these communities may be more active and hold different roles in each (Wenger et al., 2002).

A successful online learning network or community for educators increases communication, collaboration, and support among participants (Booth, 2011; Yen et al., 2019). Accordingly, "these communities enable educators to gain equitable access to human and information resources that may not be available locally" (Booth, 2011, p. 1). Community members often feel comfortable freely sharing ideas that contribute to learning and new knowledge development. By leveraging the affordances of open digital ubiquitous technologies, these communities are forming online via social media within Facebook, Twitter, Google+, and others. Based on above thoughts, similarities and differences of three learning communities are presented: Communities of Practice (CoPs), Professional Learning Communities (PLCs), and Professional Learning Networks (PLNs). Interviews of three connected educators are also presented in order to identify themes and commonalities regarding their views, perceptions, and experiences of the various learning communities and how technology (specifically Twitter) is used as part of their learning in an open community.

This chapter further provides clear definitions of these types of learning communities (PLCs, PLNs, and CoPs). This includes descriptions of their key characteristics, practices, and underlying theory, which are also synthesized in the review of literature. The development and design of personal and professional learning networks, generally, are explored in the review of literature. Current trends and the use of social media for developing learning networks are analyzed to inform the development of interview questions. Such an approach allowed explanation of how social media was used for professional learning and to explore the differences exhibited by legitimate peripheral participants (sometimes called lurkers), core contributors, and other community leaders in such environments. The authors clarify how and why learning networks are formed, the characteristics of these networks, and the role technologies play in a learning community. Additionally, emergent themes not tied to these topics of inquiry were identified from the interviews.

LITERATURE REVIEW

Communities of Practice (CoPs)

The term community of practice (CoP) was coined by Lave and Wenger (1991). The concept was first used in a book focused on the rethinking or theorization of learning, in which learning is characterized as legitimate peripheral participation within a CoP (Lave & Wenger, 1991). Expanding on these original works, Wenger et al. (2002) defined a CoP as: "groups of people who share a concern, a set of problems, or a passion about a topic, and who deepen their knowledge and expertise in this area by interacting on an ongoing basis" (p. 9). Learning communities develop into CoPs over time through interaction, collaboration, knowledge creation and sharing. The focus on CoPs in business and education has come to the forefront of research because of the overall value of knowledge as an asset, and is seen as a key to success for gaining a competitive advantage (Saint-Onge & Wallace, 2003; Wenger et al., 2002). Multiple CoP models exist. They differ in the structure of the community and theoretical grounding. Further, it is a shared belief that, in a CoP, knowledge is created and shared within the community; participation is voluntary (Brown & Duguid, 1991; Saint-Onge & Wallace, 2003; Wenger et al., 2002).

The nature of knowing and learning is a foundation for understanding how learning communities behave and create new knowledge. There are multiple theoretical foundations such as social learning, situated learning, and knowledge management. Each of these learning theories underpins the CoP model (Bandura, 1986; Lave & Wenger, 1991; Saint-Onge, 2012).

Social learning theory is one such theoretical foundation for a CoP. It is an integration of behavior and cognitive theories. Bandura (1986) who is a leading researcher on social learning used the concept of modeling. Bandura (1986) presented three types of modeling within this theory: live modeling, verbal instruction, and symbolic modeling. Bandura explained that when people display a certain behavior, they are modeling a behavior they learned or observed, which is something he called *live modeling* which, as a social learning process, "occurs on the basis of casual or studied observation of exemplary models" (Bandura, 1971, p. 10). Behavioral or live modeling is replaced by verbal modeling as verbal skills are developed and this is called *verbal instruction* (Bandura, 1971; 1986). *Symbolic modeling* from television or media, or emotional responses and behavior patterns learned from such media are the final type of modeling in Bandura's theory (1971; 1986). Social learning and knowledge sharing are part of a community. In various models of a CoP, this social environment and interaction is how members of the community advance in their particular trade (Brown & Duguid, 1991; Lave & Wenger, 1991).

Three structural elements of a CoP work together to make up a knowledge structure: domain, community, and practice (Wenger et al., 2002). The first, the *domain,* is a common ground or territory for members of the CoP and "knowing the boundaries and the leading edge of the domain enables members to decide exactly what is worth sharing…" (Wenger et al., 2002, p. 18). The members of the community have a personal commitment or shared passion to the domain of the CoP; the domain inspires members and defines the identity of the community (Bates, 2014; Wenger et al., 2002; Wenger, 2011).

The *community,* a second element of a CoP, is the activity or engagement of members within the domain. It is the social component of the CoP and is considered a critical element to the overall CoP. Development of an online community is empowering, as the members within the community share ideas and work collaboratively (Palloff & Pratt, 2007). The discourse and relationships developed by members through interaction is the community element of a CoP (Palloff & Pratt, 1999; Wenger et al., 2002; Wenger, 2011).

The third structural element of a CoP, *practice*, is more specific than the domain element. In a CoP, practice, it is the collection of the resources developed over time by the members, such as "a set of frameworks, ideas, tools, styles ... that community members share" (Wenger, et al., 2002, p. 18). The *practice* of a CoP is the knowledge that the community develops, shares and maintains (Wenger et al., 2002; Wenger, 2011).

Wenger's theory is valuable in that it considers the ways in which CoP are formed and developed; notions of trajectories of belonging, legitimate participation, and boundary objects/crossings have provided useful lenses to describe many interactions observed in online spaces. (Conole, Galley & Culver, 2010, p. 123)

Along these lines, Saint-Onge and Wallace (2003) also explained the range of formality in various models of CoPs from informal communities to those groups who are highly motivated and more structured. The types of practices within this model are informal, supported, and structured (Saint-Onge & Wallace, 2003). There may also be a growth or development in formality of a CoP as time passes. Brown and Duguid (1991) also elucidated how informal groups in a CoP, as well as the benefits they can offer their organization in terms of developing solutions to problems. Generally, CoPs use productive inquiry to seek answers to their questions within their area of practice (Saint-Onge & Wallace, 2012).

Professional Learning Communities

A PLC is an "environment that fosters mutual cooperation, emotional support, and personal growth" (Dufour & Eaker, 1998, p. xii). It is one in which individuals, namely educators; work together to accomplish goals as a team. The Dufour and Eaker model of a PLC has six characteristics that are identified and differentiate this model from other PLCs. These are: (1) a shared mission, vision and values, (2) collective inquiry, (3) collaborative teams, (4) action orientation, (5) continuous improvement, and (6) results orientation. The PLC was designed to give voice and agency to educators, parents, and the community. The ultimate goal, described by Dufour and Eaker, was to allow the PLC to play a key role in school improvement shifting from a top down factory model into a collaborative and inclusive educational community.

Similarly, Hord's (1997; 2004) PLC model consists of five themes or dimensions: (1) supportive and shared leadership, (2) shared values and vision, (3) collective learning and application of learning, (4) supportive conditions, and (5) a shared practice. Both the Dufour & Eaker (1998) and Hord (1997; 2004) models were developed to address the teacher workplace and the support needs of teachers for learning, teacher networks, and teacher self-efficacy.

Senge (1990), who is the leading researcher of this theory, crafted the term *learning organization* which is one of the theoretical foundations for a PLC. Senge's paradigm was instrumental in the education field and the development of what a PLC is defined as today (Hord, 2004). Senge defined a learning organization as "a place where people are continually discovering how they create their reality and how they can change it…" (Senge, 1990, p. 13). Senge developed five dimensions for establishing a learning organization, which have had a profound impact on education (Lin, 2002). According to Senge (1990), the five dimensions of a learning organization are: (1) personal mastery, (2) mental models, (3) shared vision, (4) team learning and (5) systems thinking (Figure 1).

Figure 1. The five dimensions of a learning organization (Adopted from Senge, 1990)

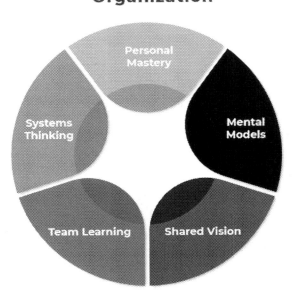

Systems thinking is the fifth discipline that Senge (1990) describes as being critical. However, without a clear understanding of the big picture, or a shared achievable goal, these parts may well come together in a non-cohesive manner. *Personal mastery* is a concept of self-exploration and growth, but also includes the commitment of the individual and the organization in learning (Senge, 1990). A *mental model* is an awareness of an individual's thinking but may be enhanced by an effective leader encouraging inquisitively (Lin, 2002, Nejad, Abbaszadeh, Hassani, & Bernousi, 2012; Senge, 1990). A *shared vision* or understanding of the interests of the individuals and the group helps those members achieve the overarching goals. With *team learning*, the expertise of the group increases and is desirable to all members. *Systems thinking*, or process thinking is a shift in focus to the system rather than individual parts or units of a system (Lin, 2002; Senge, 1990). This is helpful because "when people in organizations focus only on their position, they have little sense of responsibility for the results produced when all positions interact" (Senge, 1990; p. 19). The five dimensions, as a whole, are a connected unit. The successes of the individuals, as well as the organization, form the collective goals of a learning organization (Nejad et al., 2012; Senge, 1990).

Learning organizations are possible because not only is it our nature to learn, but we love to learn. Most of us at one time or another have been a part of a great team, a group of people who functioned together in an extraordinary way - who trusted one another, who complemented each other's strengths and compensated for each other's limitations, who had common goals that were larger than individual goals, and who produced extraordinary results...The team that became great didn't start off great - it learned how to produce extraordinary results. (Senge, 1990; p. 4)

Learning Communities

The team and collaborative work is at the heart of a PLC, for participants in this type of learning setting can freely express new ideas in an attempt to solve problems (Dufour, 2004; Hord, 2004). Implementing the concepts of a PLC is a challenge, as "initiating and sustaining the concept is hard work" (Dufour, 2004, p. 6). There is a shift from teaching to learning using a PLC model, and the development of a shared vision by the PLC sharpens this focus (Dufour, 2004; Hord, 2004). A PLC requires discipline and dedication to sustain its work, as Dufour (2004) explains:

[T]he rise or fall of the professional learning community concept depends not on the merits of the concept itself, but on the most important element in the improvement of any school—the commitment and persistence of the educators within it (p. 6).

Accordingly, a successful PLC fosters the conditions that allow for the changes needed to increase student learning and overall improvement in a school setting (Hord, 1997).

Professional Learning Networks (PLN)

Predictions that the Internet would change the way we learn, and that connectivity would become as important as electricity to society, as it moved from being a one-way or "push" of content to a two-way medium or "push-pull" (Brown, 2002). Connectivism, a conceptual framework developed for the digital age (Siemens, 2004), situates the student at the center of his or her own learning (Bell, 2011; Boishwarelo, 2011; Dunaway, 2011; Kop & Hill, 2008; Mackness & Tschofen 2012; Ravenscroft, 2011). Connectivism proposes that we connect to knowledge through our digital connections and engagements at online networks, while concurrently harnessing the power of the Internet and PLNs. Acknowledging the complexities of learning in the digital age, connectivism offers insight into how learning can be managed through the better understanding of emerging technologies and their relationship to knowledge networks (Couros, 2010).

Connectivism conceptually supports the notion of a community of practice or a PLN where like-minded people share ideas with their peers across a variety of Web 2.0 tools facilitating development of a networked learner. Blogs, Twitter, Facebook, LinkedIn, and other social media networks are a part of this development. The PLN leverages social media sites that have become prevalent and commonplace, creating an emergent opportunity for learning (Visser, Evering, & Barrett, 2014). PLNs tend to be self-organized on the web which has created conditions that allow for the emergence of self-organized learning to flourish as the number of blogs, tweets, emails, and texts has grown to the billions. An example of this is the PLC that surround MOOCs where participants begin utilizing social media and commenting on each others' blogs as an extension of the learning experience such as #Rhizo15 (Cormier, 2015) and #HumanMOOC (Crosslin, 2016).

Informal learning and knowledge seeking rather than formal education is the main form of learning for adults in like and work (Misko, 2008). Formal learning no longer comprises the majority of our learning. Knowledge is acquired in a variety of ways through completion of work-related tasks, our personal networks, and CoPs (Siemens, 2005). A learning network is a rich set of connections that help us to achieve our learning pursuits (Richardson & Mancabelli, 2011). Today, we can connect digitally and communicate immediately with others that share similar passions from all around the world. In other words, information technologies are a participatory medium that is continually reshaped by the participation (Thomas & Brown, 2011).

Table 1. Community comparison

	Theory Base	Membership	Knowledge Sharing	Formation	Example
CoP	Social Learning Situated Learning Knowledge Management	Voluntary participation and membership	Created and shared within the community	People with common interests coming together to improve their practice	Conference Special Interest Groups (SIGs)
PLC	Learning Organization	Assigned roles, expected as educator or faculty member	Collaborative, teams create new knowledge	People brought together to learn from one another	Groups formed within a particular school to solve challenges
PLN	Connectivism	Voluntary participation	Shared and created across communities	Voluntary digital connections with global reach	MOOCs Hashtags Unconference Events

We can see that the internet is enabling communities to form, which would have been previously limited by geographic factors, and the removal of these barriers has seen an unprecedented growth in communities for whom learning is a key objective (Weller, 2011).

Current Trends in Learning Communities

Wiley and Hilton (2009) pointed to six significant shifts that support network building. These include the shift from (1) analog to digital, (2) tethered to mobile, (3) isolated to connected, (4) generic to personal, (5) consumption to creation, and (6) closed systems to open systems. Accordingly, "people are more connected to people, content is more connected to content, and systems are more connected to other systems than ever before" (Wiley & Hilton, 2009, p 2.). These connections allow learners to share and learn on demand; seeking and sharing information to solve problems. Research indicates that the affordances of social media allow the creation of formal and information learning spaces (Dabbagh & Kitsantas, 2012). Lewis and Rush (2013) reported results of a narrative case study showing that small groups of professionals linked to each other through social media can develop a network and community. The authors followed the development of a social media presence based on the professional practice of one participant. The number of original followers and the growth of the online presence were analyzed. Profile categories, interactions in the network, tweet counts, frequently occurring hashtags, and frequently occurring mentions were some of the information points that contributed to the case. "The activity of operating the account has been of value to the holder in her professional life, through the immediate sharing of information and making contacts which have subsequently developed into longer lasting relationships and collaborative working" (Lewis & Rush, 2013, p. 11).

Twitter for Teaching and Learning

Twitter is one social media tool that has allowed educators to connect, collaborate, and learn (Visser, et. al, 2014). In essence, it is an online social networking and microblogging service. This free messaging service serves as a platform for micro blogging, or small-scale blogging and content sharing.

Learning Communities

Messages sent through Twitter can be no more than 280 characters. The use of hashtags in a message (i.e. #cecs6220) connects Twitter users and is also used for organizing and searching content. Twitter chats are hashtag chats that are similar to public discussions, in which groups of users address various topics by "tweeting" messages, posting questions, and responding to questions posed by others. A pre-set hashtag is commonly used to connect the separately occurring, often non-chronological conversations of a Twitter chat. Proponents of Twitter believe that these Web 2.0 technologies are a resource for growing a PLN (Lalonde, 2011).

Although Twitter was not originally developed for developing learning networks, utilizing the symbols for "hashtag" and the "at" symbol (# and @) allows Twitter contributors to engage in conversations and collaboration (Lewis & Rush, 2013; Veletsianos, 2011). The development of a CoP can be supported by electronic communications (Murillo, 2008; Wasko, Tiegland & Faraj 2009) but it is the psychological feeling of connectedness, the human connection using these technology mediums, which allow the community to form. A successful community for professional learning can grow through Twitter, (Lewis & Rush, 2013). Additionally, Twitter is linked to significant teacher learning in an online CoP (Wesely, 2013).

According to Trust (2012), educators who immerse themselves in a PLN through the use of social media and use the learning community to improve their practice and skills, transition from an isolated teacher to a connected educator and lifelong learner. This occurs when they manage information overload, gather the information of importance for their growth, share information within the PLN, and model the behavior of a lifelong learner by continuing this process (Trust, 2012). The affordances of technology are "giving voice to the ideas of people we have never had access to before and enabling us to reshape our information experiences to suit our learning needs" (Warlick, 2009, p. 13). Teachers identified Skype, Google Reader, Delicious, and blogs as a few technology tools (other than Twitter) as favorite PLN tools because the use of such tools has "freed content from the printed page" (Warlick, 2009, p. 13). Similarly, the use of Twitter as a teacher professional development tool in recent years has brought the PLC outside the traditional confines of the school itself. Learning communities that use social media form groups using the information being shared, connections created, and collaboration among members (Brooks & Gibson, 2012; Manzo, 2009).

Gunawardena et al. (2009) developed progressive phases to explain the collaborative learning journey of a CoP and how this interacts with social networking tools. The purpose of their work was to understand how a CoP utilizes social networking to reach a common goal. The framework is a social networking spiral depiction (Figure 2).

Accordingly, it is a learning environment with five phases: context, discourse, action, reflection, and reorganization, which builds and evolves to socially mediated metacognition (Gunawardena et al., 2009). The authors emphasized the importance and journey necessary to fully understand the multiple underlying "learning theories that influence learning in social networking environments, and application of these theories for learning" (Gunawardena et al., 2009, p. 15).

However, empirical research on Twitter and learning communities that leverage this tool is limited (Cho, Ro & Littenberg-Tobias, 2013; Veletsianos, 2011). Additional research is needed on the translation of professional communities and these relationships, specifically when looking at the online version of such communities through the use of social media (Cho et al., 2013). Cho et al. (2013) recommend stronger theorizing about these various issues. In addition, Veletsianos (2011) has called for more research to determine if Twitter presents opportunities to build close-knit scholarly communities.

Figure 2. Social networking spiral (Adopted from Gunawardena et al., 2009)

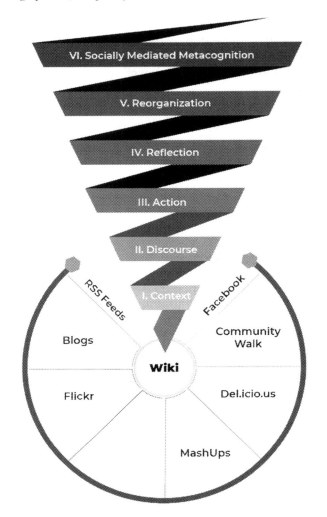

METHODOLOGY

Research Design

This study benefited from the qualitative phenomenological research design to explore the differences between CoPs, PLCs, and PLNs by discovering the participants' experiences in these contexts. The purpose of phenomenological research is to understand the essence of individuals' experiences and their interpretations (Moustakas, 1994; Scott & Morrison, 2005; Snape, & Spencer, 2003). Because these experiences and their interpretations are subjective in nature, this study is hermeneutic (Adams & Van Manen, 2008), naturalistic, and discovery-oriented (Patton, 2002).

Participants

In qualitative studies, it might be significant to interview with representative participants to better understand the research phenomena, get a deeper and comprehensive understanding (Gill, Stewart, Treasure, & Chadwick, 2008; Hammersley & Atkinson, 2007). In this regard, the participants in this study were purposefully selected based upon their voice and status represented on social media with an intention to create a representative study group. The three participants each hold different roles in K-12 education. The content of those interviews was anonymized, and each participant given a pseudonym. Two of the participants were female, one was a Caucasian educator in a private school and the other was an African-American instructional technologist in a large public-school district. The third participant was a Caucasian male principal in an intermediate school. The variety of their backgrounds, career paths, leadership roles, and their social media use was essential in learning more about their understanding of CoPs, PLNs, and PLCs as well as their use of social media.

Data Collection Tool, Procedures, and Analysis

For the purposes of the study, the researchers conducted online synchronous interviews (Fraenkel & Wallen, 2011) in which open-ended semi-structured questions were used to collect data. The interviews were recorded and transcribed in preparation for coding and analysis. The interviews and their analysis allowed researchers to seek answers to research questions, gain a deeper understanding of each community (CoP, PLN, PLN), and identify themes to emerge. More specifically, such an approach provided researchers a rich set of data to gather insights into the educators' experiences, perceptions and values related to the research topic, and further to help identify the current practices in community development and support, present the evolution from lurker to contributor to community leader, and the evolution from a community to a network.

The online interviews were conducted remotely using a private Google Hangout on Air, a form of computer conferencing, to record the session and save as an unlisted, private YouTube video. These online interviews were then transcribed and reviewed by the authors. Semi-structured online interview questions were as followings:

1. How do you describe a community of practice?
   a. How is this different in your opinion from a professional learning network?
2. Would you please describe the difference between a Professional Learning Community and a Professional Learning Network?
   a. Do you keep your personal network separated from your professional network?
3. How do you use Twitter as a part of your professional learning?
4. Can you describe the differences between lurkers, contributors, and community leaders online?
   a. Where do you see yourself in that continuum?
   b. Has that changed since you first began using social media?

In analysis procedure, the data were coded to assign them in related categories and conduct a thematic analysis (Aronson, 1995). Considering that a phenomenological research focuses on individuals' experiences, this type of studies generally provides direct quotes to validate interpretations (Giorgi &

Giorgi, 2009) and demonstrate how participants load meanings to their experiences through language (Adams & Van Manen, 2008). Therefore, when necessary, the researchers used direct quotes to support their interpretations.

FINDINGS AND DISCUSSION

Interview Themes/Systems Analysis

The interviews provided considerable insights regarding the lack of clarity surrounding the various types of communities. This confusion may be due in part to the proliferation of technology and partly due to their highly skilled use of social media as connected educators. There was no clear distinction between a PLC, CoP, and PLN in their first responses, however, there were some subtleties noted. The three interviewees did not separate professional and personal networks; however, they do mention filtering the information that they post and also discuss the evolution of their own networks as they found their voice online. Each interviewee shared how they used Twitter for their own professional learning and how to both build and sustain an online learning community.

PLCs, CoPs, and PLNs

All three interviewees mentioned a lack of clarity across the terms PLCs, CoPs, and PLNs. For example, Paul did not see any difference and equated all three terms with his PLN. Rochelle mentioned that PLCs have become too structured and that this may be due to the way they are implemented in schools. When asked about the difference between a PLC and a PLN, Rochelle responded with *"people are going to say a PLC are the people that you work with and a PLN are the people you don't necessarily work with... in order to make them different you have to go back to their micro-purposes for each one."* CoP for Rochelle are essentially a *"micro-section of a PLN."*

For these participants, like Wenger, a community is comprised of individuals who come together because they share a common interest and may even have aligned goals, ideals, and a shared vision. Communities engage in conversation and have habits and routines. Building a community takes time and requires consistent effort. Megan mentioned that, in an online environment, it is very important that the community *"know that there is a real person there."* The word community implies engagement, so a community of practice is more engaged in conversations with each other. To better differentiate a network from a community, we turn to Megan's thoughts about networks: *"A network is just a linking together of devices. It does not mean that traffic is flowing through those devices; it just means that traffic can travel if it wishes. So, the PLN is a pipe and a PLC means that the pipe has something going through it. A PLC would be an active pipeline...When you use the word community and CoP, I think that community should imply engagement."* The network allows for broadcasting of information or as Paul says *"throwing out your ideas"* as well as curation of ideas that are shared by others that may help to improve one's own teaching practice.

Technology Powered Learning Communities

There is power in a PLN due to the distributed nature of the network. It brings together people and ideas from a wide variety of industries and backgrounds that have similar interests. This *"big mess of everybody,"* as Rochelle referred to it, provides diversity of thought. She later goes on to discuss her confusion between PLCs and PLNs by stating *"I'm actually struggling with those two things because I think that social media has changed what that looks like...[w]e teach the idea of learning is something that can exist with or without walls."* Online communities tend to overlap each other, and we are all there to grow professionally. There can be some loss of control of membership in online communities, as the tools utilized may not have access controls. Using a conference hashtag creates an event-based node within a larger PLN and, while this node may become dormant at other times of the year, when active, it can be a very powerful CoP.

Finding Their Voices: The Evolution From Lurker To Contributor

The interviewees all shared a common experience of finding their voice online. Paul shared that he continually thought his ideas were not as good as others. Rochelle stated that she felt *"afraid of people judging me and not living up to the standard of what some people thought I should be."* She also mentioned that she didn't feel empowered to share, but that Twitter has changed that for her. As she put it, *"it makes me see the value of who I am."* It took a nudge from a peer to encourage Paul to share online. Megan described her first experiences on social media as play. She later realized that people read what she had written and felt a professional responsibility to be worthy of their time and attention.

When asked what a lurker was, Rochelle responded, *"a lurker is scrolling through the timelines and reading but that doesn't mean that they are not active."* A lurker, according the Lave and Wenger (1998), may be described as a legitimate peripheral participant in the community. This lurker may be looking for new ideas to implement and may try something new next week *"because someone lurked on your page and saw it."* Megan went on to say that a lurker might also be influential to their community of practice, taking ideas from the larger PLN there.

Rochelle only connected with classmates from school and family when she first began using social media. However, as she became a professional and made face to face connections with other educators she would also connect via social media, expanding her personal network by including her professional network. She also mentioned how this change in her digital network has changed what she posts as she is more careful about what she shares on social media. Rochelle shared that, as she found her voice, while she may have evolved from lurker to learner to community leader, it can be any of these roles at any time. She said *"sometimes when I'm quiet on social media, I'm still there. I'm just scrolling through my phone and reading tweets and reading blogs... I just don't feel like having a conversation."* This is legitimate peripheral participation.

Professional Learning Networks vs. Personal Networks

All participants described their personal and professional networks as being one in the same. They do not manage separate accounts for the purposes of keeping their personal and professional contacts separate. Megan commented *"My personal is my professional, I've chosen to be one person."* In small contrast,

Paul talked about the blurred line between his personal and professional network; however, he went on to mention that he still maintains an *"inner circle"* of those he reaches out to directly for advice and support. Making connections in real life after following someone on twitter was mentioned as well. Paul talked about both approaching others that he had only known from social media, and having others come up to him to introduce themselves for the first time in real life.

Using Twitter for Professional Learning

Paul described his use of Twitter to support professional learning as having changed over time. At first, he used to read other participants' tweets as a form of *"soaking stuff up"* and checked out Twitter chats to gain new ideas. However, now that he is a connected educator, he is less likely to tweet a random question to a hashtag. Instead, he is more likely to ask a specific person a direct question. Rochelle described discovering educator Twitter chats years ago at a conference. She remarked that she was surprised to learn that there were other educators on Twitter talking about things that mattered to her. Since then, she has become a connected educator and says *"now it is bigger than that because it is not just about talking to other educators it is about standing up for what I believe in…Twitter is like an extension of my voice."* Megan currently has the largest Twitter following of the interviewees and uses Twitter differently. She said that Twitter is more like a focus group for her; she sees what content is retweeted and resonating with educators. This helps her to *"keep her finger on the pulse"* of the connected educator community. She mentioned that she has become very *"intentional about setting up my own media diet."*

Tools

There were a variety of social media and collaborative tools mentioned in the interviews including: Google Hangouts, Voxer, Twitter, Pinterest, Facebook, Edmodo, Feedly, FlipBoard, Pocket, and Buffer. However, Megan stated an important point about collaborative tools, *"when you have digital tools, collaborative tools without a community of practice, they are just tools, and they are not collaborative."* The diagram in Figure 3 shows a representation of various tools and where they fit into the various community types.

As the reach of the community grows, the technologies are extended. This is done in order to provide the communicative and collaborative opportunities that are needed to build and sustain connectedness.

The PLC, known for it's structured meetings, may leverage systems like email or other tools outside of their scheduled meeting times for communications. In contrast, CoP typically forms across organizations or schools, mainly where the members come together with a shared purpose and may leverage a wider variety of communication and meeting tools. The PLN, an unstructured collection of connected educators across multiple CoPs, allows each individual to reach far beyond the physical world with their ideas.

Community Leadership/Management/Support

Community developers typically spend a great deal of time connecting and bringing the community together and establishing the norms (habits and routines) for the group. Nurturing, encouraging, and mentoring community members requires consistent effort. In keeping with the research and theory

Figure 3. CoP, PLC, and PLN comparison with tools

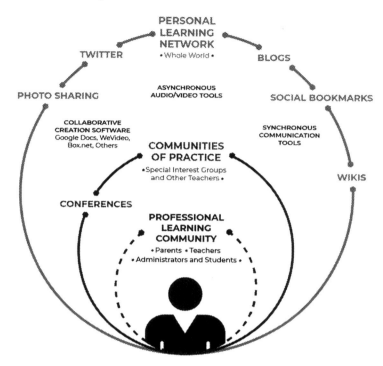

centered on community development, legitimate peripheral participants must feel comfortable, so they can become core-contributing participants. Internet trolls, an abusive or obnoxious user who uses shock value to promote arguments and disharmony online, according to Megan *"are the underbelly of the online community."* It is important to the participants that they feel safe in their environment; therefore, it is important to handle inappropriate actions swiftly and transparently while modeling good digital citizenship.

CONCLUSION

There were several topics brought up during the interviews that were outside the scope of this chapter but warrant further exploration. For example, some organizations have strong social media policies that limit the use of social media; this may impact a community member's participation. The ethics of social media posting related to an individual's affiliation to companies and the disclosure of this information was mentioned and should be considered in future research. There is a need for additional research into the online personas of educators and what impact these have on the formation of community. Finally, there was a mention of antisocial, or troll-like behavior and research should explore this management aspect further.

This chapter provided a number of topics for discussion. It included definitions for three types of learning communities, as well as the learning theory they were founded upon. Further, we examined the tools that these communities make use of and how they are formed and supported by both the tools and the people. Recommendations regarding the development of a PLN are included as well. These recommendations include:

1. Connect with people who challenge your ideas not just those who agree with you.
2. Share your successes and failures openly.
3. Be reflective and transparent. If you make a mistake admit it publicly, no one is perfect.

The themes from a small number of cases that emerged from interviews point to the lack of clarity among educators about the various types of communities. This may be due to the proliferation of ubiquitous technology-based communities to which they belong. From the participants' perspectives, the difference between *community* and the *network*, is clearly related to the conversations or engagement within the group. They also believe that a PLN is functionally a larger collection of CoPs and acts as a broadcast system rather than a community. What is different for these participants is that a community is engaged in sharing information that is useful to the work practices of those who are members of the community. This suggests that the community of practice is much like a cell, which it has a semi-permeable membrane around it. The conversations within the community may be visible to those beyond its borders; open learning communities. However, it takes some form of active transport to bring information into the community. This may occur in a variety of ways (e.g.: a community member may bring the new information into the community, or the PLN observer may use a hashtag to push the information into the community.) It is apparent from the interviews that informal learning communities are adding value to educators as they serve as social learning hubs with 24/7 access to expertise across a wide variety of areas.

REFERENCES

Adams, C., & Van Manen, M. (2008). Phenomenology. In L. M. Given (Ed.), *The Sage Encyclopedia of Qualitative Research Methods* (pp. 614–619). Thousand Oaks, CA: Sage.

Aronson, J. (1995). A pragmatic view of thematic analysis. *Qualitative Report, 2*(1), 1–3.

Bandura, A. (1971). *Social learning theory*. New York, NY: General Learning Press.

Bandura, A. (1986). *Social foundations of thought and action: A social cognitive theory*. Englewood Cliffs, N.J: Prentice-Hall.

Bates, T. (2014). *Teaching in a digital age*. Open Textbook.

Bell, F. (2011). Connectivism: Its place in theory-informed research and innovation in technology-enabled learning. *International Review of Research in Open and Distance Learning, 12*(3), 98. doi:10.19173/irrodl.v12i3.902

Boishwarelo, B. (2011). Proposing an integrated research framework for connectivism: Utilizing theoretical synergies. *International Review of Research in Open and Distance Learning, 12*(3). Retrieved from http://www.irrodl.org/index.php/irrodl/article/view/881

Booth, S. (2011). *Cultivating knowledge sharing and trust in online communities for educators: A multiple case study* (Unpublished doctoral dissertation). North Carolina State University, Raleigh, NC.

Brooks, C., & Gibson, S. (2012). Professional Learning in a Digital Age. *Canadian Journal of Learning and Technology, 38*(2), n2. doi:10.21432/T2HS3Q

Brown, J. S. (2002). *Growing Up Digital: How the Web Changes Work, Education, and the Ways People Learn*. United States Distance Learning Association. Retrieved from http://www.usdla.org/html/journal/FEB02_Issue/article01.html

Brown, J. S., & Duguid, P. (1991). Organizational learning and communities-of-practice: Toward a unified view of working, learning, and innovation. *Organization Science, 2*(1), 40–57.

Cho, V., Ro, J., & Littenberg-Tobias, J. (2013). What Twitter will and will not do: Theorizing about teachers' online professional communities. *Learning Landscapes, 6*(2), 45–62.

Conole, G., Galley, R., & Culver, J. (2010). Frameworks for understanding the nature of interactions, networking, and community in a social networking site for academic practice. *The International Review Of Research In Open And Distributed Learning, 12*(3), 119-138. Retrieved from http://www.irrodl.org/index.php/irrodl/article/view/914/1666

Cormier, D. (2015). What was #rhizo15. *The Association for Learning Technology (ALT) Newsletter*. Retrieved from https://newsletter.alt.ac.uk/2015/07/what-was-rhizome15/

Couros, A. (2010). Developing Personal Learning Networks for Open and Social Learning. In G. Veletsianos (Ed.), *Emerging technologies in distance education*. Edmonton: Univ of British Columbia Pr.

Crosslin, M. (2016). *Customizable Modality Pathway Learning Design: Exploring Personalized Learning Choices through a Lens of Self-Regulated Learning* (Doctoral dissertation). University of North Texas. Retrieved from https://digital.library.unt.edu/ark:/67531/metadc849703/

Dabbagh, N., & Kitsantas, A. (2012). Personal learning environments, social media, and self-regulating learning: A natural formula for connecting formal and informal learning. *Internet and Higher Education*, *15*(1), 3–8. doi:10.1016/j.iheduc.2011.06.002

DuFour, R. (2004). What is a "professional learning community?". *Educational Leadership*, *61*(8), 6–11.

Dufour, R., & Eaker, R. (1998). *Professional learning communities at work: Best practices for enhancing student achievement*. Alexandria, VA: Association for Supervision and Curriculum Development.

Dunaway, M. (2011). Connectivism: Learning theory and pedagogical practice for networked information landscapes. *RSR. Reference Services Review*, *39*(4), 675–685. doi:10.1108/00907321111186686

Fraenkel, J. R., & Wallen, N. E. (2011). *How to design and evaluate research in education*. New York: McGraw-Hill Humanities.

Gill, P., Stewart, K., Treasure, E., & Chadwick, B. (2008). Methods of data collection in qualitative research: Interviews and focus groups. *British Dental Journal*, *204*(6), 291–295. doi:10.1038/bdj.2008.192 PMID:18356873

Giorgi, A., & Giorgi, B. (2009). Phenomenology. In J. A. Smith (Ed.), *Qualitative psychology: A practical guide to research methods* (pp. 26–52). Los Angeles, CA: Sage.

Gunawardena, C. N., Hermans, M. B., Sanchez, D., Richmond, C., Bohley, M., & Tuttle, R. (2009). A theoretical framework for building online communities of practice with social networking tools. *Educational Media International*, *46*(1), 3–16. doi:10.1080/09523980802588626

Hammersley, M., & Atkinson, P. (2007). *Ethnography: Principles in practice*. Routledge. doi:10.4324/9780203944769

Hord, S. M. (1997). *Professional learning communities: Communities of continuous inquiry and improvement*. Austin, TX: Southwest Educational Development Laboratory.

Hord, S. M. (2004). Professional learning communities: An overview. In S. Hord (Ed.), *Learning together, leading together: Changing schools through professional learning communities* (pp. 5–14). New York: Teacher College Press.

Kop, R., & Hill, A. (2008). Connectivism: Learning theory of the future or vestige of the past? *International Review of Research in Open and Distance Learning*, *9*(3). doi:10.19173/irrodl.v9i3.523

Lalonde, C. (2011). *The Twitter experience: The role of Twitter in the formation and maintenance of personal learning networks* (Doctoral dissertation). Royal Roads University.

Lave, J., & Wenger, E. (1991). *Situated Learning: Legitimate peripheral participation*. New York: Cambridge University Press. doi:10.1017/CBO9780511815355

Lewis, B., & Rush, D. (2013). Experience of developing Twitter-based communities of practice in higher education. *Research in Learning Technology, 21*.

Lin, H. C. (2002). Current research in organizational systems: Higher education. *Futurics, 26*(1-2), 11–19.

Mackness, J., & Tschofen, C. (2012). Connectivism and dimensions of individual experience. *International Review of Research in Open and Distance Learning, 13*(1). Retrieved from http://www.irrodl.org/index.php/irrodl/article/view/1143

Manzo, K. K. (2009). Twitter lessons in 140 characters or less. *Education Week, 29*(8), 1–14.

Misko, J. (2008). *Combining formal, non-formal and informal learning for workforce development*. Adelaide: National Council for Vocational Education Research.

Moustakas, C. (1994). *Phenomenological research methods*. Thousand Oaks, CA: Sage. doi:10.4135/9781412995658

Murillo, E. (2008). Searching usenet for virtual communities of practice: using mixed methods to identify the constructs of Wenger's theory. *Information Research, 13*(4). Available at: http://InformationR.net/ir/13-4/paper386.html

Nejad, B. A., Abbaszadeh, M. M. S., Hassani, M., & Bernousi, I. (2012). Study of the entrepreneurship in universities as learning organization based on Senge model. *International Education Studies, 5*(1).

Palloff, M. R., & Pratt, K. (1999). *Building Learning Communities in Cyberspace*. San Francisco: Jossey-Bass.

Palloff, M. R., & Pratt, K. (2007). *Building online learning communities: effective strategies for the virtual classroom*. San Francisco, CA: Jossey-Bass.

Patton, M. Q. (2002). *Qualitative research and evaluation methods*. Thousand Oaks: Sage.

Ravenscroft, A. (2011). Dialogue and connectivism: A new approach to understanding and promoting dialogue-rich networked learning. *International Review of Research in Open and Distance Learning, 12*(3), 139. doi:10.19173/irrodl.v12i3.934

Richardson, W., & Mancabelli, R. (2011). *Personal learning networks: using the power of connections to transform education*. Solution Tree Press.

Saint-Onge, H., & Wallace, D. (2003). *Leveraging communities of practice for strategic advantage*. Boston: Butterworth-Heinemann.

Saint-Onge, H., & Wallace, D. (2012). Leveraging communities of practice for strategic advantage. Boston: Routledge. doi:10.4324/9780080496085

Scott, D., & Morrison, M. (2005). *Key ideas in educational research*. A&C Black.

Senge, P. M. (1990). *The fifth discipline: The art and practice of the learning organization*. New York: Doubleday/Currency.

Siemens, G. (2004). *Connectivism: A Learning Theory for the Digital Age*. Elearnspace. Retrieved January 8, 2014, from http://www.elearnspace.org/Articles/connectivism.htm

Siemens, G. (2005). Connectivism: A learning theory for the digital age. *International Journal of Instructional Technology and Distance Learning, 2*(1), 3–10.

Snape, D., & Spencer, L. (2003). The foundations of qualitative research. In J. Ritchie & J. Lewis (Eds.), *Qualitative Research Practice: a guide for social science students and researchers* (pp. 1–23). Thousand Oaks: Sage.

Thomas, D., & Brown, J. S. (2011). *A new culture of learning: Cultivating the imagination for a world of constant change* (Vol. 219). Lexington, KY: CreateSpace.

Trust, T. (2012). Professional learning networks designed for teacher learning. *Journal of Digital Learning in Teacher Education, 28*(4), 133–138. doi:10.1080/21532974.2012.10784693

Veletsianos, G. (2011). Higher education scholars' participation and practices on Twitter. *Journal of Computer Assisted Learning, 28*(4), 336–349. doi:10.1111/j.1365-2729.2011.00449.x

Visser, R. D., Evering, L. C., & Barrett, D. E. (2014). #TwitterforTeachers: The implications of Twitter as a self-directed professional development tool for K–12 teachers. *Journal of Research on Technology in Education, 46*(4), 396–413. doi:10.1080/15391523.2014.925694

Warlick, D. (2009). Grow Your Personal Learning Network: New Technologies Can Keep You Connected and Help You Manage Information Overload. *Learning and Leading with Technology, 36*(6), 12–16.

Wasko, M. M., Teigland, R., & Faraj, S. (2009). The provision of online public goods: Examining social structure in an electronic network of practice. *Decision Support Systems, 47*(3), 254–265. doi:10.1016/j.dss.2009.02.012

Weller, M. (2011). *The Digital Scholar: How Technology is Transforming Scholarly Practice*. Bloomsbury Academic. doi:10.5040/9781849666275

Wenger, E. (2011). *Communities of practice a brief introduction*. Retrieved from http://wenger-trayner.com/wp-content/uploads/2013/10/06-Brief-introduction-to-communities-of-practice.pdf

Wenger, E., McDermott, R., & Snyder, W. (2002). *Cultivating communities of practice*. Boston: Harvard Business School Press.

Wesely, P. M. (2013). Investigating the community of practice of world language educators on Twitter. *Journal of Teacher Education, 64*(4), 305–318. doi:10.1177/0022487113489032

Wiley, D., & Hilton, J. III. (2009). Openness, dynamic specialization, and the disaggregated future of higher education. *The International Review of Research in Open and Distributed Learning, 10*(5).

Yen, C., Bozkurt, A., Tu, C., Sujo-Montes, L., Rodas, C., Harati, H., & Lockwood, A. (2018). A predictive study of students' self-regulated learning skills and their roles in the social network interaction of online discussion board. *Journal of Educational Technology Development and Exchange, 11*(1). doi:10.18785/jetde.0901.03

Learning Communities

KEY TERMS AND DEFINITIONS

Community: The condition of sharing or having certain attitudes and interests in common.

Community of Practices (CoPs): A CoP is a group of people who share a common interest and learn it better by interacting regularly.

Network: A group or system of interconnected people or things.

Professional Learning Communities (PLCs): A PNC is a group of people that come together to learn from one another.

Professional Learning Networks (PLNs): A PLN is defined voluntary digital connections with global reach.

Social Learning: Learning through social communication, interactions, and exchanges.

Social Media: Online spaces (websites, platforms, applications etc.) that enable users to create and share content or to participate in social networking; or enable users to facilitate the building of online networks and communities.

Chapter 5
Enhancing Personal Professional Development Through Technology Integration:
The Need for Ubiquitous Learning

Özden Şahin İzmirli
Çanakkale Onsekiz Mart University, Turkey

Gökhan Çalışkan
Çanakkale Onsekiz Mart University, Turkey

ABSTRACT

In this chapter, personal professional development trainings, which need to include ubiquitous learning environments, are discussed. First of all, professional development is explained. Then, the authors discussed factors affecting the efficiency of professional development activities and how they can incorporate new technologies into professional development activities to meet the needs of adult learners. After that, based on the definition of ubiquitous learning, ways of using technology in terms of meeting adult needs with professional development are examined. Finally, the process that was evaluated within the framework of technology integration is presented to readers.

Enhancing Personal Professional Development Through Technology Integration

PROFESSIONAL DEVELOPMENT

It is seen that the educational practices which have been successful in societies are always compatible with the characteristics and attitudes of the societies where they were implemented. In addition to this, it is essential to meet the needs of societies when it is a necessity to make some radical changes or radical practices. Such a situation is an indicator of the fact that socio-cultural values and structures are influential in the educational processes. It is possible to understand the power of societies to influence cultures with the observation of two simple examples from two different societies regarding lunch time hours of the schools. In some societies, you can see that families fill their schoolyards waiting to feed their children at lunchtimes. In some societies, children have full control over their food and nutrition-related tasks. These characteristic differences of the societies obviously influence the developmental progress of the children. In addition to this, it may also be influential on the duration of lunch, the physical needs of schools and even the expectations of their families and schools.

In addition to the ability of societies to influence the schools, schools and teachers also have the power to influence societies. This mutual influence constitutes an endless cycle of shaping both sides. However, it would be meaningless to leave such important facts on their own in such processes. For this reason, processes should be supported and guided periodically. These supports and guidance often go through the education of adults. It is obvious that parents are also informed about the processes within the scope of the education of adults. However, most of the teachers' sustainable education is planned and carried out within the scope of "professional development". In the trilogy of community, education and future, professional development activities are one of the vital factors feeding this trilogy.

The main purpose of professional development is to provide individuals with the necessary knowledge, skills and attitudes regarding their work and to support their compliance with their organization (Nadler, 1965). The process of acquiring knowledge, skills and attitudes of adults starts with their being uncomfortable with the existing processes and being demanding individuals. Professional development is a process based on the needs of adults. The ability of an adult to demand an individual development task is an indication of a need. In addition; needs are (1) shortcomings determined as a result of evaluations, (2) the changes in laws and regulations, (3) the need for continuously raising qualified individuals who meet the needs of the day, (4) the employment of new employees, the use of a new equipment added to the work environment, the appointment of a new manager (interpretation of the changing vision, etc.) and making decisions on the transition to a new technology.

Planning of professional development is based on individuals' recognition of their needs and being demanding individuals. However, the provision of professional development activities to the staff for institutions is almost a necessity. The complex business relations in business life, achieving the institutional goals, motivation, access to the targeted quality (lack of supervisor and quality work) all make professional development activities a necessity for institutions (Aydın, 2011). Therefore, besides the benefits of professional development for individuals, it is also necessary to see its benefits for institutions.

In addition to all these general situations, what wears off adults' knowledge and skills is the rapid change and developmental mobility of technology in the 21st century. In fact, the main cost of this quick mobility in such technologies is to bring the new technology to the institution. The technological and software requirements of the institutions to keep their existing requirements up to date constitute a serious cost for them. For adult educators, however, the main handicap is how to give the training regarding the new technology to the employee rather than purchasing the most up to date devices so that the staff can use the constantly updated technology (Thompson, Chuang and Sahin, 2007). By allocating some shares from institutions' budgets, they can purchase the technologies to the institutions with a single transaction. However, what makes the staff training process difficult is about how to plan the working hours and training hours, how to give training that will be application-oriented, the diversity in the need for training among the personnel and the diversity of the time intervals of the personnel.

These situations reveal the necessity that the process of professional development should be managed in an individual-based way. Individual-based management of these processes in professional development activities does not only aim to get rid of these dilemmas. It is recommended that professional development activities based on adult education should be practised in accordance with the needs of small and homogeneous groups by considering their differences in age, experience and learning situations (Taymaz, 1997). In other words, the nature of professional development activity requires this process. In fact, these mishaps in the process are not the result of a setback, but perhaps a result of not considering the nature of the adult.

WHY DO WE NEED PERSONAL PROFESSIONAL DEVELOPMENT (PPD)?

Nowadays, individuals need to keep up with the changes brought about by the era by constantly improving themselves. Individuals generally carry out this development process by participating in professional development activities. Professional development activities are often organized by the institutions to which individuals are affiliated. In other words, individuals receive in-service training through their institution, which is accepted as an authority. It is expected in their professional development activities that individuals acquire the knowledge and skills that will enable them to effectively use the new technologies that they encounter in their daily life or working environments.

This situation can be evaluated considering the teaching profession. Teachers are a key element in shaping societies. In other words, teachers play important roles in the adoption of the changes of the era by society. The point to note here is that first of all teachers need to have the full competence in using such changes effectively. The Ministry of National Education (MoNE) has been offering relevant training in helping teachers gain these competencies through some professional development activities. For example, various in-service teacher training activities have been organized by the Ministry in order to train teachers for the changes to be integrated into their lives as part of FATİH project in Turkey, which started in 2010. However, it is seen in the researches that the teachers do not find these activities in the FATİH project efficient and that these training are insufficient in terms of gaining the required competencies regarding the project (eg Alabay, 2015; Vural & Ceylan, 2014). This situation can be interpreted that the teachers do not always get full efficiency from the professional development activities they participated in, and they have problems in transferring the information they acquired in these training activities to the real life.

Professional development activities organized for the purpose of helping individuals gain the knowledge and skills should be reviewed. It is necessary to find out the obstacles in achieving the full effect of such activities and to take necessary precautions to eliminate these obstacles. The relevant literature review reveals that studies are carried out to determine the factors that prevent individuals from achieving sufficient efficiency from their professional development activities. Drage (2010) defines the barriers to teachers' professional development activities as (1) inappropriate time for teachers (2) lack of budget and (3) lack of professional development activities meeting teachers' individual needs. Organization for Economic Co-operation and Development (OECD) (2009) and OECD (2010) grouped the obstacles preventing teachers from participating in professional development activities in the European countries in the Teaching and Learning International Survey as (1) mismatch of the times of the activities for teachers, (2) lack of appropriate professional development activities, (3) family responsibilities, (4) expensive activities, (5) lack of institutional / employer support, and (6) lack of necessary preconditions. Diaz-Maggioli (2004) emphasizes the factors limiting the professional development activities as; the organization of professional development activities by the managers, the lack of professional development activities meeting the needs of teachers, the organizing the activities without considering teachers' learning styles, the lack of the diversity of the channels which could be used in delivering the professional development activities, the inability of teachers to participate in the planning process and teachers' failing in adapting to the professional development activities that they participate. As seen in the researches, time, budget and teacher (teachers' needs, differences etc.) factors are seen as the common points in the lack of efficiency in traditional professional development activities. In this context, it is recommended to pay attention to these three elements in order to obtain the desired level of efficiency from professional development activities. In other words, while planning effective and successful professional development activities, the obstacles caused by these elements should be minimized. However, Lee (2005) suggests that (a) multiple professional development strategies should be used for a successful professional development activity (e.g., observation, guided individual development, etc.); (b) a prolonged period of professional development rather than a short process, (c) the establishment of an effective communication network among teachers involved in a professional development; and (d) the development of professional development activities within the scope of the strategy, which should provide teachers with theoretical knowledge and practice. Diaz-Maggioli (2004) emphasizes the importance of meeting individuals' needs on the basis of effective professional development.

Considering the factors affecting the effectiveness and efficiency of professional development activities, it is seen that using technology in professional development activities makes a significant contribution to the process. In the relevant literature, many professional development activities in the form of distance education using Internet technologies (e.g.in Turkey,the Ministry of National Education organizes professional development activities at http://e-hizmetici.meb.gov.tr/ address and http://uzem.eba.gov.tr/) and it is also seen that there are some other research in the field regarding this issue (e.g. Chen, Chen, & Tsai, 2009; Erickson, Noonan & McCall, 2012; Rienties, Brouwer & Lygo-Bake, 2013; Vrasidas & Glass, 2004). Considering the flexibility of distance education in the training process in terms of time and space, the time factor, which is one of the obstacles affecting the efficiency of professional development activities, can be partially eliminated. In other words, the teachers who are not able to participate in the traditional professional development activities due to the fact that the schedule does not comply with their working hours can participate in the professional development activities organized with distance education within the most appropriate time slots for themselves. Even though the time barriers in front of the professional development activities can be minimized with the help of distance education environments, such activities can still be designed in a way to give training to more than one teacher as in the traditional environment. It could be said that the professional development activities carried out in distance education environments make it difficult to organize the environments in line with the individuals' professional development and learning styles. Considering this, it could be suggested that professional development activities conducted with the use of distance education technologies limit teachers' individual professional development. At this point, the availability of the other technologies allowing teachers to develop their individual professional development, except distance education technologies, should be questioned. One of these technologies is the Ubiquitous Computing (u-computing) technologies. U-computing technologies can be used to bring a new dimension to professional development. With the professional development activities conducted with the use of U-learning technologies in U-learning environments, professional development could be brought down to individual level. With this scope, teachers could benefit from the U-computing technologies available in the U-learning environment for their personal professional needs and learning styles, and thus can achieve their professional development more effectively without any time, space and budget-related obstacles. At this point, the concept of u-learning needs to be well understood.

WHAT IS THE UBIQUITOUS LEARNING?

Nowadays, technology is constantly renewing itself or new technologies are being developed to replace old technologies. Especially in recent years, developments in internet and mobile device technologies have made these technologies an indispensable part of the lives of individuals. As technology has got more and more a place in the daily lives of individual's day by day, various changes have occurred in the learning needs of 21st century individuals. Individuals have started to solve their all needs which depending on these learning changes using technological tools such as internet, computers, tablets and smart phones. This case leads to the various transformations in the learning environment in order to use the best use of the benefits brought by new technologies (Kolomvatsos, 2007). As a result of technological developments, the transformation trend in learning support systems is given in Figure 1 in detail.

As seen in Figure 1, each new transformation includes the previous transformation (Arkün & Aşkar, 2010; Cheng et al., 2005). The transformation in the learning support system began in the early days when computers began to enter into individuals' daily lives. In this term, computer assisted learning has

Figure 1. The transformation trend in learning support systems (Cheng, Sun, Kansen, Huang, & He, 2005)

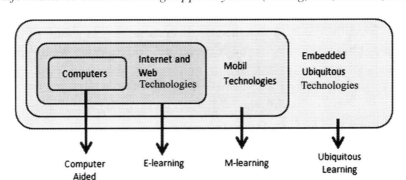

become widespread in the learning environment. This transformation was followed by web-based learning (e-learning) as a result of the development and widespread use of internet technologies, and then followed by mobile learning (m-learning) with the rapid development and widespread use of mobile technologies in the recent past. Nowadays, Ubiquitous Learning (u-learning), which consists of embedded information systems, has started to become widespread (Cheng and et al., 2005). The term of U-learning is based on the term of Ubiquitous Computing (U-computing) which introduced to literature by Weiser (1991). On the basis of U-computing as a term, get a place as an invisible positioning of developing technologies in individuals' daily lives. When the literature is examined, it is seen that there are many definitions about U-computing. Tan, Liu and Chang (2007) define u-computing as embedded computer technologies that have become part of daily life, where individuals can interact at any time. Kolomvatsos (2007) defines u-computing as technologies such as sensors embedded in objects or computers that are spread out to the environment that enables individuals to access the source of information at anywhere and at any time. Learning activities in daily life using U-computing technologies can be defined as u-learning (Bomsdorf, 2005; Marinagi, Skourlas & Belsis, 2013; Sahrir, Yahaya, Nasir & Hamid 2018). In other words, U-learning environments are supported by u-computing technologies embedded in the environment such as GPS, RFID, QR code, wireless sensor networks and badges (Marinagi et al., 2013; Sakamura & Koshizuka, 2005). U-computing technologies allow individuals to learn in the environment at any times (Ng, Nicholas, Loke & Torabi, 2010). In other words, individuals can achieve the best learning with U- learning in their living environment without the limitations of traditional learning environments (Kinshuk & Huang, 2015). In this context, the process of U-learning environments is shown in Figure 2.

As seen in Figure 2, the individual can access information by using u-computing technology (QR code, etc.), mobile devices, internet or wireless network technology. An Example, a person visiting the zoo can access to the information they want by using his mobile device, the internet technology which owned and the QR code on the signboard. U-learning environments can provide personalized learning activities, feedback and context-awareness to individuals in their environment and time (Marinagi et al., 2013; Wu, Hwang & Tsai, 2013). In this context, there are some criteria for u-leaning environments. Virtanen, Haavisto, Liikanen and Kääriäinen (2018) defined these criteria as below.

Figure 2. U-learning environment

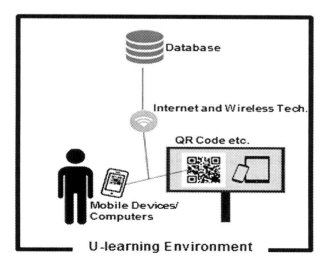

- **Context-Awareness:** Learning systems including mobile devices, cameras, internet and wireless network technologies, RFID, QR code and sensor technologies.
- **Interactivity:** Usage of technologies that individuals have such as mobile technologies, internet, wireless technologies and sensors, in order to realize learning.
- **Personalization:** Based on the location of the individual, presenting learning content and guiding to them (An Example. sensing of students' position by using RFID technology and presentation of best learning content to them)
- **Flexibility:** Providing the opportunity to study and learn at anytime and anywhere, which is appropriate for the individual's time and learning goals.

In addition to these criteria of U-learning, U-learning also has various characteristics. When the literature is examined, it is seen that these characteristics of u-learning are categorized based on the mobile learning environment characteristics which defined by Chen, Kao, Sheu and Chiang(2002) and also Curtis, Luchini, Bobrowsky, Quintana and Soloway (2002) which their study about handheld computers. The characteristics of the U-learning determined based on these two studies are given below (Li, Zheng, Ogata, and Yano, 2005; Ogata et al., 2004; Ogata and Yano, 2004).

- **Permanency:** In the U-learning environment, individuals do not lose the records of their learning activities unless they want to delete themselves. These activities are recorded continuously.
- **Accessibility:** Individuals can access their materials from anywhere
- **Immediacy:** Individuals can access the information, which they want to access, instantly whenever they want.
- **Interactivity:** It's easy to reach experts. Individuals can communicate with their teachers, peers and experts simultaneously and asynchronously.
- **Situating of Instructional Activities:** Learning can be integrated of individuals' daily lives as embedded. In this context, the individual can encounter and associate with the necessary information and problems in the natural environment.

Nowadays, developing technologies have become invisible in all fields of our lives. In other words, individuals started to live every moment of their daily lives as become integrated with the technology. Now, individuals can access any information they want to access anytime and anywhere, with technologies, called as u-computing, which they carry with them at any moment. At this point, individuals are able to shape their learning as u-learning according to their own needs by the u-computing technologies which provide to gain them elements such as accessibility, memory, interaction and flexibility. Considering all of these, professional development activities can be realized in u-learning environments in more individualized way by using u-computing technologies. In this context, the contribution of u-learning to personal professional development process and its importance for the process should be known.

WHY DOES PERSONAL PROFESSIONAL DEVELOPMENT (PPD) NEED UBIQUITOUS LEARNING

When the ongoing learning support systems are examined (i.e. Cheng et al., 2005), it is seen that they have been influenced by the developing technologies. For example, a computer-aided system was born with computer technology. E-learning was formed with the emerge of the Internet and Web technologies. With the formation of mobile technologies, m-learning was born. However, u-learning is not a concept that arose from the birth of a new tool and technology. The concept of u-learning was formed by combining the superior aspects of developing technologies and considering their contribution to educational environments. Regardless of the fact that all other technologies are old or new and mobile or not, u-learning has been formed by bringing together the superior features of the tools and facilities with the aim of meeting the requirements of educational content and target audience. Then there is a need to determine the requirements of Personal Professional Development (PPD) and examine what requirements u-learning meets.

What is PPD?

The fact that adults are aware of their individual strengths is an important step in creating areas both in their daily and work life. Support training may be on the subjects that we sometimes fail to achieve, but they may also be on the subjects which we want to achieve. Support training can sometimes be in the areas we have achieved and, on the subjects, that we want to be better at. Kruckeberg, Amann and Green (2011) associates the second option with a happy life-successful career. She expresses this as "a situation which is too good to be true in the world" because it is a process in which we are strong and that we will work on the topic we love. But what is magical here is the "learning process". What is mentioned as "magic" is to meet the needs and demands of individuals and planning the process accordingly. In this definition, it is tried to explain that individuality is not only a "singularity", but it is also a group of individuals with similar characteristics. When we give PPD training, what characteristics should be considered in gathering individuals in groups to establish PPD environments?

1. **The Level of Knowledge Possessed:** The fact that individuals will have a similar level of knowledge in the related subjects through the training will be connective for PPD. The level of knowledge of the target audience, where to start the training, the pace at which the training will be maintained and the objectives the training will cover are all important. Homogeneity cannot be achieved in contexts where people at different levels of learning or who have different opinions about the related subject exist. The fact that individuals are at similar levels in their level of knowledge will support the homogeneity of the individuals as well as supporting individualization.
2. **Targeted Development Level:** It may be appropriate to categorize the participants according to the target level of the knowledge for the participants in the relevant education. In this homogenization approach, as it determines the point which participants target to reach, it supports the "individualization", in other words, the pace of the participants in the education process. In order to support individualization here, the homogenization of "level of knowledge owned", which is mentioned above, will further support PPD.

3. **The Similarity of the Problem Situation:** Another approach in homogenizing participants is to organize their educational activities with those having similar problem situations. The similarity of the problem situation shows that the participants roughly have similar field knowledge. In addition, the participants' targeted level of development is also clear: *solving the problem situation*. In such cases, it is necessary to define the problem situation well, and it is necessary to ensure that the module covers a problem. Participants are expected to be relatively more willing and demanding since this approach to homogenization is based on the participants' own problems. Participants expect to solve their problems. Here, the problem was tried to be homogenized by taking advantage of the similarity of the situation.
4. **Joint Responsibilities:** The individuals who have taken joint responsibilities on an issue may worry about the quality-raising related concerns such as quality standard or adopting a joint approach. In addition, individuals may need professional development activities in order to enable them to work in collaboration, to clarify their boundaries and responsibilities, or to understand the whole-part relationship in their responsibilities. Participants' being in a joint task or having a joint responsibility to complete a task may bring the participants closer to "individualization" as it homogenizes the "problem", in other words, "the scope". The participants can have different preliminary information about the subject. However, taking joint action will enable them to homogenize.

The mentioned situations are expected to categorize the participants in professional development activities into groups and thus to increase the efficiency of the activities performed. When homogeneity is fulfilled in the categories stated above, the individuality in PPD can be achieved. In this way, it is expected that the opportunities for individuals to benefit from the professional development activities will increase and their satisfaction levels will change in a positive way. While the individualization and quality expectation that are provided in the professional development training are expected to progress in a positive way, there may be some limitations that the adults' existing lives dictate.

An adult individual should make some calculations for his / her own development when deciding on professional development activities. These are; (a) planning of their work-related responsibilities, (b) planning of their daily life, (c) planning of family and other environmental elements, and (d) economic-related planning. In addition, the fact that the educational opportunities are far away from where they live or that the person that they will receive the training from is at a distant place can be a problem. In other words, even if those who prepare professional development activities aim to achieve homogeneity and increase the quality of the education by categorization, the responsibilities of adult lives or the problems of accessing field experts may still remain as a problem. On the other hand, it is expected that employers and even consumers will be able to sacrifice some of their workforces in business hours. When we look at the great scheme, besides the quality preparations of the trainers, the conditions of the employers and working groups on the receiving side are important in the participation in the training. "Ubiquitous Learning" could be used to complete the learning time, space and training hours demanded by the receivers of the training.

What Needs Does U-Learning Cover?

U-learning eliminates the necessity for individuals to be in a certain place while taking professional development training and does not force individuals to be at the location of the tool as in the process of computer-aided process. As u-learning provides space flexibility, it does not force individuals to the place of the Internet (as in e-learning). Even at this point, rather than getting to technology or intermediary centre, it is on the side of meeting the needs and it is based on using the necessary tool (old or new) without making any discrimination. It is important that u-learning is invisible but functional. So what is invisibility mentioned here?

Tan et al. (2007) explained the invisibility of u-learning as technology's becoming a part of their daily lives. Here, while living an individual's daily life, u-learning refers to the fact that he can take his education without adding a new variable to his life regarding his professional development. Thus, individuals can access the documents through different devices, write responses to them, can set up a calendar reminder and share it with the groups they want, access the videos of the lessons learned, ask questions and get his answers. This process, of course, takes place in the virtual world in the background, while individuals are living their daily life. Individuals undertake the responsibilities of their visible and invisible (virtual) worlds and write their results for their benefits. In addition to these opportunities provided by U-learning, quick communication in the invisible world, the speed of the transfer of information and documents use the cognitive capacity, 24 hours, attention, energy and effort of individuals in the world that is still visible. This combination facilitates the works of individuals while increasing their workload. Today, human beings are trying to fight the dilemma, and trying to bear the burdens. This process can be put on the track by integrating the u-learning and other technologies appropriately into daily life and professional work life.

LOOKING AT THE PROCESS THROUGH TECHNOLOGY INTEGRATION LENSES

When the current trends in the world are analyzed, adult education is provided to meet their own needs. It is expected that adults determine the needs for education. In addition, systems have been created in such a way that an individual can carry out their own lives. What Illich (2006, p: 110) says "I can learn to play the guitar by receiving guitar lessons, picture music books, tape-recorded guitar tutorials as well as buying a new guitar" could be given as a good example to that. However, it is important that the content of the training should be taken in line with the technology used and the instructional-designed content. In addition, it is important to maintain their life while meeting their needs with the unique learning environments in their intensive work and life cycle.

The correct use of technologies embedded in our daily lives will enable us to get the quality education we need without hindering our daily lives. The use of the right technology is the job of "technology integration" (TE). Here, with the help of the embedded technologies, educators will actin line with the principles of technology integration and they will relax the users. In addition, the integration of technology into users' lives and training under a disciplinary approach will increase their efficiency and they will not be affected by the potential damages. In other words, there are two perspectives. The person who will have the PPDshould also have TE in his / her personal and professional life, and that the PPD should be implemented with the use of u-learning.

Embedded technologies are technologies that can continuously collect data from us and send notifications as we live our daily lives. The notifications could be very critical, and they affect our decisions, and they can also quickly change our moods during the day and make us weary in the cognitive dimension. So far, we have mentioned about the superior aspects of this intensive information gathering and information orientation process. However, this density may be at a level that may be exhausting. We may need to limit the topic titles, the frequency, scope and intensity of the notifications from different sources. In the U-learning process, we can expect this restriction from units from which training are received. Sometimes this adjustment task will be the individual's own responsibility. In other words, the fact that the u-learning process is an invisible cognitive load enhancer could be prevented with the use of the TE process.

In the process of TE, units providing u-learning and professional development training will need some information regarding those receiving the training. The process of monitoring participation in the process and the most appropriate time will be understood. In addition, some information can be obtained from the participants regarding the content filtering and identification of keywords. The following points could be requested from the participants to prepare the u-learning environment;

- Reasons for getting an education,
- Preliminary information,
- Which channels could be used for training,
- For which purpose they will use the training,
- The keywords regarding the content about which they expect to receive training,
- Preference for field expert,
- The daily-weekly schedule for training

REFERENCES

Alabay, A. (2015). *Ortaöğretim öğretmenlerinin ve öğrencilerinin EBA (eğitimde bilişim ağı) kullanımına ilişkin görüşleri üzerine bir araştırma* (Unpublished master's thesis). İstanbul Aydın University, İstanbul, Turkey.

Amann, W., Kruckeberg, K., & Green, M. (Eds.). (2011). *Leadership and personal development: a toolbox for the 21st century professional.* IAP.

Arkün, S., & Aşkar, P. (2010). *Çevreleyen Öğrenme: Kavramsal Çerçeve Ambient Learning: Conceptual Framework.* In Uluslararası Öğretmen Yetiştirme Politikaları ve Sorunları Sempozyumu II. Hacettepe University.

Aydın, İ. (2011). *Kamu ve özel sektörde hizmet içi eğitim el kitabı.* Ankana: Pegem Akademi.

Bomsdorf, B. (2005). Adaptation of learning spaces: Supporting ubiquitous learning in higher distance education. In *Dagstuhl Seminar Proceedings*. Schloss Dagstuhl-Leibniz-Zentrum fr Informatik.

Chen, Y., Chen, N. S., & Tsai, C. C. (2009). The use of online synchronous discussion for web-based professional development for teachers. *Computers & Education*, *53*(4), 1155–1166. doi:10.1016/j.compedu.2009.05.026

Chen, Y. S., Kao, T. C., Sheu, J. P., & Chiang, C. Y. (2002). A mobile scaffolding-aid-based bird-watching learning system. In *Proceedings. IEEE International Workshop on Wireless and Mobile Technologies in Education* (pp. 15-22). IEEE. 10.1109/WMTE.2002.1039216

Cheng, Z., Sun, S., Kansen, M., Huang, T., & He, A. (2005). A personalized ubiquitous education support environment by comparing learning instructional requirement with learner's behavior. In *19th International Conference on Advanced Information Networking and Applications (AINA'05)* (Vol. 2, pp. 567-573). IEEE. 10.1109/AINA.2005.46

Curtis, M., Luchini, K., Bobrowsky, W., Quintana, C., & Soloway, E. (2002). Handheld use in K-12: A descriptive account. In *Proceedings. IEEE International Workshop on Wireless and Mobile Technologies in Education* (pp. 23-30). IEEE. 10.1109/WMTE.2002.1039217

Diaz-Maggioli, G. (2004). *Teacher-centered professional development.* ASCD.

Drage, K. (2010). Professional Development: Implications for Illinois Career and Technical Education Teachers. *Journal of Career and Technical Education*, *25*(2), 24–37. doi:10.21061/jcte.v25i2.477

Erickson, A. S. G., Noonan, P. M., & McCall, Z. (2012). Effectiveness of online professional development for rural special educators. *Rural Special Education Quarterly*, *31*(1), 22–32. doi:10.1177/875687051203100104

Illich, I. (2006). *Okulsuz toplum.* İstanbul: Oda Yayınları.

Kinshuk & Huang. (2015). *Ubiquitous Learning Environments and Technologies*. Berlin, Germany: Springer Berlin Heidelberg.

Kolomvatsos, K. (2007). Ubiquitous Computing Applications in Education. In *Ubiquitous and Pervasive Knowledge and Learning Management: Semantics, Social Networking and New Media to Their Full Potential* (pp. 94–117). London: IGI Global.

Lee, H. J. (2005). Developing a Professional Development Program Model Based on Teachers' Needs. *Professional Educator*, *27*, 39–49.

Li, L., Zheng, Y., Ogata, H., & Yano, Y. (2005). A Conceptual framework of computer-supported Ubiquitous Learning Environment. In *4th IASTED International Conference on Web-Based Education, WBE 2005* (pp. 243-248). Academic Press. 10.2316/Journal.208.2005.4.208-0861

Marinagi, C., Skourlas, C., & Belsis, P. (2013). Employing ubiquitous computing devices and technologies in the higher education classroom of the future. *Procedia: Social and Behavioral Sciences*, *73*, 487–494. doi:10.1016/j.sbspro.2013.02.081

Nadler, L. (1965). *Employee Training in Japan*. Education and Training Consultants.

Ng, W., Nicholas, H., Loke, S., & Torabi, T. (2010). Designing effective pedagogical systems for teaching and learning with mobile and ubiquitous devices. In T. T. Goh (Ed.), *Multiplatform e-learning systems and technologies: Mobile devices for ubiquitous ICT-based education* (pp. 42–56). New York: IGI Global. doi:10.4018/978-1-60566-703-4.ch003

OECD. (2009). *Creating Effective Teaching and Learning Environments First Results from TALIS*. Retrieved 30.03.2019 from http://www.oecd.org/education/school/43023606.pdf

OECD. (2010). *Teachers' Professional Development: Europe in international comparison*. Retrieved 30.03.2019 from http://www.dgeec.mec.pt/np4/105/%7B$clientServletPath%7D/?newsId=157&fileName=Teachers__Professional_Development.pdf

Ogata, H., Akamatsu, R., Mitsuhara, H., Yano, Y., Matsuura, K., Kanenishi, K., ... Morikawa, T. (2004). TANGO: supporting vocabulary learning with RFID tags. *Proc. Int. Workshop Series on RFID*.

Ogata, H., & Yano, Y. (2004). Context-aware support for computer-supported ubiquitous learning. In *The 2nd IEEE International Workshop on Wireless and Mobile Technologies in Education, 2004. Proceedings.* (pp. 27-34). IEEE. 10.1109/WMTE.2004.1281330

Rienties, B., Brouwer, N., & Lygo-Baker, S. (2013). The effects of online professional development on higher education teachers' beliefs and intentions towards learning facilitation and technology. *Teaching and Teacher Education*, *29*, 122–131. doi:10.1016/j.tate.2012.09.002

Sahrir, M. S., Yahaya, M. F., Nasir, M. S., & Hamid, M. F. A. (2018). Design and Development of Mobile EZ-Arabic. Net for Ubiquitous Learning Among Malaysian Primary School Learners from Experts' Perspective. In *Mobile and Ubiquitous Learning* (pp. 341–361). Singapore: Springer. doi:10.1007/978-981-10-6144-8_20

Sakamura, K., & Koshizuka, N. (2005). Ubiquitous computing technologies for ubiquitous learning. In *IEEE International Workshop on Wireless and Mobile Technologies in Education (WMTE'05)* (pp. 11-20). IEEE. 10.1109/WMTE.2005.67

Tan, T. H., Liu, T. Y., & Chang, C. C. (2007). Development and evaluation of an RFID-based ubiquitous learning environment for outdoor learning. *Interactive Learning Environments*, *15*(3), 253–269. doi:10.1080/10494820701281431

Taymaz, H. (1997). *Hizmetiçi Eğitim*. Ankara: Tokav Tapu ve Kadastro Vakfı Matbaası.

Thompson, A. D., Chuang, H. H., & Sahin, I. (Eds.). (2007). *Faculty mentoring: The power of students in developing technology expertise*. Charlotte, NC: Information Age.

Virtanen, M. A., Haavisto, E., Liikanen, E., & Kääriäinen, M. (2018). Ubiquitous learning environments in higher education: A scoping literature review. *Education and Information Technologies*, *23*(2), 985–998. doi:10.100710639-017-9646-6

Vrasidas, C., & Glass, G. V. (Eds.). (2004). *Online Professional Development for Teachers*. Greenwich, CT: Information Age Publishing.

Vural, A. R., & Ceylan, V. K. (2014). *Fatih Projesi Eğitimde Teknoloji Kullanım Kursunun Öğretmen Görüşlerine Göre Değerlendirilmesi. 19. Türkiye'de İnternet Konferansı*. İzmir: Yaşar University.

Weiser, M. (1991). The Computer for the 21 st Century. *Scientific American*, *265*(3), 94–105. doi:10.1 038cientificamerican0991-94 PMID:1675486

Wu, P. H., Hwang, G. J., & Tsai, W. H. (2013). An expert system-based context-aware ubiquitous learning approach for conducting science learning activities. *Journal of Educational Technology & Society*, *16*(4), 217–230.

Chapter 6
Seamless Learning Design Criteria in the Context of Open and Distance Learning

Erkan Yetik
Eskişehir Osmangazi University, Turkey

Nilgun Ozdamar
Anadolu University, Turkey

Aras Bozkurt
https://orcid.org/0000-0002-4520-642X
Anadolu University, Turkey & University of South Africa, South Africa

ABSTRACT

Seamless learning is a form of learning whereby, regardless of location, the learning process, as it relates to learning needs and readiness, can continue through the aid of technology. Seamless learning environments are spaces that can be accessed independent of time and place through mobile or stationary devices, and that are equipped with technologies capable of meeting learning needs. With the advancements in technology, seamless learning environments are becoming increasingly popular. In this regard, the design of environments that are suitable for seamless learning in open and distance learning (ODL) fields is of critical importance. This study aimed to determine the criteria for the design of seamless learning environments in the context of ODL. In line with this aim, the Delphi technique, a qualitative research approach, was used. A total of 47 criteria under 10 different themes were identified in the study.

DOI: 10.4018/978-1-5225-9779-7.ch006

Seamless Learning Design Criteria in the Context of Open and Distance Learning

INTRODUCTION

Sharoles et al. (2012) defined seamless learning as the unrestricted continuity of technology-based learning regardless of place, time, and social environments. Seamless learning is identified as a special form of mobile and accessible learning that has been and continues to be improved through technology. In looking at the definitions of technology-based learning approaches presented in the literature, ubiquitous learning is defined as the availability of learning resources at any time and in any place, whereas seamless learning is defined as a form of learning that also enables, in addition to what is provided through ubiquitous learning, a shift to different learning habits and scenarios. According to an alternative definition offered by Wong et al. (2012), seamless learning is a learning approach that has the potential to include learning models which encompass many fields of learners' daily lives and which are supported by various technologies, from virtual classrooms to e-learning.

With the advancements in mobile technologies, seamless learning environments have become more widespread. In order to design these environments to meet learners' and teachers' needs in the learning process, appropriate design criteria are required. Keeping this in mind, the purpose of the present research is to identify seamless learning environment criteria for open and distance learning (ODL). The following research question was developed to guide the research: What are the themes and criteria for evaluating seamless learning environments?

BACKGROUND AND RELATED LITERATURE

Seow et al. (2008), in their study, highlighted that researchers are interested in seamless learning environments that are capable of combining informal and formal learning once mobile devices and network access become more widespread. Based on studies related to the design of a learning environment using mobile devices and online portals for environmental education and inquiry-based science learning, the following components of seamless learning environments were identified: community, place, time and context, and cognitive devices and constructs. Using these components, they proposed a framework based on the theory of distributed cognition for seamless learning.

Kukulska-Hulme and Viberg (2018), in their study, presented a review of the literature published between 2012–2016 which focused on mobile collaborative language learning in order to identify the mobile technologies used to support collaborative learning between second- and foreign- language students. Their results highlighted the elements of flexible use, feedback on-time, customization, socialization, personal assessment, active participation, peer coaching, outdoors sources of inspiration, and cultural originality.

Sharples (2015), who investigated seamless learning in terms of its capacity to deliver a continuous meaning flow despite the changes in the physical and social context, reported that one of the ways to achieve this was to provide a flow state whereby learners lose their awareness about their environment. It was further stated that mobile educational games can serve as one of the means to reach such as flow; however, it was noted this was neither easy nor necessarily effective on learning. Another approach suggested in the same study was to interconnect learning processes that take place in different contexts, such as in-class and home learning contexts. This approach requires that the learning process be strongly organized to ensure a smooth integration of one learning environment with that of another. Whatever the context may be, seamless learning is a learning concept that integrates self-directed learning and teacher guidance through the support of mobile technology toolkits.

Hwang et al. (2011) pointed out that mobile and wireless communication technologies not only provide ubiquitous learning but also presents opportunities for developing learning environments capable of integrating the resources of the real world and digital world. They suggested an interactive concept map approach to support mobile learning activities. An experiment was carried out in a primary school natural sciences course to evaluate the effectiveness of the method suggested. The experimental results showed that the method not only fostered positive attitudes towards learning but also improved students' level of achievement in learning.

In their review study on seamless learning, Wong and Looi (2011) identified 10 distinct dimensions of seamless learning. This review study examined previous studies on seamless learning and identified these dimensions based on their common aspects.

Milrad et al. (2013) indicated that it is of critical importance for researchers and implementers to figure out effective means for designing, implementing, and assessing innovative learning environments and technologies in various learning settings. They also highlighted the importance that the design of learning activities reflects students' cultural diversity and that the assessment of seamless learning is conducted in the latest educational contexts.

Wong and Looi (2011) defined the term seamless learning as "the continuous inclusion of learning experiences in formal and informal learning contexts, individual and social learning, and real and virtual environments." This clearly highlights that the most important feature of seamless learning is that "it provides a continuous learning flow between different contexts (Wong & Looi, 2011). According to Chan et al. (2006), seamless learning refers to "the students' ability to learn about anything in which they are interested in different scenarios and their ability to shift from one context to another in an easy and fast way." Wong (2012) further identified the following 10 components of mobile-aided seamless learning:

- **MSL1**: Encompasses formal and informal learning
- **MSL2**: Encompasses personalized and social learning
- **MSL3**: Operates across time
- **MSL4**: Operates across locations
- **MSL5**: Ubiquitous access learning resources
- **MSL6**: Encompasses physical and digital worlds
- **MSL7**: Combined use of multiple device types
- **MSL8**: Seamless switching between multiple learning tasks
- **MSL9**: Knowledge synthesis
- **MSL10**: Encompasses multiple pedagogical and learning activity models

Figure 1. Visualization of the 10D-MSL dimensions (Wong 2012)

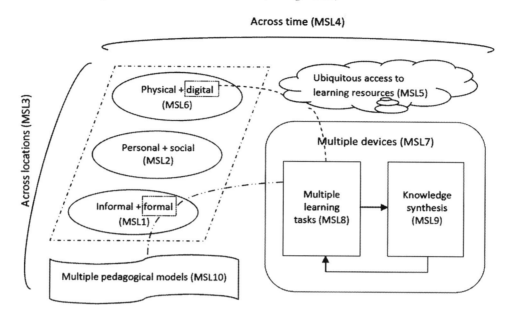

METHODOLOGY

In this study, the Delphi technique, a qualitative research model, was used. The Delphi technique is widely used in educational studies (Green, 2014). This technique, which aims to collect creative, reliable data for forecasting and decision-making (Bozkurt, 2013), has a range of characteristic features. With this technique, data is collected from panels of experts in a structured process and then shaped in a comprehensive manner (Adler & Ziglio, 1996). The panelists' anonymity is secured throughout the entire process in order to prevent the panelists from influencing one another and to free them from any prejudices they may have (Helmer, 1997; Şahin, 2001). The basic features of the Delphi technique can be summarized as follows (Dalkey, 1972):

- Confidentiality in participation (anonymity),
- Statistical analysis of panelist responses,
- Controlled feedback on the Delphi process.

There are different opinions on the size of panelist groups, with some suggesting that they should consist of at least seven individuals (Şahin, 2001) and others recommending 10–15 individuals (Adler & Ziglio, 1996). In the present study, purposeful sampling and snowball techniques were employed for the selection of the Delphi expert panelists. The expert panel group consisted of 10 academics who work in Turkey. These panelists had expertise in at least one of the following fields: distance education, open and distance learning, mobile learning, and ubiquitous learning. The criteria for participation on the Delphi panel was that the experts had either produced academic studies on the topics of distance education, open and distance learning, mobile learning, or ubiquitous learning, or that they were actively working on these topics in institutions operating in the relevant fields.

Data Collection Tools

Interview (1st Delphi Round)

In semi-structured interviews, a data tool widely used in educational studies, the aim is to gather responses and reactions to open-ended questions on a particular topic (McMillan, 2004). Ten panelists participated in the first Delphi round, for which the data were collected through semi-structured interviews conducted with three of these panelists.

Questionnaire (2nd and 3rd Delphi Rounds)

Questionnaires are defined as research material that consists of a range of questions to determine individuals', beliefs, or attitudes (Thomas, 1988). Compared to other data collection methods (interviews, observations), questionnaires are particularly advantageous insofar as they are low cost and allow data to be rapidly collected from larger groups from different regions. Online questionnaires forms used in the 2nd round of the Delphi technique.

Data Analysis

Various measurement instruments for data analysis can be used in Delphi studies, and different consensus levels, such as those derived from arithmetic mean, mode, median, and standard deviation, can be designated according to the scope of the study (Powell, 2003). Outlier responses at the extremes can influence the results of the study in a non-realistic manner; therefore, the median and interquartile range (IQR) values are frequently used for data analysis in Delphi studies (Cochran, 1983; Mullen, 2003; Giannarou & Zervas, 2014).

In order to meet the consensus criteria in this study, the median and interquartile range values were calculated. The consensus level is the sum of the *agree* and *strongly agree* responses on the five-point Likert-type scale, which was used in the 2nd and 3rd rounds of the Delphi technique. The median is the exact middle value when the responses are arranged in order from greatest to smallest. The first quartile is the point that separates 25% of the responses on the left-hand-side and 75% of the responses on the right-hand side, while the third quartile is the point that separates 25% of the responses to the right-hand-side and 75% of them to the left-hand side. The interquartile range (IQR) refers to the difference between the first and third quartiles, where a low value of IQR indicates agreement and a high value of IQR indicates disagreement. The consensus criteria designated for the second and third rounds are presented in Table 1.

Table 1. Consensus criteria designated for the second and third rounds

2. Round	Median $\geq$ 4, IQR $\leq$ 1, Frequency 4-5 $\geq$ 70%
3. Round	Median $\geq$ 4, IQR $\leq$ 1, Frequency 4-5 $\geq$ 80%

Delphi Rounds

- **First Round:** A total of 10 open-ended questions were posed in the first round. These questions were developed based on the themes identified by Wong (2012), Wong and Looi (2011), and Milrad et al. (2013). Ten panelists participated in this round. Based on the panelists' responses to the semi-structured interview and open-ended questions, 59 criteria on 10 different themes were identified.
- **Second Round:** In this round, the panelists' opinions on the 59 criteria governing the 10 different themes identified in the first round were taken. Ten panelists participated in this round. The panelists' responses in this round were analyzed according to the consensus criteria designated. Five items that were below the consensus criteria were eliminated, leaving 54 items remaining.
- **Third Round:** In this round, the items that met the consensus level designated based on the responses were once again posed to the panelists, and they were asked to evaluate them. In this last Delphi round, 10 panelists participated. The responses given in this round were analyzed according to the consensus criteria. Four items that were below the consensus criteria were eliminated, leaving 50 items remaining. The 6 items that were determined to overlap with each other were further analyzed and then combined, leaving a total of 47 criteria remaining.

Reliability

To confirm the reliability of the study, apart from the researcher, a university faculty member who was an expert in the field of distance learning, was asked to code the criteria for the design of seamless learning environments in open and distance education, and the intercoder reliability was found to be 93.2%.

FINDINGS

The Criteria for the Design of an Environment that Encompasses Formal and Informal Learning in the Context of Seamless Learning.

Integrating Social Networks to Learning Environments

Murray (2008) indicated that social networks and software has changed the way individuals communicate and their share of knowledge in today's societies. From this point of view, social networks that are integrated into the learning environment can directly contribute to the education process. In the context of seamless education, a nexus between formal and informal learning can be established. Learners can build digital profiles and express themselves rather than being restricted to isolated settings, such as traditional classrooms and learning management systems. In this way, the capacity and content of seamless learning can be enlarged by integrating them with social networks, which play an active role in the daily lives of individuals

SCORM-Compliant E-Learning Materials

The Shareable Content Object Reference Model (SCORM) is a reference model which is formed based on the standards of being durable, reusable, compatible with other software, and accessible for e-learning material. Various devices and environments are needed in order to establish a bridge between formal and informal learning. Therefore, it can be proposed that the use of SCORM-compliant materials is necessary to facilitate a complete seamless learning process.

Use of Cross-Platform Applications and Content

The use of such applications and designs is necessary to provide the sustainability of learners' seamless learning between devices that have different technologies and backgrounds.

The Criteria for the Design of an Environment Encompassing Personalized and Social Learning in the Context of Seamless learning

Use of Web-Based Environments, Like Social Networks, Forums, and Blog Pages, For Social Interaction

Social networks, with their many features and opportunities, assist teachers in supporting educational processes by facilitating active, creative and collaborative learning, foster student-student, student-content and teacher-student interaction, and help students to use and develop research, inquiry, and problem-solving skills (Gülbahar et al., 2010). In addition, the communication tools, like forum or discussion pages, available in many learning management systems have social add-ons, and furthermore, in systems that are capable of being integrated to social networks, the content created in learning environments can be shared, thus enabling learning experiences to be transported to social networks.

Developing a Design That Conforms to Learners' Individual and Social Preferences

Under the theory of independent study, Wedemeyer (1981) presented six guidelines of distance learning, which included the personalization of learning, conforming learning to students' own setting, and giving students the ability to determine their own pace of study and the responsibility to make all these decisions themselves. As these criteria make clear, the personal characteristics of the learners should be considered, and designs that are suitable to students' personal and social preferences should be made.

Identifying the Characteristics of the Target Audience

Karimi (2016) highlighted the importance of personal characteristics in the adaptation of learning and further emphasized that the awareness of students, in terms of directing themselves and adapting the learning processes to their needs and desires, influences the use of the e-learning system. The personal characteristics of learners can serve to either raise or diminish their motivation to use the learning environment. For this reason, knowing the characteristics of the students who will be provided with the education can contribute to improving seamless learning.

Use of Learning Environments Appropriate to Collaboration

Collaborative learning refers to a state of learning that involves peers who are at more or less the same academic level, carry out actions, have a common goal, and study together to achieve this goal (Dillenbourg, 1999). A design that is appropriate to seamless learning in the context of ODL should be enriched with collaboration-based learning opportunities.

The Criteria for the Design of an Environment Providing Ubiquitous Access Learning Resources

Designing Learning Materials That Can be Used Online and Offline

The IEEE Learning Technology Standards Committee (LTSC) describes Learning Objects as "any entity, digital or non-digital, which can be used, re-used or referenced during technology- supported learning". (Premlatha & Geetha, 2015). In order to provide seamless learning, it is essential to have access to learning materials in environments other than online ones. Therefore, designing the learning environment and/or materials in such a way that they can be used offline was determined as an important criterion in this study.

Design of the Learning Process in the Context of Mobile Learning and Ubiquitous Learning

Hwand et al. (2008) stated that in seamless learning, learning services should not be interrupted in the shifts between devices or networks (the internet networks) that learners' make in their movement between spaces. One of the most important aspects of seamless learning is that there is no discontinuity in the learning process; in other words, learners should be able to engage in learning at any time and place they desire. The use of educational approaches and techniques and learning theories that encompass mobile learning and ubiquitous learning in seamless learning processes helps to enrich learning processes

Search Engine Integrated Learning Devices

Users have a low tolerance for browsing beyond the results displayed on the first page of search engines. Instead of accepting the list of results delivered, they tend to redefine the web inquiry (Jansen & Spink, 2006). Learners also might need to access the data they require without shifting between the environments or devices. Therefore, integrating search engines into the learning environments and devices is necessary to achieve the feeling of seamless learning in the learning environment or with the device used, as revealed by this criterion of the study.

Use of Learning Environments Designed With the Architecture of Cloud Computing

Cloud technologies refer to platforms, servers, and software that can be accessed via the internet and whose continuity is guaranteed in all aspects. This criterion implies that the use of safe environments, ones that function with backup, do not have any performance problems, and can be extended – in other words, environments equipped with the architecture of cloud computing – is necessary in order to ensure ubiquitous access to learning resources. However, it is important to note that cloud-based e-learning environments are not currently used very frequently due to their high costs. Nevertheless, platforms that are capable of providing seamless learning which encompasses all the hardware, software, and data processing resources required for e-learning can be created.

The Criteria for the Design of Course-Environments Encompassing Multiple Device Types

Use of Devices Providing Cross-Platform Support

Devices that provide cross-platform support are those that are supported by a large variety of platforms, which mainly function via browsers. Developers of mobile learning applications can develop complex applications that are compatible with different devices by using HTML5, JavaScript, and CSS (Özdamar-Keskin & Kılınç, 2015). The use of these platforms can enable designs that encompass multiple device types. Devices that are capable of providing cross-multiplication support in the context of seamless learning can minimize learners' dependence on particular devices and therefore provide the continuance of the seamless learning experience, as this criterion indicates.

Making a Responsive Design

Kim (2013) highlights that the purpose of responsive web design is to allow webpages to be displayed at the same rate regardless of the screen size of a device. Cell phones, which today are the most actively used mobile devices, provide different user experiences depending on the device models and screen resolutions. Specific mobile devices are selected based on what they will be primarily used for, such as for traveling, exercising or playing sports, studying, or other activities. The variety of screen sizes available on devices has therefore increased in line with the advancements made in technology. Responsive designs function as an important criterion for the design of seamless learning environments in the context of ODL, particularly in the sense that learners who make use of different devices can resume their learning process in more fluid manner.

Use of Mobile Applications

Mobile applications are generally designed to give users who are mobile access to the services and data they need. Considering mobile applications in terms of the course-environment criteria encompassing multiple device types, there is a need for applications that can function in multiple operating systems.

Creating the Same Visual and Sensory Design in Different Devices

Creating the design of an interface on the basis of specific criteria is of critical importance in terms of providing an effective, efficient and attractive learning experience (Bhaskar et al., 2011). Considering the variety of mobile devices people use, the same content, when opened in different devices, should yield the same configuration. In the shifts between devices that occur in the shift of spaces, the course content should remain the same and the learner should be able to follow the content with the same motivation. This criterion highlights an important point for seamless learning.

Use of Devices That Can Communicate With Each Other

The most significant factors that distinguish seamless learning from other modes of learning are that the shifts between platforms are smooth over multiple device types, and that the learning process encompasses real and virtual environments and involves multiple educational approaches (Yetik & Özdamar, 2016). In this context, the need to ensure that devices can communicate with each other is quite clear. The seamless resumption of course content is required for seamless learning in the context of ODL. The resume point in the learning when there is a shift between environments can be detected by transforming to a new device in the cloud system, by directly providing the communication between devices, or with the help of a device serving as a bridge. These features can contribute to the seamless learning process.

Use of Applications/Content Designed With the Use of Platform-Independent Coding Languages

Bohl et al. (2002) highlighted that the basic purposes of the SCORM standard are the easy transportation of a learning management system or learning content, as well as the reusability of learning material. In addition to platform-independent applications, this criterion indicates that platform-independent course content should be developed. For example, HTML5, a new generation technology, can be used to develop such content.

Using the Internet of Things Technology in Devices

It has been argued that Internet of Things will popularize the integration of all devices by the mediation of their interactions through grounded systems and therefore create a device network which communicates with other devices as well as with humans (Xia et al., 2012). This criterion represents the interactions and dependence that learning environments have with one another.

The Criteria for the Seamless Shift in Multiple Learning Tasks

Determining the Learner's Own Learning Needs and Shifting Accordingly Between Tasks

Grant (2002) argued in his study that learning is more subjected to change when the learning analysis of learners is performed in connection with the ongoing professional development, that education is related to the practice, and that individual reinforcements direct the educational effort and contribute to the learning. This criterion underlines the importance of identifying the learning needs of learners and determining what types of content should be being delivered according to these identified needs.

Providing Individual Learning Opportunities Using Learning Analytics

The Society for Learning Analytics Research (SOLAR) defined learning analytics as the measurement, collection, analysis, and interpretation of data related to the contexts of learner behaviors and the optimization of learning processes and environments (Siemens & Gasevic, 2012). With these analytics, the learners' means of accessing content, their device preference according to setting type, and their content preference are determined to achieve more effective seamless learning.

Microlearning Design: Presenting Learning Content in the Form of Bite-Size Pieces

Microlearning (Jomah, Masoud, Kishore, & Aurelia, 2016) is one of the significant component of seamless learning. The design of learning content in the form of small modules within the scope of learning outcomes enables the development of content that lasts a shorter time, which results in quickening the shifts between multiple learning tasks. As underlined by this finding, learning content can be presented in small pieces in order to provide rapid shifts between multiple learning tasks.

Carrying Out Activities to Reinforce the Learner's Intrinsic Motivation in Order to Continue the Learning Activity in Different Environments

Motivation is an important ingredient of learning processes (Uçar and Kumtepe, 2018). The decreased motivation learners experience in transitions to a different activity can be a problematic issue in the rapid shift of multiple learning tasks. As a result, new tasks that are assigned should not require a deviation from the previous context and learning content should be managed based on an algorithm or some other like arrangement. In addition, provisions such as informing learners about the progress they have covered to reach the learning outcome and about the approximate remaining time can contribute, in the context of seamless learning, to learner motivation.

Providing Learning Opportunities Appropriate to Different Technology Literacy Levels

Technology literacy is a vital factor for technology-enhanced learning processes (Ezziane, 2007), including seamless learning. Not all learners have the same level of technological understanding, albeit the increasing trend in technology literacy today. For this reason, environments that require only a basic level of technological literacy should be preferred, and different levels of technological literacy should be provided, if necessary, for the learning content, as this criterion highlights.

Resumption of the Online Content While Shifting From One Environment/Device to Another

The rapid shift in multiple learning tasks is one of the most important characteristics that distinguish seamless learning from other learning approaches. The shift between educational applications should be autonomous and smooth (Yetik & Özdamar-Keskin, 2016). This criterion suggests that the learner should be able to readily resume studying course content. An example of this could be that a learner, after watching a portion of video course content on a mobile device, can resume watching this video on the television at home.

The Criteria for the Design of an Environment Encompassing Physical and Digital Worlds

Creating Learning Designs Where Connectivist Principles Can be Used

Connectivism in terms of learning is defined as the development of a network through the forming of connections (Siemens, 2004). Learners who are curious or have high levels of motivation can access data by forming connections. Therefore, the design of environments that enable learners to achieve the aforementioned stands as an important criterion for seamless learning processes.

Use of Gamified Learning Processes

Gamification is defined as the use of digital game elements in situations outside the game context in order to boost user experience and appeal (Sezgin, Bozkurt, Yılmaz, & van der Linden, 2018). Gamification mechanics create a social setting for learners and direct the learning process to the targeted outcome by keeping motivation high. The use of gamified course content is of critical significance in terms of fostering learners' motivation and commitment and sustaining the learning process. Therefore, the use of gamified learning processes is an important criterion for enhancing learners' motivation and for providing the sustainability of learning processes in seamless learning.

Reinforcing Online Content With Offline Activities

This criterion highlights that online content that is presented in such a way that it is adapted to real-life situations as part of a design of an environment that encompasses both the physical world and the digital world can contribute to seamless learning. An example of this would be an experiment presented in an online course being given as an assignment in a laboratory setting.

The Criteria for the Design of a Course Where Prior and New Knowledge Can Be Synthesized

Searching for New Knowledge and Providing Rapid Access to Prior Knowledge

Learning content starts with a reference to learning outcomes and, then, identification of the topics upon which additional content touches. In this way, students are taught how to construct knowledge. This criterion involves presenting a course syllabus to students, followed by communicating the learning outcomes targeted at the beginning and end of course content. In addition, providing shortcuts for students who want to access previous topics can further develop their understanding of how to search for knowledge and quicken their access to prior knowledge.

Use of Constructivist Learning Processes With the Constructivist Approach

Learning theories like constructivism stress the importance of providing appropriate instructional support and guidance in order to facilitate meaningful learning and maximize students' learning outcomes (Lee, 2012). When the content and designs of seamless learning are organized on the basis of the constructivist approach, this can contribute to the seamless learning process, as this criterion implied.

Recognition of Prior Learning

Recognition of prior knowledge is central to the earning of credits in higher education, which includes adult education and professional education (Anderson et al., 2013). With the fostering of communication between digital databases, the transference of credits between institutions increases, allowing learners' recognition of prior knowledge to enlarge and be accepted by institutions. Recognition of learners' previous knowledge and the acceptance of this knowledge by institutions is essential in terms of the synthesis of previous and new knowledge.

Providing Opportunities for Personalized Learning

Each person's perceptions and learning styles differ from each other (Martinez, 2001). While some students learn by reading, others learn by experiencing or solving. Hence, considering the personal characteristics that distinguish students' learning styles can improve the effect of seamless learning processes, as this criterion reveals.

Creating Learner-Centered Learning Designs

In learner-centered designs, particular attention is given to ensuring that all activities are carried out by students. Learners take the initiative in determining the content and in carrying out the assessment of the activities. They are also given the opportunity to perform activities that are related to their own interests and abilities. In other words, the learner should be the one who is at the center of the seamless learning experience, and the learning frame should be designed in line with the learner's learning needs.

The Critera for the Design of Courses Appropriate to Seamless Learning Using Multiple Pedagogical Model or Andragogy

Use of Different Content Types (Audio, Text, Visual, Animation, Video etc.)

The use of multimedia contents that corresponds to a particular purpose is a factor that positively affects learning processes (Mayer, 2001). In a seamless learning design that considers learners' individual preferences, it is necessary that the content can be applied to every user. Delivering content that is appropriate to learners' circumstances is a primary feature of seamlessness. In addition, contents addressing the specific needs of the learners should be developed due to individual learning differences.

Presenting Learning Content According to the Dual-Coding Theory and Designing Learning Content That Does Not Encumber Cognitive Load

The Dual-Coding Theory, which provides a theoretical framework for multimedia designs, is based on the assumption that coding of the same data in two forms supporting each other raises the efficiency and effectiveness of learning (Mayer, 1997). Thus, in order for seamless learning to also take place at the cognitive level, designs need to be created according to the dual-coding theory and not overburden cognitive load, as this criterion underlines.

Ability to Shift Between Different Learning Approaches

Basic components of the seamless learning design can be developed using the multidimensional-user modeling of learning support based on the meta-cognitive, cognitive and affective development of the student and the environment (Specht, 2015). This multidimensionality can be realized through designs that include different learning approaches. This criterion revealed that learning approaches should be changed according to different spaces and contexts. It was also determined that learners' individual preferences can change once they are determined and that the system should be able to accommodate these changes by applying a situation-focused approach.

Equipping Learners With Self-Regulated Learning Skills

In a learning design where learners are at the center, the learners can achieve better outcomes when they regulate themselves. In this way, learners can direct the seamless learning process and also develop their seamless learning skills, allowing them to be more active in and have greater control of their present and future learning experiences.

Design of the Seamless Learning Processes on the Basis of Cultural Diversity

Providing Cultural Integration by Including Students From Different Cultures in the Social Interaction

Cultural context may affect learning from various aspects (Bozkurt, Yazıcı, Erdem-Aydın, 2018) and therefore should be considered in seamless learning processes. Learners should have respect for the values of individuals outside of their own culture, be free from prejudices about different cultures, and consider differences as an asset for humanity. The design of learning environments that nurture this cultural understanding can change learners' perspectives on life as well as contribute to their education.

Assigning Task/Homework That Helps Learners to Feel a Sense of Belongingness to the System

Belongingness can be defined as the sense of noticing that members develop towards each other and the group, and the belief that their needs are met thanks to the unity of the members (Ilgaz & Aşkar, 2009). Through the massive number of people participating in ODL, there has been an increased opportunity for individuals to attend courses with other individuals from different cultures. Therefore, considering learners' cultural characteristics and assigning tasks accordingly can boost their motivation and sense of belongingness to the system. Learners with a high sense of belongingness can engage in more active participation, and their activities in learning processes will be based on intrinsic motivation.

Exclusion of Sensitive Learning Content (Language, Religion, Race Etc.)

The presentation of content which learners may have sensitivity towards or feel uncomfortable about (Banks, 1993) can interrupt the seamless learning process by alienating their perceptions and feelings from the learning process and content. This criterion highlights that the learning content developed should be universal, and that any content that could cause discomfort to learners should be avoided so as not to interrupt the learning experience.

Design of the Assessment and Evaluation Process in Seamless learning

Use of Questions Encompassing Formal and Informal Learning in the Assessment and Evaluation Process

According to Kargın (2007), the evaluation and assessment process is a formal process, for which formal assessment tools should be supported with the data obtained by informal assessment tools. Informal assessment tools, such as observations, interviews, written exams, error analysis, analysis of study example, homework, worksheets, and criterion-based tools, aim to determine the student's mastery of a particular skill. Wong and Looi (2011) defined seamless learning as the seamless formal and informal inclusion of physical and digital worlds in individual and social learning processes. Based on this, the assessment and evaluation process should be included in these environments, as this criterion indicates.

Use of Methods Where Students Can Assess Themselves

According to Shearer (2003), the course design should provide enough self-assessment levels that can accommodate, as much as possible, different cognitive styles. These types of control variables provide a positive learning experience for students who are self-directed. For example, portfolios can be considered as reflections of what learners know and how they construct the knowledge. Portfolios can also be included in the alternative assessment and evaluation applications. Learners who engage in portfolio activity can assess themselves and boost their motivation regarding related topics.

Providing Rapid Feedback in Learning Processes

Particular attention was given to adult learners, since this study was carried out in the context of ODL. Regularly provided feedback helps to facilitate a sense of success and professional development in adult learners, as it is important that they can track their progress and understand whether they took steps correctly or incorrectly (Malone, 2014). This criterion underlines how important it is to provide feedback in a rapid manner.

Use of Personalized Assessment and Evaluation Processes With Learning Analytics

Learning analytics is defined as the collection and interpretation of large-scale data produced by learners in order to evaluate academic achievement, predict future performance, and determine current issues (Johnson et al., 2011). Learning analytics enables the presentation of personalized learning opportunities to provide more effective learning experiences (Bozkurt, 2016). From this point of view, the use of learning analytics in assessment and evaluation processes is important in that it helps learners to track their progress in seamless learning processes.

Use of Assessment and Evaluation for the Process Rather Than the Outcome

This criterion stresses that learners should be assessed during the process rather than at the end of the process. The combined use of learning analytics and self-assessment within the process can contribute to seamless learning.

Use of Biometric Data, Such as Those Involving the Eyes and Face, in Order to Enhance Reliability in the Assessment Process

Seamless learning processes are based on the assumption that learning should be independent of time and place, and this assumption extends to the evaluation and assessment processes, where it is expected that the same flexibility is applied. However, one of the chief challenges to this same flexibility in online assessment and evaluation processes is the current authentication methods (Bozkurt & Uçar, 2018), which have proven to be largely inadequate (Flior & Kowalski, 2010). Yet, with that said, there are a number of mobile applications available to learners to ensure the reliability of the assessment and evaluation. For example, retinal scan and fingerprint scan features, which are already available in new model phones, can be used to ensure this criterion. In this way, learners can participate in the assessment and evaluation processes at any time and place they desire, and reliable assessments can be carried out through these biometric authentication processes.

CONCLUSION

This study aimed to determine criteria for the design of a seamless learning ODL system based on the themes identified by Wong (2012), Wong and Looi (2011), and Milrad et al. (2013). The study used the Delphi technique, a qualitative research method for gathering data, from which a total of 47 criteria under 10 themes were identified.

Based on the findings of the study, the following suggestions can be taken into consideration. First, learning management systems (LMS), which are widely used nowadays, do not yet have the capacity to detect learners' positions. Therefore, future studies on context-aware learning and seamless learning can examine ways to improve learning management systems and enrich seamless learning experiences. Second, this study was carried out in the context of ODL; thus, conducting studies on criteria for the design of seamless learning in different contexts can further contribute to the related literature. The themes and criteria developed within the scope of this study can be periodically updated according to features developed by new technologies, and future studies can be carried on this issue.

ACKNOWLEDGMENT

This research was supported by Anadolu University, Scientific Research Project Commission under the grant numbers 1602E062, 1805E123 and 1905E079.

This research is an extended version of master thesis entitled "Identifying Seamless Learning Environment Design Criteria in the Context of Open and Distance Learning" by Erkan Yetik which was conducted at Anadolu University, Graduate School of Social Sciences, and supervised by Dr. Nilgun Ozdamar and Dr. Aras Bozkurt.

REFERENCES

Açıkgöz, K. Ü. (2003). *Etkili Öğrenme ve Öğretme*. İzmir: Eğitim Dünyası Yayınları.

Adler, M., & Ziglio, E. (1996). *Gazing into the oracle*. Bristol, PA: Jessica Kingsley Publishers.

Andersson, P., Fejes, A., & Sandberg, F. (2013). Introducing research on recognition of prior learning. *International Journal of Lifelong Education*, *32*(4), 405–411. doi:10.1080/02601370.2013.778069

Banks, J. A. (1993). Multicultural education: Characteristics and goals. In J. A. Banks & C. A. M. Banks (Eds.), *Multicultural education: Issues and perspectives* (2nd ed.; pp. 3–28). Boston: Allyn & Bacon.

Bhaskar, N. U., Naidu, P. P., Babu, S. R. C., & Govindarajulu, P. (2011). Principles of good screen design in websites. *International Journal of Human-Computer Interaction*, *2*(2), 48–57.

Bohl, O., Schellhase, J., Sengler, R., & Winand, U. (2002). The Sharable Content Object Reference Model (SCORM) – A Critical Review. In *Proceedings of the International Conference on Computers in Education (ICCE02)* (pp. 950-951). Auckland, New Zealand: Academic Press.

Bozkurt, A. (2013). *Açık ve uzaktan öğrenmeye yönelik etkileşimli e-kitap değerlendirme kriterlerinin belirlenmesi*. Eskişehir: Anadolu Üniversitesi, Sosyal Bilimler Enstitüsü, Uzaktan Eğitim Anabilim Dalı.

Bozkurt, A. (2016). Öğrenme analitiği: E-öğrenme, büyük veri ve bireyselleştirilmiş öğrenme. *Açık Öğretim Uygulamaları ve Araştırmaları Dergisi*, *2*(4), 55–81.

Bozkurt, A., & Uçar, H. (2018). E-Öğrenme ve e-sınavlar: Çevrimiçi ölçme değerlendirme süreçlerinde kimlik doğrulama yöntemlerine ilişkin öğrenen görüşlerinin incelenmesi. *Mersin Üniversitesi Eğitim Fakültesi Dergisi*, *14*(2), 745–755. doi:10.17860/mersinefd.357339

Bozkurt, A., Yazıcı, M., & Erdem Aydın, İ. (2018). Cultural diversity and its implications in online networked learning spaces. In E. Toprak (Ed.), *Supporting Multiculturalism in Open and Distance Learning Spaces* (pp. 56–81). Hershey, PA: IGI Global. doi:10.4018/978-1-5225-3076-3.ch004

Chan, T. W., Roschelle, J., Hsi, S., Kinshuk, Sharples, M., Brown, ... Hoppe, U. (2006). One-to-one technology-enhanced learning: An opportunity for global research collaboration. *Research and Practice in Technology Enhanced Learning*, *1*(1), 3–29. doi:10.1142/S1793206806000032

Cochran, S. W. (1983). The Delphi method: Formulating and refining group judgments. *Journal of Human Sciences, 11*(2), 111–117.

Dalkey, N. C. (1972). The Delphi method: An experimental study of group opinion. In N. C. Dalkey, D. L. Rourke, R. Lewis, & D. Snyder (Eds.), Studies in the quality of life: Delphi and decision-making (pp. 13-54). Lexington, MA: Lexington Books.

Dillenbourg, P. (1999). *What do you mean by collaborative learning? Collaborative-learning: Cognitive and Computational Approaches.* Oxford, UK: Elsevier.

Erdoğdu, E., & Kesim, M. (2015). Ağ günlüklerinin kurumsal düzeyde kullanılması. *Açıköğretim Uygulamaları ve Araştırmaları Dergisi, 1*(2), 8–23.

Ezziane, Z. (2007). Information technology literacy: Implications on teaching and learning. *Journal of Educational Technology & Society, 10*(3).

Flior, E., & Kowalski, K. (2010, April). Continuous biometric user authentication in online examinations. In *Seventh International Conference on Information Technology (ITGN2010)* (pp. 488-492). Las Vegas, NV: Academic Press. 10.1109/ITNG.2010.250

Giannarou, L., & Zervas, E. (2014). Using Delphi technique to build consensus in practice. *International Journal of Business Science and Applied Management, 9*(2), 65–82.

Grant, J. (2002). Learning needs assessment: Assessing the need. *BMJ (Clinical Research Ed.), 324*(7330), 156–159. doi:10.1136/bmj.324.7330.156 PMID:11799035

Green, R. A. (2014). The Delphi technique in educational research. *SAGE Open, 4*(2), 1–8. doi:10.1177/2158244014529773

Gülbahar, Y., Kalelioğlu, F., & Madran, O. (2010). Sosyal ağların eğitim amaçlı kullanımı. *XV. Türkiye'de İnternet Konferansı*. İstanbul Teknik Üniversitesi.

Helmer, O. (1977). Problems in futures research: Delphi and causal cross-impact analysis. *Futures, 9*(1), 17–31. doi:10.1016/0016-3287(77)90049-0

Holmberg, B. (1995). *Theory and practice of distance education* (2nd ed.). London: Routledge.

Hwang, G. J., Tsai, C. C., & Yang, S. J. H. (2008). Criteria, strategies and research issues of context-aware ubiquitous learning. *Journal of Educational Technology & Society, 11*(2), 81–91.

Hwang, G. J., Wu, P. H., & Ke, H. R. (2011). An interactive concept map approach to supporting mobile learning activities for natural science courses. *Computers & Education, 57*(4), 2272–2280. doi:10.1016/j.compedu.2011.06.011

Ilgaz, H., & Aşkar, P. (2009). Çevrimiçi uzaktan eğitim ortamında topluluk hissi ölçeği geliştirme çalışması. *Turkish Journal of Computer and Mathematics Education, 1*(1), 27–34.

Jansen, B. J., & Spink, A. (2006). How are we searching the World Wide Web? A comparison of nine search engine transaction logs. *Information Processing & Management, 42*(1), 248–263. doi:10.1016/j.ipm.2004.10.007

Johnson, L., Smith, R., Willis, H., Levine, A., & Haywood, K. (2011). *The 2011 Horizon Report*. Austin, TX: The New Media Consortium.

Jomah, O., Masoud, A. K., Kishore, X. P., & Aurelia, S. (2016). Micro learning: A modernized education system. BRAIN. *Broad Research in Artificial Intelligence and Neuroscience, 7*(1), 103–110.

Kargın, T. (2007). Eğitsel değerlendirme ve bireyselleştirilmiş eğitim programı hazırlama süreci. *Ankara Üniversitesi Eğitim Bilimleri Fakültesi Özel Eğitim Dergisi, 8*(1), 1-16.

Karimi, S. (2016). Do learners' characteristics matter? An exploration of mobile-learning adoption in self-directed learning. *Computers in Human Behavior, 63*, 769–776. doi:10.1016/j.chb.2016.06.014

Kim, B. (2013). Responsive web design, discoverability and mobile challenge. *Library Technology Reports, 49*(6), 29–39.

Kukulska-Hulme, A., & Viberg, O. (2018). Mobile collaborative language learning: State of the art. *British Journal of Educational Technology, 49*(2), 207–218. doi:10.1111/bjet.12580

Laisema, S., & Wannapiroon, P. (2013). Development of a Collaborative Learning with Creative Problem-Solving Process Model in Ubiquitous Learning Environment. *International Journal of e-Education, e-Business, e- Management Learning, 3*(2), 102–106.

Lee, Y. J. (2012). Developing an efficient computational method that estimates the ability of students in a Web-based learning environment. *Computers & Education, 58*(1), 579–589. doi:10.1016/j.compedu.2011.09.008

Martinez, M. (2001). Key design considerations for personalized learning on the web. *Journal of Educational Technology & Society, 4*(1), 26–40.

Mayer, R. E. (1997). Multimedia learning: Are we asking the right questions? *Educational Psychologist, 32*(1), 1–19. doi:10.120715326985ep3201_1

Mayer, R. E. (2001). *Multimedia learning*. New York: Cambridge University Press. doi:10.1017/CBO9781139164603

McMillan, J. (2004). *Educational research fundamentals for the consumer* (4th ed.). Hershey, PA: Pearson Education.

Milrad, M., Wong, L.-H., Sharples, M., Hwang, G.-J., Looi, C.-K., & Ogata, H. (2013). Seamless learning: an international perspective on next-generation technology enhanced learning. In Z. L. Berge & L. Y. Muilenburg (Eds.), Handbook of Mobile Learning (pp. 95-108). New York: Routledge.

Mullen, P. M. (2003). Delphi: Myths and reality. *Journal of Health Organization and Management, 17*(1), 37–52. doi:10.1108/14777260310469319 PMID:12800279

Murray, C. (2008). Schools and social networking: Fear or education. *Synergy Perspectives: Local, 6*(1), 8–12.

Nicholas, H., & Ng, W. (2009). Ubiquitous Learning and Handhelds. In P. Rogers, G. Berg, J. Boettcher, C. Howard, L. Justice, & K. Schenk (Eds.), *Encyclopedia of Distance Learning* (2nd ed.; pp. 2171–2176). Hershey, PA: IGI Global. doi:10.4018/978-1-60566-198-8.ch321

Özdamar-Keskin, N., & Kılınç, H. (2015). Mobil öğrenme uygulamalarına yönelik geliştirme platformlarının karşılaştırılması ve örnek uygulamalar. *Açıköğretim Uygulamaları ve Araştırmaları Dergisi, 1*(3), 68–90.

Powell, C. (2003). The Delphi technique: Myths and realities. *Journal of Advanced Nursing, 41*(4), 376–382. doi:10.1046/j.1365-2648.2003.02537.x PMID:12581103

Premlatha, K. R., & Geetha, T. V. (2015). Learning content design and learner adaptation for adaptive e-learning environment: A survey. *Artificial Intelligence Review, 44*(4), 443–465. doi:10.100710462-015-9432-z

Saban, A. (2002). *Öğrenme Öğretme Süreci*. Ankara: Nobel Yayın Dağıtım.

Şahin, A. E. (2001). Eğitim araştırmalarında Delphi tekniği ve kullanımı. *Hacettepe Üniversitesi Eğitim Fakültesi Dergisi, 20,* 215–220.

Seow, P., Zhang, B., So, H. J., Looi, C. K., & Chen, W. (2008). Towards a framework for seamless learning environments. In *Proceedings of the 8th international conference on International conference for the learning sciences. International Society of the Learning Sciences*, (pp. 327-334). Utrecht, The Netherlands: Academic Press.

Sezer, A., & Tokcan, H. (2003). İş birliğine dayalı öğrenmenin coğrafya dersinde akademik başarı üzerine etkisi. *Gazi Üniversitesi Gazi Eğitim Fakültesi Dergisi, 23*(3), 227–242.

Sezgin, S., Bozkurt, A., Yılmaz, E. A., & van der Linden, N. (2018). Oyunlaştırma, eğitim ve kuramsal yaklaşımlar: Öğrenme süreçlerinde motivasyon, adanmışlık ve sürdürülebilirlik. *Mehmet Akif Ersoy Üniversitesi Eğitim Fakültesi Dergisi, 45,* 169–189. doi:10.21764/maeuefd.339909

Sharples, M. (2015). Seamless learning despite context. In Seamless learning in the age of mobile connectivity (pp. 41-55). Springer Singapore. doi:10.1007/978-981-287-113-8_2

Sharples, M., McAndrew, P., Weller, M., Ferguson, R., FitzGerald, E., Hirst, T., ... Whitelock, D. (2012). *Innovating Pedagogy 2012: Open University Innovation Report 1*. Milton Keynes, UK: The Open University.

Shearer, R. (2003). Instructional design in distance education: An overview. In M. G. Moore & W. G. Anderson (Eds.), *Handbook of Distance Education* (pp. 275–286). Mahwah, NJ: Lawrence Erlbaum Associates.

Siemens, G. (2004). *Connectivism: A learning theory for the digital age*. Retrieved from http://www.elearnspace.org/Articles/connectivism.htm

Siemens, G., & Gasevic, D. (2012). Guest editorial–Learning and knowledge analytics. *Journal of Educational Technology & Society, 15*(3), 1–2.

Specht, M. (2015). Connecting Learning Contexts with Ambient Information Channels. In *Seamless Learning in the Age of Mobile Connectivity* (pp. 121–140). Singapore: Springer. doi:10.1007/978-981-287-113-8_7

Thomas, R. M. (1998). *Conducting educational research: A comparative view*. Greenwood Publishing Group.

Uçar, H., & Kumtepe, A. T. (2018). Integrating Motivational Strategies into Massive Open Online Courses (MOOCs): The Application and Administration of the Motivation Design Model. In K. Buyuk, S. Kocdar, & A. Bozkurt (Eds.), *Administrative Leadership in Open and Distance Learning Programs* (pp. 213–235). Hershey, PA: IGI Global. doi:10.4018/978-1-5225-2645-2.ch009

Wang, W., & Wang, Z. (2008). Leveraging on u-learning to nurture a society of learning. *China Educational Technique & Equipment*, 22, 33–35.

Wedemeyer, C. A. (1981). *Learning at the back door: Reflections on the non-traditional learning in the lifespan*. Madison, WI: University of Wisconsin Press.

Wong, L. H. (2012). A learner-centric view of mobile seamless learning. *British Journal of Educational Technology*, 43(1), 19–23. doi:10.1111/j.1467-8535.2011.01245.x

Wong, L. H., & Looi, C. K. (2011). What seams do we remove in mobile-assisted seamless learning? A critical review of the literature. *Computers & Education*, 57(4), 2364–2381. doi:10.1016/j.compedu.2011.06.007

Xia, F., Yang, L. T., Wang, L., & Vinel, A. (2012). Internet of things. *International Journal of Communication Systems*, 25(9), 1101–1102. doi:10.1002/dac.2417

Yetik, E., & Keskin, N. Ö. (2016). Açık ve uzaktan eğitimde kesintisiz öğrenmenin kullanımı. *Journal of Research in Education and Teaching*, 5(1), 98–103.

KEY TERMS AND DEFINITIONS

Delphi Technique: As a primary source of data to be able to get expert opinions from different disciplines, the Delphi technique is based on a structured process for collecting and distilling knowledge from a group of experts by means of a series of questionnaires interspersed with controlled opinion feedback.

Distance Education (DE): Planned and organized teaching and learning in which learners are separated from teachers or facilitators in time and space.

Electronic Learning (E-Learning): It is a learning paradigm that uses educational technologies in employing the principles of multimedia learning.

Mobile Learning (M-Learning): As an extension of e-learning, it is a learning paradigm that uses mobile technologies to provide a just in time, just in place, and just for me experience.

Open and Distance Learning (ODL): Any learning activities within formal, informal, and non-formal domains that are facilitated by information and communication technologies to lessen distance, both physically and psychologically, and to increase interactivity and communication among learners, learning sources, and facilitators.

Open Education: Teaching and learning that are independent of time and place with a special focus on social justice, equity and elimination of barriers in educational processes.

Seamless Learning: It is integration of the learning experiences across various dimensions including formal and informal learning contexts, individual and social learning, and physical world and cyberspace.

Ubiquitous Learning (U-Learning): As an extension of e-learning and m-learning, it is a learning paradigm that uses ubiquitous technologies to provide a seamless, just in time, just in place, and just for me experience.

Chapter 7
Supporting Learners with Special Needs in Open and Distance Learning

Hakan Genc
Anadolu University, Turkey

Serpil Kocdar
Anadolu University, Turkey

ABSTRACT

Open and distance learning (ODL) systems provide learners with a flexible learning environment independent of time and place. However, the advantage of this flexibility may turn out a disadvantage if the learners do not find a solution to problems they may face before, during, and after the learning process. In eliminating this disadvantage, learner support services play an important role. The quality of support services has a direct impact on learner retention and academic success. Especially, for the learners with special needs, the quality of support services has a particular importance. Within this context, in this chapter, the authors address accommodations for learners with special needs in ODL. First, this chapter focuses on support services in ODL, then learners with special needs in ODL and what accommodations learners with special needs require according to their disability type. Finally, the authors exemplify the accommodations for learners with special needs in ODL institutions and offer recommendations.

DOI: 10.4018/978-1-5225-9779-7.ch007

INTRODUCTION

In open and distance learning, the learner and instructor are geographically separated from one another. For this reason, learner support, in the distance education context, takes on a different sense of importance (Brindley; Walti & Zavachki-Richter, 2004, p. 9–11). Traditional learners have access to support services for affairs like admission, student enrollment, financial aid, registration, help desk, and library – all of which are main components of the education process – through facilities present on the campus. However, distance learners, since they are not present on the physical campus, encounter limitations in access to support services. Therefore, distance learners can feel alone in the learning process, lose their motivation, and eventually even fail (Lapadula, 2003, p. 119–120). To prevent this, support services offered to traditional learners should also be accessible to distance learners. According to Dirr (1999, as cited in Lapadula, 2003, p. 119-128), there is a need to create a comprehensive support service approach, one that completely addresses the needs of distance learners, rather than simply adjusting the traditional learner services for distance learners, as they possess different characteristics. Dirr also states that this approach will provide a learner-centered environment whereby distance learners will be able to capture the same learning experience as traditional learners, meet the expectations of accreditation authorities, allow institutions to completely benefit from the advantages of the up-to-date technologies and to be more competitive in the highly intense, fluctuating educational environment, all of which will contribute to sustaining learners within the system. Similarly, Floyd and Casey-Powell (2004, p. 57) are of the opinion that traditional learner support services must be redefined by taking the needs of distance learners into consideration.

Institutions offering ODL should initiate the process of planning support services for distance learners by identifying learner needs (Rumble, 2000, p. 223). However, in this planning process, one should not ignore the fact that ODL programs are focused on providing educational opportunities to individuals who are unable to attend traditional education due to various reasons; in other words, the learner group has a heterogeneous structure. One of the groups constituting this structure is learners with special needs. Thus, it would not be useful to organize support services without considering the learner characteristics (Fiege, 2010, p. 13). In the light of the facts mentioned above, it can be concluded that one of the crucial matters should be taken into consideration in designing an online course in ubiquitous learning environment is accommodations for learners with special needs. In this context, the purpose of this chapter is to describe learner support services in ODL and accommodations for learners with special needs in ODL institutions.

Support Services in Open and Distance Learning

Learner support, in the broad sense, is defined in open and distance learning as "besides the design and presentation of course materials, all activities supporting students' progress in their studies" (Simpson, 2002, p. 6). Brindley et al. (2004, p. 9–11) described learner support as "all services which help learners to gain knowledge and skills and to attain the learning objectives necessary for them to be successful"

There are various studies in the literature that present the importance and necessity of support services. For example, Mills and Ross (1993, as cited in Scheer and Lockee, 2003, p. 178) stressed the necessity of learner support services in forming a high-quality distance education environment. Sewart

(1993, p. 9) directly associated learner support with learner achievement and stated that an increase in the variety of support services leads to an increase in the learner achievement. Rumble (2000, p. 221) pointed out the importance of support services by arguing, "The unsupported learner likely completes the program late or completely quits it." The insufficiency in the learner support services, according to Chute, Thompson and Hancock (1999, p.192), is a common mistake sabotaging distance education practices. Simpson (2002, p. 9–10) discussed the necessity of support services under three categories: practical reasons, theoretical reasons, and moral reasons, all of which are explained below.

1. Practical Reasons
    a. **Retention**: It has been observed that ODL institutions, compared to traditional educational institutions, have higher dropout rates. This indicates that there is a problem regarding the sustainability of student attendance in ODL.
    b. **Students' Demands**: As a result of the increase in the number of ODL institutions, learners have more opportunities to choose from among institutions. One of the factors affecting learners' choices is undoubtedly the qualifications of the learner support services an institution provides.
2. Theoretical Reasons
    a. **Student Isolation**: In ODL, the learner is geographically separated from the instructor, the institution and other learners. Compared to traditional education, this serves as a disadvantage in the learner-instructor, learner-institution, and learner-learner interactions and can result in the isolation of the learner in the process. However, by offering environments that enable the learner to interact through support services, it is possible to prevent the learner from being isolated in the process.
    b. **Democracy vs Authoritarianism:** ODL can be thought of as an authoritarian system, one that delivers education through specific materials and environments. However, learner support services offer a more flexible service approach by providing some options to the learner.
3. Moral Reasons

While one of the reasons governing the importance of learner support is to help learners advance in their studies, there may be some inner obligations that contradict this situation. There is a fine line between these two scenarios: supporting learners who experience negative events in their lives, such as illness, divorce, or loss of a relative, to continue the program at all costs, or to let them quit the program. Paying regard to the circumstances that learners face and helping them to make the right decisions is only possible by having comprehensively designed learner support principles and methods.

The importance and necessity of learner support can also be touched upon examining the functions of learner support. According to Tait (2000, p. 289), learner support has mainly three different functions, all of which play a supplementary role with one another.

a. **Cognitive**: Improving and supporting the learning process for learners through learning sources and course materials.
b. **Affective**: Providing a learner-supportive climate, facilitating a sense of belonging, and boosting self-esteem.
c. **Systemic**: Establishing information management systems and managerial processes that are effective, transparent, and completely learner-friendly.

Supporting Learners with Special Needs in Open and Distance Learning

Even though there exists no international model of support services for distance learners, the literature has reported that learner support services mainly include: a) distance learning orientation, b) access to the library, c) academic counseling, d) registration for online course, e) personal counseling, f) technical support, g) financial aid, h) monitoring, and i) social interaction (Beede and Burnett, 1999; Chute et al., 1999; Kovel-Jarboe, 1997; Nunan, 1992; Sewart, 1992 as cited in Scheer and Lockee, 2003, p. 179). Tait (2000, p. 289-290), on the other hand, listed the elements of the content of support services as: a)enquiry, admission, pre-study advisory services b) tutoring, c) guidance and counseling services, d) assessment of prior learning and credit transfer, e) study and exam centers, f) residential schools, g) library services, i) individualized correspondence teaching, j) archive, information management and other management systems, k) services for learners with special needs (convicts, disabled, etc.), and l) materials supporting the improvement of study skills, programme planning or career development

The increase in the number of students enrolled in distance education programs suggests an effective and collaborative learner service system (Floyd and Casey-Powell, 2004, p. 57). Various studies on the planning of a system for learner support services are included in the literature. Tait (2000, p. 287–299) indicated that the planning of learner support services can be carried out within the framework of six primary elements: student characteristics, course or program demands, geography, technology, scale, and management systems. According to Tait:

1. The characteristics of learners play a determinative role as it relates to identifying their needs. Hence, learner characteristics should be taken into consideration in the design of learner support services. The elements constituting these characteristics can be listed as age, gender, occupational status, income status, educational background, geographical situation, special needs (disability, etc.), language, ethnicity and cultural background, and communication technology connectedness.
2. Elements required by the course or program are another factor affecting the provision of support services. For example, the fact that a course or program includes certain applications and requires the need to engage in face-to-face education makes it necessary to offer a support service suitable to this condition.
3. The characteristics of distance learners' residential area play a decisive role in the way services are provided to them. For example, factors such as transportation, opportunities in the area, or cultural perspective (negative perception towards leaving the home) can pose an obstacle to interactions between the learner and instructor.
4. The technologies with which learner services are going to be presented should be analyzed. To this purpose, the technologies to which learners have access and the current technologies in the institution should be determined. Variables such as learner characteristics, their occupational status, their means to access the information and communication technologies, and the technological infrastructure of their residential area should be considered in the selection of technologies to be used. For example, while for some learners, the use of e-mails is unfeasible due to the technological infrastructure, for others, the use of it can be a rather effective service. In addition to these, the paradigmatic shift in information and communication technologies, such as that from printed materials to a web-based online environment, video conferences, and CD-ROMs has an impact on the technologies used in learner support services.

5. The size of the group of distance learners in an institution is a factor considered in determining an institution's allocation of investments to the specific services it provides. Therefore, the extent to which learner support services is presented is related to the size of the learner group. For example, the size of the learner group could justify the need for a residential office or study center that are some of the learner support services. The size of the learner group in an institution also can differ from program to program. In some cases, the size of the group of open and distance learners in institutions offering dual-mode education can be relatively small compared to the size of their counterparts receiving traditional education. In these cases, separate service approach should be adopted for each learning group.

6. In the context of support service, the amount of the institutional budget to be allocated to each service, and in turn, the benefits to be yielded, should be decided upon. It is here that the administrative systems get involved. Moreover, information management plays a significant role in ensuring an efficient provision of learner services. Data collected within the process are used to evaluate the services offered and facilitate continuous development.

Floyd and Casey-Powell (2004, p. 58–61) developed the Inclusive Student Services Process Model, which offers a framework for the design of the process of learner support in both traditional and online programs. This model addresses learner support services in five phases (Table 1). The main focus during *the learner intake phase* is to evaluate learners' readiness level for distance education. In order to ensure that the system supports prospective learners, admission information should be presented on the homepage of the institution's website in a clear, concise way, a user-friendly website that explicitly distinguishes the services intended for distance learners and traditional learners should be created, information regarding the testing procedures, contact phone numbers, career planning opportunities, and assessment instruments should be provided, a virtual or online orientation should be presented to help learners get involved in their course of study and remain permanent within the system, information on

Table 1. Inclusive student services process model

Learner intake phase	Learner intervention phase	Learner support phase	Learner transition phase	Measurement phase
Admission	Instruction on strategies of being successful	Academic advising	Career development and counseling services (interview strategies development, coping with life problems)	Evaluating the program's efficiency
Pre-enrollment Assessment	Student help desk support	Instructional support	Getting a job	
Registration	Technology training	Tutoring		
Financial Aid	Online faculty advising	Library and bookstore services		
Information Technology		Services intended for individuals with special needs		
Orientation		Network		

(Floyd and Casey-Powell, 2004)

application dates for scholarships/loans should be provide for learners who are in need of financial aid, payment schemes, or payment options and links enabling learners to access various scholarships and loans should be included. *The learner intervention phase* is where the online program is presented. The main purpose of this phase is to support learner's self-development and independent learning. At *the learner support phase*, the learner acquires self-developing strategies in order to take charge of his or her own learning. Services like career development and counseling are the focuses of *the learner transition phase*, while in *the measurement phase*, the focus is on the evaluation of the effectiveness of the program, which is analyzed on the basis of the current population and graduation and attendance rates in the system. Feedback on learner services is taken in order to improve the quality of service.

Another study, titled *Good Practices in student services*, that was conducted on the planning of learner services was carried out by the Western Interstate Commission for Higher Education. This study introduced a comprehensive framework for the planning of learning services (Western Interstate Commission for Higher Education [WICHE], 2002 as cited in Ströhlein, 2003, p. 62–76):

1. Informing Prospective Learners
    a. Clearly express the online learning opportunities on the website of the institution, b) Indicate the institutional vision and distance learning offerings, c) Provide prospective learners the opportunity to evaluate their readiness level for distance education, d) Provide information and/or tools for assessing hardware and software adequateness, e) State how to access additional information on online programs and how to contact relevant people for getting extra info about any issue, and f) Include information on relevant equipment, duration, transferability and fees in a Frequently Asked Questions section.
2. Admission
    a) Explain the admission process, b) State the necessary qualifications for admission, c) State how the admission process is carried out, d) Provide an online admission form that includes clear instructions, e) List the deadlines, f) Provide options to save, update, and track admission information, g) Provide multiple payment options.
3. Financial Aid
    a) Provide general information on financial aid, b) Define financial aid types available, c) State the cost of attendance, d) Explain the application process, e) Specify the institution's policy on financial aid, f) List the dates for application submission, g) Provide other applications and related forms, h) Include the links of relevant websites, and i) Provide counseling service on the online learner loan process.
4. Registration
    a) Explain the registration process, b) Define what needs to be followed for registration, c) State the relevant policies, d) Provide an online schedule planner, and e) Provide an online registration form that includes clear instructions.
5. Orientation Services
    a) Present perspectives on being a distance learner, b) Deliver an online virtual tour for a real or hypothetical course, c) Provide tips for being successful in online environments, d) Provide information on or link to all requirements, essential policies, fees, learner services and how to receive help, e) Explain the stages of access to the online course and define the necessary technical knowledge, and f) Include all the links of the learner services provided to distance learners.

6. Academic Counseling
    a) Enable one-on-one access to consultants, b) Define the entire education process and fundamental requirements, c) Give suggestions for personal development, d) Provide a link to automated transfer/articulation information, e) Provide online access to the counseling manual for the learner, instructor and consultants, and f) Enable learners to access their own records.
7. Technical Support
    a) Explain the service and provide introductory information, b) Announce the times the network will be under maintenance or out of use, c) Provide online courses or documents, d) Provide learners with training on this issue to help them efficiently use software and hardware and to minimize requests for technical personnel, e) Provide self-help tools, and f) Offer support through hotline/help desk.
8. Career Services
    a) Define the services and make clear who is eligible for current students, graduates, community members, and employers, b) Offer self-help career tools, including online tutorials, c) Provide information on career opportunities within the institution, d) Give support for career planning, e) List local and national job opportunities, f) Deliver a comprehensive online guidebook related to different occupations, g) Design an online forum and automatic e-mail service for learners registered for the service, and h) Get in contact with alumni.
9. Library Services
    a) Give orientation materials, b) Specify how to contact a librarian who has expertise in the field of distance education, c) Provide remote access to electronic resources and present instructions for remote access of electronic resources, d) Give reference support through e-mail and/or telephone, e) Offer document delivery services and ensure that necessary forms are downloadable or completable online, f) Provide online tutorials on how to conduct library research, and g) Provide online electronic reservations.
10. Services Intended for Learners With Special Needs
    a) Present general information, b) List the eligibility requirements and required documentation, c) Define the current services, d) Provide support in identifying assistive technology requirements, e) Include links to relevant websites, f) Deliver guidance to academic personnel/personnel working with learners with special needs, and d) State career opportunities specific to learners with special needs.
11. Personal Counseling
    a) Explain personal counseling services, b) Provide assistance to learners with mental disorders, c) List and introduce the counseling personnel, d) Present self-help articles, e) Offer access to self-help materials developed by the counseling centers of other organizations, f) Attach importance to confidentiality, g) Provide counseling to academic personnel/relevant personnel working with a distressed learner, h) Offer referrals to off-campus counseling resources, i) Offer 24-hour information hotlines, and j) Create forums providing learners the opportunity to express their concerns.
12. Instructional Support and Tutoring
    a) Provide online tutorials on learner-instructor interaction to instruct learners on how to engage with the instructor through tools such as e-mail, chat, or online conference, b) Provide necessary contact details to enable learners to ask questions or receive support through phone and/

Supporting Learners with Special Needs in Open and Distance Learning

or fax, c) Include links to external education resources, d) Present tips on test techniques and study skills, and e) Consider to provide an online writing lab.

13. Bookstore
    a) Create online environments where learners can access books and services, b) Indicate the relevant policies, c) Present an online method whereby learners can browse course textbooks and materials, d) List the methods available for ordering books, e) Offer an order form to assist in giving orders via fax or phone, f) Offer the opportunity to order textbook online, g) Deliver purchases to off-campus addresses, h) Present an online payment system, i) Present an online booking system, and j) Offer order tracking option.

14. Services Intended for Improving Sense of Community
    a) Form a student administration for distance learners, b) Form a news bulletin for distance learners, c) Provide access through the website to chatrooms and links to particular announcements that might be of interest to distance learners, and d) Create a virtual community through an accessible network, multiple participants, and virtual reality.

Classification of Support Services in Open and Distance Learning

When the literature was reviewed, different types of classification of support services were encountered (Bozkurt, 2013, p. 396). Keast (1997, p. 49–50) categorized support services under four different categories: administrative, instructional, technical, and counseling and tutorial support. According to Keast, registration, admission, provision of texts, equipment, library resources, maintenance of document transfer, scheduling, and other administrative acts are within the scope of *administrative support*; integral parts of the services of graduate assistants, technology personnel, instructional designers and communication with tutorial support personnel are within the scope of *instructional support*; monitoring the effective process of delivering mediums and providing technical support to instructors are within the scope of *technical support*; and guidance, academic support for learners and the interactions between the learner and instructor are within the scope of *counseling and tutorial support.*

Rekkedal and Qvist-Eriksen (2003, p. 29-30) classified support services in terms of the process and categorized the support services offered at NKI Online University under five headings: prospective phase, start-up phase, learning phase, graduation and post-graduation. According to Rekkedal and Qvist-Eriksen, information about courses, counseling on the selection of courses and program, loan/scholarship, financial issues, and guidance for practical issues are included in the *prospective phase*; provision of physical learning materials, registration/information/user id/password, etc., introduction to online learning techniques, initial follow up, and technical support are included in the *start-up phase*; teaching/tutoring, academic support, organization of learning, social support, evaluation, practical support, follow-up, technical support, resources/library, learning group support, local learning support, local management support, local technical support, local social/practical support are included in the *learning phase*; diploma/accreditation is included in *graduation* and counseling for further studies, counseling for career opportunities, and graduate services are included in the *after graduation.*

Keegan (2003, p.1–2) classified learner support services under two categories: *learner support* and *learning support*. According to Keegan, learner support is all the support that is offered by the distance education system and that overlaps with the opportunities provided to achieve success in face-to-face education. These supports are further addressed in seven different processes: information, guidance, registration, integration, final results, accreditation assistance, and guidance on further study. Learning support, on the other hand, is the support provided in the process of learning to assist in the attainment of learning objectives. Included within the scope of learning support services are the provision of printed documents and other learning materials, instruction on online learning techniques, bulletin boards enabling learners to post comments and questions, e-mail service to facilitate learner-learner or learner-instructor interaction, face-to-face and online tutorials to meet learning objectives, online access to library services and other additional resources, provision of online environments enabling self-evaluation of the learning process for learners, automated evaluation carried out at the end of the course, the opportunity to send studies to the instructor for correction or evaluation, electronic or manual feedback, and personal portfolios through which learners have the opportunity to introduce themselves to other learners, share knowledge and/or present their studies.

Thorpe (2003, p. 201-203) defined support services as all elements responding to the needs of a learner or a group of learners before, during and after the learning process. Under this approach, support services can be discussed within two contexts: *institutional* and *teaching*. Learners' need for support in the institutional context includes being acquainted with services offered, making course selections, rendering payments, and claiming a refund of payment, etc. In the instruction context, the needs related to matters such as properly completing an assignment, communicating and collaborating with other learners, and sense-making of knowledge are addressed.

Berge (1995) indicated that several conditions need to be met for quality online learning and categorized those conditions under four groups: *pedagogical, social, managerial,* and *technical*. Berge's classification is discussed in the literature as support types (Aydın, 2011, p. 63; Okur, 2012, p. 14; Durak, 2017, p. 163). Services related to academic skills and course content can be listed under pedagogical support; services related to improving human affairs, strengthening group dynamics, enhancing learner-learner or learner-instructor non-academic interaction, and minimizing the sense of isolation can be listed under the social support; services related to registration procedures, administrative acts, timetable, organization, evaluation, and procedural rules can be listed under administrative support; and services related to the elimination of software- and hardware-related problems encountered by distance learners can be listed under technical support (Berge, 1995; Okur, 2012, p. 14; Durak, 2017, p. 163).

Simpson (2012, p. 13) noted that learner needs should be determined first in order to decide upon the learner support services to be offered in open and distance learning and he addressed distance learners' needs for support under three headings: cognitive, organizational, and emotional. Simpson (2012) classified support services into two groups: academic and non-academic support. Support for cognitive issues related to a certain course or courses, instruction-related issues, are considered under academic support, while affective and organizational aspects of learners' studies are considered under non-academic support.

Academic Support

1. **Defining the Territory**: Generally, in open and distance learning systems, the scope of the course is clarified in the course material.
2. **Explaining the Course**: Generally, in open and distance learning systems, the course is explained in the course materials. These materials can be available in printed form, online, on CD-ROM or video and through audio and other tools. The explanation can be done by the instructors for particular topics, as well.

3. **Assessment (Formal/Informal):** Providing learners with feedback on the progress they make in the course is the informal assessment. Self-assessment questions are included in the course materials in distance education programs. However, the students' nonuse of these questions, which provides passive feedback, can create a sense of guilt and inefficacy in them. For this reason, interactive instructor feedback is of great importance in the informal assessment.

   Formal assessment is a process wherein the computer or instructor makes the evaluation and does the grading accordingly. While more standardized feedback is delivered with computers, the feedback by the instructor can be more specific.

4. **Progress Chasing:** Periodical monitoring of learner progress is one of the responsibilities of the instructor in open and distance learning and as such, functions as a support service directly addressing learner motivation.

5. **Learning Skills Development:** By the nature of open and distance learning, students who are deprived of effective learning skills and coming from educationally disadvantaged backgrounds can be present in the system. Therefore, instructors play an important role to help students develop these skills.

6. **Exploring, Enthusing, Enriching:** The instructor plays a substantial role in processes related to building a sense of learning in the learner through eliciting a continuity of learning by bringing the learning experience outside the course boundaries and deepening the learning experience (through gallery/concert events, experiments, presentations, discussions, additional reading recommendations).

Non-Academic Support

1. **Advising:** Assisting the learner in the selection of a particular course/program, helping the learner to develop beneficial learning skills (e.g. concentration), providing vocational guidance, offering support on time management, providing support for any personal problems that may affect the learner's studies, offering support for problems the learner might experience with the organization, and providing motivational guidance are all included within the scope of advising.

2. **Assessment:** In order to direct the learner to a particular course or program, interest, motivation, and qualifications can be assessed. With computer-aided diagnosis software learners' learning styles can be determined. Learners' interests and skills can also be analyzed with computer-aided software such as CASCAID, and appropriate career advising can be carried out. Moreover, self-assessment materials that enable learners to set forth their needs and current qualifications can be applied.

3. **Action:** Practical assistance, like scheduling face-to-face interviews with the instructor, establishing contact between two learners with similar needs, or providing a learner transportation home, can sometimes be the most effective learning support.

4. **Advocacy:** In the open and distance learning system, the learner may not get sufficient recognition by the organization, making it difficult for the organization to be a reference for a variety of issues (financial opportunities, additional programs, occupation/career). In order to eliminate this disadvantage, particular information on learners can be gathered.

5. **Agitation**: it is making some regulations within an institution for the benefit of learners. Learner support services personnel may propose some changes in existing policies in line with their experience. Although it is not possible for a system to respond to all learner needs, it is nonetheless important that systems be designed to benefit the learner to the greatest extent possible, as this will be a factor in competition between institutions and attracting potential learners.
6. **Administration**: The organization of support services may differ according to the organizational models in ODL. For example, in a centralized organization model, all learner support, assessment and production are carried out by one center; in a localized organization model, learner support is carried out by local services.

Learners With Special Needs in Open and Distance Learning

An individual with special needs refers to "a person who lost their physical, mental, emotional, or social abilities in various degrees due to congenital or subsequent diseases or accidents and therefore faces challenges in fulfilling the requirements of normal life" (Department of Disability Research and Statistical, Turkey, 2006, p. 2). According to the *Special Education Services Regulation*, individuals with special needs could have attention deficit hyperactivity disorder, speech and language impairment, emotional and behavioral disorder, visual impairment, mild or moderate to severe or profound mental disability, hearing impairment, physical disability, multiple deficiencies, learning difficulties, autistic spectrum disorder, cerebral palsy, or a chronic disease, or be gifted (Ministry of National Education [MoNE], Turkey, 2006, p. 3). According to these broad characteristics, individuals with special needs constitute 12.29% of the total population in Turkey. Considering their education level, 7.7% of the individuals with special needs who are at the age of six or above in Turkey have at least a high school education level (Turkish Statistical Institute, 2010), which suggests that the participation rate of individuals with special needs in higher education needs to be improved.

It is believed that ODL can play an important role in providing individuals with special needs access to higher education opportunity. The inherent flexibility of time and place in ODL allows for accommodation of individual needs and requests in education. Considering that individuals with special needs have certain personal preferences and needs, ODL should be regarded as a higher education option for those individuals. ODL institutions should offer a wide range of services to meet the needs of learners with special needs accordingly (Ommerborn, 1998, p. 91–97).

The support services offered by ODL institutions to learners with special needs vary; however, there are general categories that do emerge from the variety of services offered. These categories include assistive technologies, additional arrangements for exam services, and alternative learning materials. Assistive technologies, alternative learning materials, serve to support the learning process of learners with special needs, and exam services may also vary according to disability type (Burgstahler, 2002a; Edmonds, 2004, p. 59–60; http://www.open.ac.uk/; http://www.uoc.edu/portal/en/; https://www.unisa.edu.au/; http://www.ouj.ac.jp/eng/):

Learners with visual impairment can benefit from a variety of tools, including screen reading software (e.g., Jaws/Voiceover), screen magnifier software (e.g., Zoomtext), text magnifying glass, text to speech converters, digital audio recorders, DAISY digital talking books, speech recognition software

Supporting Learners with Special Needs in Open and Distance Learning

(e.g., Dragon), A4 scanners, which scan printed materials into digital format, A3/A4 printers allowing material to be printed in enlarged text, Magnilink magnifier tools, Pearl readers which provide access to screen readers by converting printed materials to electronic format, speech synthesizers, Braille refreshable display, text-only browsers (e.g., Lynx), and large-screen monitors. They can also benefit from alternatives, like larger print, audio records, digital audiobooks, Braille prints, electronic texts, verbal explanations, tactile drawings, and distinctive color use on websites instead of printed materials, video, projection etc. Access to HTML sources can be provided by designing websites that take into consideration accessibility standards. Access to non-HTML presentations, such as PowerPoint can be provided by converting the presentation to an HTML document or by adding readable explanations to visual elements in the presentation by screen readers. To accommodate visually impaired learners, exam services can give them opportunity to use, if requested, magnifying glasses, computers, screen reading or speech recognition software, tape recorder or any other needed assistive technology. Besides that, they can give these learners the opportunity to answer in Braille, provide them with extra time or an amanuensis, allow them to take oral exams, or provide them with electronic exam paper or exam paper in Braille, large font size, colorized, or audio.

Learners with special learning disabilities can experience difficulties in reading, writing and information processing; to ease their reading difficulties, they can benefit from video clips, audio recordings or screen-enhanced systems. Communication paths like email can be offered in place of synchronous communication. The exam service can provide them with extra time, a separate room, or rest breaks. It should be taken into consideration that understanding complicated information on websites can be challenging to these individuals.

Learners with physical disability can use an alternative keyboard and mouse, speech recognition software, and speech input tools in order to access Internet-based sources. Regarding their physical access to buildings and other physical activities, foldable wheelchairs, height-adjustable tables, ergonomic furniture, ramps, and elevators can be used. For exams, exam services can provide scribe support and give extra time to these individuals.

Learners with hearing impairment can benefit from text telephone, walkie-talkie support systems, induction loop systems, and conference microphones. The provision of captioning or transcripts for all audio material is of utmost importance to these individuals. Furthermore, the lack of support elements, such as sign language translator, real-time captioning, separate chat windows, and transcription can serve as a barrier to these learners' engagement with technologies like phones and video conferencing. For exams, the exam service can provide these individuals with separate rooms, extra time and communication support. Learners with speech and language impairment may also be unable to participate in phone and video conferences. To address this, they can be supplied with text telephone or participate through e-mail.

The technological opportunities offered by the world of the 21st century directly concern the field of distance education. Today, distance education, whose the first form was correspondence in the past, uses various presentation ways altogether. Printed materials, radio, and television are accompanied by today's technology, the Web (Burgstahler, 2002a). One of the chief barriers for learners with specials needs to overcome in ODL programs is accessibility to web environments (Edmonds, 2004, p. 55). Web accessibility, as it relates to individuals with special needs, involves challenges in terms of helping these individuals to perceive, understand, navigate, interact with and participate in web environments (https://www.w3.org/WAI/). In the literature, several standards were developed to serve as guides to the Web accessibility. The World Wide Web Consortium developed WCAG 2.0 standards to make web services accessible to individuals with special needs. (https://www.w3.org/TR/WCAG20/). Similarly, Section 508 of the U.S. Rehabilitation Act developed certain standards to improve the accessibility of individuals with special needs to information and communication technologies (http://www.section508.gov/). Center for Persons with Disabilities in Utah University (WebAIM) also developed web accessibility standards (https://webaim.org/).

Another practice applied to provide accessibility is the *Universal design*, which was formed by *The Center for Universal Design* at North Caroline State University. It is defined as the design of products and environments capable of being used by all people, to the greatest extent possible, without the need for adaptation or specialized design. (https://projects.ncsu.edu/ncsu/design/cud/about_ud/about_ud.htm). The universal design principles aim to ease life for everyone; thus, considering these principles in the design of ODL programs will be a step in the right direction to making distance education accessible for everyone (Burgstahler, 2002b, p. 32–61).

Accommodations for Learners With Special Needs in Open and Distance Learning Institutions

ODL institutions offer a wide variety of accommodations for learners with special needs. In this part, we exemplify them within pedagogical, social, managerial and technical context. Accommodations mentioned here below are limited to information presented on the website of the related university (http://www.open.ac.uk/; https://www.athabascau.ca/; https://www.uoc.edu/portal/en/index.html; https://www.ouj.ac.jp/eng/; https://www.unisa.edu.au/; https://www.anadolu.edu.tr/acikogretim; http://engelsizaof.anadolu.edu.tr; https://aosdestek.anadolu.edu.tr).

The Open University

Examination of the managerial support services offered by the Open University shows that individuals who are eligible to receive special needs support are those with physical or sensory disability, ongoing health condition, ongoing mental health difficulty, specific learning difficulty, autism spectrum disorder, and/or speech or language difficulty. In the context of financial aid, a grant for learners with special needs is provided. With this grant, transportation and non-medical assistive support expenses are met. Support services related to diagnosing students are also offered by the Open University. Specifically, this support service finds an expert trained in evaluating and diagnosing special learning difficulties. In addition to these, there are online forms available to all learners with special needs to request the support service they need, including a proxy support form to allow learners with speech and language impairment to appoint a proxy in their interviews with the university. In the context of exams, there are various services available. For example, there is an application form that allows individuals to report that the support provided on exams remain insufficient or to request electronic exam paper, exam paper in Braille, large-font size, colored, or audio, extra time in exams, rest breaks of up to 30 minutes, and

Supporting Learners with Special Needs in Open and Distance Learning

the use of special equipment, such as a pillow, special chair, inclined table, magnifying glass, spelling check, food-beverage permission during exams when deemed necessary, and alternative answering methods, like answering in Braille or recording answers with a tape recorder. Communication support is provided during exams for learners with hearing impairment, an amanuensis is offered for learners with visual impairment to read questions and fill in answers. In addition to exam centers, learners can take the exam in a separate room or office, or at home. Moreover, an online exam checklist for the conditions to be met in the home environment is presented for exams taken at home. The opportunity to use a computer or needed software is offered to learners who cannot take the exam at the exam center. An assessment guidebook that informs learners on how the assessment procedure is also provided. Assistant support, assistive technologies, such as foldable wheelchairs, scooters, freight elevators, shower tuffets, portable refrigerators, induction loop systems, conference microphones, and walkie-talkies are provided for boarding school learners with special needs. In addition to these, links to relevant units within the university and other organizations, from which all learners with special needs can benefit, are included, and principles for international learners are specified.

Examination of the pedagogical support services offered by the Open University shows that the learning needs of learners with special needs are evaluated by evaluation centers or at home by experts. Financial aid for learners with special needs is provided for academic-related expenses. Study materials in alternative formats are offered, including electronic books, Kindle electronic books, word documents compatible with screen readers, DAISY digital talking book versions of module materials, audio or audio and text versions of printed materials, Braille products, detailed written explanations of important visual contents, tactile materials in some modules, printed versions of online modules, and captioning for audio-visual components. In addition to these, services such as recorded versions of some online modules and the provision of an assistant without visual impairment in order to narrate some explanations are provided. The Open University also offers various services to learners with special needs in face-to-face learning environments. For example, the additional accommodations according to learner needs in settings where face-to-face courses are carried out, the opportunity to request printed text prior to the course, the opportunity to make or request written contact with instructors, communication support, portable induction loops for those who wear hearing aids, and environments suitable for lip-reading and listening are provided. The support via phone calls or e-mails, and home visits for students who cannot attend face-to-face courses are also offered. Moreover, brochures that present information on learning with dyslexia, visual impairment, hearing impairment are presented. The Open University also offers various services to learners with special needs within the scope of distance and on-site library services. In the context of distance library services, library chats access through screen readers, explanations on the accessibility of databases, a guidebook on searching for resources with screen readers, and accessible library websites for screen reader users are offered. In addition to these, other services, like links to accessible formats (e.g., audiobooks, talking newspaper, Braille books, and tactile diagrams) presented by other organizations, online automatic file format converter and instructions for its use, and conversion of visuals in e-books or e-articles to word format in some circumstances, are provided. In the context of on-site library services, tactile signage in the library, elevators, assistive technologies, such as multidimensional adjustable chairs, magnifying glasses, compact+video magnifying glasses, trackerballs, and assistive software, like JAWS screen reader, Zoomtext, TextHELP read and write, CCTV magnifier, and Kurzweil scan and read, are provided. Lastly, the Open University provides opportunities for voluntary participation in the production of audio-format materials and in support assistance to learners with special needs.

When the social support services offered by the Open University to learners with special needs are investigated, it is seen that these services are delivered: brochures on staying mentally healthy and coping with anxiety, support and counseling service in each boarding school, and encouraging learners to make share with other learners through social media groups, forums, e-mails, phone and face-to-face communication.

Examination of the technical support services offered by the Open University to learners with special needs shows that learners who are unable to receive the special needs grant are able to borrow assistive technologies, including digital audio recorders, digital pencils, DAISY digital talking books, text magnifiers, magnifier software, text telephone, walkie-talkie, speech recognition software, screen reading software, text to speech converters etc. In addition to these, learners are provided with information on the required level of computer use for admission to the Open University and relevant contact details, given recommendations on special hardware and software that might be needed, and also provided with technical support for boarding school request process, homework preparation and submission. WCAG 2.O web accessibility principles are applied in the university's website design.

There are some services offered by the Open University that is outside of the managerial, pedagogic, technical and social support services. These services include job seeking resources and opportunities brochures, comprehensive information on job applications for learners with special needs, other links related to occupations, and comprehensive information on points necessary to consider during job interviews.

Athabasca University

Examination of the managerial support offered by Athabasca University to learners with special needs shows that an online form to request what is needed by a learner and information on what needs to be done to receive a need-based support service are provided. Besides that, accessibility office where all support services for learners with special needs are provided, referrals to various institutions for the services that are unavailable at the institution, a web interface introducing the services offered to learners with special needs, a privilege on the calculation of course loads of certain learners with special needs, the opportunity to request an extension for completing a course under certain conditions, the opportunity to withdraw from a course for a particular period of time under certain conditions, contact details of assistants in charge of exams, managerial issues, assistive technology, learner support services are also provided. Furthermore, various online forms are available to request services such as alternative format course materials, extension of time and additional supports. As for financial aid, the services available include links to scholarships for learners with special needs, the support during the funding appeal process. Various exam services are offered by Athabasca University to learners with special needs. These services include providing the opportunity to take the exam at home in the company of a volunteer or salaried attendant or at alternative exam sites, the implementation of the exam part by part, longer exam duration, oral exams or tests, sign language translator, the opportunity to use assistive technologies, the opportunity to bring food, beverage, medicine, or certain equipment to the exam under particular conditions, amanuensis support, personal room, ergonomic chair, etc. In addition, an online form through which learners can access the days available to book a personal room in exam centers in certain regions and forward their support request is available. The institution also has a set of written policies for learners with special needs.

Examination of the pedagogical support offered by Athabasca University to learners with special needs shows that individual support service plan is developed with the learner himself or herself in order to determine their specific support services and need for assistive technologies and academic support. In addition, tailored made services, such as color of the page, font type or line spacing and large print, alternative course materials, such as electronic text, Braille, tactile graphs and mp3 audio files, and transcription in audio/video materials are provided.

Examination of the technical support offered by Athabasca University to learners with special needs shows learners with special needs are supported with links to audio recorders, sticky notes, smart pencils, and software facilitating the organization of ideas (e.g., Evernote, Mindnote) that can be used to take notes. Links to screen readers (e.g., window-eyes, Voiceover), talking browsers (e.g., Opera, Atbar), text-readers (e.g., Balabolka, natural reader), software converting text to audio file (e.g., Spoken text), screen magnification software (e.g., Zoomtext, izoom), and electronic text and audiobooks that can be used for reading, are provided. Links to software with the handwriting recognition feature (e.g., Ink equation), voice recognition software (e.g., Dragon naturally speaking), screen keyboard, alternative mouse, alternative keyboard, and eye-tracking systems that can be used for writing, are provided. Links to software supporting time management (e.g., Toodledo, Rescue time), spelling and grammar tools (e.g., Grammarly), graph calculators (e.g., Audio Mmath Trax), and mobile applications (e.g., Voiceover, easy text speech) are also provided. In addition to these, services like an expert evaluation of learners' need for assistive technologies, tutorial support on how to use assistive technologies, and links to some ergonomic equipments are provided.

Universitat Oberta de Catalunya

Examination of the managerial support services offered by Universitat Oberta de Catalunya to learners with special needs shows that a discount is made in the registration fee for learners with 33% disability or higher. Moreover, Erasmus+internship scholarships are available based on the disability rate, and if the learner has 65% or above disability, support for additional expenses, such as sign language translator or personal assistant, etc. are provided. Links to other organizations, like Fundacion Prevent and Fundacion Universia, which offer scholarship opportunities in cooperation with the university, are presented. For exams, the support services include buildings with elevator and ramp, easily accessible, large classrooms, wheelchair-compatible desks, computer use when deemed necessary, assistive software, like JAWS and Zoomtext, stand-alone classrooms or with few people, larger font size texts, Braille texts, and extra time. Moreover, an online request form of special need is available for learners to convey their needs, and secondary exams are offered for learners who have justified reasons for not taking the exam. Additional services provided include material delivery to home addresses, and special accessibility features, such as disabled parking spots, sign language translators, ramps, etc. for on-site events like graduation ceremonies and activities in residential centers, and there is an online request form for additional support needed for these types of events. The institution also has an accessibility improvement plan for learners with special needs.

Examination of the pedagogical support services offered by the Universitat Oberta de Catalunya to learners with special needs shows that these learners are provided alternative material to accommodate their special needs; these include formats such as PDF, HTML, karaoke, audiobooks, e-books, DAISY, and Braille. In addition to these, learners are provided with the opportunity to request additional support to meet their needs for their current study materials. There is also a Curriculum Adaptation Committee which makes modifications on the content, method, and skills in the curriculum based on learner needs.

Examination of the technical support services offered by Universitat Oberta de Catalunya to learners with special needs shows that adaptations conforming to the W3C Consortium WAI AA standards (www.w3c.org/wai) have been made in the Virtual Campus interfaces and on the website to help learners with visual impairment navigate the system. A request form to borrow equipment, devices, or software from the Support Product Bank is presented to learners who have 33% or higher disability within the scope of the agreement made with Fundacion Universia.

The support services offered by Universitat Oberta de Catalunya that are considered to be outside the managerial, pedagogical, technical and social support include links to career guidance, job and internship offers delivered by other organizations that work in cooperation with the university, like Fundacion Prevent and Fundacion Universia.

The Open University of Japan

Examination of the managerial support services offered by the Open University of Japan to learners with special needs shows that they hold annual meeting to determine these learner's need. They also excuse them from university entrance exam. As exam support services; extra time, an amanuensis, personal rooms, the use of tape recording, word processors, Braille reading glasses etc., and exam papers with larger font, in Braille are offered. Moreover, the institution has a support systems report on learners with special needs, which includes the current support systems and a future action plan.

Examination of the pedagogical support services offered by the Open University of Japan to learners with special needs shows that digital text formats of broadcasts and online courses for screen reader users; and Braille formats of digital texts for Braille users are provided. In addition to these, captions in online and television courses and transcriptions of radio courses are offered. Some face to face services are also offered. These services include parking spaces, provision of necessary worksheets prior to the course, communication with the instructor on the needs prior to the course, assistant support for learners with hearing impairment, transportation support, and wheelchair-compatible desks etc. Furthermore, the opportunity to take courses from OUJ and transfer the credit is also given to learners with special needs studying at other universities.

University of South Australia

Examination of the managerial support services offered by the University of South Australia to learners with special needs shows that various exam services are provided, including extra time on tests, rest or toilet breaks, food-beverage permit during exams when deemed necessary, provision of equipment, such as laptops, trackballs and spell checker, and assistant support like a scribe or reader. In addition to these, alternative sitting arrangements, such as ergonomic chairs or footrests, alternative exam centers, oral exams, special parking spaces, and the use of software, like a screen reader, and speech synthesizers are provided. The opportunity to do secondary exam is given to those whose exam performance was

Supporting Learners with Special Needs in Open and Distance Learning

negatively affected by lack of support service or to those who were unable to take the exam at the normal schedule due to valid excuses. In terms of financial aid, the University of South Australia includes the links of scholarships offered by other organizations and also provides assistive technology scholarships for learners with special needs. Other services provided include an online system to get an appointment for support on phone or face-to-face, a disability services unit, a website highlighting the support services offered to learners with special needs, an introductory video on services, and printed material delivery to the home addresses. The institution has an action plan and online accessibility action plan for learners with special needs. Moreover, the institution presents a tab on its website that offers hints for creating accessible content, control lists of accessible content, links to useful accessibility resources, and the list of standards needed to be considered for accessibility in non-textual resources.

Examination of the pedagogical support services offered by the University of South Australia to learners with special needs shows that in addition to the provision of assistive technology support, the institution has on-campus adaptive technology suits which offer Dragon Naturally Speaking speech recognition software, a 20-inch LCD monitor, Zoomtext software, A4 scanner allowing hard copy materials to be converted into electronic text, an A3-A4 printer allowing material to be printed in enlarged text, Read&Write software providing features such as word prediction, spelling and grammar checking and screen reading, ergonomic furniture, an internal phone for contacting the library loans, and a height-adjustable desk. University of South Australia provides alternative format materials such as, large print, electronic, Braille and audio. In addition, simultaneous captioning, transcripts for video/audio content and captioning in all videos and online resources are provided. In the context of remote access to library services, the University of South Australia delivers services such as a tab on the website for the library services for learners with special needs, a disability services unit support, electronic resource delivery, introduction to library services, and online or on-phone librarian support. In addition to these, the University of South Australia has Access&Inclusion advisor support to determine the needs of learners and any additional services they may require in education activities and to develop individual access plan. In the context of individual access plan the services such as, support in academic writing, writing references, time management, planning study load, reading&writing strategies and organization skills, portable FM system, sign language translator support, Closed-circuit television displaying printed materials in larger font size are provided. Furthermore, they offer the learners opportunity to report problems encountered in the accessibility of online materials to the disability hub via e-mail.

Examination of the social support services offered by the University of South Australia to learners with special needs shows that they offer disability advisers, counseling, and a webpage providing tips for wellbeing and links to relevant resources.

Finally, the examination of the technical support services offered by the University of South Australia to learners with special needs shows that adaptations conforming to the W3C Consortium WAI AA standards have been made on the website design to help learners with visual impairment navigate the system.

Anadolu University (Open Education System)

Examination of the managerial support services offered by Anadolu University to learners with special needs shows that learners with 40% or higher disability are exempt from education expenses and tuition fees, and that learners with disability rate below 40% only pay the education expenses. During registration procedures, these learners are given priority in local offices. In the context of the exam services, Anadolu University provides scribe and/or reader support, an at least two question exemption in each course, an exam paper and answer key with large font for learners with visual impairment, while for learners with physical disability, they are allowed to take exams on the ground floor, they receive scribe support, and in cases of bedbound learners, they are allowed to take exams at home. In addition to these, depending on their specific needs, the learners can take the exam in a separate room, are allowed to bring equipment, food and drink, or medicine, etc. Furthermore, a website which is available specifically for learners with special needs is provided (engelsizaof.anadolu.edu.tr). Live support for registration procedures, exam services via audio, video, and text message, an online Turkish sign language translator and access to frequently asked questions are also provided on this website. Besides that, Anadolu University provides 7/24 call center and 81 local offices working in cooperation with the Central office and organize Open Education workshop for learners with special needs annually. Open Education System Support Unit for Disabled Learners, the Central office, the Computer Research Center, the Test Research Unit, and the Learning Technologies Research and Development Unit all work cooperatively to support learners with special needs.

In the context of pedagogical support services, Anadolu University offers materials in alternative formats like DAISY digital talking books, mp3, PDF, Word, videos, e-pub and interactive videos. In order to ensure future access to online courses, their recorded versions are also included. In addition to these services, subtitle and sign language support for audio/video contents, description for visual contents, access to contents through mobile application (Anadolu Mobil), academic advising within the scope of project courses are provided. Furthermore, e-advising which includes services like giving tips for study techniques and strategies is also offered on a website (https://ekampus.anadolu.edu.tr/). For its on-site library services, the university offers Braille books and printouts, computer with screen reader softwares, and audiobooks. Moreover, the open library service including audiobooks, and digital magazines is provided.

Examination of the social support services offered by Anadolu University to learners with special needs shows that the Open Education Faculty formed a visual and hearing impaired choir. University also organizes concerts in which visual and hearing impaired choir takes part.

Finally, the examination of the technical support services offered by the Anadolu University to learners with special needs shows that a website conforming to the *Level A Conformance to Web Content Accessibility Guidelines 2.0* is available specifically for learners with special needs (engelsizaof.anadolu.edu.tr) and technical support for e-learning management system (Anadolum eKampüs) navigation is provided.

CONCLUSION

The flexible structure of ODL supports the accessible education approach. However, this reality can become meaningful only if all learners benefit equally from all services provided in ODL systems. Services which are accessible to all can be designed by taking the all distance learner's characteristics into consideration. In this context, one of the elements that has to be taken into account in design of learner support is disability. Examination of support services offered by ODL institutions included in this study show that they offer some accommodations for learners with special needs. The services provided by institutions have both similarities and differences.

Supporting Learners with Special Needs in Open and Distance Learning

Some of the managerial support services offered for learners with special needs in ODL institutions are financial aid, alternative exam arrangements, online forms and access plans. As a matter of fact, ODL has evolved into a web-based learning model in 21st century world. Accordingly, in access to this model offering e-learning contents, assistive technologies play a crucial role for learners with special needs. Considering that such technologies are costly, assistive technology financial aid is an essential support element. Therefore, provision of scholarships or link to scholarships offered by other institutions has great importance. One of the other essential support element for learners with special need is exam services. ODL institutions provide a wide variety of alternative exam arrangements such as alternative exam papers in large font size, audio or Braille, an amanuensis, separate exam rooms, extra time, rest breaks, the use of assistive technologies, alternative answering methods like answering in Braille or recording answers with a tape recorder, exam centers with elevator and ramp, easily accessible large classrooms, wheelchair-compatible desks, oral exams, the opportunity to take exam at home for bedbound learners, secondary exams, and online exams. Examination of the services offered in ODL institutions included in this study show that some of the universities do not offer online exam service. It is a matter of fact that not all ODL institutions have the same technological infrastructure. In order to develop an online exam system, ODL institution need to have sufficient technological infrastructure enabling to eliminate potential problems in exam security and identity verification. In other words, ODL institutions need to keep up with latest technology and offer online exam services accordingly. This will be a step in the right direction to enhance accessibility especially for learners with physical disability. Some of ODL institution included in this study also offer a secondary exam for learners who have justified reasons for not taking the exam. Considering that these learners may be absent on the day of an exam due to medical condition or disability, giving a second chance will be a good practice on behalf of these learners. In the context of managerial support, the other services are online forms and access plans. Nearly all of ODL institutions included in this study offer online forms which are used to request support services and some of them offer individual access plans for learners with special needs. Considering that these learners' need may also vary according to their disability rate, online forms and individual access plans which are helpful tool for determining the learners' specific needs should be provided by all ODL institutions.

Within the context of pedagogical support, ODL institutions offer learning materials in alternative formats such as DAISY digital talking books, e-books, audio books, mp3, PDF, Word, videos, interactive videos, e-pub and HTLM. Considering that learners with visual impairment use voice recognition or screen reading software to access e-learning contents, all materials must be compatible with assistive software. Description for non-text content must also be provided. For learners with hearing impairment captioning, sign language translation and transcripts for all audio/video content are of vital importance in accessibility. To conclude, accessibility of the learning materials is a crucial matter. Therefore, a unit testing the accessibility of learning materials and courses can be formed in ODL institutions. In addition, institutions can offer tutor support well prepared for learners with special needs to guide learners throughout their studies. In the context of pedagogical support, another crucial element is library services. Examination of the services offered in ODL institutions included in this study show that accessibility in library services and remote access to library services are limited. Considering the library services are an integral part of the learning process, ODL institutions should enhance the accessibility in remote library services for learners with special needs.

Within the context of social support, some of ODL institutions offer services like disability adviser, counseling, forums, visual and hearing impaired choir, and self-help materials for staying mentally healthy and coping with anxiety. These services are some of the important factors fostering sense of belongings in ODL. Distance learners can feel isolated and lose their motivation because they are not physically present on campus. Especially, for learners with special needs this situation may be much more critical. They may be more likely to feel isolated due to their disability. Therefore, giving counseling services to help learners with special needs cope with anxiety and depression, organizing social responsibility projects, graduate ceremonies and activities, building mobile apps, forums and alumni networking platforms will be a step in the right direction to overcome isolation and create sense of social presence.

Within the context of technical support, most of the ODL institutions included in this study provide a website conforming to the web accessibility standards. Considering that the most of the services are offered through websites and mobile apps in ODL, institutions' commitment to continuous improvement on their web and mobile accessibility must be reflected in practice. In addition to that, mechanism enabling learners to give feedback on web and mobile accessibility must be provided. Informing learners on assistive technologies, providing tutorials on how to use assistive technologies and university's learning management system are also crucial technical supports.

In addition to managerial, pedagogical, social and technical support, institutions can also offer *vocational support*. Within this context, services like information on disability rights at work, employment resources such as job boards and social media platforms, job applications, job interviews and CV preparation, and links to job boards should be provided.

To conclude, learner support systems need to be designed to the greatest extent possible. ODL institutions should conduct researches to determine the needs of learners with special needs and the degree of learners' satisfaction in perception of current services accordingly. Besides that, they should investigate what accommodations other ODL institutions offer for learners with special needs in more detail.

ACKNOWLEDGMENT

This chapter is the reviewed and improved version of a section in the dissertation "Determining Needs and Priorities in Support Services for Students with Special Needs in Open and Distance Learning", completed in the Distance Education Department of Social Sciences Institute at Anadolu University in 2018.

REFERENCES

Aydın, H. C. (2011). *Açık ve uzaktan öğrenme: Öğrenci adaylarının bakış açısı* [Open and distance learning: The perspective of prospective learners]. Ankara: Pegem.

Berge, Z. L. (1995). Facilitating Computer Conferencing: Recommendations From the Field. *Educational Technology, 15*(1), 22–30.

Bozkurt, A. (2013). Mega üniversitelerde öğrenci destek hizmetleri [Support services in mega universities]. In *Proceedings of the Academic Informatics Conference* (pp. 395-401). Antalya: Akdeniz University. Retrieved October, 15, 2017, from https://www.academia.edu/2536907/Mega_%C3%9Cniversitelerde_%C3%96%C4%9Frenci_Destek_Hizmetleri

Brindley, E. J., Walti, C., & Zavachki-Richter, O. (2004). The current context of learner support in open, distance and online learning: An introduction. In J. E. Brindley, C. Walti, & O. Zawacki-Richter (Eds.), *Learner support in open, distance and online learning environments* (pp. 9–27). Oldenburg: BIS-Verlag der Carl von Ossietzky Universität Oldenburg.

Burgstahler, S. (2002a). Universal design of distance learning. *Information Technology and Disabilities E-Journal, 8*(1). Retrieved December 17, 2017, from http://itd.athenpro.org/volume8/number1/burgstah.html

Burgstahler, S. (2002b). Distance learning: Universal design, universal access. *AACE Journal, 10*(1), 32–61.

Chute, A., Thompson, M., & Hancock, B. (1999). *McGraw-Hill handbook of distance learning: An implementation guide for trainers and human resource professionals.* New York: McGraw-Hill.

Department of Disability Research and Statistical Turkey. (2006). *Türkiye özürlüler araştırması temel göstergeleri* [Main indicators of Turkey disability research]. Retrieved October 20, 2017, from http://www.engelsiz.hacettepe.edu.tr/belge/ozida.pdf

Durak, G. (2017). Uzaktan eğitimde destek hizmetlerine genel bakış: Sorunlar ve eğilimler [A general outlook on the issue of support services in open and distance learning: trends and problems]. *Açıköğretim Uygulamaları ve Araştırmaları Dergisi, 3*(4), 160–173.

Edmonds, D. C. (2004). Providing access to students with disabilities in online distance education: Legal and technical concerns for higher education. *American Journal of Distance Education, 18*(1), 51–62. doi:10.120715389286ajde1801_5

Fiege, K. (2010). *Successful practices in supporting students in distributed learning; Meeting the needs of diverse students engaging in e-learning.* Calgary, Canada: Bow Walley.

Floyd, L. D., & Casey-Powell, D. (2004). New roles for student support services in distance learning. *New Directions for Community Colleges, 2004*(128), 55–64. doi:10.1002/cc.175

Keast, A. D. (1997). Toward an effective model for implementing distance education programs. *American Journal of Distance Education, 11*(2), 39–55. doi:10.1080/08923649709526960

Keegan, D. (2003). Introduction. In H. Fritsch (Ed.), The role of student services in e-learning systems (pp. 1-6). ZIFF.

Lapadula, M. (2003). Comprehensive look at online student support services for distance learners. *American Journal of Distance Education, 17*(2), 119–128. doi:10.1207/S15389286AJDE1702_4

Ministry of National Education Turkey. (2006). *Özel eğitim hizmetleri yönetmeliği* [Special education services regulation]. Author.

Okur, R. M. (2012). *Açık ve uzaktan öğrenmede öğretim elemanlarına yönelik çevrimiçi destek sistemi tasarımı* [Designing online faculty support system for open and distance learning] (Unpublished doctoral dissertation). Anadolu University.

Ommerborn, R. (1998). *Distance study for the disabled: National and international experience and perspectives*. Hagen, Germany: FernUniversität.

Rekkedal, T., & Qvist-Eriksen, S. (2003). Internet based e-learning, pedagogy an support systems. In H. Fritsch (Ed.), The role of student services in e-learning systems (pp. 8-32). ZIFF.

Rumble, G. (2000). Student support in distance education in the 21st century: Learning from service management. *Distance Education, 21*(2), 216–235. doi:10.1080/0158791000210202

Scheer, B. S., & Lockee, B. B. (2003). Addressing the wellness needs of online distance learners. *Open Learning: The Journal of Open, Distance and eLearning, 18*(2), 177-196.

Sewart, D. (1993). Student support systems in distance education. *Open Learning, 8*(3), 3–12. doi:10.1080/0268051930080302

Simpson, O. (2002). *Supporting students in online open and distance learning*. London: Kogan Page.

Simpson, O. (2012). *Supporting students for success in online and distance education*. New York: Routledge.

Ströhlein, G. (2003). On the use of information and telecommunication technology to support learning. In H. Fritsch (Ed.), The role of student services in e-learning systems (pp. 62-76). ZIFF.

Tait, A. (2000). Planning student support for open and distance learning. *Open Learning, 15*(3), 287–299. doi:10.1080/713688410

Thorpe, M. (2003). Collaborative on-line learning: transforming learner support and course design. In A. Tait & R. Mills (Eds.), *Rethinking learner support in distance education* (pp. 198–210). London: Routledge.

Turkish Statistical Institute. (2010). *Özürlülerin sorun ve beklentileri araştırması* [The problems and expactations of people with disability research]. Retrieved 10 December 2017, from http://www.tuik.gov.tr/PreTablo.do?alt_id=1017

KEY TERMS AND DEFINITIONS

Accommodation for Learners With Special Needs: It refers to assistance or arrangement meeting the needs of learners with special needs.

Assistive Technology: It refers to any equipment, device, software or product which helps individuals with special needs fulfill the requirements of their daily life.

Open and Distance Learning: It refers to education in which the instructors and learners are separated by place or time or both time and place, requiring learner-learner, leaner-instructor, learner-content interaction through technologies.

Web Accessibility: It refers to the web which can be used by learners with special needs.

Chapter 8
The Contribution of Information Communication Technologies in Online Career Counseling:
Case Study of an Online Community Within Higher Education

Nikolaos Mouratoglou
https://orcid.org/0000-0001-6653-7810
Aristotle University of Thessaloniki, Greece

George K. Zarifis
Aristotle University of Thessaloniki, Greece

ABSTRACT

Information communication technologies have undoubtedly affected the discipline of career counselling. Nevertheless, online career counselling remains a rather limited practice in Greece; therefore, the chapter attempts to contribute to the wider dialogue that has been addressed so far, by focusing on the design, implementation, and assessment of an online career counselling program for higher education students and graduates. The purpose of the study is to present the main parameters related to participants' learning experience, such as motivation, barriers to participation, as well as adopted strategies for overcoming these barriers during the online program. The researchers conducted 15 semi-structured interviews to collect data for summative assessment. The analysis of the data indicates that prior acknowledgement of learners' motivation, educator/career counsellor's role, the learning environment, the methods utilized, and the teaching material can maximize the effectiveness of equivalent programs, due to the fulfillment of their needs, goals, and expectations.

DOI: 10.4018/978-1-5225-9779-7.ch008

The Contribution of Information Communication Technologies in Online Career Counseling

INTRODUCTION

Aristotle University of Thessaloniki is the largest University in Greece and one of the largest in Southeast Europe including 11 Faculties, 41 Schools and almost 74.000 students.[1] The Career Services Office delivers face to face and online counseling sessions, organizes various capacity building workshops as well as other activities related to personal and vocational growth (Career Days, CV and Cover Letter workshops, seminars for searching postgraduate programs, placements, grants). At the same time, Online Career Counseling is not a widely known, and therefore implemented, practice in Greece. As a result, research data concerning the dimensions, conditions, factors and outcomes of Online Career Counseling remain rather limited.

The above-mentioned framework formed the context as well as the need of the present research study. The researchers designed an online program for students and graduates of the Aristotle University, based on data which were collected in an earlier phase referring to specific needs, concerns and expectations. Afterwards, the program was adapted on the Google+ space in the form of an online community. The title of the program was "Prepare & Present Yourself: a personal branding approach", it lasted one month and included four thematic modules: a) Curriculum Vitae: Studies and Work, b) Postgraduate Studies, Grants and Cover Letter, c) Interview: Studies and Work and d) Job seeking techniques and Social Media management. Each week the researchers uploaded the corresponding material (articles, videos, templates) and set the activities that should be completed by the end of the week (writing the Curriculum Vitae, creating LinkedIn profile). At the same time, the researchers encouraged the community members to actively participate in the discussions developed in the forum, exchange ideas, share experiences and express their views and concerns. In the meantime, personal communication among participants and one of the researcher that is Career Counselor also took place via personal e-mails and Skype sessions. Personal communication was a redeeming feature for those who did not wish to share information openly and functioned also as a way of protecting participants' personal data, for instance, personal information included in the Curriculum Vitae and Cover Letter.

BACKGROUND

The study is grounded in four interdisciplinary fields; Lifelong Learning, Distance Learning, Instructional Design and Online Career Counseling. This section will briefly discuss dimensions of these disciplines, in order to form the framework of the present research.

The notion of Lifelong Learning can be approached as a twofold, because it reflects different epistemological and semantic background. On the one hand, Lifelong Learning is described as a process in which a person can learn new things, in new ways and for various reasons. Although this process seems to be an individual case, it is governed and guided by social or inter-subjective characteristics and factors that bring change both at the individual and the social level. On the other hand, Lifelong Learning seems to be outlined, in the post-modern era, through a variety of conceptual definitions, such as the empirical implementation of educational policy in western culture, the institutionalization of education throughout the life-span, as well as the perception that human life itself constitutes a learning journey (Karavakou, 2011).

Lifelong Learning has also been described in terms of settings, namely formal, informal and non-formal learning settings. This division gives prominence to the influence that learning environments can have on people, describe the differential conditions that exist as well as the goals that each one addresses. However, this division of learning is convenient for researchers, educational developers, educational policies and governments; yet, remains undivided for the person itself. Regarding Lifewide Learning[2], a term which denotes that learning occurs in multiple learning environments, has been introduced in an institutional text of the Swedish National Agency for Education (Skolverket, 2000). Skolverket's institutional text describes the relationship between Lifelong Learning and Lifewide Learning and concludes that the term "Lifelong Learning" refers to the learning that occurs throughout the life-span, while "Lifewide Learning" emphasizes that learning can occur in various settings and environments (formal, informal and non-formal). Hence, Lifewide Learning is not an opposite concept of Lifelong Learning. Instead, Lifewide Learning is a complementary concept that emphasizes spatial factors, encompasses formal, non-formal and informal learning and enriches the concept of Lifelong Learning. According to Jackson (n.d.), attempting to represent those two terms on an axis system, Lifelong Learning would be placed on the vertical axis with its distinct time frames, while Lifewide Learning on the horizontal axis with the various learning settings.

As stated earlier, Lifelong Learning –and learning in general– is subjected to social or inter-subjective characteristics and factors. Van Merriënboer and Stoyanov (2008) discuss in their research that both trainees and trainers are part of a rapidly changing landscape, in which both the content and the context are constantly differentiated. The wide utilization of Information Communication Technologies (ICT) in the learning process transformed the learning framework in terms of time and space independency, inducing major changes in the learning process. One of these changes is Distance Education (DE) and Open Distance Learning (ODL). Since 1980s, DE has globally been expanded due to socio-economic factors and the rapid development of technological advances (Gunawardena & McIsaac, 2004). However, it was not until the late 1990's that DE began systematically to develop in Greece, mainly through the establishment of the Hellenic Open University (Gkiosos, Mavroeidis, &Koutsoumpa, 2008).

According to Keegan (1980), DE can be defined through six key features, namely teacher-student/learner separation, the influence of an educational institution in the planning process and students' support, the use of technical media, the provision of two-way communication, the participation in an industrialized form of education and the organization of the learning process at an individual level. Nevertheless, some of the above-described features have been perceived both as advantages and as disadvantages of DE. Skikos, Louka, Zwgopoulos and Moschoudi (2010) suggest that DE has abolished the geographical constraints and greatly expanded the dissemination of knowledge. Through DE, every person across countries is provided with equal opportunities, notably in cases where hindering factors like distance, time and limited options are present. Furthermore, DE has contributed in continuing training and education and consequently many learners have improved their knowledge and skills by attending higher education courses (Kentnor, 2015).

Similarly, ODL provides flexibility. Bergamin, Ziska, and Groner (2012) identified 22 dimensions of flexibility and classified them in seven categories: time, space, methods, learning styles, content, organization and infrastructure, as well as requirements (p. 104). On the other hand, two main disadvantages of DE are the absence of social dimensions in the learning process and trainees' isolation (Panagiotakopoulos, Lionarakis & Xenos, 2003). According to the same researchers, those two factors often result in low academic performances and high dropout rates. Moreover, Rodriguez (2012) also concluded that the majority of participants (80% -90%) are not socially engaged in their learning process. Instead, participants tend to watch, listen or read the educational material, while those who actively participate in the activities are almost 10%. Inter alia, Gravani, Hatzinikita and Zarifis (2012) discuss in their research that deficiencies in infrastructure such as audiovisual equipment and the digital platform can influence trainees' attitudes towards DE in a negative way.

Palloff and Pratt (2003) describe the characteristics that virtual students should have in order to be successful and therefore minimize the potential pitfalls that they may face in DE. According to the researchers, learners need to have the required technological equipment as well as the skills to use that equipment; they should be open-minded and feel comfortable with sharing personal information, as well as not be obstructed in case that audio or visual dimensions of communication are not present. Furthermore, virtual learners need to be self-motivated and self-disciplined, willing to devote enough time for studying and showcase (or develop) their critical thinking and reflecting skills. Finally, virtual learners need to believe that *"high-quality learning can happen anywhere and anytime"* (p.8). Nevertheless, the qualities of successful virtual learners need to be transformed into specific principles that will inform Instructional Designers and therefore support and enhance students' success.

Instructional Design (ID) refers to the *"systematic and reflective process of translating principles of learning and instruction into plans for instructional materials, activities, information resources, and evaluation"* (Smith & Ragan, 2005, pp. 4). Many ID models have been proposed, in order to describe the content of ID (Gagné, Wager, Goals & Keller, 2005; Dick, Carey & Carey, 2009; Merrill, 2007, 2009; Branch, 2009; Van Merriënboer, Clark & de Croock, 2002; Kirschner & Van Merriënboer, 2008). Models constitute a simplified outline of a process by capturing the basic elements, the interactions between these elements, and can be used in guiding the design process of various educational activities (Caffarella, 2002). The Four-Component Instructional Design (4C/ID) model proposed by Van Merriënboer and his colleagues (2002), that later on was enriched (Kirschner & Van Merriënboer, 2008), is based on the complex learning approach, while at the same time successfully incorporates elements of the critique that was formulated regarding the most frequently used model ADDIE (Analysis, Design, Development, Implementation and Evaluation). The four components and ten steps of the model are presented below in Table 1.

Table 1. The four blueprint components of 4C-ID and the ten steps to complex learning

Blueprint Components of 4C-ID	Ten Steps to Complex Learning
Learning Tasks	1. Design Learning Tasks 2. Sequence Task Classes 3. Set Performance Objectives
Supportive Information	4. Design Supportive Information 5. Analyze Cognitive Strategies 6. Analyze Mental Models
Procedural Information	7. Design Procedural Information 8. Analyze Cognitive Rules 9. Analyze Prerequisite Knowledge
Part-Task Practice	10. Design Part-Task Practice

Source: (Kirschner & Van Merriënboer, 2008)

The 4C/ID model aims at designing learning environments that will improve cognitive skill and focuses on skills that contribute in the completion of complex cognitive activities based on cognitive schemata, allowing multiple iterations. Therefore, programs that are based on the 4C/ID model, aim at learning transference, in which the learner can apply the acquired skills in a wide range of real-life situations (Van Merriënboer et al, 2002).

This is also the aim of Career Counseling. Learning transference, skills' applicability in real-life situations as well as the self-management of career constitute the main ways of transforming clients into active, self-managed and self-motivated individuals. According to Kidd (2006) career counseling[3] is *"a one-to-one interaction between practitioner and client, usually ongoing, involving the application of psychological theory and a recognized set of communication skills. The primary focus is on helping the client make career-related decisions and deal with career-related issues"* (p. 1). Furthermore, OECD and European Commission (2004) define Career Guidance as *"services and activities intended to assist individuals, of any age and at any point throughout their lives, to make educational, training and occupational choices and to manage their careers..."* (p. 10).Therefore, Online Career Counseling refers to professional counseling sessions delivered through Information Communication Technologies and focus on assisting people – of any age and at any point throughout their lives– make career-related decisions, educational, training and occupational choices, deal with career-related issues and manage their careers[4].

Even though most of the research conducted refers to Online Counseling (OC), however, the results and conclusions reached can be applied in Online Career Counseling merely, as the context and therefore the conditions remain the same, but the content of the sessions is different. Online counseling sessions can be delivered in various modes by using telephones (Van den Bos & Williams, 2000), asynchronous written messages (Gatti, Brivio & Calciano, 2016), synchronous written messages (Dowling & Rickwood, 2013) and video conferencing (Tyler & Guth, 2003). Notably, text-based online counseling is associated with the healing feature of writing (Finfgeld, 1999; Wright, 2002), as clients reflect on their problem and in attempt to communicate effectively with the counselor they may realize elements and meanings that they have earlier overlooked. This process relates to what Suler (2000, 2011) described as "reflection zone".

Inquiring the characteristics and specific conditions related to OC, the literature review offers interesting insights regarding the advantages and disadvantages of delivering online counseling sessions. OC provides clients the opportunity to access counseling services directly, when they need to (Skinner & Zack, 2004), while at the same time ensures access to those who otherwise would not be able to attend counseling sessions (Sussman, 2004). People living in remote areas where counseling services do not exist (Boer, 2001), or when people do not trust the local counselors or fear that they may be exposed (Efstathiou, 2009), are indicative examples. Furthermore, people who can benefit the most, are those who face difficulties in attending f2f sessions due to workload, other social obligations and/or people with mobility disabilities (Maples & Han, 2008; Pelling, 2009). Other advantages include the permanent nature of the written messages (Suler, 2011), counselors' flexibility and fewer cancellations (Bischoff, 2004), comfort (Barak, 1999), lower costs (Chester & Glass, 2006) and the limited resistance due to the perceived anonymity (Young, 2005; Salleh, Hamzah, Nordin, Ghavifekr & Joorabchi, 2015).

On the other hand, OC has also drawbacks that have been addressed in research studies and mainly focus on the absence of visual contact with the client. Therefore, the lack of non-verbal cues (Richards & Vigano, 2013) result in hindering the communication process (Barak, 1999). In the research conducted by Zamani, Nasir and Yusooff (2010), counselors reported that forming a strong therapeutic relationship with the client during online counseling is difficult, due to the absence of non-verbal cues. Other disadvantages may include problems of misunderstanding and therefore incorrect diagnosis of the client's request (Beel & Court, 2000), the risk of personal data disclosure from cyber-attacks (Mallen, Vogel & Rochlen, 2005), clients' social isolation (Barak, 1999), the exposure of vulnerable groups over the internet (Finn & Banach, 2000) and the difficulty the counselor may face regarding referral (Finn, 2002). Finally, disadvantages may also refer to technical problems that discourage both the counselor and the client (Haberstroh, Parr, Bradley, Morgan-Fleming & Gee, 2008).

RESEARCH STUDY

Aim and Research Questions

The purpose of the present study is to investigate parameters linked to the development, implementation and assessment of an online career counseling program by Higher Education students and graduates. The research attempts to provide answers to the following research questions:

R.Q. 1: Which factors motivated and hindered participants' engagement?

R.Q. 2: What kind of strategies have the participants adopted in order to overcome their difficulties?
R.Q. 3: How did participants assess the online career counseling program?

Data Collection Techniques and Data Analysis Methods

The present study has been developed based on the creation of an online community in Google+. By using the term community, the researchers adopt Sergiovanni's (1994) conceptualization regarding the sense of belonging, the common sharing of ideas and values among the members of a group and its' discrete characteristics in relation to other groups. Additionally, the online community was developed based on the model that Amy Jo Kim proposed (Kim, 2000). The contribution of the model lies in the multiperspective approach of the online communities and simultaneously in the multifactorial view of their success. Kim's model includes nine basic principles:

Principle 1: Define the purpose.
Principle 2: Create Distinct, Member-Extensible Gathering Places.
Principle 3: Create Member Profiles that Evolve Over Time
Principle 4: Promote Effective Leadership and Hosting
Principle 5: Define a Clear-Yet-Flexible Code of Conduct
Principle 6: Accommodate a Range of Roles
Principle 7: Facilitate Member-Created Subgroups
Principle 8: Organize and Promote Cyclic Events
Principle 9: Integrating with the Real World.

Regarding data collection, quantitative and qualitative techniques were used. The researchers administered two questionnaires and conductedfifteenf2f semi-structured interviews with average duration of 20 minutes. Questionnaires provide the opportunity of collecting a great extent of data from a large sample of subjects (Cohen, Manion & Morrison, 2018), while semi-structured interviews enable researchers to explore themes for a given framework by inquiring deeper experiences and understandings (Rubin & Rubin, 2012). The first questionnaire aimed at inquiring participants' needs, goals and expectations (pre-assessment/diagnostic assessment) and informed the researchers about the designing phase of the informal, online career counseling program. The second questionnaire collected data during the program's formative assessment, while semi-structured interviews were used for summative assessment.

The participants that were invited to the interviews were chosen based on two criteria; first their will to participate and secondly the level of their participation in the online community. According to Wenger's model of participation (1999), communities of practice –but also most of the social learning settings– usually involve the core group, the active participants, the occasional participants, the peripheral participants and the transactional participants. In order to classify the participants of the present study, the researchers used data analytics for their online behavior and recorded participants' entry frequency in the community, the duration of their activity, the interactions that they developed with the rest of the community members as well as their contributions in the dialogue and the activities. Finally, the quantitative data analysis was carried out with statistical tests using the Statistical Package for Social Sciences (SPSS) 23.0, while the qualitative data, from the open-ended questions that were included in the questionnaires, as well as the data collected via the semi-structured interviews, were analysed based on the Qualitative Content Analysis and the inductive category development (Mayring, 2000). In the present chapter, the researchers will discuss the qualitative data of the study, as the quantitative data reflect the formative assessment of the program.

Participants

The researchers aimed at forming a medium size community, in which the number of the participants would be limited. The underlying reason was to ensure that each member of the community would feel safe and comfortable in contributing and actively participating in the online community; yet, there would be the potentiality of developing multiple interactions with each other. Hence, the online community is consisted of thirty-five participants, twenty-nine women and six men. Their age average is 26.5 years old and most of them live in urban areas in Greece (88.6%), while three participants reside abroad. Regarding their study level, fifteen participants are undergraduate students, ten participants are graduates and ten other are graduates from postgraduate programs. Most of the participants (82.9%) attend or have attended the School of Social Sciences, 14.2% the School of Engineering and 2.9% the School of Sciences. In addition, 60% of the participants are highly skilled in using computers, 51.4% are employed, 74.3% have not participated earlier in online programs and 80% have never visited the Career Services Office of the Aristotle University.

RESULTS

Factors Motivating and Hindering Participants' Engagement

The first section of the semi-structured interviews aimed at exploring students' motivation and barriers to participation, as well as the strategies that participants adopted in order to overcome these barriers. The subcategories are presented in Table 2.

Inquiring participants' motivation for attending the online career counseling program, the most important factors included the relevance of the program with their needs, as well as the interesting topic of the program. A student reported, *"It was something I was interested in; something I needed especially now that I am completing my studies and will be looking for work and postgraduates. It was something I needed"*, while another commented, *"It seemed really interesting to me because the content was related with curriculum vitae, the way that I can build my profile, my qualifications, the personal statement... The feedback was really useful, as I had not prepared my tools and that program was a great opportunity"*.

Nine participants highlighted that one of the main reasons for participating in the program was the practical dimension. In other words, students applied the theoretical knowledge they acquired during the program and developed their personal branding tools (CV, Personal Statement, Cover Letter, LinkedIn profile). One participant stated, *"Because I could use the knowledge to make a good CV. It was not theoretical, and this was something I liked from the beginning"*. Two other participants mentioned, *""I learned practical things with guidance and this is very important. I was applying, what I was learning"* and *"The program was practical. If it was theoretical, I would not participate. I am tired of theory"*.

Eight participants responded that the online delivery mode of the program was also an important factor that impacted their participation, mainly due to the time and distance flexibility and flexible learning in general. One of them expressed his view, *"it was an online program and not a face to face course; I participated from the comfort of my home"*, while another commented *"I attended the course because there were not any meetings. Working all day leaves me with little free time"*. A final indicative statement by a graduate student living in Germany described, *"It was a distance program. Living in Germany means that I would not have access otherwise"*.

Seven students reported that the absence of cost was also a crucial reason for their participation. A community member stated, *"It would be difficult for me if there was a cost. I am currently unemployed, so free of charge participation was a motive for me"*. Another one said, *"A free personal improvement opportunity, I would not miss it"*.

Table 2. Subcategories of reasons for participation

Subcategories	Frequency
Relevance of the program with their needs	14
Interesting topic of the program	12
Practical dimension of the program	9
Online delivery mode	8
Free of charge	7
Curiosity	2

Finally, two of the participants joined the online career counseling program because they were feeling curious about it. The first one was curious about the content, *"I was curious to see what kind of program was"*, while the second one curious about the delivery mode, *"Online Career Counseling? I was curious about the online thing. How can you deliver career counseling online and with so many people?"*.

Therefore, participants stated that the primary reason for participating was their desire to compose their personal branding tools (CV, Cover Letter, LinkedIn account), in order to meet their career goals and personal needs. The interesting topic of the program in combination with the applicability and its' practical orientation were also perceived as important motivational factors. Some of them, also reported that the online delivery mode of the program, the absence of costs and curiosity were also determining reasons for participating.

Regarding barriers related to their participation, the subcategories that emerged, are presented in Table 3.

All of the participants stated that the main obstacle they faced during the implementation phase of the program was the limited time they had due to their work and studies. A consequence of this barrier, according to their statements, was the inadequate engagement in the discussions and interactions with the rest of the community members. A participant commented, *"I had limited time due to my work and other personal obligations"*, while another one stated, *"hmmm I would say my demanding daily routine... the limited free time I had... I could not enter the platform as much as I wanted and did not interact with the rest"*. An undergraduate student reported, *"The fact that I had a lot of stuff going on with my examinations. That is, many times I did not have the time to answer the questions raised by the trainer and did not have time to write my answers or the questions I wanted to do. I was less involved than I should have"*.

A relevant difficulty that many participants faced was the period that the program was delivered. The program was implemented in September, a demanding period both for those who work and for those who attend the University due to the ongoing examinations. An employed graduate reported, *"It was at the beginning of September when the new school year started, so it was a bit difficult"*, while an undergraduate student commented, *"the program took place during a transitional period in September, when I did not have a stable program yet"*.

Finally, two participants stated that Google+ community space was a difficult task, as they had no prior experience in using it. However, this holdup subsided during the program. The first participant responded, *"The truth is that I found difficult using the platform. I had not used it before, and it seemed very difficult at first. Of course, I got used to it"*, while the second one commented, *"What caused me difficulties was the Google platform. I have not used it, even though I have a Google account but mostly for e-mails. Nevertheless, I got used to it after the first week"*.

According to participants' views, the main barrier they faced was the limited time they had, due to various obligations related to their work and/or studies. Furthermore, they perceived this difficulty as

Table 3. Subcategories of barriers to participation

Subcategories	Frequency
Limited time due to work and studies	15
The time period that the program was delivered	7
Google+ community space was difficult	2

The Contribution of Information Communication Technologies in Online Career Counseling

the reason for not being actively engaged in the discussions. Moreover, the program started on September, a period that participants were not fully available due to work and studies obligations. As far as the learning environment is concerned, Google+ was an unfamiliar environment for two participants and consequently they faced difficulties in that interface. However, both became used to the platform as the online career counseling program was in progress.

Participants' Strategies in Order to Overcome Difficulties

Regarding the above-mentioned barriers, participants developed and adopted strategies, in order to make their engagement in the community feasible and effective. The subcategories of these strategies are presented in Table 4.

All of the participants reported that they used their mobile phones in order to enter the online community. In particular, participants mentioned that they were able to acquire information and notifications, as well as interact with the activities and the rest of the community, while travelling to work, to the University or during their breaks. A graduate commented, *"The fact that it was online helped me. I could check the community, what others have commented or uploaded, while I was on the train. Instead of being on Facebook and WhatsApp, I was reading the material and the conversations of the community"*. An undergraduate student mentioned, *"It was great that it could be accessed through mobile phones. As mobile phones are computers, it was easier. When I was going to the University, I was reading the discussions from the trainer and the trainees. I was working on them. I could respond no matter where I was. I think this resolved many issues"*.

Eight participants decided to dedicate a specific day of the week for completing their assignments and participating in the community. One of them said, *"I was entering the community multiple times per week via my mobile phone, but I had one day set to carry out my assignments"*. Another student reported, *"The program offered me information, so I decided to dedicate a specific day for completing the activities"*.

Another strategy adopted by the participants was rearranging their free time. According to their statements, some of them decided to devote their personal time, namely from relaxation and hobbies. A participant commented, *"...with effective time management. I was trying to use my free time"*, while another one stated, *"by organizing effectively my time and by dedicating time from my hobbies to engaging with the community"*. An employed graduate mentioned, *"I was trying to steal time from my sleep. It was the easiest way"*.

Some of the participants took advantage of a technological option provided by Google+; namely, they activated the e-mail notifications, so when a community member shared something, an e-mail notifica-

Table 4. Subcategories of participants' strategies for overcoming barriers

Subcategories	Frequency
Using mobile phones	15
Define a specific day of the week	8
Rearranging personal free time	5
Activating Google+ e-mail notifications	2
Getting reminders from other members of the community	1
Prioritizing tasks	1

tion was sent. One of them mentioned, "*I was getting e-mails. Therefore, I was entering the community and was able to be updated*".

Another student referred that she was communicating with other participants and sometimes they reminded each other of activities that should be completed by the end of the week. She described, "*I was texting with some people that we came closer, and we were supporting each other. I remember once that I had forgotten to upload a video and X reminded me to do so*".

Finally, one student reported that he had to set priorities even though this was a difficult task. "*I managed to handle it* [the time constraints related to his work] *by prioritizing my learning. Of course, this was not easy*".

Therefore, participants reported that the main strategy to overcome the barriers they faced was by using their mobile phones. This strategy is linked with the online and distance delivery mode of the program. Due to time and space flexibility, all of the participants used their phones to access the community, interact with the material, share their views and communicate with the members of the community. Another common strategy was that participants set a specific day of the week for engaging with the activities. The strategy constitutes a result of personal time management, as well as flexible learning. Similarly, several participants adopted strategies such as free-time rearrangement and prioritizing, while others preferred either a social strategy by which they reminded activities and assignments to each other or a technological strategy by activating Google+ e-mail notifications.

Participants' Assessment for the Online Career Counseling Program

The second section of the semi-structured interviews aimed at inquiring participants' views regarding the assessment of the online career counseling program and includes the positive and negative features of the program. The subcategories of the positive features reach the second level of analysis and are presented in Table 5.

One of the features that participants positively assessed was the learning material. According to their views, the learning material developed for the program, was complete, well organized and of high quality. Furthermore, the learning material was perceived as useful and intuitive, linked to both participants' real needs and labor's market requirements, while the use of multiple media (videos, text, webpages and other resources) was also addressed. A student commented, "*Positive elements were the completeness of information, the practical advice I received and material's connection with my needs*". Another one referred, "*The usefulness of the training material*", while a graduate student stated, "*The material is relevant to my real needs and the requirements of the labor market*".

The trainer/career counselor of the program was also perceived as a positive feature of the online career counseling program. Participants described that the trainer was punctual, directly responding to their questions and concerns and was constantly available in the community. The fact that he promoted the discussions, encouraged active engagement and ownership, as well as provided participants with feedback were also positive attributes. A student mentioned, "*My personal communication with the trainer regarding the practical part, as well as his feedback and recommendations were very important to me*". Another participant commented, "*The trainer was excellent, he was actually there! Constantly present and explained in detail all the questions that I had*", while a graduate stated, "*The fact that the trainer provided us with challenges and stimuli for discussion and reflection. He was not providing answers directly. Instead he encouraged me to find them on my own*".

Table 5. Subcategories of program's positive features

Subcategories	Frequency
1 LEARNING MATERIAL	15
1.1 Complete	
1.2 Well organized	
1.3 Quality	
1.4 Useful	
1.5 Intuitive	
1.6 Multimodal	
2 TRAINER/CAREER COUNSELOR	15
2.1 Punctual	
2.2 Encouraging	
2.3 Direct response	
2.4 Provided feedback	
2.5 Continuous presence in the community	
3 ONLINE DELIVERY MODE	13
3.1 Time flexibility	
3.2 Spatial flexibility	
3.3 Informal dimension of the program	
4 PROGRAM'S ORGANISATION	12
4.1 Program structure	
4.2 Clear instructions	
4.3 Implementation period	
5 PROGRAM'S CONTRIBUTION	11
5.1 Social learning	
5.2 Reflection	
5.3 Misconceptions' resolution	
5.4 Self-management skills	
6 LEARNING APPLICABILITY	11
6.1 Linking theory and practice	
6.2 Preparation of personal branding tools	
7 PROGRAM'S GENERAL FEATURES	11
7.1 Free	
7.2 Useful	
7.3 Interesting	

A third positive feature of the program refers to the online delivery mode; namely, the program afforded flexibility in terms of time and accessibility. Participants were able to access the community via any device that has internet anytime and in any place. In addition, the online community established the sense of an informal process, a feature that enabled participants to feel more comfortable. Some students reported, "*It was online and therefore time and space flexible*", "*I liked the flexibility; I could access the community wherever I was*", "*I was able to keep up with what was happening everywhere through my mobile phone*". Another student made the following comment, "*I liked the informal way of the whole process. I could talk more openly and freely both with the rest of the participants and our trainer. Perhaps because we were in distance... I do not know*".

Twelve participants acknowledged the program's organization as one of the positive features of their experience. In particular, they refer to the structure and clarity of the instructions. The implementation of the program was also a positive feature for some participants, as September is the month that most of the postgraduate programs start and more job vacancies are announced. One student described, "*The structure of the program was very well organized and of course it was easy to understand it's function*", while another one stated, "*I knew from the beginning what I was doing, how I would do it and when. It was very organized. To be honest, I did not expect that. I have participated in other programs, but there was not such organization and support*". Furthermore, a participant reported, "*It was at the beginning of the year, when calls for postgraduate studies and job vacancies are published*".

Some additional positive features that participants perceived can be classified in a broad category, namely the contribution of the online career counseling program. Some participants liked –and a specific student realized for the first time– the fact that they were able to learn from each other, while others laid more emphasis on the reflection related to the program. Some students referred to the resolution of misconceptions they had regarding their personal branding tools and fewer participants highlighted the acquisition of skills related to these tools. Indicative references include, "*We also learned from each other. First, I did not realize it, but I learned many new things from the rest*", "*I loved the section "I did not know that... I learned to..." I found it very original*" [this section was part of each unit and encouraged participants to reflect on their learning]. A participant commented, "*It helped me to solve misconceptions I had. For example that I will write a CV and send it to multiple job vacancies*", while another one reported, "*I have learned how I can write my resume and to effectively manage my LinkedIn profile*".

The applicability of learning has also been addressed as a positive characteristic of the online career counseling program. Participants pointed out that one of the most important feature was that they were able to put into practice everything they have learned during the program. Some statements refer, "*It was the practical aspect of the program. By the end of it, I have learned how to build my CV, write my Cover Letter and manage my LinkedIn account*", "*I enjoyed the process of applying what I have learned and not remain at the level of theory*" and "*The practical dimension of the program is the most positive element*".

Finally, eleven participants numbered the absence of cost, the interest and the usefulness among the positive features of the program. Some students commented, "*It was free and beneficial*", "*The program was free, interesting and useful to me*" and "*It was free and something I needed*"

Therefore, according to participants' views the quality and usefulness of the program in general, as well as aspects such as the learning material, the trainer/career counselor, the delivery mode and the applicability of learning constituted the positive features of the online career counseling program.

Participants' views regarding the negative features of the program formed five subcategories that are presented in Table 6.

The most frequent negative feature that participants referred to, was the short length of the online career counseling program and therefore the limited time they had. According to their statements, due to limited time, the development of sufficient interactions with the community members was hindered,

Table 6. Subcategories of program's negative features

Subcategories	Frequency
1 PROGRAM'S SHORT LENGTH	11
1.1 Insufficient time for developing interactions	
1.2 Insufficient time for developing personal branding tools	
1.3 More time for extra modules	
2 COMMUNITY SPACE	5
2.1 Difficult interface	
2.2 Notifications	
3 NUMBER OF PARTICIPANTS	
4. THE EXISTENCE OF A SINGLE TRAINER/CAREER COUNSELOR	3
5. LACK OF F2F INTERACTION	2

while at the same time there was not enough time for completing the assignments and activities of the program. A participant described, *"My limited time did not allow me to adequately engage in communicating with others"*, while another one reported, *"The thematic units of the program did not last long. If there was more time, it would surely be better"*. Moreover, limited time also influenced participants social behavior in a negative way. Namely, some participants did not communicate with other members, as they were feeling shy. Therefore, there was not sufficient time for participants to get to know with each other. One of the students mentioned, *"In the beginning, we did not talk to each other, maybe we were shy"*. In relation to personal branding tools' development, participants commented, *"The practical part needed a lot of time"*, *"I needed too much time to prepare my tools (CV, Cover Letter). Sometimes, it was difficult for me; perhaps one week for each unit was not enough"*. However, four participants reported that they would need an extended version of the program to integrate additional modules. Those students made the following comments, *"The duration of the program was short. I would like more time and more topics covered"* and *"I would like extra topics, such as work placement. But time was limited...I think"*.

Google+ community space was another negative feature, highlighted by five participants. Having no prior experience and familiarization with the Google+ community space caused navigation difficulties. Other students referred to Google+ email notifications they received when community members shared or commented on a post. Therefore, the amount of e-mails per day was vast. Some indicative statements described, *"I was struggling with the platform as I have not used it before"*, *"Google+ may confuse the user. Especially a novice just like me"* and *"The Google+ platform made it hard for me to focus on each module"*. Other participants mentioned, *"I've been getting a lot of community notifications in my email"*, *"Google+ Platform and notifications were really inconvenient"*.

Furthermore, three community members have also assessed participants' number in the community negatively. The reasons lie on the fact that too many members created a great extent of content via sharing, posting and commenting, while at the same time was a hindering factor for those who did not feel comfortable enough in contributing to the dialogue. One of them commented, *"It was not easy to join all of the discussions; there were so many"*. Similarly, others stated, *"I think thirty-five people were too many. It was not easy to keep up with the discussions"* and *"You could not talk comfortably with 35 people in the community... it was difficult"*.

Two community members reported that the existence of a single trainer/career counselor was also a negative feature of the online career counseling program. In particular, their arguments refer to the fact that in case at least another trainer/career counselor was present, they would gain additional perspectives on the topics discussed, but also would be easier and more flexible for the current trainer/career counselor. A student stated, *"I would like extra trainers to get involved, in order to have an extra view"*, while another mentioned, *"I think another trainer would be better both for us and the trainer because he would also have more flexibility"*

Finally, the lack of f2finteractionwas also a negative feature of the program. Participants did not have the opportunity to meet with the rest of the participants and the trainer, while the only source of visual representation were the profile photos. A student reported, *"There was no f2f communication both with the trainer and the trainees"*. Similarly, another participant made the following comment, *"I have not seen (beyond the profile photo) neither the instructor nor the others"*.

Therefore, according to participants' views the program's length and the consequent insufficiencies regarding social interactions, completion of the activities and assignments were perceived as negative features. In addition, Google+ community space, e-mail notifications and participants' number also formed feelings of inconvenience. The existence of a single trainer/career counselor as well as the lack of f2f interactions also emerged as negative features of the program.

SOLUTIONS AND RECOMMENDATIONS

A few suggestions for improving the quality of the services provided in the online career counseling program were formulated by the researchers. These recommendations may benefit future iterations of the program, but also other career counselors, trainers and researchers while designing corresponding programs.

Firstly, the duration of the program could be extended to accommodate participants' needs and ease their concerns. Consequently, time flexibility would contribute in adequate and effective interaction with their peers and the learning material. At the same time, the extension of the program implies the potentiality of enriching the learning material with additional resources and activities, as well as adding new modules and topics of discussion. Therefore, the second suggestion refers to content and context enrichment. Content enrichment has already been discussed; Context enrichment may include the participation of experts, such as HR Employees, Employers, Professors and Career Counselors, that they will add multiple perspectives in the dialogue, provide insights and real-life experiences, as well as promote the applicability of participants' learning. Context enrichment may also imply the use of synchronous messaging via chatting, as well as videoconference platforms and tools. Thirdly, the online delivery mode of the program did not make it possible for the participants to meet and communicate f2f. Therefore, a blended mode in which online and f2f meetings of the community members will take place may bring added value. However, a blended approach of the program may hinder the participation of people who cannot attend. As a result, an alternative suggestion would be to set up non-compulsory and informal meetings at cafes or at the university, in which community members will have the opportunity to become familiar with each other and discuss.

Regarding Google+, at this moment, the community space has been permanently closed. According to MacMillan and MacMillan (2018), Google has discovered a bug that enabled outside developers to gain access in personal private data. Therefore, an alternative platform should be sought to meet the needs and goals of the program. Participants' number constitutes another important recommendation. The number of participants should be less in order both trainees and trainers to be effective and keep up with the flow of the community. In that way, social interactions may be enhanced, and more introverted participants may be benefited. Finally, reflection needs to be emphasized and promoted in the framework of online career counseling programs. Guiding and assisting participants to reflect on what they learn, is one of the most important things of their learning. This reflective process empowers participants to apply what they have learned in real-life situations and therefore promotes their career self-management skills.

FUTURE RESEARCH DIRECTIONS

The present study resulted in suggesting some future research directions regarding Distance Education, Open Distance Learning and Online Career Counseling. It would be rather interesting to inquire whether participants' diversity may influence the social interactions among community members, as well as learning achievement. Which benefits and pitfalls would emerge if a community would be highly homogeneous or heterogeneous respectively? Are there any adaptation patterns? If so, what do these patterns reflect and how could they inform research and practitioners? Another, research attempt may focus on exploring the effectiveness of a blended approach in Online Career Counseling, given that no verified data exist for determining which delivery mode –f2f, DE, or a combination of two– is more effective (Simonson, Smaldino, Albright, & Zvacek, 2014). However, the combination of online and f2f meetings is expected, at least, to differentiate both the learning environment and participants' relationships and behaviors. However, how would a blended career counseling program evolve? What parameters may facilitate or hinder the learning process? What kind of learning principles and techniques may prove to be more effective?

CONCLUSION

The vast majority of the participants reported that the primary reason for attending the online counseling program was their interest and perceived usefulness of the topics covered. In addition, participants assessed positively the program's effectiveness in terms of importance, usefulness and interest. This finding is supported by the research that Hartnett, St. George and Dron (2011) conducted and implies that both identified regulation and intrinsic motivation were equally important for the participants of the present study. Another factor that shaped participants' motivation was the applicability of learning and the practical orientation of the program according to their needs. According to Baldwin and Ford (1988) in order students' learning experience to be meaningful, learning should be applicable. Similarly, Merrill (2002) suggests that learners need to apply the knowledge they acquire to facilitate learning, while Collis and Moonen (2006) mention that learning is facilitated when contribution-oriented activities relate to real-world problems. Several participants also reported that the online delivery mode of the program and the consequent time and distance flexibility enhanced their participation in the online program. Barron (1999) as well as Sun, Tsai, Finger, Chen, and Yeh (2008) reached, among other, to the same conclusions. The absence of costs and curiosity were also factors that influenced participants' motivation. Regarding the element of curiosity, it has also emerged in the research conducted by Panagiotakopoulos, Lionarakis and Xenos (2003).

According to participants' views, the main difficulties that they faced during the program was their limited time, due to various obligations related to their work and/or studies. It should be noted, that most of the students who drop out of DE are facing issues related to their work, studies, as well as to family responsibilities (Oliveira, Oesterreich, &Almeida, 2017). Another important barrier that participants faced, mainly at the beginning of the program, was the Google+ community space that caused various difficulties. As Valentine (2002) describes, problems related to hardware and software in the learning environment can be frustrating.

Nevertheless, to overcome these difficulties, participants adopted various strategies. The main strategy adopted by the majority of the participants was mobile phone use. This strategy is linked with the online and distance delivery mode of the program. Due to time and space flexibility, all of the participants used their phones to access the community, interact with the material, share their views and communicate with the members of the community. The present finding is in line with the content presented in the Horizon Report. In particular, as the processing power of technological devices increases dramatically, mobile learning provides learners the opportunity to access materials anywhere, often across various devices (Adams Becker, Cummins, Davis, Freeman, Giesinger, &Ananthanarayanan, 2017). Another common strategy among the participants was setting a specific day of the week for engaging with the activities of the program. This finding suggests that participants were highly self-motivated and self-disciplined, characteristics that have been pointed out in research conducted by Palloff and Pratt (2003).

The practical implication that can be set out from these findings is that the program accommodated participants' motivational factors, as most of them were included in the positive elements of the program in the summative assessment and therefore highlights the need of inquiring not only participants' needs but also their motivation. Furthermore, according to participants' views, the online career counseling program was perceived as effective, even though that negative elements existed. Hence, when participants' needs and expectations are met, some factors are still perceived of minor importance. However, further studies are necessary in order to reach safe conclusions.

REFERENCES

Adams Becker, S., Cummins, M., Davis, A., Freeman, A., Hall Giesinger, C., & Ananthanarayanan, V. (2017). *NMC Horizon Report: 2017 Higher Education Edition*. Austin, TX: The New Media Consortium.

American Psychological Association Dictionary. (n.d.a). *Career Counseling*. Retrieved May 20, 2019, from https://dictionary.apa.org/career-counseling

American Psychological Association Dictionary. (n.d.b). *Counseling Psychology*. Retrieved May 20, 2019, from https://dictionary.apa.org/counseling-psychology

Baldwin, T. T., & Ford, J. K. (1988). Transfer of learning: A review and directions for future research. *Personnel Psychology*, *4*(1), 63–105. doi:10.1111/j.1744-6570.1988.tb00632.x

Barak, A. (1999). Psychological applications on the internet: A discipline on the threshold of a new millennium. *Applied & Preventive Psychology*, *8*(4), 231–245. doi:10.1016/S0962-1849(05)80038-1

Barron, A. (1999). *A Teacher's Guide to Distance learning*. Florida Center for Instructional Technology, College of Education, University of South Florida. Retrieved May 20, 2019, from https://fcit.usf.edu/distance/

Beel, N. & Court, J.H. (2000). Ethical issues in counselling over the internet: an examination of the risks and benefits. *Ethical Issues in Internet Counselling*, *4*(2), 35-42.

Bergamin, P. B., Ziska, S., & Groner, R. (2012). The relationship between flexible and self-regulated learning in open and distance universities. *International Review of Research in Open and Distributed Learning*, *13*(2), 102–123. doi:10.19173/irrodl.v13i2.1124

Bischoff, R. J. (2004). Considerations in the use of telecommunications as a primary treatment medium: The application of behavioral telehealth to marriage and family therapy. *The American Journal of Family Therapy*, *32*(3), 173–187. doi:10.1080/01926180490437376

Boer, P. M. (2001). *Career counseling over the internet: An emerging model for trusting and responding to online clients*. Mahwah, NJ: Lawrence Erlbaum Associates Publishers.

Branch, R. M. (2009). *Instructional design: The ADDIE approach*. New York, NY: Springer. doi:10.1007/978-0-387-09506-6

Chester, A., & Glass, C. A. (2006). Online counselling: A descriptive analysis of therapy services on the internet. *British Journal of Guidance & Counselling*, *34*(2), 145–160. doi:10.1080/03069880600583170

Cohen, L., Manion, L., & Morrison, K. (2018). *Research methods in education*. New York, NY: Routledge.

Collis, B., & Moonen, J. (2006). The contributing student: Learners as co-developers of learning resources for reuse in web environments. In D. Hung & M. S. Khine (Eds.), *Engaged learning with emerging technologies* (pp. 49–67). Dordrecht: Springer. doi:10.1007/1-4020-3669-8_3

Dick, W., Carey, L., & Carey, J. O. (2009). *The systematic design of instruction*. Upper Saddle River, NJ: Merrill/Pearson.

Dowling, M., & Rickwood, D. (2013). Online counseling and therapy for mental health problems: A systematic review of individual synchronous interventions using chat. *Journal of Technology in Human Services*, *31*(1), 1–21. doi:10.1080/15228835.2012.728508

Efstathiou, G. (2009). Students' psychological web consulting: Function and outcome evaluation. *British Journal of Guidance & Counselling*, *37*(3), 243–255. doi:10.1080/03069880902956983

Finfgeld, D. L. (1999). Psychotherapy in cyberspace. *Journal of the American Psychiatric Nurses Association*, *5*(4), 105–110. doi:10.1177/107839039900500401

Finn, J. (2002). MSW student perceptions of the efficacy and ethics of internet-based therapy. *Journal of Social Work Education*, *38*(3), 403–419. doi:10.1080/10437797.2002.10779107

Finn, J., & Banach, M. (2000). Victimization online: The down side of seeking human services for women on the internet. *Cyberpsychology & Behavior*, *3*(5), 243–254. doi:10.1089/109493100316102

Gagné, R. M., Wager, W. W., Goals, K., & Keller, J. (2005). *Principles of instructional design*. Belmont, CA: Wadsworth.

Gatti, F. M., Brivio, E., & Calciano, S. (2016). Hello! I know you help people here, right? A qualitative study of young people's acted motivations in text-based counseling. *Children and Youth Services Review*, *71*, 27–35. doi:10.1016/j.childyouth.2016.10.029

Gkiosos, I., Mavroeidis, I., & Koutsoumpa, M. (2008). Η έρευνα στην από απόσταση εκπαίδευση: Ανασκόπηση και προοπτικές [Distance education research: Review and prospects]. *Open Education-The Journal for Open and Distance Education and Educational Technology*, *4*(1), 49–60.

Gravani, M. N., Hatzinikita, V., & Zarifis, G. K. (2012). Factors influencing adult distance teaching and learning processes: The case of the Open University. *International Journal of Learning*, *18*(5), 307–319.

Gunawardena, C. N., & McIsaac, M. S. (2004). Distance education. In D. H. Jonassen (Ed.), *Handbook of research on educational communications and technology*. London: Lawrence Erlbaum Associates Publishers.

Haberstroh, S., Parr, G., Bradley, L., Morgan-Fleming, B., & Gee, R. (2008). Facilitating online counseling: Perspectives from counselors in training. *Journal of Counseling and Development*, *86*(4), 460–470. doi:10.1002/j.1556-6678.2008.tb00534.x

Hartnett, M., St. George, A., & Dron, J. (2011). Examining motivation in online distance learning environments: Complex, multifaceted, and situation-dependent. *International Review of Research in Open and Distance Learning*, *12*(6), 20–38. doi:10.19173/irrodl.v12i6.1030

Jackson, N. J. (n.d.) Lifewide learning and education in universities & colleges: Concepts and conceptual Aids. In N. Jackson & J. Willis (Eds.), *Lifewide learning and education in universities & colleges* (pp. 1-27). Academic Press. Retrieved May 20, 2019, from http://www.learninglives.co.uk/uploads/1/0/8/4/10842717/chapter_a1.pdf

Karavakou, V. (2011). Το φάσμα και η πρό(σ)κληση της δια βίου μάθησης [The spectrum and call/challenge for lifelong learning]. In V. Karavakou (Ed.), *Lifelong learning: Interdisciplinary approaches* (pp. 1–32). Thessaloniki, Greece: University of Macedonia Press.

Keegan, D. J. (1980). On defining distance education. *Distance Education*, *1*(1), 13–36. doi:10.1080/0158791800010102

Kentnor, H. (2015). Distance education and the evolution of online learning in the United States. *Curriculum and Teaching Dialogue*, *17*(1 &2), 21–34.

Kidd, J. M. (2006). *Understanding career counselling: Theory, research and practice*. London: Sage Publications.

Kim, J. A. (2000). *Community Building on the Web: Secret strategies for successful online communities*. Berkeley, CA: Peachpit Press.

Kirschner, P. A., & Van Merriënboer, J. J. G. (2008). Ten steps to complex learning: A new approach to instruction and instructional design. In T. L. Good (Ed.), *21st century education: A reference handbook* (pp. 244-253). Thousand Oaks, CA: Sage. doi:10.4135/9781412964012.n26

MacMillan, D., & MacMillan, R. (2018). Google exposed user data, feared repercussions of disclosing to public. *The Wall Street Journal*. Retrieved May 20, 2019, from https://www.wsj.com/articles/google-exposed-user-data-feared-repercussions-of-disclosing-to-public-1539017194

Mallen, M. J., & Vogel, D. L. (2005). Introduction to the major contribution: Counseling psychology and Online Counseling. *The Counseling Psychologist*, *33*(6), 761–775. doi:10.1177/0011000005278623

Mallen, M. J., Vogel, D. L., & Rochlen, A. B. (2005). The practical aspects of online counselling: Ethics, training, technology and competency. *The Counseling Psychologist*, *33*(6), 776–818. doi:10.1177/0011000005278625

Maples, M. F., & Han, S. (2008). Cybercounseling in the United States and South Korea: Implications for counseling college students of the millennial generation and the networked generation. *Journal of Counseling and Development*, *86*(2), 178–183. doi:10.1002/j.1556-6678.2008.tb00495.x

Mayring, P. (2000). Qualitative content analysis [28 paragraphs]. *Forum Qualitative Sozialforschung/Forum: Qualitative. Social Research*, *1*(2), 20. Retrieved from http://nbn-resolving.de/urn:nbn:de:0114-fqs0002204

Merrill, M. D. (2002). First principles of instruction. *Educational Technology Research and Development*, *50*(3), 43–59. doi:10.1007/BF02505024

Merrill, M. D. (2007). First principles of instruction: a synthesis. In R. A. Reiser & J. V. Dempsey (Eds.), *Trends and issues in instructional design and technology* (pp. 62–71). Upper Saddle River, NJ: Pearson.

Merrill, M. D. (2009). First principles of instruction. In C. M. Reigeluth & A. Carr (Eds.), *Instructional design theories and models: Building a common knowledge base* (Vol. 3). New York, NY: Routledge Publishers.

Oliveira, P. R. d., Oesterreich, S. A., & Almeida, V. L. d. (2017). School dropout in graduate distance education: Evidence from a study in the interior of Brazil. *Educação e Pesquisa, 44*, 1–20.

Organisation for Economic Co-operation and Development & European Commission. (2004). *Career guidance: A handbook for policy makers.* Retrieved May 20, 2019, from http://www.oecd.org/education/innovation-education/34060761.pdf

Palloff, R. M., & Pratt, K. (2003). *The virtual student: A profile and guide to working with online learners.* San Francisco, CA: Jossey-Bass.

Panagiotakopoulos, C., Lionarakis, A., & Xenos, M. (2003). Open and distance learning: tools of information and communication technologies for effective learning. *Proceedings of the 6th Hellenic European Research on Computer Mathematics and its Applications Conference.*

Pelling, N. (2009). The use of email and the internet in counselling and psychological service: What practitioners need to know. *Counselling, Psychotherapy, and Health, 5*(1), 1–25.

Richards, D., & Vigano, N. (2013). Online counseling: A narrative and critical review of the literature. *Journal of Clinical Psychology, 69*(9), 994–1011. doi:10.1002/jclp.21974 PMID:23630010

Rodriguez, C. O. (2012). MOOCs and the AI-Stanford like courses: Two successful and distinct courses formats for massive open online courses. *European Journal of Open Distance and E-Learning, 2*, 1–13.

Rubin, H. J., & Rubin, I. S. (2012). *Qualitative interviewing: The art of hearing data.* Thousand Oaks, CA: Sage Publications.

Salleh, A., Hamzah, R., Nordin, N., Ghavifekr, S., & Joorabchi, T. N. (2015). Online counseling using email: A qualitative study. *Asia Pacific Education Review, 16*(4), 549–563. doi:10.100712564-015-9393-6

Sergiovanni, J. T. (1994). *Building community in schools.* San Francisco, CA: Jossey-Bass.

Simonson, M., Smaldino, S., Albright, M., & Zvacek, S. (2014). *Teaching and learning at a distance: Foundations of distance education.* Charlotte, NC: IAP–Information Age Publishing, Inc.

Skikos, N., Louka, V., Zwgopoulos, E., & Moschoudi, A. (2010). Η μεθοδολογία εκπαίδευσης ενηλίκων στην εξ αποστάσεως επιμόρφωση εκπαιδευτικών [Adult education methodology in distance learning teachers' training]. *Proceedings of the 2ndPanhellenic Educational Conference of Imathia "Digital and Online Applications in Education".*

Skinner, A., & Zack, J. S. (2004). Counseling and the internet. *The American Behavioral Scientist, 48*(4), 434–446. doi:10.1177/0002764204270280

Skolverket. (2000). *Lifelong learning and lifewide learning*. Retrieved May 20, 2019, from https://moodle.fct.unl.pt/pluginfile.php/32501/mod_glossary/attachment/10340/lifelong_and_lifewide.pdf

Smith, P. L., & Ragan, T. J. (2005). *Instructional design*. New York, NY: John Wiley & Sons, Inc.

Suler, J. (2000). Psychotherapy in cyberspace: A 5-dimensional model of online and computer-mediated psychotherapy. *Cyberpsychology & Behavior*, *3*(2), 151–159. doi:10.1089/109493100315996

Suler, J. (2011). The psychology of text relationships. In R. Kraus, G. Stricker, & C. Speyer (Eds.), *Online counseling: A handbook for mental health professionals* (pp. 21–53). San Diego, CA: Academic Press. doi:10.1016/B978-0-12-378596-1.00002-2

Sun, P., Tsai, R., Finger, G., Chen, Y., & Yeh, D. (2008). What drives a successful e-learning? An empirical investigation of the critical factors influencing learner satisfaction. *Computers & Education*, *50*(4), 1183–1202. doi:10.1016/j.compedu.2006.11.007

Sussman, R. J. (2004). Counseling over the internet: Benefits and challenges in the use of new technologies. In G. R. Waltz & C. Kirkman (Eds.), *Cyberbytes: Highlighting compelling uses of technology in counseling* (pp. 17–20). Greensboro, NC: ERIC Clearinghouse on Counseling and Student Services.

Tyler, M. J., & Guth, L. J. (2003). Understanding online counseling services through a review of definitions and elements necessary for change. In J. W. Bloom & G. R. Walz (Eds.), Cybercounseling and cyberlearning: An encore. ERIC Document Reproduction Service No. ED 481146.

Valentine, D. (2002). Distance Learning: Promises, Problems, and Possibilities. *Online Journal of Distance Learning Administration*, *5*(3). Retrieved from https://www.westga.edu/~distance/ojdla/fall53/valentine53.html

Van Merriënboer, J. J. G., Clark, R. E., & de Croock, M. B. M. (2002). Blueprints for complex learning: The 4C/ID-model. *Educational Technology Research and Development*, *50*(2), 39–64. doi:10.1007/BF02504993

Van Merriënboer, J. J. G., & Stoyanov, S. (2008). Learners in a changing learning landscape: Reflections from an instructional design perspective. In J. Visser & M. Visser-Valfrey (Eds.), *Learners in a changing learning landscape: Reflections from a dialogue on new roles and expectations*. Dordrecht: Springer. doi:10.1007/978-1-4020-8299-3_4

Wenger, E. (1999). Communities of practice: The structure of knowledge stewarding. In C. Despres & D. Chauvel (Eds.), *Knowledge horizons: The present and the promise of knowledge management* (pp. 205–225). Boston, MA: Butterworth – Heinemann.

Wright, J. (2002). Online counselling: Learning from writing therapy. *British Journal of Guidance & Counselling*, *30*(3), 285–298. doi:10.1080/030698802100002326

Young, K. S. (2005). An empirical examination of client attitudes towards online counseling. *Cyberpsychology & Behavior*, *8*(2), 172–177. doi:10.1089/cpb.2005.8.172 PMID:15938657

Zamani, Z. A., Nasir, R., & Yusooff, F. (2010). Perceptions towards online counseling among counselors in Malaysia. *Procedia: Social and Behavioral Sciences, 5*, 585–589. doi:10.1016/j.sbspro.2010.07.146

ADDITIONAL READING

Brookfield, S. (1986). *Understanding and facilitating adult learning.* San Francisco, CA: Jossey-Bass.

Burns, M. (2011). *Distance education for teacher training: Modes, models and methods.* Washington, DC: Education Development Center.

Jackson, N. (2011). *Learning for a complex world: A lifewide concept of learning, education and personal development.* Authorhouse.

Jackson, N. (2016). *Exploring learning ecologies.* Chalk Mountain. Retrieved May 20, 2019, from http://www.normanjackson.co.uk/uploads/1/0/8/4/10842717/lulu_print_file.pdf

Jones, G., & Stokes, A. (2009). *Online counselling: A handbook for practitioners.* Basingstoke: Palgrave Macmillan. doi:10.1007/978-0-230-23085-9

Kraus, R., Stricker, G., & Speyer, C. (2011). *Online Counseling: A handbook for mental health professionals.* San Diego, CA: Academic Press.

Moore, M. G., & Anderson, W. G. (2003). *Handbook of distance education.* Mahwah, NJ: Lawrence Erlbaum Associates Publishers.

Reiser, R. A., & Dempsey, J. (2017). *Trends and issues in instructional design and technology.* Upper Saddle River, NJ: Pearson.

Rheingold, H. (1993). *The virtual community: Homesteading on the electronic frontier.* New York, NY: Harper Collins.

Saar, E., Ure, O. B., & Holford, J. (2013). *Lifelong learning in Europe: National patterns and challenges.* Cheltenham: Edward Elgar Publishing.

KEY TERMS AND DEFINITIONS

Flexible Learning: Learning in which specific factors such as content, time, space, mode, and pace are determined by the learner.

Instructional Design: The process of inquiring participants' needs, goals, expectations, motivation and barriers to participation in order to define specific learning outcomes, which are expected to be achieved upon completion of the teaching and learning activities, as well as of the assessment tasks that have been designed in an earlier phase.

Lifelong Learning: Learning that occurs throughout the life span including formal, informal and non-formal learning.

Lifewide Learning: Learning that occurs in various settings including formal, informal and non-formal learning.

Online Career Counseling: Professional counseling sessions delivered through Information Communication Technologies and focus on assisting people—of any age and at any point throughout their lives—make career-related decisions, educational, training and occupational choices, deal with career-related issues and manage their careers.

Online Community: An online space in which members of the community interact with each other and share at least one common belief, aim or concern.

Personal Branding Tools: Tools that introduce an individual, in terms of personality traits, aptitudes, knowledge, skills, and attitudes; indicative forms include curriculum vitae, resume, personal statement, LinkedIn profile.

ENDNOTES

[1] Institutional profile retrieved on May 20, 2019, from https://www.auth.gr/en/uni.

[2] Further information regarding Lifewide Learning research can be found in Norman Jackson's work (2011, 2016), one of the main researchers who thoroughly examines the concept of Lifewide Learning. See the additional reading section.

[3] Counseling Psychology and Career Counseling are two different disciplines. According to the American Psychological Association, Counseling Psychology is *"the branch of psychology that specializes in facilitating personal and interpersonal functioning across the lifespan. Counseling psychology focuses on emotional, social, vocational, educational, health-related, developmental, and organizational concerns—such as improving well-being, alleviating distress and maladjustment, and resolving crises—and addresses issues from individual, family, group, systems, and organizational perspectives. The counseling psychologist has received professional education and training in one or more counseling areas, such as educational, vocational, employee, aging, personal, marriage, or rehabilitation counseling"* (American Psychological Association Dictionairy, n.d.b), while Career Counseling is defined as *"consultation, advice, or guidance specifically focused on a person's career opportunities, most often provided in educational, work, and some community settings. It also may have the specific goal of enabling a person to change the direction of his or her career. The counseling will take account of an individual's preferences, intelligence, skill sets, work values, and experience. Such counseling is offered to groups as well as individuals. Also called career guidance"* (American Psychological Association Dictionairy, n.d.a).

[4] According to Mallen and Vogel (2005), Online Counseling is defined as "any delivery of mental and behavioral health services, including but not limited to therapy, consultation, and psychoeducation, by a licensed practitioner to a client in a non-FtF setting through distance communication technologies such as the telephone, asynchronous e-mail, synchronous chat, and videoconferencing" (p. 764). However, the researchers of the present study have not located any definition for Online Career Counseling. Therefore, they define Online Career Counseling as "professional counseling sessions delivered through Information Communication Technologies and focus on assisting people—of any age and at any point throughout their lives—make career-related decisions, educational, training and occupational choices, deal with career-related issues and manage their careers".

Chapter 9
Ubiquitous Learning for New Generation Learners' Expectations

Tarık Kişla
Ege University, Turkey

Bahar Karaoğlan
Ege University, Turkey

ABSTRACT

It cannot be denied that environmental influence has a great effect on the characteristics of individuals: reason why people can be profiled with their generation. Generation is a collection of lifespans which fall into a time duration when major changes have occurred. The last decades are labeled as information and technology era where the world is witnessing great changes in lifestyles that go in parallel with the speed of evolving digital technology. Young people born after 2000 are categorized as "Generation Z," who are born into a world of IT technology and are independent, social individuals competent in using technology and mostly interested in technology-driven/enabled events and devices. Due to this fact, portable/wearable smart devices may be used to offer new opportunities for delivering education tailored according to situational needs and preferences of these people. In this chapter, after touching distinctive characteristics of the generations, concepts regarding ubiquitous learning and how it aligns with the aspirations and values of Generation Z are highlighted.

DOI: 10.4018/978-1-5225-9779-7.ch009

INTRODUCTION

The major changes that happen over time have a considerable impact on the behaviors, beliefs, attitudes and habits of the individuals. Such individuals, who have been subject to similar life events and who have accumulated similar life experiences growing up, tend to have similar attitudes, beliefs, habits and characteristics. The term 'generation' defines a group of people who are born within the same timeframe and who, generally, have similar experiences. In literature, all generations, past to present, have been classified under 6 titles: G.I Generation, the Silent Generation, the Baby Boomers, Generation X, Generation Y/Millennial and Generation Z (McCrindle, & Wolfinger, 2009; DelCampo, Haggerty & Haney, 2010). Grose (2011) has expressed his opinion on generation as "Gender, religion and social classes may influence you, but it is your generation that defines and distinguishes who you are. It defines your identity". When considered from this aspect, learning expectations and needs of each generation are different. Today, many educators are clearly aware that they need to adjust education strategies according to the needs of the learners (McCrindle, 2008). In order to provide efficient education and learning, we need to understand the new generation's expectations from education and then, re-evaluate our approaches, methods and techniques, and maybe even our learning environments to ensure that they meet the expectations and values of our students. Thus, the real issue is to understand how to handle the complexity of this new generation and to be able to offer them meaningful and creative learning and education tools. At this point, enabling technology-supported learning environments becomes quite important.

Technological developments that have occurred over the years are one of the most important reasons that have caused changes in learning and education. For example, the rise and widespread use of the Internet introduced the concept of e-learning and caused considerable changes on the structure of distance education. Similarly, mobile technologies that have emerged within the last years, allow the users to access information that matches their needs "anytime, anywhere". This opportunity increased the potential of the researches, who wish to advance the quality and prevalence of education, to create new learning environments. At this juncture, development of learning approaches, especially e-learning, m-learning, and p-learning, accelerated. Ubiquitous learning is one of the new approaches that have evolved from these developments. Ubiquitous learning, which is based on the "Ubiquitous Computing" concept introduced by Mark Weiser towards the end of the 1980s, aims to set up a learning process that is constantly in interaction with the individuals and that is geared towards the needs of the individuals (Zhang, 2008). According to Graf, ubiquitous learning has emerged from combination of mobile learning and informal learning (Graf, 2008).

The objective of this section is to determine how well the ubiquitous learning approach meets the expectations of the new generation students (generation Z). In line with this objective, ubiquitous learning, generations, distinctive characteristics of the new generation and the new generation's expectations from education are discussed under section entitled "Background". Afterwards, the findings of the mixed methods research, carried out by the researchers to determine the expectations of Generation Z students from education and how well the characteristics of ubiquitous learning correspond to these expectations, are presented.

BACKGROUND

Ubiquitous Learning

Ubiquitous learning can be defined as a daily learning environment that is supported by mobile/ embedded computers and wireless networks with the aim to provide learners content and interaction anytime and anywhere (Hwang, Tsai, & Yang, 2008; Ogata, Matsuka, El-Bishouty, & Yano. 2009). Ubiquitous learning involves real life experience. Learning process, content, targets and activities are designed according to the areas of interest, cognitive characteristics, past experiences and the environment of the learner (Kinshuk & Graf, 2012). According to Ogata and Yano (2004), ubiquitous learning combines the informal learning environments and high mobility, whereby the student acts with a mobile device and the system supports learning in a dynamic way by communicating with the embedded computers in the environment.

One of the pedagogical approaches underlying ubiquitous learning is called situated learning (Lave, 1991; Clancey, 1995). Situated learning is based on the idea that real learning is acquired from real activities of daily life. This approach argues that learning is acquired via relationship between individuals and by associating past information with informal and, usually, unwanted contextual learning. One other pedagogical approach underlying ubiquitous learning is learning based on collaboration involving social interaction.

Learning is evolving and improving. In this context, Yahya, Ahmad, and Jalil (2010) state that e-learning has transformed into m(mobile)-learning, and m-learning has evolved to ubiquitous learning. From many aspects, it can be said that ubiquitous learning is more flexible and has a more dynamic structure when compared to e-learning and m-learning (Park, 2011). The main characteristics of ubiquitous learning are shown in Table 1 (Curtis, Luchini, Bobrowsky, Quintana & Soloway, 2002, Ogata & Yano, 2004).

In order for a true ubiquitous learning experience, (i) technologically, mobile devices with high processing capacities, high communication speed and high-capacity data storage systems are required. Additionally, in order to ensure reliability and scalability of ubiquitous learning systems, they need to be totally cloud-based. Today, these technologies are accessible. The next step is to set up smart and

Table 1. Main characteristics of ubiquitous learning

No.	Characteristic	Explanation
1	Permanency	All learning processes can be continuously recorded. Learners never lose their work unless they purposefully delete it.
2	Accessibility	Learners can access their data, work, documents and multimedia tools anytime and anywhere they like.
3	Immediacy	It is quite easy for learners to access information. The students can access the required data promptly and easily when they encounter a problem.
4	Interactivity	Learners can interact with specialists, teachers or peers in a synchronized or non-synchronized manner. In this way, accessing specialists, therefore trusted information, becomes easier.
5	Situatedness	Learning becomes available anytime and anywhere in our daily lives. This allows the student to encounter problems and issues in a natural way as they arise during daily life.
6	Adaptability	Learners can have the right information at the right place in a learning environment that is customized to them.

customizable learning environments. Developments in the fields of artificial intelligence and educational data mining are promising. (ii) Pedagogically, education programs, education contents, materials and tools are required to be designed to support this dynamic and flexible structure.

Generations

Groups of people, who are born within the same timeframe are referred to as generations. Each generation shares a common social past. In other words, to a large extent, they experience similar social events and they tend to have similar attitudes, behaviors and characteristics. In literature, each generation includes individuals, who were born within a 20-year period. In Table 2, generations defined in the 20th and the 21st centuries (McCrindle, & Wolfinger, 2009; DelCampo, Haggerty & Haney, 2010). Currently, most of the world's living population falls into either of the 4 generations. The starting and ending years shown in Table 2 may slightly change in different sources.

G.I Generation and the Slient Generation

G.I. generation is comprised of individuals born between the years 1900 and 1921. While the individuals of this generation spent their youth going through major income inequality, economic and social upheavals in the world, they were the ones, who experienced the effects of World War II. The Silent generation is comprised of individuals who were born between 1922 and 1943 during the time of great depression.

The Baby Boomers

This generation is known as the generation of individuals, who were born between 1944 and 1960, after World War II. To emphasize the spike in the birth rates during that time, which occurred due to more than one reason, this generation is named as "Baby Boomers". The Baby Boomers have considerable power on economy as they form the majority of the consumers. According to the age wave theory, the economic slowdown has started with the retirement of the Baby Boomers. Being self-centered, deliberate, focused and independent are listed among the characteristics of this generation.

Table 2. Generations

Cohort	Year of Birth
G.I Generation	1900 – 1921
The Silent Generations	1922 – 1943
The Baby Boomers	1944 – 1960
Generation X	1961 – 1980
Millenial / Generation Y	1981 – 2000
Generation Z	2001 - …

Generation X

This generation, which is also known as GenX, is comprised of individuals born between 1961 and 1980. The fall of Berlin Wall, ending of the Cold War, ending of imperialism, rise of the hippies and protests are among the important social events during this period. Additionally, the individuals of this era are considered to be quite affected by the media to the extent that they are named as the MTV Generation in some sources. One of the most important events of this generation, when many technological developments occurred, is personal computers becoming accessible. One other factor that makes this generation important is the fact that Generation X is educating Generation Z.

Generation Y/Millennial

This generation, which covers individuals born between 1981 and 2000, is known as the Millennials, Generation Y or Gen Next. During the childhood of this generation, computers and internet connection were available almost in all of the homes. Therefore, this generation is quite knowledgeable on technology and they are comfortable and confident in the use of technology. During the youth of this generation, the Internet rapidly grew and, the social media emerged and became widespread. This generation not only benefits largely from the Internet for their school studies, but they also the social media tools to communicate with their friends and socialize (Oblinger, 2003). Furthermore, concepts such as flexible working hours, working from home, and freelancing have emerged during the time of this generation.

Generation Z

Following the Millennials generation comes Generation Z, also referred to as iGeneration (iGen), Gen Tech, Gen Wii, Net Gen, Digital Natives, and Plurals. Even though the date range defined for Generation Z is from the mid-90's through the second decade of this century, the date range differs from source to source (Taylor, 2011; Seemiller and Grace, 2016). Of all the generations, Generation Z embodies the highest number of individuals. When compared to the other generations, the members of this generation have more of the global citizen characteristics as they were born into a world with an advanced communication means.

Gen Z is growing up in a highly advanced social media and digital environment and with ubiquitous mobile communication opportunities. This generation never experienced a world without smartphones or social media. Most of the members of Generation Z, unlike the other generations, have gained their reading skills on technological tools. Furthermore, Generation Z is the first generation to access the Internet widely. In many sources, this generation is defined as Digital Natives. Based on a study done by Pew Research Center, USA, called "Teens, Social Media and Technology", Figure 1 shows the rate of ownership of technological devices among ages 13 through 17. Accordingly, while 95% of the teens, between the ages of 13 and 17, own smart phones, 88% of them have either desktop computers or laptop computers and 84% own gaming consoles.

The main characteristics of Generation Z can be summarized as follows:

- Socializing with different ethnical, religious and racial groups (multicultural)
- Global citizen
- Digital native

Figure 1. Rate of ownership of technological devices among teens, between the ages of 13 and 17 (Source: Pew Research Center's Teens, Social Media & Technology Survey, 2018, http://www.pewinternet.org)

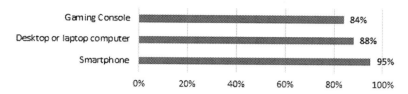

- Aptitude for entrepreneurship
- Independent
- Focused on problem-solving
- Multitasking
- Spending more time online
- Using phone for entertainment rather than TV
- Less reliant on the economy
- Request flexible working
- Request remote working
- Request project-based working
- Prone to work collaboratively using various technological tools
- Prefer leaving less permanent digital trail on social media
- Geared towards rational choices.
- Prefer taking less risks.
- Prefer learning on demand
- Differences in their family structures (higher number of single-parent or same-sex parents)

Learning Expectations of Generation Z

In the face of the characteristics, requests and expectations of Generation Z, the education system has no other choice but to make changes in many respects. Many countries are reviewing their education programs in consideration of the generation's needs. One of the most striking examples is the fact that a class on "entrepreneurship" has been added to the curriculums of high schools and universities in many countries. Generation Z can put many ideas into practice via the Internet. The power of social media platforms provides various new entrepreneurship opportunities to Generation Z.

Even though there is a consensus on the fact that the conception of education must change with regards to the education of Generation Z, the findings of the studies reveal two major avenues. While some of the studies are in favor of the opinion that technologies, such as smart phones and tablets, contribute to the learning of the individuals (Tindell & Bohlander, 2012; Briz-Ponce, Pereira, Carvalho, Juanes-Méndez & García-Peñalvo, 2017; Crompton & Burke, 2018), others claim that such usage would cause technology addiction and deficiency in self-regulation skills, thus influence the teens negatively (Gerhart, 2017; Kim, Jung, Jung, Ko, & Lee, 2017; Rosen, Carrier, Pedroza, et al. 2018). Here, the important point is to ensure that the potential of technology is adapted to education in the right way and benefited from to the maximum extent possible. At this juncture, implementation of technological integration becomes important. Therefore, we must understand the new generation and integrate technology in education according to the characteristics/ expectations of the generation. When the characteristics of ubiquitous learning are considered, it is strongly believed that it has the potential to meet the learning expectations of the new generation learners.

A CASE STUDY: NEW GENERATION LEARNERS' EXPECTATIONS

The objective of the case study is to identify the learning expectations of Generation Z learners and to determine how well the characteristics of ubiquitous learning meet these expectations. In line with this objective, research problems have been defined as follows:

- What are the learning expectations of Generation Z?
- How well do the characteristics of ubiquitous learning meet the learning expectations of Generation Z learners?

The method applied to find answers to the research problems defined above, data collection tool, information regarding the participants taking part in this study, and findings concluded from the collected data are presented in the following headings.

Methodology

In this study, mixed methods research methodology has been applied. Mixed methods research is defined as qualitative and quantitative methods, approaches and notions used in combination by the researcher in a study or in a series of studies (Tashakkori & Teddlie, 2010; Creswell & Creswell, 2017; Johnson & Onwuegbuzie, 2004). Application of qualitative and quantitative methods together, allows us to better understand and interpret the research problems compared to applying the two methods separately (Creswell & Creswell, 2017). In other words, when used within the same framework, the qualitative and quantitative techniques support one another and corroborates the research findings. Mixed methods researches can be of different types based on how and in what order the qualitative and quantitative methods are applied. In this research, sequential explanatory design has been utilized. According to this design, findings obtained through a method define the methods or phases applied in later stages of the research. In other words, the two methods are applied sequentially whereby the qualitative data help develop the quantitative aspect of the study (Greene, Caracelli & Graham, 1989). The research phases are shown in Figure 2.

In the study, qualitative method is applied to answer the first sub problem. For this purpose, focus group discussion were held with the participants. Krueger (2014) defines focus group discussions as carefully structured discussions held in an environment where the individuals could freely speak their minds. Detailed data obtained through focus group discussions provide a solid basis for one-on-one in-

Figure 2. Phases of methodology

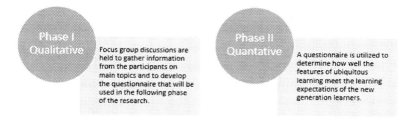

terviews and questionnaires (Kitzinger, 1995). Interview method applied in focus group discussions may be structured or unstructured. Whereas the structured interviews do not allow any discussions outside the list of questions, unstructured interviews are more flexible and allow the discussions to proceed in their own course. The questions asked should serve a purpose, should be as clear and simple as possible so that they are easily understood by the participants, should be constructed in daily language and easily answerable (Krueger, 2014). In this research, unstructured focus group discussions are employed. In the focus group discussions held with the participation of 15 generations Z individuals, in three groups of five, questions were posed on ubiquitous learning and learning expectations. Data collected from these discussions were analyzed and used in support of development of the quantitative phase of the research.

In the second phase of the research, in order to find an answer to the sub-problem of how well the characteristics of ubiquitous learning meet the learning expectations of generation Z individuals, quantitative method is applied. Survey method is utilized in the quantitative phase. Survey method can be defined as collection of data by asking questions to those individuals, who are assumed to have the required knowledge, and to interpret such collected data (Groves, Fowler, Couper et al., 2011; Jackson 2011). In this technique, questionnaires, scales or individual or group discussions can be utilized to collect data. Here, a questionnaire was utilized within the scope of the quantitative research to be able to reach higher number of individuals within a short period of time.

Qualitative Research

Participants

A total of 15 individuals took part in the qualitative phase of the research. Discussions were held in 3 sessions in groups of 5. Information on the groups is presented in Table 3.

As depicted in Table 3, the age range of the 15 participants change from 14 to 19. Five participants attended from each age range defined. It can further be seen that 9 of the participants were males and 6 of them were females, and 5 of them were university students, whereas 10 were high school students.

Data Collection Tool

Questions asked during unstructured focus group discussions in the research are listed in the table below. Questions asked during the focus group discussions were prepared by the researchers and then finalized after consulting with the experts.

Table 3. Demographics of participants

	N	%
Gender Male Female	9 6	60.0 40.0
Age 14-15 16-17 18-19	5 5 5	33.3 33.3 33.3
School Type High School University	10 5	66.6 33.3

Collection and Analysis of Data

The participants attended focus group discussions in three different age groups. Each of the discussions last approximately 1 hour. Certain demographical data pertaining to the participants of the three groups are presented in Table 5.

Since generalization was not going to be applied, quantification was not utilized in the analysis of the collected data (Fern & Fern, 2001). Content analysis method was used for analyzing the data in the study. In line with this purpose, while analyzing the data, key topics were identified under certain headings. Brief notes taken by the researcher during the discussions were used in the analysis of the data.

Findings

A total of ten topics were defined as a result of the analysis of the data collected from the focus group discussions held, to determine the expectations of Generation Z learners from learning (Table 6).

Table 4. Questions asked in focus group discussions

No	Questions
1	What do you learn faster, easier and better?
2	You learn better doing what?
3	Do you believe that there is a place and a time for learning?
4	What do you expect from your teacher in support of your learning?
5	Do your friends support your learning?
6	Do you use the Internet for learning?
7	Would you like your mobile devices to support your learning?
8	Which learning activities do you prefer?
9	Do you keep the activities/ homework/ projects that you complete throughout your education?
10	Do you believe that learning environments presented are appropriate for you?
11	Do you learn information and acquire skills that help you solve problems in your daily life?
12	Who do you think is responsible for your learning? (Yourself, teachers, friends, parents etc.)

Table 5. Information pertaining to participants attending focus group discussions

Group no	N	Gender	Age	Type of School
1	5	3 Male 2 Female	14-15 ages	High School
2	5	2 Male 3 Female	16-17 ages	High School
3	5	4 Male 1 Female	18-19 ages	University

Table 6. Topics defined from the data analysis

Topic No	Topic
1	Place and time of learning
2	Better learning
3	Learning support
4	Peer collaboration
5	Internet and mobile technologies in learning
6	Learning activities
7	Saving learning materials and activities
8	Proximity to life
9	Customized learning environments
10	Learning responsibility

Students' opinions regarding these topics are given below. Discussions group (G#) and sequence number (S#) are used to represent students. In other words, G1S3 identifies the third participant in the first discussion group. In addition, "Q #" represents the expression in which the question of discussion is being discussed. For example, Q5 indicates that the statement was said during the fifth question discussion in Table 4.

The first topic is determined as "place and time of learning". When the responses of the participants are reviewed, it can be gathered that the new generation expects learning anywhere and anytime. Student opinions on this topic can be summarized as follows:

I definitely think that learning does not have a place and a time. I learn something even when I see something as I am walking on the street. (G1S2) (Q3)

For example, when I am playing a strategy game, I learn new things regarding history and geography. (G1S4) (Q3)

I would like to access videos, written material, etc. that would help me learn anytime and anywhere. In this way, my learning can be better. For example, when I think of something on the subway, I immediately research the Internet and find information. (G2S3) (Q3)

I can learn as I read the written content on social media. Of course, I do not assume that these are always correct. I wish there was someone or something that could help me determine whether such writings are true... (G3S1) (Q3)

The next topic was determined as "better learning". Analysis of the collected data shows that students expect topics that interest them and that meet their expectations for better learning. Opinions of the students stated in line with this statement can be found below:

It depends. For example, some of the subjects are too easy for me, but the subjects that are easy for me may be hard for my friend. I think this has to do with fields of interest. (G1S1) (Q2)

If I think that a topic is something that I need to know, then I learn it easier. (G3S2) (Q1)

In addition to these opinions, some of the students have stated that learning would be better if learning was towards solving problems in real life through practice.

I learn much better with practice. (G1S2) (Q2)

Yes, if it is information that benefits me in real life, I absolutely try to learn it. (G2S2) (Q1)

When I solve a problem I encounter, I learn much better. I guess knowing what it is used for and using it makes me learn it better. (G3S5) (Q2)

One other topic was "learning support". Regarding this topic, many of the students expressed that they would like to be in touch with their teachers through social platforms outside of school. When the responses are analyzed, it can be deducted that students especially would like accurate and reliable resources to be identified and, when in doubt, would like to receive support from their teachers in the form of learning guidance. Student opinions on this topic can be stated as follows:

I expect (my teacher) to be close to me in school, support me and to pay attention to me. But, since there are too many students, this is not really possible. I would like to contact (my teacher) through social platforms outside of school. That way, I can ask (my teacher) the questions that come into my mind. (G1S1) (Q4)

I would like to be able to ask questions whenever I want to. I can contact a couple of my teachers via WhatsApp. For example, I can ask right away when I do not understand a subject. (G3S3) (Q4)

Sometimes I doubt the accuracy of the content I see on the Internet. In such instances, it would be better if I could ask my teacher. (G2S1) (Q4)

I would like it very much if my teacher sent me videos, written content, etc., materials that are suitable for me to support my learning. (G3S2) (Q4)

Under this topic, there were also the opinions of the students, who did not want to get in touch with their teachers on social platforms. Additionally, one student has stated that teachers would be insufficient as the number of students is very high and that automatic systems should be developed for this purpose instead.

Actually, I would not really want to get in touch with my teacher outside of school due to different reasons. I do not even want to stay in contact with my parents on social platforms. Other than that, a teacher does not event pay enough attention to all of his/her students at school, so expecting this outside of school would not be realistic. It would be great if there were smart systems that could support my learning. (G3S4) (Q4)

I would not want to get in touch with my teachers outside of class/on online social platforms. I feel like I would not be able post as freely if I knew that my teacher was following me. (G3S1) (Q4)

In light of the collected data, the next topic was determined as "Peer Collaboration" The participants stated that when they learn with their peers, they are much more comfortable and that it was beneficial for them to study in collaboration. Student opinions on this topic can be stated as follows:

Yes, absolutely. Sometimes, learning from my friend is much easier than learning from the teacher. Because I can ask anything to my friend and my friend can ask me anything. (G1S3) (Q5)

It is very useful for me to study with my friends. We fill in for where we lack. We explain to one another. (G1S1) (Q5)

Time and place are not important when I am studying with my friends. Especially, we can write to one another and we can share on social platforms. (G2S2) (Q5)

One other topic in the research was determined as "Internet and mobile technologies in learning". The students have stated that especially the Internet held an important place in their learning, but that the reliability of the information obtained from the Internet should be questioned. Additionally, they stated that they needed more mobile educational applications for mobile devices. Some of the student opinions on this topic are given below:

I definitely use the Internet when learning. In fact, I research for and learn many things online. Because, all information is available on the Internet. (G3S4) (Q6)

I certainly agree with my friend, but not everything on the Internet is true. If there was a way to validate that information, that would have been awesome. (G2S3) (Q6)

When I do research online, I also check for the source of information I find. I especially find the pages of the educational institutions or known experts more reliable. (G3S1) (Q6)

I also check the information I find from a couple other places to validate its accuracy. (G3S5) (Q7)

I use mobile technologies for learning. For example, I do not use the computer too much. I find everything I am looking for using my mobile phone. (G1S5) (Q7)

I believe that mobile devices should support our learning. However, for right now, I think that there aren't enough mobile applications that could support our learning. (G3S1) (Q7)

We already use the Internet on our mobile devices constantly. But, in my opinion, mobile applications that offer controlled and accurate information may be more reliable. (G2S5) (Q7)

On "Learning activities" topic, the students have expressed that they preferred project activities to be more of delivering a product, practical, problem-based, etc. The student opinions on this topic are below:

Yes, homework is boring, but I love doing projects. I learn better when I do a project; I especially like to create a product at the end of it. (G1S1) (Q8)

We do projects frequently and these projects support my learning in a positive way. But of course, it is very important to provide the necessary conditions when doing a project. (G2S4) (Q8)

In fact, I believe that many learning activities are important. But I surely prefer doing projects. We enhance what we have learned hands on and learn new things when doing projects. (G2S1) (Q8)

When student opinions are reviewed, it was revealed that there was a need to organize the group dynamics and find interesting problems for project activities.

I find some of the projects very beneficial for me. I especially enjoy doing projects that are related with me areas of interest. But, some of them are really painful... sometimes, my friends do not make enough effort in group projects. I have difficulties in situations like this. (G2S3) (Q8)

I also prefer project activities, but the problem has to be interesting. At this point, I believe that the problem should motivate us. (G1S5) (Q8)

On the topic stated as "Saving learning materials and activities". Almost all of the students opted for saving class materials, activities and end products. Student opinions on this matter are summarized below.

Not all of them, but I save the activities I enjoyed doing since kindergarten. (G1S2) (Q9)

I take short notes and I keep them. I believe I learn better this way. But of course, when they accumulate, it is hard to find what I am looking for among old notes. (G1S4) (Q9)

I believe that all should be saved, because they show my progress. Yes, I would very much like everything I do in learning activities to be saved automatically. This way, I can easily access what I did in the past. (G3S2) (Q9)

I would like all of our class notes to be saved, not just the projects or homework we do. (G3S4) (Q9)

Another topic determined as a result of the analysis of the date was "Proximity to life". When the opinions grouped under this topic are reviewed, it can be seen that the prevailing opinion of the students was that it would be more beneficial if learning was structured around daily problems and potential problems that they could enter in their lives.

I think that we learn too much useless information. Learning based on daily problems would be more enjoyable. (G1S3) (Q11)

What we in fact need is to learn information that is useful for us. I prefer to know all of the things that are useful for me rather than knowing little of everything. (G1S2) (Q11)

Especially, my expectation from my university education is to be taught the knowledge and skills that would help me overcome the problems I would encounter in my professional life. (G3S4) (Q11)

When the student opinions were reviewed on the topic determined as "Customized learning environments", it was seen that the students expected learning environments to support their learning. Student opinions on this topic can be stated as follows:

For me, this question does not have a clear answer, some of them are suitable for me, some are not. In the end, none of them is designed towards my wishes and expectations. …. I would very much like to have learning environments specially designed for me. (G1S4) (Q10)

School environment is not suitable for me. I get very bored. It is very tedious to have everything structured in certain times; I would like to study when I want and as I want. For example, I love to read laying down wearing headphones. I can concentrate better when I listen to music. (G1S3) (Q10)

Learning environments at school do not bother me, but can they be better? The answer to this question, especially with my friends in mind, is a definite yes. Because not everyone learns in the same way and at the same pace. (G2S2) (Q10)

One of our teachers mentions customizable learning. If this can be implemented, it would be really nice. Everyone can learn as they wish… (G3S1) (Q10)

Within the scope of the final topic, "Learning responsibility", the students have stated that the learning responsibility should reside with them especially during their university education. On the other hand, some of the students said that the responsibility was rather on the teacher.

I think that the responsibility of our learning is on our teacher, because they decide what we should learn. (G1S5) (Q12)

I cannot speak for early ages, but as we grow older, and especially at university, we should be responsible. We should assume the responsibility of our learning. Because at this point, we learn professional information that we will be putting to use for the rest of our lives. If I learn well, then I can be successful in my business life. With this in mind, I believe I should assume the learning responsibility. (G3S4) (Q12)

Learning is in fact an individual concept and concerns the learner; therefore, the responsibility to learn should rest with the learner. But my observations show the contrary. (G3S2) (Q12)

Findings obtained from the focus group discussions data that were collected and analyzed under 10 topics, were utilized for developing the quantitative phase of the research.

QUANTITATIVE RESEARCH

Data Collection Tool

Data collection tool used in this study has been developed by the researchers. Data collection tool consists of two parts: demographical information form and learning expectations survey. In the demographic information form, questions on gender, age, school type, social media accounts, Internet access, smart phone ownership and tablet ownership.

The second part of the form includes the survey on "learning expectations of students", which is composed of 19 questions. In the quantitative phase of the research, an item pool, composed of 34 questions, was developed using the findings of the focus group discussions held for the qualitative phase of the research. As the next step, 9 of the overlapping items were removed from the item pool. 25-item draft form was presented to three experts for their opinions. As a result of the expert opinions obtained, 6 more items were removed from the form. The resulting survey "Learning Expectations of Students", which is composed of 19 items, is presented in Table 8. The third column in Table 8 indicates that the survey item is related to the topics that were identified as a result of the analysis of the data collected from the focus group discussions. For example, the second item of the survey has been prepared based on the topic of "Saving Learning Materials and Activities", which is listed as the seventh topic in Table 6.

The participants were asked to evaluate the items based on a five-point Likert scale. Accordingly, the items were graded as 1: Strongly Disagree; 2: Disagree; 3: Neutral; 4: Agree; 5: Strongly Agree.

In Table 7 under the fourth column, each question is matched against the 6 different aspects of ubiquitous learning (1: Permanency, 2: Accessibility, 3: Immediacy, 4: Interaction, 5: Situatedness and 6: Adaptability). Accordingly, questions 1, 2, and 3 reference the "permanency" feature of ubiquitous learning, questions 4 and 5 reference "accessibility", questions 6 and 7 reference "immediacy", questions 8, 9, 10, and 11 reference interaction, questions 13, 14, and 15 reference "situatedness", and lastly, questions 16, 17, 18, and 19 reference "adaptability". Here, the aim is to determine how well the characteristics of ubiquitous learning meet the learnings expectations of the students from the responses given by the students.

Participants of Quantitative Research

Demographical information of the 297 individuals, who participated in the quantitative phase of the research, can be found in Table 7. Individuals participating in the research filled out the form based on voluntariness. Monographic sample selection technique is utilized for sample selection. In this instance, a sample is selected based on the information on the characteristics of the phase and according to the purpose of the research (Lin, 1976). Since the individuals had to be members of Generation Z, data that did not fit this condition were not included in the analysis.

Table 7. The survey on "students' expectations from ubiquitous learning"

No	Item	Mapping (Reference in Table 6)	Mapping (Reference in Table 1)
1	I would like to access the materials on my previous projects, homeworks, etc. that belong to me	6, 7	1
2	I would like the learning activities and products that belong to me to be saved.	7	1
3	I would like to access previous class materials.	7	1
4	I would like to access resources that support my learning any time I want to.	1	2
5	I would like to access resources that support my learning any place I want to.	1	2
6	I would like to access information easily on the Internet.	5	3
7	I would like to quickly access the resources I need to solve the problems I encounter.	5, 8	3
8	I would like to contact my teachers on digital platforms.	3	4
9	I would like my teachers to guide my learning in online environments.	3	4
10	I would like to collaborate with my friends while learning.	4	4
11	I like to engage in other activities while learning.	9	4
12	I learn by using social media.	1, 5	4
13	I would like to take responsibility of my learning.	10	5
14	I would like to learn through real life activities.	2, 8	5
15	I learn better as I solve problems in my daily life.	2, 8	5
16	I would like customized learning resources to developed for me and presented.	9	6
17	I would like to learn at my own pace without a time restriction.	9	6
18	I would like to learn based on my own methods.	9	6
19	I would like learning environments to be designed according to my needs.	9	6

As can be seen in Table 7, out of the 297 individuals, who participated in the research, 153 (51.5%) of them were males and 144 (48.5%) were females. Participants, aged between 15 and 19, were evaluated in 2 groups. Accordingly, the number of participants between the ages of 15 and 17 was 123 (41.4%) and the number of participants between the ages of 18 and 19 was 174 (58.6%). The number of participants attending high school was 161 (54.2%) and the number of participants attending university was 136 (45.8%).

In the next part of the form, the participants were asked about the social media applications they used. Even though there are currently many social media applications, 6 different social media applications of different categories were listed and presented as options in this question: YouTube, Facebook, Instagram, Twitter, Swarm, and LinkedIn. All of the participants stated that they used at least one social media application. The number of participants using YouTube was 271 (91.2%). According to the collected data, YouTube was determined as the social media application with the most user count. While the number of individuals with an Instagram account was 248 (83.5%), the number of individuals using Snapchat was 241 (81.1%). Additionally, the number of participants with a Facebook account was 235 (79.1%). It was also determined that the number of individuals with a Swarm account was 210 (70.7%) and with a Twitter account was 201 (67.7%). The least used social media application among the participants was

Table 8. Demographics of participants

	N	%
Gender Male Female	153 144	51.5 48.5
Age 15-17 18-19	123 174	41.4 58.6
School Type High School student University student	161 136	54.2 45.8
Social Media Youtube Instagram Snapchat Facebook Twitter Swarm LinkedIn	Yes 271 (91.2%) 248 (83.5%) 241 (81.1%) 235 (79.1%) 201 (67.7%) 210 (70.7%) 114 (38.4%)	No 26 (8.8%) 51 (16.5%) 56 (18.9%) 64 (20.9%) 96 (32.3%) 89 (29.3%) 185 (61.6%)
Other Features Internet Access Smart Phone ownership Tablet Ownership	Yes 262 (88.2%) 282 (94.9%) 182 (61.8%)	No 35 (11.8%) 17 (15.1%) 117 (38.2%)
Aims of mobil device usage Take a picture or video Communication Social media Game Education Personal data storage Shopping	289 (97.3%) 281 (94.6%) 270 (90.1%) 245 (82.4%) 223 (75,0%) 198 (66.7%) 160 (53.8%)	

LinkedIn with 114 participants (38.4%). When 114 participants with LinkedIn accounts were further analyzed, it was seen that 81 of them were attending university. Findings obtained here show similarity with findings of the research, "Teens, Social Media & Technology", conducted by Pew Research Center (Figure 3). According to the findings of that research, it was determined that the most prevalent social media application among the teens was YouTube (85%), Instagram (72%), Snapchat (69%), Facebook (51%), and Twitter (32%), respectively.

Of the participants, 262 of them (88.2%), which makes up the majority, stated that they have uninterrupted internet connection. Also, a majority of the participants (n=828, 94.9%) owned smart phones. The number of participants, who owned tablets, was 182 (61.8%). When these figures are evaluated, we can say that almost all of Generation Z participants were closely related with technology. Furthermore, it can be seen that the figures obtained from the participants parallel with those that were reported under Teens, Social Media & Technology Survey, conducted by the Pew Research Center in 2018 (Figure 3).

In the last part of the demographic information form that was used as a data collection tool, participants were asked about the purpose of their mobile device use. For this question, 7 different options were

Ubiquitous Learning for New Generation Learners' Expectations

Figure 3. Social media use of young people aged between 13 and 17 (Source: Pew Research Center's Teens,Social Media & Technology Survey, 2018, http://www.pewinternet.org)

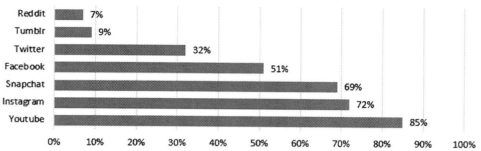

provided: education, shopping, game, social media, communication, personal data storage, and taking pictures/videos. Participants were allowed to select more than one option. When the answers of the participants were analyzed, it was found that 289 (97.3%) of the participants used their mobile devices to take pictures or videos. The number of participants, who stated that they used their mobile devices for communication, was 281 (94.6%), the number of participants, who stated they used their mobile devices for social media purposes, was 270 (90.1%) and the number of those who used their mobile devices for games was 245 (82.4%). It can also be said that the number of participants, who stated that they used their mobile devices for educational purposes, was rather high (n=223, 75.0%). The options least selected by the participants were personal storage (n=198, 66.7%) and shopping (n=160, 53.8%).

Collection and Analysis of Data

Data were collected online between the dates 25 January 2019 and 14 February 2019. A total of 324 individuals filled out the online form. Forms with missing responses and filled by those outside the age group of the research were eliminated from the scope of evaluation. Analysis was done on data collected from 297 forms.

Findings

Findings obtained from the data collection tool are evaluated within the framework of the six different characteristics of the ubiquitous learning.

Analysis results obtained from the first three items that match the "permanency" feature of ubiquitous learning are shown in Table 9. In the tables below that depict the analysis results, columns f1, f2, f3, f4,

Table 9. Analysis results of items that reference the permanency feature of ubiquitous learning

Item No	f1	f2	f3	f4	f5	Average
1	0 (0.0%)	19 (6.4%)	41 (13.8%)	127 (42.7%)	110 (37.0%)	4.10
2	0 (0.0%)	6 (2.0%)	40 (13.5%)	145 (48.8%)	106 (35.7%)	4.18
3	0 (0.0%)	8 (2.7%)	38 (12.7%)	151 (50.1%)	100 (33.7%)	4.15

Ubiquitous Learning for New Generation Learners' Expectations

and f5 show the frequency of the Reponses given by the participants, "strongly disagree", "disagree", "neutral", "agree", "strongly disagree", respectively.

As can be seen in Table 9, the average of the responses given by the participants to the first three questions, is above 4. While the average of the students' response to the first question is 4.10, the averages for the second and third questions are 4.18 and 4.15, respectively. Thus, we can say that the students would like the learning materials that they use in the learning processes, the activities that they have completed and the products they delivered during these processes to be permanent.

Analyses of the two items that match the "Accessibility" feature are shown in Table 10. The averages of the responses given by the participants to questions 4 and 5, which reference the "accessibility" feature of the ubiquitous learning, are 4.18 and 4.17, respectively. According to the results, it can be gathered that Generation Z participants would like to access their learning resources at anytime and anywhere.

The analysis of the two items that reference the "immediacy" feature of ubiquitous learning can be found in Table 11. When Table 11 is reviewed, we see that the averages of the responses given by the participants to the items that reference the "immediacy" feature of ubiquitous learning, are quite high (4.48 and 4.35, respectively). Based on these results, we can conclude that the members of the new generation would like to access information sources quickly and easily. It is believed that with the opportunities offered by technology, ubiquitous learning can easily meet this expectation of the students.

In the survey, items 8 through 12 were matched against the "interaction" feature. The analysis of these items is presented in Table 12. Here, even though the averages of the results for questions 8 (ave. 3.5) and 9 (3.66) are above 3 (neutral), it strikes as being lower than other items. When these questions

Table 10. Analysis results of items that reference the accessibility feature of ubiquitous learning

Item No	f1	f2	f3	f4	f5	Average
4	0 (0.0%)	13 (4.4%)	42 (14.1%)	120 (40.4%)	122 (41.0%)	4.18
5	0 (0.0%)	3 (1.0%)	37 (12.5%)	164 (55.2%)	93 (21.3%)	4.17

Table 11. Analysis results of items that reference the immediacy feature of ubiquitous learning

Item No	f1	f2	f3	f4	f5	Average
6	0 (0.0%)	0 (0.0%)	17 (5.8%)	118 (39.7%)	162 (54.5%)	4.48
7	0 (0.0%)	0 (0.0%)	22 (7.4%)	150 (50.5%)	125 (42.1%)	4.35

Table 12. Analysis results of items that reference the interaction feature of ubiquitous learning

Item No	f1	f2	f3	f4	f5	Average
8	16 (5.4%)	24 (8.1%)	82 (27.6%)	146 (49.2%)	29 (9.8%)	3,50
9	8 (2.7%)	21 (7.1%)	75 (25.3%)	154 (51.9%)	39 (13.1%)	3,66
10	0 (0.0%)	5 (1.7%)	42 (14.1%)	131 (44.1%)	119 (40,1%)	4.23
11	2 (0.6%)	8 (2,7%)	54 (18.2%)	152 (52.2%)	81 (27.2%)	4.02
12	0 (0.0%)	2 (0.6%)	33 (11.1%)	119 (40.1%)	143 (48.1%)	4.36

are reviewed, it is seen that they are about online interaction with the teacher. In the focus group discussions, there were divided opinions on this topic. 10. The averages for questions 10, 11, and 12 are 4.23, 4.02, and 4.36, respectively.

Analysis of items 13, 14, and 15, which reference "Organization of learning activities", can be found in Table 13. Under this topic, the average for item 13, i.e. "I would like to take responsibility of my learning", is 3.77. Even though this average is not low, it is not as high as the other averages. It is believed that the reason for this result is due to the different opinions the students have on who should assume the learning responsibility. Focus group discussions had a similar result. It can be seen that averages for items 14 (4.24) and 15 (4.32) are also high. Thus, we can easily conclude that the students expect the learning activities to reference daily life problems.

The analyses of the four items that reference the "adaptability" feature of ubiquitous learning are presented in Table 14. When the averages of the four items are evaluated, it can be seen that they are all above 4. It can be stated that Generation Z students expect customized learning environments and methods to be developed.

Graphical projection of points obtained for all items in the survey is shown in Figure 4. The lowest of averages obtained for survey items is 3.50 for Item 8 (I would like to contact my teachers on digital platforms). The highest average is 4.48 for Item 6 (I would like to access information easily on the Internet). As seen in Figure 4, the average score of all items except 8, 9 and 13 items is above 4.00 ("agree" statement). Moreover, general average of all items yields 4.11 points. Based on this value, it can be interpreted that the characteristics of ubiquitous learning meet the learning expectations of the new generation students to a great extent.

Table 13. Analysis results of items that reference the feature of ubiquitous learning related with organization of learning activities

Item No	f1	f2	f3	f4	f5	Average
13	9 (3.0%)	18 (6.1%)	73 (24.6%)	128 (43.1%)	69 (23.2%)	3.77
14	0 (0.0%)	0 (0.0%)	67 (22.6%)	92 (30.1%)	138 (46.5%)	4.24
15	0 (0.0%)	0 (0.0%)	54 (18.2%)	94 (31.7%)	149 (50.1%)	4.32

Table 14. Analysis results of items that reference the adaptability feature of ubiquitous learning

Item No	f1	f2	f3	f4	f5	Average
16	0 (0.0%)	0 (0.0%)	61 (20.5%)	173 (58.2%)	63 (21.2%)	4.01
17	0 (0.0%)	0 (0.0%)	36 (12.1%)	124 (41.8%)	137 (46.1%)	4.34
18	0 (0.0%)	0 (0.0%)	73 (24.6%)	134 (45.1%)	90 (30.3%)	4.06
19	0 (0.0%)	0 (0.0%)	58 (19.5%)	173 (58.2%)	66 (22.2%)	4.03

Figure 4. Average points of survey items

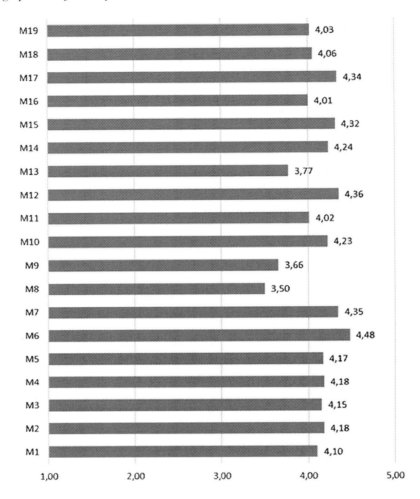

FUTURE RESEARCH DIRECTIONS

Smart phones are replacing laptops, tablets, e-reading devices as the storage capacity and the speed of the wireless communication increase. They have started to serve as another limb, especially for the young generation. They feel like impaired whenever they are left without them. This great bonding between the young people and their smart phones can be a great advantage to engage and motivate students learning. For the future work, it will be focus on how smart phones can be used for ubiquitous learning and what kind of applications can be developed to improve the educational aspects.

CONCLUSION

Education has been among the top three concerns together with health and law. As the information technology pushed its way into our lives many studies are carried about the impact of technology in education and how it should be integrated. Today, there is no doubt that education not embracing technology will not be influential. Therefore, a good understanding of the behavioral aspects and expections of the new generation is needed to formulate tools and environment for educational forms.

New generation kids, born into a world of digitally enabled computation and communication, IT technology is like part of nature and anything that is not making use of it is absurd. They are independent, social, multicultural in character, thus are in favor of flexible (in time and space) project based working. They are digital native: handle most of their needs online, own and use smart phones for many purposes besides communication. They are Prone to work collaboratively using various technological tools.

It can be seen that portable smart devices (smart phones, wearable smart devices, etc.), becoming accessible by the whole community, will be pulling and bearing agents for new educational incentives. With these devices students can participate in inter/intra national groups which goes along with their multicultural and global personalization. Since they are always with their smart devices, any time they have a new idea they can immediately share it with their friends and bring up new projects which is in line with their entrepreneurship. Being able to store and reach learning material when and where needed is termd as Ubiquitous learning.

In this chapter, it is intended to show how the general characteristics of generation z is aligned with the ubiquitous educational features enabled by IT, based on a qualitative analysis of the thoughts of the generation on ubiquitous learning.

REFERENCES

Briz-Ponce, L., Pereira, A., Carvalho, L., Juanes-Méndez, J. A., & García-Peñalvo, F. J. (2017). Learning with mobile technologies–Students' behavior. *Computers in Human Behavior*, *72*, 612–620. doi:10.1016/j.chb.2016.05.027

Clancey, W. J. (1995). A tutorial on situated learning. In *Proceedings of the International Conference on Computers and Education (Taiwan)*. Charlottesville, VA: AACE.

Creswell, J. W., & Creswell, J. D. (2017). *Research design: Qualitative, quantitative, and mixed methods approaches*. Sage Publications.

Crompton, H., & Burke, D. (2018). The use of mobile learning in higher education: A systematic review. *Computers & Education*, *123*, 53–64. doi:10.1016/j.compedu.2018.04.007

Curtis, M., Luchini, K., Bobrowsky, W., Quintana, C., & Soloway, E. (2002). Handheld use in K-12: A descriptive account. In *Proceedings. IEEE International Workshop on Wireless and Mobile Technologies in Education* (pp. 23-30). New York: IEEE Computer Society Press. 10.1109/WMTE.2002.1039217

DelCampo, R. G., Haggerty, L. A., & Haney, M. J. (2010). *Managing the multi-generational workforce: From the GI generation to the millennials*. Gower Publishing, Ltd.

Fern, E. F., & Fern, E. E. (2001). Advanced focus group research. *Sage (Atlanta, Ga.)*.

Gerhart, N. (2017). Technology Addiction: How Social Network Sites Impact Our Lives. *Informing Science*, 20.

Graf, S. (2008). Adaptivity and personalization in ubiquitous learning systems. In *Symposium of the Austrian HCI and Usability Engineering Group* (pp. 331-338). Springer. 10.1007/978-3-540-89350-9_23

Greene, J. C., Caracelli, V. J., & Graham, W. F. (1989). Toward a conceptual framework for mixed-method evaluation designs. *Educational Evaluation and Policy Analysis*, *11*(3), 255–274. doi:10.3102/01623737011003255

Grose, M. (2011). *XYZ: The new rules of generational warfare*. Random House Australia.

Groves, R. M., Fowler, F. J. Jr, Couper, M. P., Lepkowski, J. M., Singer, E., & Tourangeau, R. (2011). *Survey Methodology*. John Wiley & Sons.

Hwang, G.-J., Tsai, C.-C., & Yang, S. J. H. (2008). Criteria, strategies and research issues of context-aware ubiquitous learning. *Journal of Educational Technology & Society*, *11*(2), 81–91.

Jackson, S. L. (2011). Research methods and Statistics: a critical approach. *Cengage Learning, 17*.

Johnson, R. B., & Onwuegbuzie, A. J. (2004). Mixed methods research: A research paradigm whose time has come. *Educational Researcher*, *33*(7), 14–26. doi:10.3102/0013189X033007014

Kim, I., Jung, G., Jung, H., Ko, M., & Lee, U. (2017). Let's FOCUS: Mitigating Mobile Phone Use in College Classrooms. *Proceedings of the ACM on Interactive, Mobile, Wearable and Ubiquitous Technologies, 1*(3), 63. 10.1145/3130928

Kinshuk, & Graf, S. (2012). Ubiquitous Learning. In *Encyclopedia of the Sciences of Learning*. Springer.

Kitzinger, J. (1995). Qualitative research: Introducing focus groups. *British Medical Journal, 311*(7000), 299–302. doi:10.1136/bmj.311.7000.299 PMID:7633241

Krueger, R. A., & Casey, M. A. (2014). *Focus groups: A practical guide for applied research*. Sage publications.

Lave, J. (1991). Situating learning in communities of practice. *Perspectives on Socially Shared Cognition, 2*, 63-82.

Lin, N. (1976). *Foundations of social research*. McGraw-Hill Companies.

McCrindle, M. (2008). *The ABC of XYZ: Generational diversity at work*. McCrindle Research Pty Ltd.

McCrindle, M., & Wolfinger, E. (2009). *The ABC of XYZ: Understanding the global generations*. The ABC of XYZ.

Oblinger, D. (2003). Boomers gen-xers millennials. *EDUCAUSE Review, 500*(4), 37–47.

Ogata, H., Matsuka, Y., El-Bishouty, M. M., & Yano, Y. (2009). LORAMS: Linking physical objects and videos for capturing and sharing learning experiences towards ubiquitous learning. *International Journal of Mobile Learning and Organisation, 3*(4), 337–350. doi:10.1504/IJMLO.2009.027452

Ogata, H., & Yano, Y. (2004). Context-aware support for computer-supported ubiquitous learning. In *The 2nd IEEE International Workshop on Wireless and Mobile Technologies in Education, 2004. Proceedings* (pp. 27-34). IEEE. 10.1109/WMTE.2004.1281330

Park, Y. (2011). A pedagogical framework for mobile learning: Categorizing educational applications of mobile technologies into four types. *The International Review of Research in Open and Distributed Learning, 12*(2), 78–102. doi:10.19173/irrodl.v12i2.791

Rosen, L. D., Carrier, L. M., Pedroza, J. A., Elias, S., O'Brien, K. M., Lozano, J., & Ruiz, A. (2018). The role of executive functioning and technological anxiety (FOMO) in college course performance as mediated by technology usage and multitasking habits. *Educational Psychology, 24*(1), 14–25.

Seemiller, C., & Grace, M. (2016). *Generation Z goes to college*. John Wiley & Sons.

Tashakkori, A., & Teddlie, C. (Eds.). (2010). *Sage handbook of mixed methods in social & behavioral research*. Sage Publications. doi:10.4135/9781506335193

Thomas, M. (Ed.). (2011). *Deconstructing digital natives: Young people, technology, and the new literacies*. Taylor & Francis. doi:10.4324/9780203818848

Tindell, D. R., & Bohlander, R. W. (2012). The Use and Abuse of Cell Phones and Text Messaging in the Classroom: A Survey of College Students. *College Teaching, 60*(1), 1–9. doi:10.1080/87567555.2011.604802

Yahya, S., Ahmad, E., & Jalil, K. A. (2010). The definition and characteristics of ubiquitous learning: A discussion. *International Journal of Education and Development Using ICT, 6*(1).

Zhang, J. P. (2008). Hybrid learning and ubiquitous learning. In *International Conference on Hybrid Learning and Education* (pp. 250-258). Springer. 10.1007/978-3-540-85170-7_22

Chapter 10
Considering Social Presence in the Designing of Ubiquitous Learning Environments

Serkan İzmirli
Çanakkale Onsekiz Mart University, Turkey

ABSTRACT

Ubiquitous learning is an emerging research area in which learning occurs at the right time, in the right place, with the help of various technologies. Since ubiquitous learning helps to improve learning, motivation, and creativity, effective ubiquitous learning environments should be designed. Theories, models, and strategies should be considered to design these environments. One of these models is the community of inquiry approach, which has three elements: social presence, teaching presence, and cognitive presence. In this study, social presence is selected as a focus. In this context, the purpose of the study is to present techniques for establishing social presence in ubiquitous learning environments. In line with this purpose, first, ubiquitous learning and social presence are explained. Then, techniques to establish social presence in ubiquitous learning environments are expressed. Following on, a sample ubiquitous learning environment (a ubiquitous history museum) is designed and presented, considering social presence as a specific element.

DOI: 10.4018/978-1-5225-9779-7.ch010

INTRODUCTION

The development of mobile and wireless technologies provides new opportunities to improve and redesign educational settings (Saccol et al., 2009). Shifts in learning are occurring in parallel with the needs of learners and technological developments. These shifts include those away from conventional learning to e-learning, from e-learning to mobile learning (m-learning), and currently from m-learning to ubiquitous learning (u-learning) (Yahya, Ahmad, & Jalil, 2010). M-learning involves learning that occurs anytime and anywhere, and as such, provides high mobility. However, to be effective, learning anytime and anywhere must be supported by personalization. 'Personalization' in this context means providing learning content to the learner at the right time and in the right place. In short, it can be said that context-aware environments are needed to facilitate this form of learning (Leone & Leo, 2011). This is the context in which u-learning arises. U-learning is therefore an expanded form of e-learning and m-learning (Huang, Chiu, Liu, & Chen, 2011).

Since u-learning is more dynamic and flexible than m-learning and e-learning (Park, 2011), effective u-learning environments must be designed. Theories, models, and strategies should be taken into account to design these environments. One of these models is the community of inquiry approach (Garrison, Anderson, & Archer, 2000). This model comprises three elements: social presence, teaching presence, and cognitive presence. In this study, social presence is adopted as a specific focus. In this context, the purpose of the study is to present techniques to establish social presence in u-learning environments. First, u-learning and social presence will be explained. Following on, techniques to establish social presence in u-learning environments are expressed. Finally, a sample u-learning environment is designed and presented, considering social presence, in the form of a history museum.

UBIQUITOUS LEARNING

Different definitions have been put forward to explain 'u-learning'. It is an approach to learning that seamlessly combines virtual environments and physical spaces, and is therefore a step beyond e-learning. In u-learning environments, learners access content at the right time and place (Bomsdorf, 2005). U-learning can occur in situations when the learner is mobile, such as visiting a museum, as well as in formal learning environments (Saccol et al., 2009). Yahya et al. (2010) define u-learning as learning the right thing at the right time and place, and in the right way. U-learning provides high mobility using mobile devices such as smartphones and tablets. It also provides high embeddedness through radio frequency identification (RFID), quick response codes (QR codes), and sensor networks. Embedded devices communicate with mobile devices through wireless communication (Leone & Leo, 2011). As such, u-learning can be described as learning at the right time and place via embedded technologies, such as RFID, QR codes, and sensor networks.

The use of ubiquitous and networked mobile devices is increasing in educational settings (Wang, Wiesemes, & Gibbons, 2012). U-learning environments can help motivate learners (Altınışık & Adıgüzel, 2016; Chen & Huang, 2012; Chen & Li, 2010; Tan, Liu, & Chang, 2007) and improve learning (Chen & Huang, 2012; Chen & Li, 2010; Hwang, Wu, Tseng, & Huang, 2011; Tan et al., 2007). Moreover, u-learning environments support peer-to-peer collaborative learning (Yang, 2006) and improve learner creativity (Chen & Huang, 2012; Tan et al., 2007). Since they help learning in many ways, it is important to design, develop, and use these environments in educational settings.

Considering Social Presence in the Designing of Ubiquitous Learning

Yahya et al. (2010) propose five characteristics of u-learning: permanency, accessibility, immediacy, interactivity, and context-awareness. Huang et al. (2011) denote ten characteristics of u-learning, giving it a broader scope. These characteristics are: providing urgent learning needs, providing knowledge acquisition, interaction, a situation of instructional activity, context-awareness, personalization, self-regulated learning, constructivist learning, adaptive learning, and learning community. These characteristics are explained below (Huang et al., 2011).

- **Providing Urgent Learning Needs:** Learners can access their learning needs from u-learning environments immediately.
- **Providing Knowledge Acquisition**: U-learning systems provide information to learners.
- **Interaction**: Learners can communicate with other learners and teachers.
- **Situation of Instructional Activity**: Instructional activities are embedded in daily life.
- **Context-Awareness**: U-learning systems detects the learner's location and other related information. Contextual information is location, time, preference, device, and network (Yang, 2006).
- **Personalization**: Based on learner position, the system provides related content. Leone and Leo (2011) state that QR codes can help to improve the personalization of learning.
- **Self-Regulated Learning**: Learners have control of their learning process.
- **Constructive Learning**: Learning activities should be planned based on learners' prior knowledge.
- **Adaptive Learning**: The learning process is adaptable to individual learners. Learners will progress differently, based on their specific learning pace.
- **Learning Community**: The learner can interact in online communities via web-based tools such as blogs.

A number of techniques and technologies such as actuators and sensors, RFID tags, QR codes, and mobile devices have been used to develop context-aware ubiquitous computing environments (Hwang, Tsai, & Yang, 2008). Hwang et al. (2011) propose a number of items to be prepared/completed to develop a context-aware ubiquitous computing environment. These are: (1) instructions on how to use a ubiquitous computing environment; (2) instructions on how to download and install software required (e.g. QR code software); (3) instructions on the aims of the learning activity; (4) an authentic learning environment with a wireless network; (5) a server; (6) a database. Virtanen, Haavisto, Liikanen and Kääriäinen (2018) state a number of criteria for the u-learning environment. These are context-awareness, flexibility (thanks to learning management systems such as Moodle), interactivity, personalization, functional objects (e.g. RFID tags and QR-codes), wireless networks, and mobile devices.

A number of u-learning environments have been developed in different contexts. Tan et al. (2007) developed a u-learning environment for outdoor learning called 'Environment of Ubiquitous Learning with Educational Resources' (EULER). EULER includes RFID, embedded systems, database technologies, a wireless network, and internet access. EULER has design features such as interactivity, permanency, museum-likeness, collaboration, accessibility, and context awareness. EULER provides interactivity with multiple functions via virtual classes. Learning statuses are recorded and stored in the database, which provides permanency. Outdoor teaching using EULER provides a museum-like experience. Sharing experiences among students with mobile devices is an example of collaboration. In the case of EULER, teachers and students can easily access learning resources. Context-aware learning resources can be delivered via RFID functions at the right time and in the right place. An experimental design was used in Tan et al.'s study. Participants of the study were elementary school students and their teachers. In the experimental group, EULER was used to teach elementary school students about wetland creatures and an ecosystem in a park in Taiwan. In the control group, students were taught via traditional methods (paper-pencil). Results showed that student motivation, learning, and creativity were improved by EULER. At the conclusion of the study, the u-learning environment (EULER) was deemed to have been effective.

Chen and Li (2010) developed a personalized, context-aware ubiquitous learning system (PCULS) to teach English vocabulary. This system is based on the situational learning approach, which asserts that context is extremely important in learning. This PCULS includes a neural-network-based WLAN positioning technique and database technologies. Participants in this experimental study were high school students from Taiwan. In the experimental group, students learned English vocabulary using the PCULS, which included a context-aware service. In the control group, students learned English vocabulary from a system without a context-aware service. Results showed that students using a personalized context-aware u-learning system were more successful than students using the system without context-awareness. Most of the students stated that the PCULS and its context-aware service motivated them to learn. Moreover, students expressed that using the PCULS to learn English made them happy. It can therefore be argued that context-awareness is an important factor in u-learning environments.

Hwang et al. (2011) developed a context-aware ubiquitous learning platform (CULP). The CULP includes embedded cameras, internet access, and QR-codes. In this experimental study, participants were university students from Taiwan. The experimental group completed the 'Personal Computer-Assembling' course via CULP, while the control group took the course using the traditional method. According to the results, students who used the CULP showed significantly higher learning performance than students who used the traditional method. The CULP therefore rendered learning more effective. Besides, survey results showed that studying using the CULP satisfied students.

Chen and Huang (2012) proposed a context-aware ubiquitous learning system (CAULS). The CAULS includes RFID, embedded systems, database technologies, and a wireless network. In this experimental study, participants were elementary school students and their teachers in Taiwan. In the experimental group, students learned about aboriginal artifacts in a museum environment using the CAULS. The CAULS can identify students' location and guide them to find specific artefacts. Students used personal digital assistants (PDAs) with a RFID reader. When students reached an artefact, learning material about said artefact was provided by the CAULS. In the control group, students learned aboriginal artifacts in the museum environment using the tour-based u-learning method. The control group used PDAs for each artefact, but had no assistance, which was provided using the CAULS. Results obtained in the study showed that teaching using the CAULS increased students' learning, motivation, and creativity. Most of the students stated that the CAULS was easy to use. It can be said that this system was therefore effective in terms of enhancing learning.

As shown in the literature, a range of design strategies are available for designing u-learning environments. Saccol et al. (2009) proposed a framework for designing u-learning applications in which they considered four elements, given below.

- **Learners' Profiles and Needs**: Learners' profiles and needs should be known when designing u-learning environments.

- **Context**: Technologies and applications should be context-aware to meet learners' needs. Context information includes physical (location), temporal, and social environments.
- **Educational Paradigm**: An educational paradigm should be considered when designing u-learning environments. Educational design principles based on an educational model can help guide the instructional designer and instructor.
- **Possibilities and Limitations of Mobile and Wireless Technologies**: The possibilities and limitations of using mobile and wireless technologies should be taken into account, since interface problems may arise. For example, mobile devices may not have user-friendly interfaces.

SOCIAL PRESENCE

According to the community of inquiry model, learning occurs within the community via the interactions among three elements: social presence, cognitive presence, and teaching presence. As shown in Figure 1, the intersection of these elements represents educational experience (Garrison et al., 2000).

Garrison et al. (2000, p. 89) define cognitive presence as "the extent to which the participants in any particular configuration of a community of inquiry are able to construct meaning through sustained communication". Cognitive presence is based on critical-thinking and focuses on higher-order thinking processes (Garrison, Anderson, & Archer, 2001). Teaching presence is "the design, facilitation, and direction of cognitive and social processes for the purpose of realizing personally meaningful and educationally worthwhile learning outcomes" (Anderson, Rourke, Garrison & Archer, 2001, p. 5). Social presence is "the degree of salience of the other person in the interaction and the consequent salience of interpersonal relationships" (Short, Williams, & Christie, 1976). Athabasca University in Canada hosts a web site (https://coi.athabascau.ca/) that presents the community of inquiry model and publications related to this model. Each of the above-noted three elements of community of inquiry is studied in the

Figure 1. The community of inquiry model (Garrison et al., 2000, p. 88)

literature. In the present study, social presence is taken as a focus. Learners may feel that an instructor is absent, and that they are alone in u-learning environments, implying that they perceive no or low social presence. To overcome this problem, u-learning environments should be designed considering the aspect of social presence. Adding social presence features to these environments will help motivate students to learn, and eventually, to learn better.

Developing a sense of belonging with others (students, instructors, and programs of study) may be negatively affected in computer-mediated communication. To overcome this problem, the topic of creating social presence has emerged (Swan, Garrison, & Richardson, 2009). Social presence is the perception of interaction with other people in an e-learning environment (Akcaoglu & Lee, 2016; Choi, 2016). According to another definition, social presence is defined as the degree of illusion to which an individual perceives another as a real person in synchronous or asynchronous communication environments (Kreijns, Kirschner, Jochems, & Van Buuren, 2007). Social presence positively affects satisfaction (Akyol & Garrison, 2008; Gunawardena & Zittle, 1997; Johnson, Hornik, & Salas, 2008), and there is a positive relationship between social presence and perceived learning (Richardson & Swan, 2003). The absence of social presence weakens learning experience. Establishing social presence is important to have a successful learning experience (Dunlap & Lowenthal, 2014). Social presence enhances learning interactions (Wei, Chen, & Kinshuk, 2012) and as such, it can be argued that learners need to have high social presence perceptions. Rourke, Anderson, Garrison and Archer (1999) state, however, that social presence perception level should be at an optimum level; if it rises above this level, it can harm learning. Therefore, this issue should be closely studied.

Social presence includes three categories: affective expression, open communication, and group cohesion (Garrison et al., 2000). Affective expression is where learners express their emotions, feelings, values, and beliefs. Open communication is where learners interact with activities and tasks. Group cohesion is where learners create and maintain group commitment (Swan et al., 2009). Indicators of the social presence categories and their definitions are presented in Table 1.

As shown in Table 1, indicators of the 'affective expression' category are paralanguage, emotion, value, humor, and self-disclosure. Indicators of the 'open communication' category are acknowledgement, agreement, approval, asking questions, personal advice, and continuing a thread. Indicators of the 'group cohesion' category are greetings and salutations, vocatives, group reference, social sharing, and self-reflection.

Establishing warm and intimate relationship with others is key to maintaining longer relationships (Choi, 2016). Social presence may help to establish such relationships in the u-learning environment. Therefore, it can be said that designing a u-learning environment that incorporates social presence features can help students to interact within the learning environment for longer. Since social presence makes the learning experience enjoyable in the e-learning environment (Aragon, 2003), it has the same potential in the u-learning environment. Additionally, Jones-Roberts (2018) states that if social presence is successfully implemented, students will be more motivated and successful. Creating social presence in e-learning environments is thus a necessity (Izmirli, 2017). It can be stated that creating social presence in the u-learning environments is necessary as well.

Table 1. Social presence categories and indicators (Rourke et al., 1999; Swan, 2003)

Categories	Indicators	Definition
Affective expression	Paralanguage	Showing emotion by using informal features of text such as emoticons, repetitious punctuation, and spelling.
	Emotion	Using descriptive words to show feelings (hatred, sadness, etc.).
	Value	Expressing values, beliefs and attitudes.
	Humor	Teasing, sarcasm, cajoling, and irony.
	Self-disclosure	Sharing personal information.
Open communication	Acknowledgement	Quoting from others' messages or referring to them.
	Agreement	Expressing agreement/disagreement.
	Approval	Praising and encouraging.
	Asking questions	Asking questions/inviting response.
	Personal advice	Offering advice.
	Continuing a thread	Using a 'reply' feature of software instead of starting a new thread (blog comments, etc.).
Group cohesion	Greetings and salutations	Greetings, salutations, and closures.
	Vocatives	Addressing participants by name.
	Group reference	Addressing or referring to the group as 'we', 'us', 'our'.
	Social sharing	Sharing information that is unrelated to the course (celebrating a birthday, etc.)
	Self-reflection	Participants' reflection on the course.

TECHNIQUES TO ESTABLISH SOCIAL PRESENCE IN UBIQUITOUS LEARNING ENVIRONMENTS

U-learning refers to learning anywhere, and anytime. Students learn content in an authentic context that had been specifically designed to facilitate this. Instructors are not physically present in u-learning environments. Social presence is used in e-learning and online learning environments, and can also be used in u-learning environments. In this part, techniques for establishing social presence in the u-learning environment are presented.

U-learning includes ubiquitous connection. With the ubiquitous connectivity features of smartphones, people can connect to others anytime and anywhere. This ubiquitous connectivity increases social presence (Choi, 2016). Similarly, u-learning environments should have social presence features to facilitate effective learning. Therefore, it can be argued that u-learning and social presence affect one another to some degree.

Researchers and practitioners use different techniques to create social presence (Lowenthal & Dunlap, 2018) in a bid to overcome feelings of isolation. Social presence strategies that are suggested for e-learning and online learning environments, and that can be used in u-learning environments, are provided below.

- **Orientation**: Orientation activities can be used to help students. These activities include orientation videos and weekly announcements (Dunlap & Lowenthal, 2014). In a learning environment, there should be a welcoming message in the form of an orientation video at the start of the course.

For example, the instructor can welcome students and provide information about the course via a streamed video to help orient students. This strategy specifically creates the social presence of the instructor (Aragon, 2003; Lowenthal & Dunlap, 2018).

- **Providing Feedback**: Students need feedback about their assignments and participation. Individual feedback creates social presence (Aragon, 2003). Some feedback types are one-to-one emails, audio feedback, and video feedback (Dunlap & Lowenthal, 2014; Jones-Roberts, 2018). In promoting social presence, audio or video feedback can be more effective than text-only feedback which is time-consuming for instructors (Jones-Roberts, 2018; Oyarzun, Barreto & Conklin, 2018).
- **Organic Interactions**: Social networking tools such as Twitter and Facebook can be used to establish social presence. These tools provide an informal environment in which to connect with participants (Dunlap & Lowenthal, 2014). For example, Izmirli (2017) offered an online course via Moodle and a Facebook group, and found evidence in the Facebook group for each of the social presence categories, i.e. affective expression, open communication, and group cohesion. He concluded that the Facebook group established social presence. Additionally, Dunlap and Lowenthal (2009) found that Twitter also established social presence.
- **Using Audio and Video**: Audio and video can be used in the design. If there is only text, meanings of words may be interpreted incorrectly. When instructors use audio and video, it can help students to create social presence (Aragon, 2003; Jones-Roberts, 2018).
- **Using Emoticons**: Emoticons are non-verbal cues, generally expressed via facial expressions. When emoticons are used, they can help participants interpret a message correctly (Aragon, 2003). For example, smile emoticons, i.e. ':)', are created using punctuation, while '☺' references a facial expression.
- **Using Humor**: Social distance is reduced by humor (Aragon, 2003).
- **Greetings and Salutations**: Greeting participants creates social presence (Rourke et al., 1999; Swan, 2003).
- **Addressing Participants by Name**: Addressing participants by name establishes social presence (Aragon, 2003).
- **Social Sharing**: Sharing information that is unrelated to the course can help to establish social presence (Swan, 2003).
- **Self-Reflection**: Reflecting on the course enhances social presence (Swan, 2003).
- **Asking Questions**: Learners can ask questions of other learners (Rourke et al., 1999; Swan, 2003).

Although these strategies are essentially used in online and e-learning environments, they can be transferred and adapted into u-learning environments.

A SAMPLE UBIQUITOUS LEARNING ENVIRONMENT DESIGNED CONSIDERING SOCIAL PRESENCE: A UBIQUITOUS HISTORY MUSEUM

Social presence strategies can be used in u-learning environments to facilitate, establish, and maintain social presence. For better understanding of this concept, a sample u-learning environment, **'Ubiquitous History Museum'**, including social presence features, is presented below. Social presence techniques will be indicated in bold.

Considering Social Presence in the Designing of Ubiquitous Learning

Envision a history museum that provides u-learning. At the entrance of this museum, there is a video that provides instructions about how to utilize the museum effectively. This is an **orientation video (technique: 'orientation')**. This video informs participants where to start, what directions to follow, what tasks to accomplish, and how to finish a tour. In short, this video informs the student what will happen during their visit. After the orientation video, there is a kiosk that instructs participants how to install the mobile application used in the museum. The kiosk screen exhibits the greeting, 'Hi!' **(technique: 'greeting and salutation')** to the participant, both in audio and text format. On important national days, there will be a celebratory message **(technique: 'social sharing')** on the kiosk screen. The kiosk will then provide instructions for how to install the mobile application to a mobile device (smartphone or tablet). The participant installs the mobile application, creates an account, and logs into the application. The mobile application addresses the participant using their name, which was entered into the database upon creating the account. For example, 'Hello, Serkan! Welcome to the History Museum. You will have fun and learn at the same time'. **(techniques: 'addressing participants by name' and 'greeting and salutation')**. Consider that the museum has five rooms/parts. In each part, there are different types of historical artifacts. In the first part, historical rocks are exhibited. Beneath these artifacts are QR codes with instructions. Adding an emoticon to the QR code instruction can add a social presence feature, resulting in intimation, and making the visitor smile. For example, the instruction may be, "To view the video, please scan this QR code with your mobile app that you installed at the entrance of the museum. Now smile ☺ and ready, set, go!" **(technique: 'using emoticons')**. In this way, the participant may experience the feeling of a teacher smiling at them. Once the participant scans the QR code, they will be able to view a video describing the history and features of the item exhibited. While watching a video, the participant will put on a headset. In this video, the participant will hear a human voice, which further increases social presence **(technique: 'using audio and video')**. At the end of the each section of the museum, there will be a QR code to test the participant, where questions will be asked about the section they have completed. Below the QR code, there will be an instruction, "Are you ready to be tested? You are going to rock today!" **(technique: 'using humor')**. The participant scans the QR code and is tested with questions. After being tested, the participant is provided with audio feedback **(technique: 'providing feedback')**. Once the participant has completed the tour, the mobile application will provide feedback about the participant's visit throughout the museum **(technique: 'providing feedback')**. Once the participant has finished viewing all five parts of the museum, they will go to a room located near the museum exit. There will be a kiosk where visitors can ask questions if they require clarification about historical elements **(technique: 'asking questions')**. This will be a live chat with a museum expert at the kiosk. After the question-and-answer part, the kiosk will provide closure, e.g. "I hope you learned and enjoyed your visit. Please come back again" **(technique: 'greeting and salutation')**. Prior to leaving the museum, in the mobile application, the participant will be asked to reflect on the informative museum tour **(technique: 'self-reflection')**. A social networking account (Twitter) registered to the museum, and which can be accessed via the mobile application will help participants interact with one another **(technique: 'organic interaction')**.

Although it may seem that the above u-learning environment will be easy to design, this is not the case. Social presence techniques are only briefly explained in this paper to facilitate better understanding of what they comprise. It should be kept in mind that the purpose of this study is not to develop a u-learning environment from the start, but rather, to add the aspect of social presence to the u-learning environment.

CONCLUSION

Effective u-learning environments must be designed, as u-learning improves learning, motivation, and creativity. In this study, social presence techniques in the designing of u-learning environments were presented. It is expected that this study will help instructional designers and instructors. The example presented in this paper, the 'Ubiquitous History Museum', includes some assumptions and limitations. Participants/visitors are assumed to have digital literacy skills, as they will need to use technological devices such as a kiosk and smartphone in the museum. Visitors will need such a device to use the u-learning system. Parents should help their children to take a tour of the museum if they are too young to use or have a mobile device.

The techniques for establishing and maintaining social presence refer to a type of teaching presence (Lowenthal & Dunlap, 2018). Using these techniques can help to establish a teaching presence, which is an aspect of the model of community of inquiry. User interface (e.g. ease of use) positively affects social presence (Wei et al., 2012). It can be said that ease of use of systems in u-learning environments has positive effects on social presence. In addition to considering social presence techniques in designing u-learning environments, u-learning environments should be well-designed overall.

Social presence strategies that can be used in u-learning environments include orientation, providing feedback, organic interaction, using audio and video, using emoticons, using humor, greetings and salutations, addressing participants by name, social sharing, self-reflection, and asking questions. The social presence techniques presented in this study should be tested with research studies for u-learning environments. Experimental studies can be conducted; in this way, the effectiveness of social presence techniques can be determined. Additionally, the effectiveness of each technique should be determined via research studies.

ACKNOWLEDGMENT

This research received no specific grant from any funding agency in the public, commercial, or not-for-profit sectors.

REFERENCES

Akcaoglu, M., & Lee, E. (2016). Increasing social presence in online learning through small group discussions. *International Review of Research in Open and Distributed Learning, 17*(3), 1–17. doi:10.19173/irrodl.v17i3.2293

Akyol, Z., & Garrison, D. R. (2008). The development of a Community of Inquiry over time in an online course: Understanding the progression and integration of social, cognitive and teaching presence. *Journal of Asynchronous Learning Networks, 12*(3–4), 3–22.

Altınışık, H. Z., & Adıgüzel, T. (2016). A brief review of ubiquitous learning. *Ardahan Üniversitesi İktisadi ve İdari Bilimler Fakültesi Dergisi, 2*(3), 121–130.

Anderson, T., Rourke, L., Garrison, D. R., & Archer, W. (2001). Assessing teaching presence in a computer conference context. *Journal of Asynchronous Learning Networks, 5*(2).

Aragon, S. R. (2003). Creating social presence in online environments. *New Directions for Adult and Continuing Education, 100*(100), 57–68. doi:10.1002/ace.119

Bomsdorf, B. (2005). *Adaptation of learning spaces: Supporting ubiquitous learning in higher distance education.* Paper presented at the meeting of Mobile Computing and Ambient Intelligence: The Challenge of Multimedia, Schloss Dagstuhl, Germany.

Chen, C. C., & Huang, T. C. (2012). Learning in a u-Museum: Developing a context-aware ubiquitous learning environment. *Computers & Education, 59*(3), 873–883. doi:10.1016/j.compedu.2012.04.003

Chen, C. M., & Li, Y. L. (2010). Personalised context-aware ubiquitous learning system for supporting effective English vocabulary learning. *Interactive Learning Environments, 18*(4), 341–364. doi:10.1080/10494820802602329

Choi, S. (2016). The flipside of ubiquitous connectivity enabled by smartphone-based social networking service: Social presence and privacy concern. *Computers in Human Behavior, 65*, 325–333. doi:10.1016/j.chb.2016.08.039

Dunlap, J. C., & Lowenthal, P. R. (2009). Tweeting the night away: Using Twitter to enhance social presence. *Journal of Information Systems Education, 20*(2).

Dunlap, J. C., & Lowenthal, P. R. (2014). The power of presence: Our quest for the right mix of social presence in online courses. In A. A. Piña & A. P. Mizell (Eds.), *Real life distance education: Case studies in practice* (pp. 41–66). Charlotte, NC: Information Age Publishing.

Garrison, D. R., Anderson, T., & Archer, W. (2000). Critical inquiry in a text-based environment: Computer conferencing in higher education. *The Internet and Higher Education, 2*(2-3), 87–105. doi:10.1016/S1096-7516(00)00016-6

Garrison, D. R., Anderson, T., & Archer, W. (2001). Critical thinking, cognitive presence, and computer conferencing in distance education. *American Journal of Distance Education, 15*(1), 7–23. doi:10.1080/08923640109527071

Gunawardena, C. N., & Zittle, F. J. (1997). Social presence as a predictor of satisfaction within a computer-mediated conferencing environment. *American Journal of Distance Education, 11*(3), 8–26. doi:10.1080/08923649709526970

Huang, Y. M., Chiu, P. S., Liu, T. C., & Chen, T. S. (2011). The design and implementation of a meaningful learning-based evaluation method for ubiquitous learning. *Computers & Education, 57*(4), 2291–2302. doi:10.1016/j.compedu.2011.05.023

Hwang, G.-J., Tsai, C.-C., & Yang, S. J. H. (2008). Criteria, strategies and research issues of context-aware ubiquitous learning. *Journal of Educational Technology & Society, 11*(2), 81–91.

Hwang, G.-J., Wu, C.-H., Tseng, J. C. R., & Huang, I. (2011). Development of a ubiquitous learning platform based on a real-time help-seeking mechanism. *British Journal of Educational Technology, 42*(6), 992–1002. doi:10.1111/j.1467-8535.2010.01123.x

Izmirli, S. (2017). Can we use Facebook groups to establish social presence in online courses? *World Journal on Educational Technology: Current Issues, 9*(4), 173–182.

Johnson, R. D., Hornik, S., & Salas, E. (2008). An empirical examination of factors contributing to the creation of successful e-learning environments. *International Journal of Human-Computer Studies, 66*(5), 356–369. doi:10.1016/j.ijhcs.2007.11.003

Jones-Roberts, C. A. (2018). Increasing social presence online: Five strategies for instructors. *FDLA Journal, 3*.

Kreijns, K., Kirschner, P. A., Jochems, W., & Van Buuren, H. (2007). Measuring perceived sociability of computer-supported collaborative learning environments. *Computers & Education, 49*(2), 176–192. doi:10.1016/j.compedu.2005.05.004

Leone, S., & Leo, T. (2011). The synergy of paper-based and digital material for ubiquitous foreign language learners. *Knowledge Management & E-Learning: An International Journal, 3*(3), 319–341.

Lowenthal, P. R., & Dunlap, J. C. (2018). Investigating students' perceptions of instructional strategies to establish social presence. *Distance Education, 39*(3), 281–298. doi:10.1080/01587919.2018.1476844

Oyarzun, B., Barreto, D., & Conklin, S. (2018). Instructor social presence effects on learner social presence, achievement, and satisfaction. *TechTrends, 62*(6), 625–634. doi:10.100711528-018-0299-0

Park, Y. (2011). A pedagogical framework for mobile learning: Categorizing educational applications of mobile technologies into four types. *The International Review of Research in Open and Distributed Learning, 12*(2), 78–102. doi:10.19173/irrodl.v12i2.791

Richardson, J. C., & Swan, K. (2003). Examining social presence in online courses in relation to students' perceived learning and satisfaction. *Journal of Asynchronous Learning Networks, 7*(1), 68–88.

Rourke, L., Anderson, T., Garrison, D. R., & Archer, W. (1999). Assessing social presence in asynchronous text-based computer conferencing. *Journal of Distance Education, 14*(2), 50–71.

Saccol, A. Z., Kich, M., Schlemmer, E., Reinhard, N., Barbosa, J. L., & Hahn, R. (2009, January). A framework for the design of ubiquitous learning applications. In *2009 42nd Hawaii International Conference on System Sciences* (pp. 1-10). IEEE.

Short, J., Williams, E., & Christie, B. (1976). *The social psychology of telecommunications*. New York: Wiley.

Swan, K. (2003). Developing social presence in online discussions. In S. Naidu (Ed.), Learning and teaching with technology: Principles and practices (pp. 147-164). London: Kogan.

Swan, K., Garrison, D. R., & Richardson, J. C. (2009). A constructivist approach to online learning: the Community of Inquiry framework. In C. R. Payne (Ed.), *Information Technology and Constructivism in Higher Education: Progressive Learning Frameworks* (pp. 43–57). Hershey, PA: IGI Global. doi:10.4018/978-1-60566-654-9.ch004

Tan, T.-H., Liu, T.-Y., & Chang, C.-C. (2007). Development and evaluation of an RFID-based ubiquitous learning environment for outdoor learning. *Interactive Learning Environments*, *15*(3), 253–269. doi:10.1080/10494820701281431

Virtanen, M. A., Haavisto, E., Liikanen, E., & Kääriäinen, M. (2018). Ubiquitous learning environments in higher education: A scoping literature review. *Education and Information Technologies*, *23*(2), 985–998. doi:10.100710639-017-9646-6

Wang, R., Wiesemes, R., & Gibbons, C. (2012). Developing digital fluency through ubiquitous mobile devices: Findings from a small-scale study. *Computers & Education*, *58*(1), 570–578. doi:10.1016/j.compedu.2011.04.013

Wei, C. W., Chen, N. S., & Kinshuk. (2012). A model for social presence in online classrooms. *Educational Technology Research and Development*, *60*(3), 529–545. doi:10.100711423-012-9234-9

Yahya, S., Ahmad, E. A., & Jalil, K. A. (2010). The definition and characteristics of ubiquitous learning: A discussion. *International Journal of Education and Development Using Information and Communication Technology*, *6*(1), 117–127.

Yang, S. J. H. (2006). Context aware ubiquitous learning environments for peer-to-peer collaborative learning. *Journal of Educational Technology & Society*, *9*(1), 188–201.

ADDITIONAL READING

Aragon, S. R. (2003). Creating social presence in online environments. *New Directions for Adult and Continuing Education*, *100*(100), 57–68. doi:10.1002/ace.119

Chen, C. C., & Huang, T. C. (2012). Learning in a u-Museum: Developing a context-aware ubiquitous learning environment. *Computers & Education*, *59*(3), 873–883. doi:10.1016/j.compedu.2012.04.003

Dunlap, J. C., & Lowenthal, P. R. (2014). The power of presence: Our quest for the right mix of social presence in online courses. In A. A. Piña & A. P. Mizell (Eds.), *Real life distance education: Case studies in practice* (pp. 41–66). Charlotte, NC: Information Age Publishing.

Garrison, D. R., Anderson, T., & Archer, W. (2000). Critical inquiry in a text-based environment: Computer conferencing in higher education. *The Internet and Higher Education*, *2*(2-3), 87–105. doi:10.1016/S1096-7516(00)00016-6

Lowenthal, P. R., & Dunlap, J. C. (2018). Investigating students' perceptions of instructional strategies to establish social presence. *Distance Education*, *39*(3), 281–298. doi:10.1080/01587919.2018.1476844

Oyarzun, B., Barreto, D., & Conklin, S. (2018). Instructor social presence effects on learner social presence, achievement, and satisfaction. *TechTrends*, *62*(6), 625–634. doi:10.100711528-018-0299-0

Swan, K. (2003). Developing social presence in online discussions. In S. Naidu (Ed), Learning and teaching with technology: Principles and practices (pp, 147-164). London: Kogan.

Virtanen, M. A., Haavisto, E., Liikanen, E., & Kääriäinen, M. (2018). Ubiquitous learning environments in higher education: A scoping literature review. *Education and Information Technologies*, *23*(2), 985–998. doi:10.100710639-017-9646-6

KEY TERMS AND DEFINITIONS

Affective Expression: The expressions individuals use to show their feelings, emotions, values, and beliefs.

Community of Inquiry: The learning model in which learning occurs through the interactions of social presence, cognitive presence, and teaching presence.

Group Cohesion: Behaviors that help to form and maintain a group.

Open Communication: The interactions among individuals.

QR-Code: Quick response code; a two-dimensional barcode that has hidden information.

Social Presence: The perception that a person sees another as a real person in communication environments.

Ubiquitous Learning: Learning that occurs at the right time in the right place.

Chapter 11
From Ubiquitous to Ubiquitous Blended Learning Environments

Alev Ateş-Çobanoğlu
Ege University, Turkey

ABSTRACT

As advances in information and communication technology increasingly transform learning and teaching; blended learning and ubiquitous learning concepts have gained attention and become pervasive in 21st century. With the help of recent advances in mobile learning, wireless networks, RFID tags, a new model of blended learning—ubiquitous blended learning—that takes advantage of increasing ubiquity of online devices in online phase of blended learning is considered to gain attention in designing online courses. In this chapter, the author presents a picture of ubiquitous and blended learning studies while focusing on the results of ubiquitous learning and suggesting a rationale for such designs. The author defines ubiquitous blended learning as an instructional design approach that integrates ubiquitous technologies involved on-line and/or virtual learning with face-to-face learning by decreasing seat-time in class and increasing outdoor learning activities to facilitate learning from not just the teacher but from peer to peer and on-line learning communities as well.

DOI: 10.4018/978-1-5225-9779-7.ch011

INTRODUCTION

Information and communication technology (ICT), which influences and in some ways transforms learning and teaching processes in 21st century, keeps advancing. Learning anytime and anywhere has never been possible before in today's connected world. In 21st century learning, heutagogy (self-determined learning) is a leading concept which requires learners to explore, create, collaborate, connect, share and reflect (Blaschke & Hase, 2016). In blended ubiquitous learning based instructional designs, numerous on-line learning tools and/or mobile learning applications have been on fingertips of learners. Such learning opportunities help learners to act and succeed in heutagogical learning designs.

Availability of the facilities and options for learning by means of mobile and Internet technologies, has brought new terms in learning and teaching such as ubiquity and ubiquitous learning. Ubiquitous computing was first introduced by Mark Weiser as *the calm technology, that recedes into the background of our lives* which implies the technologies surrounding us. Zhu, Yu and Riezebos (2016) define the term ubiquitous as to find out learners' needs and offer transparent visual tools of learning. The advantages of just in time, anytime, anywhere learning is realized with the help of social media and ubiquitous technologies (Hung & Zhang, 2012). And Zhu et al. (2016) claim that ubiquitous learning is a smart learning environment feature for rich, personalized and unobstructed experiences. Ubiquitous learning contains the concept of flexibility in learning situations for each learner, which means such learning activities can be completed in different space and time for individual learners. And this individualization implies personalized learning as an important concept along with flexibility (Gros, Kinshuk & Maina, 2016). Vargo (2017) mention that personalized learning includes targeted instruction, data-driven decisions, flexible content, and learner reflection and ownership, besides it encourages to use digital content and tools according to the goals of instruction. So, we can understand that both ubiquitous learning and personalized learning aim at providing learning experiences which take account of learning needs of individual learners in a digitally enriched learning environment.

Liu and Hwang (2009) remarked that development of e-learning environment has evolved towards mobile and ubiquitous learning environments recently. Mobile learning technologies have the potential to enable accessing learning materials from remote locations, collaboration, peer-to-peer interaction, engagement, and sharing knowledge and experiences (Elsafi, 2018). Ubiquitous learning, specifically context-aware ubiquitous learning compensates for authentic learning for some researchers (Looi, Zhang, Chen, Seow, Chia, Norris, & Soloway, 2011). Ubiquitous learning or u- learning model is referred to the model which aims at learning anytime, anywhere, with the help of mobile devices, RFID tags, wireless sensor networks, QR codes (Wu, Hwang & Tsai, 2013). Via those devices and embedded chips, it is asserted that learning becomes more pervasive and ubiquitous than it was in the past (Yamada, Okubo, Oi, Shimada, Kojima, & Ogata, 2016).

Peña-Ayala and Cárdenas-Robledo (2019) mention ubiquitous learning as a kind of technology enhanced learning (TEL) environment in which learners are immersed in a digital environment which involves authentic learning components, several types of tools, simultaneous stimuli and interaction possibilities. As Lombardi (2007) suggests that one of those authentic learning components includes real life relevance as much as possible which relates to the purpose of ubiquitous learning. Main idea of ubiquitous learning-based design is to involve learning activities including real-life tasks which make use of instructional technologies specifically mobile computer technologies. Chiu, Kuo, Huang, & Chen (2008) assert the basic features of ubiquitous learning as interactivity of learning process, context-awareness, situation of instructional activity, urgency of learning need, initiative of knowledge acquisition, seamless learning, self-regulated learning, adopt the subject contents, actively provides personalized services and learning community. Seamless learning is defined as a continuous learning approach which bridges private and public learning spaces for individuals and collective efforts across time and different contexts. For example, learners learn both in-class and outside the class in a seamless learning-based design (Looi, So, Chen, Zhang, Wong, & Seow, 2012). Learning outside the class or outdoor learning concept is another component of ubiquitous learning practice. As McLeod and Allen-Craig (2007) mention that outdoor learning compensates for experiential learning situations outside the class which involve interactions with people and natural resources. They conducted an experimental study for the effect of out-door learning activities on learners' life effectiveness skills as time management, social competence, achievement motivation, intellectual flexibility, task leadership, emotional control, active initiative and self-confidence. Their findings indicate the increase in the life effectiveness skills of experimental group and significantly higher level of the skills for the group with two out-door learning experiences compared to the group with one. It is considered that a well-planned and targeted instruction both inside and outside the class has the potential to develop learners in many ways, not just the academic skills but life effectiveness skills as well. About the contributions and positive effects of ubiquitous learning activities, the findings of Díez-Gutiérrez and Díaz-Nafría (2018) suggest that the use of ubiquitous technologies together with a participative methodology and the teacher's pedagogical approach facilitate a collaborative, critical, more autonomous, continuous learning and grounded in reality and the context. They also posit that new practices of citizen participation come up through experiences of technological appropriation and empowerment with the help of ubiquitous learning technologies.

Ubiquitous learning can take place for example in museums, galleries, exhibitions, ecology gardens, etc. aiming to deliver context-related content to the learners in informal settings (Liu, Ogata, & Mouri, 2015) and in the courses which deal with language-learning, the environment, engineering and computing (Hwang & Wu, 2014). Besides such personalized and increased opportunities for learning, Chiu, Tseng and Hsu (2017) pointed out the problems of traditional context-aware ubiquitous learning environments such as physical limitation problems, specifically the limited capacity of the learning targets, and the need for time to reach those targets. In order to overcome these problems, Chiu et al. (2017) propose blended context-aware ubiquitous learning framework.

Pimmer, Mateescu and Gröhbiel (2016) specify that with the help of the recent advances in mobile technology, blended or hybrid designs, learners can create multimodal representations of the content outside the class, share their experiences with their classmates and teachers. This facilitates the transfer of learners' knowledge between formal, informal and personalized learning environments. Cher-Ping and Libing (2017) suggest that blended learning plays a key role for United Nations Educational, Scientific and Cultural Organization (UNESCO) in providing inclusive education and helps learners with great need of education continue their studies despite their life conditions without physical borders.

BACKGROUND

The Term Blended Learning and Related Literature

It is asserted that especially most of the courses at higher education are shifting to blended learning as technology evolves (Hill, Sharma & Johnston, 2015). In general, blended learning is considered as a mixture of old and new as much as it is a mixture of physical and digital learning (TeachThought Staff, 2018). As Elsafi (2018) points out, blending of formal and informal learning using the affordances of mobile technologies can facilitate learning in different learning environments. The term blended learning, which in-general implies integrating face to face and on-line learning activities, has been used for almost two decades. It is also referred to hybrid learning, integrative learning, technology-mediated instruction, web-enhanced instruction or mixed-mode instruction. Moreover, as TeachThought Staff (2018) argue flipping classrooms is also mentioned with the term blended learning which is a kind of relic symbolic of the gap between traditional and digital learning and makes use of *online technology to not just supplement but transform and improve the learning process*. Curzon and Tummons (2013) suggest that like the older term e-learning, blended learning is considered as a description of learning, which implies that learning is accompanied by a variety of new tools and resources increasingly. Cross (2007) claims that blended learning can take place at many places such as grocery store or bus and can include courses, content chunks, instant messaging, blog posts etc. He implies that interaction among learner-to-content, learner-to-learner, learner-to-infrastructure is the glue which holds all those pieces together.

As a term blended learning has a couple of definitions in instructional technology literature. For example, Armstrong (2012) defines blended learning as *the use of a combination of learning methods to increase the overall effectiveness of the learning process by providing for different parts of the learning mix to complement and support one another*. This definition implies using the mixture of learning methods for more effective learning and teaching process. Blended learning, which integrates class contact hours and Internet-based learning activities, is more commonly defined as the thoughtful fusion of face-to-face and on-line learning experiences (Garrison & Vaughan, 2008). Similarly, Cher-Ping and Libing (2017) define blended learning as *the fusion of on-line and face-to-face contact time* between teachers and learners. Graham, Borup, Short and Archambault (2019) mention that the blend also needs to provide learners- especially at K-12 level- with some control over time, place, path, and/or pace which is one of the two main characteristics of personalization. In the meantime, the other main feature is customization.

On the other hand, Yamada et al. (2016) suggest that blending in blended learning correspond to the *combination of real-life learning and virtual reality* in ubiquitous learning environment. Although, the definitions of blended learning vary in instructional technology literature, pervasive implementation of blended learning especially in higher education is remarkable. And that pervasive implementations can suggest that blended learning researchers somehow share a common understanding and that blended learning has positive impacts on learning outcomes. For example, Poon (2013) implies the potential of blended learning for positively influencing learners' perceptions of the learning environment and, subsequently, their study experiences, learning outcomes, and ultimate academic achievement. Freeland Fisher and White (2017) stress that strong pedagogy is the backbone of effective blended learning practices and offer seven key tips which emerged from the Blended and Personalized Learning Conference suggestions. Those tips include:

From Ubiquitous to Ubiquitous Blended Learning Environments

1. Modify models to expand relationships and collaboration
2. Go slow to go fast when implementing competency-based models
3. Make learners agents of their learning
4. Expand the conversation about cultural relevance
5. Frame tech as one tool in the toolbox
6. Reinvent professional development for the 21st century.

Also, Graham et al. (2019) suggest that blended instruction requires four key competencies as (1) online integration, (2) data practices, (3) personalization, and (4) online interaction. Blended learning and personalized learning support each other since both take into account of learners' readiness, interest, request and learning preferences to provoke effective learning experiences and motivation for learning. How effective is blended learning? Two meta-analysis studies on blended learning reveal that in comparison with classroom instruction, blended learning is significantly successful in terms of learner achievement (Bernard, Borokhovski, Schmid, Tamim, & Abrami, 2014; Vo, Zhu & Diep, 2017). Besides, Vo et al. (2017) report that the effect of blended learning on learner performance in STEM disciplines is significantly higher than that of non-STEM disciplines. The effectiveness of on-line and blended learning is also investigated by another meta-analysis (Means, Toyama, Murphy, & Baki, 2013) concluding that on average, learners in online learning conditions performed modestly better than those receiving face-to-face instruction. Blended learning is found to be more advantageous in comparison with traditional face-to-face instruction, while the case is not the same for on-line versus face-to-face instruction which suggests blended learning instead of on-line learning for better learning outcomes. Comparing blended learning with non-blended learning (pure e-learning or pure traditional face-to-face learning) in health professions, Liu, Peng, Zhang, Hu, Li and Yan (2016) also reported significant effect size indicating knowledge gain in blended learning is higher than the other forms in their meta-analysis. In sum, the studies suggest that in comparison with traditional face-to-face interaction blended learning provides better learning outcomes in many cases (Bernard et al., 2014; Liu et al., 2016; Means et al., 2013; Vo, et al., 2017). It is a good idea to enrich the on-line part of blended learning practices with the help of cutting-edge ubiquitous technologies to provide learners better learning experiences both in-and-out of the class as well. In the next session, the findings of the recent studies on both ubiquitous learning and ubiquitous blended learning which were conducted between 2014-2019 are discussed to get the notion and the contributions of ubiquitous blended learning implementations. Those findings can enlighten the researchers with interest in developing ubiquitous learning systems and studying the effects of ubiquitous learning on several variables.

Ubiquitous Learning Studies Around the World

In this section, studies on ubiquitous learning are investigated and summarized in order to make conclusions and reach a general understanding of the effects and perceived outcomes of u-learning. Based on different pedagogical approaches, ubiquitous learning environments are used at different levels. So far both positive and negative results exist in u-learning literature. For example, Hung, Hwang, Lee, Wu, Vogel, Milrad and Johansson (2014) developed a ubiquitous problem-based learning system (UPBLS) in order to examine questioning abilities of elementary school learners in scientific inquiry activities. For conducting in-field inquiry learning activities, the UPBLS provides learning guidance, an online discussion forum, an electronic library on ecology database and a green lab for different types of geo-tagged content and sensor data which collected via mobile devices. In this study, learners are expected to gain experience in the field and link their observations with the information they get from textbooks. Peer discussion, data collection, idea sharing, and reflective diary writing in the field trip are the activities of this ubiquitous learning-based program. The study found out that both the experienced and the questioning abilities of the novice learners significantly improved. Therefore, the use of mobile/ubiquitous technologies in the field trip based on problem-based learning approach is suggested for improving inquiry and questioning abilities.

Mouri, Uosaki and Ogata (2018) argue that mobile and ubiquitous technologies can enable learner autonomously to learn and save what they have learned, share their knowledge and collaborate with their peers. They mention ubiquitous learning through ubiquitous knowledge access facility of seamless language learning which mainly aims at assisting learners to link formal, in-class and informal, out-of-class language learning experiences. As mentioned previously in this chapter, one of the characteristics of ubiquitous learning environments is the seamless learning opportunities offered by the ubiquitous learning systems as Chiu et al. (2008) suggest. By using context-aware mobile applications in museums, Wang, Liu and Hwang (2017) investigated ubiquitous language learning in socio-cultural contexts and reviewed related articles which were published between 2009 and 2014. They found out that during the years 2009–2011, learners tended to care system guidance more and in general, the activities were designed for individual learning and the level of playfulness thus found to be low. However, ubiquitous location-based systems were found to be quite popular in museums via mobile technologies between 2012–2014. Wang et al. (2017) suggested that this allowed more social interaction among learners for language learning and more improvements in linguistic developments. And they underline the shift from mobile technology-assisted learning to context-aware ubiquitous learning all over the world. Aiming at developing English listening and reading skills of English as a Foreign Language (EFL) learning learners, Wang, Lin, Hwang and Liu (2018) developed and investigated the effects of a context-aware ubiquitous language learning (CAULL) system which is a green-building English-learning application (GBELA) in combination with QR code sensor technology. By using GBELA, the learners are required to learn more about a carbon-free, ecological building that exhibits numerous authentic applications of green technology. Wang et al. (2018) mention that the type of EFL approach followed in this instructional design is called content and language integrated learning for increasing discipline-specific knowledge and foreign language skills of learners simultaneously. Having positive impacts on developing receptive skills for EFL, the researchers concluded that a well-designed context-aware learning system can assist learners enhance their self-efficacy in CAULL environment.

Another example with positive learning outcomes is from Taiwan which was conducted on K-7 learners for geography instruction. Yang and Chang (2017) developed a Ubiquitous Geography Learning System which was integrated with Location Awareness using GPS capability. With Quick Response Code (QR Code), the researchers also prepared some triggers for special questions in classroom and other learning field. Their system generated learning profile and analysis report for the activities of each learner which was proved to be effective on learners' geography learning.

From Ubiquitous to Ubiquitous Blended Learning Environments

For class teachers' adult education, Meriläinen and Piispanen (2017) developed and tried out a ubiquitous learning model based on the principles of transformational pedagogy. By utilizing virtual possibilities and e-pedagogy, they designed instruction linked to authentic learning contexts and utilized virtual possibilities. Positively, this study module offered learners flexibility for the time of the day to study, and it also provided transversal competences which are linked to transformational pedagogy, as a part of an authentic learning experience.

A SWOT analysis study provides ubiquitous computing researchers to see both sides of the coin. That study with undergraduate learners was conducted about ubiquitous computing and computer-intermediated community interaction and its effects on education (Siddiqui, Waqas, Soomrani, Qureshi, Gul & Memon, 2018). Among the findings, the researchers reported that ubiquitous computing and computer-intermediated community interaction are perceived as essential ingredients of the learners' learning process since they provide flexibility, effectiveness in terms of time, cost and the ability to acquire computer skills. On the other hand, perceived threats for ubiquitous computing and computer-intermediated community interaction also exist such as security issues, privacy, health effects and noise in the learning environment.

Besides the positive results for ubiquitous learning practices, some ubiquitous learning studies also reported *negative* aspects. For example, in health science instruction, Virtanen, Kääriäinen, Liikanen and Haavisto (2017) compared learners' satisfaction and found out that u-learning group of learners were satisfied both pedagogically and technically, however they needed more support from teacher. Web-based learning environment was perceived as easier and more supportive than ubiquitous learning environment. Ubiquitous learning environment developers need to be cautious about designing a complicated learning environment without providing enough technical and pedagogical support for learners.

Zarghami-Hamrah and de Vries (2018) discussed the changes in teachers' role and moral mission for creating changes in learning environments which involve ubiquitous learning and massive communication activities in MOOCs. They noticed that the teachers must be aware of the potential risk of reducing learners' motivation and attachment due to the decrease in interaction between individual learners and the teacher along with the substitution of conversation with texting as the means of communication. Therefore, ubiquitous learning designs need to consider the instructional variables such as learner motivation, engagement, performance etc. which affect the quality of learning and teaching process.

MAIN FOCUS OF THE CHAPTER

Managing and Designing Online Courses in Ubiquitous Blended Learning Environments

Although blended learning and ubiquitous learning are separate terms, in fact, online learning part of blended learning environments can easily be enhanced with ubiquitous learning, which offers learners personalized learning facilities, time and space independence, flexibility, and augmented learning experiences via ubiquitous technologies. The author defines Ubiquitous Blended Learning (U-blended learning) as an instructional design approach which integrates ubiquitous technologies involved on-line and/or virtual learning with face-to-face learning by decreasing seat-time in class and increasing outdoor learning activities to facilitate learning from not just the teacher but from peer to peer and on-line learning communities as well. That means, u-learning can be provided in case the learners are provided learning experiences via mobile and other ubiquitous computing devices which enable them to learn outside the class as well. U-blended designs aim to integrate in and outside class learning experiences meaningfully for reaching the goals of instruction.

It is remarkable that u-blended learning is relatively a new term in ubiquitous computing related literature and there is a lack of the studies specific to ubiquitous blended learning worldwide. In one of these studies, Zhang (2008) reported that blended or hybrid learning mixes U-learning with traditional type (Classroom-based) of learning. He implied the advantage of blended learning as uniting best of the both worlds and offering learners social interaction in class and online instruction, in which ubiquitous learning provides mobility and learning anywhere, anytime. Systematically, Pimmer et al. (2016) analyzed 36 empirical papers about mobile and ubiquitous learning in higher education settings and posit that positive outcomes of those studies stem from instructionist and hybrid or blended designs in general. They also mention a lack of empirical evidence for broad application of mobile and ubiquitous learning in higher education. About language learning, García-Sánchez (2016) integrated a ubiquitous learning approach for enhancing interaction and communication skills of ESP learners in distance and blended environments. And she showed that this design is innovative and successfully competence addressed.

In another u-blended learning study on science education, Chiu et al. (2017) proposed a navigation algorithm, B-MONS, and designed a blended context-aware ubiquitous learning system, BCAULS, with a navigation support mechanism based on B-MONS. In the National Museum of Natural Science, Taiwan, they made a field experiment. The results of their experiment showed that the performance of the learners in blended context-aware ubiquitous learning group is much better than the other two groups of the experiment which are the traditional ubiquitous learning and the e-learning groups.

As a part of a comparative study for twelve contexts, Díez-Gutiérrez and Díaz-Nafría (2018) studied the ubiquitous learning via blended instruction for the "lifelong training of trainers" and whether that model and use of open access technological tools affected development of soft skills as instrumental, cognitive-intellectual, socio-communicative, emotional and digital character. They noticed the presence of the teacher as a mediator in those learning ecologies and concluded that the ubiquitous and expanded learning provide the dilution of space-time, curricular and methodological boundaries; more horizontally and participatively knowledge-building; and the increase in the capacity for network interaction and shared effort. According to some of the findings for that large-scale study, stronger connection with social reality provided by the social media on a continuous and permanent basis through ubiquitous learning practices developed soft skills of the participant learners.

In another study about computer science instruction, Tsai, Shen and Chiang (2018) integrated ubiquitous learning and blended learning. The ubiquitous learners-as-designers improved computing skills of learners significantly while the ubiquitous self-organized learning did not. The researchers' comment on the reasons of that insignificant results is generally, the learners in Taiwan are unwilling to take responsibility for their learning. Therefore, Tsai et al. (2018) suggest self-organized ubiquitous learning to be implemented on independent and actively engaged learners. Moreover, in liberal arts education, Chin, Lee and Chen (2018) investigated the effects of the interactive ubiquitous learning system and their findings indicate that this system significantly increased overall performance.

From Ubiquitous to Ubiquitous Blended Learning Environments

A recent ubiquitous blended learning study was conducted on engineering learners regarding biofuel characterization. Manuel, Pilar, Dolores, MP, Sara and Pilar (2019) developed and facilitated three virtual labs, a web application and a social media group in their instructional design. And they found that learners are satisfied with using both the virtual labs and network web app. Social networks and the social network-based web app are found to be helpful for communication and easy access to virtual laboratories. Also, the results revealed that ubiquitous blended learning with experimental laboratory increases exam scores significantly.

The argument of this chapter is that with the help of technological advances in mobile learning, wireless networks, RFID tags; that relatively new form of u-learning - ubiquitous blended learning- is promising (Chiu et al., 2017; Manuel et al., 2019; Pimmer et al., 2016; Tsai et al., 2018; Zhang, 2008) and effectiveness of u-learning will increase by the help of blended learning models with face-to-face social interaction among learners and teachers.

SOLUTIONS AND RECOMMENDATIONS

Suggestions for Ubiquitous Blended Learning Environments

The results of blended learning, ubiquitous learning and ubiquitous blended learning studies are encouraging for further studies in general. As previously reported, blended learning practices at various levels especially in higher education and K-12 level instruction, has a positive impact on learners' performance in comparison with traditional face-to-face interaction and/or other non-blending practices in general (Bernard et al., 2014; Liu et al., 2016; Means et al., 2013; Vo et al., 2017). Besides, the literature records provide us many ubiquitous learning examples from different application areas such as scientific field-inquiry activities (Chiu et al., 2017; Hung et al., 2014); language learning in particular EFL learning-teaching (Mouri et al., 2018; Wang et al., 2017; Wang et al., 2018); computer science instruction (Siddiqui et al., 2018; Tsai et al., 2018); arts and cultural heritage instruction in museums (Chin et al., 2018); geography instruction (Yang & Chang, 2017); health science instruction (Virtanen et al., 2017), adult education (Díez-Gutiérrez & Díaz-Nafría, 2018; Meriläinen & Piispanen, 2017) and engineering education (Manuel et al., 2019) as well. Most of them have an outdoor learning component and many of them make use of QR codes, sensor technologies or specific ubiquitous learning systems or applications which are developed by the researchers. In general, the results indicate the positive impact of ubiquitous learning and ubiquitous blended learning systems (Manuel et al., 2019; Pimmer et al. 2016) on learners' motivation, performance, satisfaction and so on. Besides, Tsai et al. (2018) showed that the ubiquitous learners-as-designers group was significantly more successful than the ubiquitous self-organized-learning group, which implies that the lack of independent learning skills affect the performance of learners in a ubiquitous learning environment.

On the other hand, lack of clear instructions and teacher support (Virtanen et al., 2017) may decrease learner satisfaction while reduced face-to-face sessions (Zarghami-Hamrah & de Vries, 2018) may disengage learners and lower the motivation of learners. One can conclude from the above studies that ubiquitous learning is closely related with mobile learning and as Chiu et al. (2017) found, blended context-aware type of ubiquitous learning is more effective than traditional type on increasing learner performance. It is suggested that blended ubiquitous learning environments need to consider the implications of personalized learning. Main idea of personalized learning is to accelerate learning by tailoring instruction to the learning needs and skills of each learner.

In terms of blended learning, more commonly, it is referred to the fusion of face-to-face and online learning components (Cher-Ping & Libing, 2017; Garrison & Vaughan, 2008) while Yamada et al. (2016) claim it as the combination of real-life learning and virtual reality in ubiquitous learning environment. Therefore, it is possible to apply ubiquitous blended learning to the courses which require outdoor learning via mobile activities in order to reach their specific objectives. For example, a professor can introduce a topic in class and the next lesson he/ she can lead the learners to another learning environment which has ubiquitous systems. Or a science teacher along with the learners first may visit a herbarium and take a tour with their mobile devices and the learners independently learn by blended context-aware ubiquitous systems. Afterwards, they make a lesson in a science lab and discuss what they understand and observed. In this example, ubiquitous blended design includes flipped learning model of blended learning which suggests learners to study theoretical concepts via mobile learning before and outside the school and afterwards make practices in class.

It is suggested to the instructional designers of online courses in ubiquitous blended learning environments, first, to review blended learning models (such as flipped classroom, flex, enriched virtual, a la carte etc.) in the literature (Clayton Christensen Institute, 2019), and, second, find the best instructional design solution for their target group by analyzing their online learning readiness, learning needs and Internet access facilities; third, design and develop a ubiquitous learning environment according to course objectives which will be available online to the target group; four, plan face-to-face and on-line portions of the blended course and integrate them which will make use of ubiquitous technologies in the online phase and five, evaluate the learning outputs as a consequence of u-blended learning practices and revise the design phase accordingly.

For successful implementations of blended ubiquitous learning designs and get positive learning outcomes, several variables for learning effectiveness exist. However, it is possible to note some key factors for the practitioners, researchers and policy makers. In terms of using blended ubiquitous learning tools effectively and get productive learning solutions, Díez-Gutiérrez and Díaz-Nafría (2018) ascertain that mobile technology, contents, and the self-motivation for learning are the key factors to create learning ecologies- ubiquitous learning communities- beyond the formal and on-site traditional context. Moreover, the author suggests some other key factors for successful and effective ubiquitous blended practices which are as follows:

- Teacher's potential motivation and interest for redesigning instruction according to both face-to-face and on-line learning modalities and integrating ubiquitous learning technologies to the on-line modality
- Adaptation of policies and regulations for learning and teaching practices via ubiquitous technologies which require out-door learning.
- Readiness of learners and teachers in terms of capabilities for using online learning tools

- Matching the needs and expectations of learners and teachers
- Matching the nature and the objectives of the content area or the course
- Having and offering required technology infrastructure including high-speed Internet connection, wireless devices for ubiquitous learning and necessary software
- Learners with autonomous learning skills and inner motivation.

CONCLUSION

As an enabling and important tool, technology serves as a catalyst for change in current traditional educational settings and move towards blended learning. It is considered that main motivation for heading towards blended learning approach is the need for enhancing quality standards in learning and teaching process by forming online communities of inquiry (Garrison & Vaughan, 2008). Similarly, one of the characteristics of ubiquitous learning is to offer learners being a part of a learning community as Chiu et al. (2008) suggest. Díez-Gutiérrez and Díaz-Nafría (2018) mention the concept *ubiquitous learning ecologies* as the environments which help the formation of expanded learning networks and communities via digital tools in which knowledge is exchanged in blended learning environments. Zarghami-Hamrah and de Vries (2018) also implied the transformation by ubiquitous learning which includes the manner of interaction in a learning community from face to face to online interactions and noticed the potential disadvantages of reduced face to face interaction for the effectiveness of teaching and learning process. That risk needs to be considered while designing instruction based on ubiquitous blended learning approach.

One can realize that both ubiquitous learning and blended learning share common and similar instructional goals. Both basically aim at freeing learning activities from physical boundaries such as brick-and-mortar classrooms and provide learners opportunities to stay connected with their peers, teachers, their learning communities as well. Both ubiquitous learning and blended learning designs favor interaction between learner-and-learner, learner-and-teacher and learner-and-content. And they make use of digital tools or systems which enable these interactions.

It is rational to integrate them as u-blended learning design which makes use of u-learning facilities for 21st century learners without giving up face-to-face learning sessions with teacher guidance and peer learning facilities. As proposed in this chapter, U-blended learning takes advantage of increasing ubiquity of online devices in online phase of blended learning by decreasing seat-time in classroom and increasing on-line personalized learning facilities. It is considered that u-blended learning as a new form of u-learning approach will gain attention in designing online courses in ubiquitous learning environments. With the advantage of face-to-face interaction component, blended learning designs are suggested for the instructional designers who wish to design and apply more effective and efficient ubiquitous learning environments. As Díez-Gutiérrez and Díaz-Nafría (2018) report, ubiquitous learning must boost a critical and emancipating social knowledge for life, beyond the classroom. And this is possible with the blended learning models integrated in the instructional design. For example, Davies, Dean and Ball (2013) found that flipped classroom model facilitates learning, motivates the learners and it is effective and scalable. Therefore, the author believes that it is possible to get positive learning outcomes with applying flipped learning model in a u-blended design.

In the meantime, one of the recent trends and practices of distance learning, Massive Open Online Courses (MOOCs) can provide learners access to free information in a ubiquitous learning environment as Zarghami-Hamrah and de Vries (2018) noted. Similarly, in a u-blended design, the teacher can integrate classroom activities and MOOC activities according to instructional objectives and study the effects of such ubiquitously enhanced designs on various variables such as performance, motivation, efficacy, teaching and learning quality, etc.

Moreover, the author suggest that it would be helpful for the interested readers and researchers to present a list of the key concepts for ubiquitous blended learning. These key concepts which are briefly explained in this chapter, frequently appear in ubiquitous or ubiquitous blended learning studies. And it is considered that these key concepts are associated and sometimes complementary for each other's in terms of their purposes for improving learning of individual learners so often with the digital technologies.

- flexible learning
- authentic learning
- outdoor learning
- seamless learning
- personalized learning
- mobile learning

In conclusion, in a kind of online course design as u-blended course, learners are more self-directed and learn collaboratively with their peers, they solve problems, explore and share knowledge through both online and real-life physical learning environments. ICT have the power for both improving learners' experiences and affecting the communities surrounded by them as Cher-Ping and Libing (2017) posit. It seems that ubiquitous learning makes the world a classroom in which a user learns through computer-mediated social interaction using mobile devices (Asiimwe and Khan, 2013). Since it is at the early stages of u-blended learning studies, further studies will provide evidence for the effectiveness of that kind of u-learning environment. Nonetheless, it is considered that especially by means of recent context-aware u-blended designs, we, educators, are more able to diffuse daily routines of our learners which keep on going outside the doors of the classroom than we were in the past.

REFERENCES

Armstrong, M. (2012). *Armstrong's handbook of management and leadership: developing effective people skills for better leadership and management* (3rd ed.). Kogan Page Publishers.

Asiimwe, E. N., & Khan, S. Z. (2013, October). *Ubiquitous computing in education: A SWOT analysis by students and teachers*. Paper presented at the 12th World Conference on Mobile and Contextual Learning (mLearn 2013), College of the North Atlantic, Qatar. 10.5339/qproc.2013.mlearn.18

Bernard, R. M., Borokhovski, E., Schmid, R. F., Tamim, R. M., & Abrami, P. C. (2014). A meta-analysis of blended learning and technology use in higher education: From the general to the applied. *Journal of Computing in Higher Education*, 26(1), 87–102. doi:10.100712528-013-9077-3

Blaschke, L. M., & Hase, S. (2016). Heutagogy: A Holistic Framework for Creating Twenty-First-Century Self-determined Learners. In K. Begoña & M. Maina (Eds.), *The Future of Ubiquitous Learning. Gros* (pp. 25–41). Berlin: Springer. doi:10.1007/978-3-662-47724-3_2

Cher-Ping, L., & Libing, W. (2017). *Blended learning for quality higher education: Selected case studies on implementation from Asia-Pacific*. United Nations Educational, Scientific and Cultural Organization.

Chin, K. Y., Lee, K. F., & Chen, Y. L. (2018). Using an interactive ubiquitous learning system to enhance authentic learning experiences in a cultural heritage course. *Interactive Learning Environments*, 26(4), 444–459. doi:10.1080/10494820.2017.1341939

Chiu, C.-K., Tseng, J. C. R., & Hsu, T.-Y. (2017). Blended Context-Aware Ubiquitous Learning in Museums: Environment, Navigation Support and System Development. *Personal and Ubiquitous Computing*, 21(2), 355–369. doi:10.100700779-016-0986-9

Chiu, P. S., Kuo, Y., Huang, Y., & Chen, T. (2008). A Meaningful Learning based u-Learning Evaluation Model. *Eighth IEEE International Conference on Advanced Learning Technologies*, 77–81. 10.1109/ICALT.2008.100

Clayton Christensen Institute. (2019). *Models*. Retrieved May 9, 2019 from https://www.blendedlearning.org/models/

Cross, J. (2007). *Informal learning: Rediscovering the natural pathways that inspire innovation and performance*. San Francisco, CA: Pfeiffer/John Wiley & Sons.

Curzon, L. B., & Tummons, J. (2013). *Teaching in further education: An outline of principles and practice (7th ed.)*. Bloomsbury Academic.

Davies, R. S., Dean, D. L., & Ball, N. (2013). Flipping the classroom and instructional technology integration in a college-level information systems spreadsheet course. *Educational Technology Research and Development*, 61(4), 563–580. doi:10.100711423-013-9305-6

Díez-Gutiérrez, E., & Díaz-Nafría, J. (2018). Ubiquitous learning ecologies for a critical cybercitizenship. *Comunicar*, (54), 49–58. doi:10.3916/C54-2018-05

Elsafi, A. (2018). Formal and Informal Learning Using Mobile Technology. In S. Yu, M. Ally, & A. Tsinakos (Eds.), *Mobile and Ubiquitous Learning An International Handbook*. Singapore: Springer. doi:10.1007/978-981-10-6144-8_11

Freeland Fisher, J., & White, J. (2017). *From maverick to mainstream: Takeaways from the 2017 blended and personalized learning conference*. Retrieved June 5, 2019 from https://files.eric.ed.gov/fulltext/ED586384.pdf

García-Sánchez, S. (2016). Ubiquitous interaction for ESP distance and blended learners. *Journal of Applied Research in Higher Education, 8*(4), 489–503. doi:10.1108/JARHE-04-2014-0052

Garrison, D. R., & Vaughan, N. D. (2008). *Blended learning in higher education: Framework, principles, and guidelines*. Wiley.

Godwin-Jones, R. (2018). *Six models of blended learning: Part 2*. Retrieved June 10, 2019 from https://blog.softchalk.com/six-models-of-blended-learning-part-2

Graham, C. R. (2006). Blended learning systems: Definition, current trends, and future directions. In C. J. Bonk & C. R. Graham (Eds.), *Handbook of blended learning: Global perspectives, local designs*. San Francisco: Pfeiffer Publishing.

Graham, C. R., Borup, J., Short, C. R., & Archambault, L. (2019). *K-12 Blended Teaching: A Guide to Personalized Learning and Online Integration*. Ed Tech Books. Teacher Edition Version 1.0. Retrieved May 5, 2019 from https://drive.google.com/file/d/1P-2nftugd8ALWddD50tsXxrpZpkDvucT/view

Gros, B. K., & Maina, M. (Eds.). (2016). The future of ubiquitous learning. Berlin: Springer.

Hill, M., Sharma, M. D., & Johnston, H. (2015). How online learning modules can improve the representational fluency and conceptual understanding of university physics students. *European Journal of Physics, 36*(4), 1–20. doi:10.1088/0143-0807/36/4/045019

Hung, J.-L., & Zhang, K. (2012). Examining Mobile Learning Trends 2003-2008: A Categorical Meta-Trend Analysis Using Text Mining. *Journal of Computing in Higher Education, 24*(1), 1–17. doi:10.100712528-011-9044-9

Hung, P.-H., Hwang, G.-J., Lee, Y.-H., Wu, T.-H., Vogel, B., Milrad, M., & Johansson, E. (2014). A Problem-based Ubiquitous Learning Approach to Improving the Questioning Abilities of Elementary School Students. *Journal of Educational Technology & Society, 17*(4), 316–334.

Hwang, G.-J., & Wu, P.-H. (2014). Applications, impacts and trends of mobile technology-enhanced learning: A review of 2008-2012 publications in selected SSCI journals. *Int. J. of Mobile Learning and Organisation, 8*(2), 83–95. doi:10.1504/IJMLO.2014.062346

Liu, G., & Hwang, G. (2010). A key step to understanding paradigm shifts in e-learning. *British Journal of Educational Technology, 41*(2), E1–E9. doi:10.1111/j.1467-8535.2009.00976.x

Liu, Q., Peng, W., Zhang, F., Hu, R., Li, Y., & Yan, W. (2016). The effectiveness of blended learning in health professions: Systematic review and metaanalysis. *Journal of Medical Internet Research, 18*(1), e2. doi:10.2196/jmir.4807 PMID:26729058

Liu, S., Ogata, H., & Mouri, K. (2015). Accelerate location-based context learning for second language learning using ubiquitous learning log. In Emerging issues in smart learning. Springer. doi:10.1007/978-3-662-44188-6_7

Lombardi, M. M. (2007). *Authentic learning for the 21st century: an overview*. Retrieved June 18, 2019 from https://net. educause.edu/ir/library/pdf/ELI3009.pdf

Looi, C. K., So, H. J., Chen, W., Zhang, B., Wong, L. H., & Seow, P. (2012). Seamless Learning. In N. M. Seel (Ed.), *Encyclopedia of the Sciences of Learning*. Boston, MA: Springer. doi:10.1007/978-1-4419-1428-6_251

Looi, C. K., Zhang, B., Chen, W., Seow, P., Chia, G., Norris, C., & Soloway, E. (2011). 1: 1 mobile inquiry learning experience for primary science students: A study of learning effectiveness. *Journal of Computer Assisted Learning, 27*(3), 269–287. doi:10.1111/j.1365-2729.2010.00390.x

Manuel, P.-M., Aparicio Martinez, P., & Maria, D. R.-M., MP, D., Pinzi, S., & Pilar, M.-J.M. (2019). Characterization of biodiesel using virtual laboratories integrating social networks and web app following a ubiquitous- and blended-learning. *Journal of Cleaner Production, 215*, 399–409. doi:10.1016/j.jclepro.2019.01.098

McLeod, B., & Allen-Craig, S. (2007). What outcomes are we trying to achieve in our outdoor education programs? *Australian Journal of Outdoor Education, 11*(2), 41–49. doi:10.1007/BF03400856

Means, B., Toyama, Y., Murphy, R. F., & Baki, M. (2013). The effectiveness of online and blended learning: A meta-analysis of the empirical literature. *Teachers College Record, 115*(3), 1–47. Retrieved from http://www.tcrecord.org/library/content.asp?contentid=16882

Meriläinen, M., & Piispanen, M. (2017). Ubiquitous learning in appropriate learning environments. *International Journal of Technology and Inclusive Education, 7*(1), 1215–1223.

Mouri, K., Uosaki, N., & Ogata, H. (2018). Learning analytics for Supporting Seamless Language Learning using E-book with Ubiquitous Learning System. *Journal of Educational Technology & Society, 21*(2), 150–163.

Norberg, A., Dziuban, C. D., & Moskal, P. D. (2011). A time-based blended learning model. *On the Horizon, 19*(3), 207–216. doi:10.1108/10748121111163913

Peña-Ayala, A. & Cárdenas-Robledo, L. A. (2019). A cybernetic method to regulate learning through learning strategies: A proactive and reactive mechanism applied in U–Learning settings. *Computers in Human Behavior*. doi: .2019.03.036 doi:10.1016/j.chb

Pimmer, C., Mateescu, M., & Gröhbiel, U. (2016). Mobile and ubiquitous learning in higher education settings. A systematic review of empirical studies. *Computers in Human Behavior, 63*, 490–501. doi:10.1016/j.chb.2016.05.057

Siddiqui, S., Waqas, A., Soomrani, M. A. R., Qureshi, F., Gul, M., & Memon, I. (2018, July). *U-learning: A modern paradigm shift of learning from higher education students' perspective.* Paper presented at the 2018 International Conference on Information and Communication Technology for the Muslim World (ICT4M), Kuala Lumpur, Malaysia. 10.1109/ICT4M.2018.00043

TeachThought Staff. (2018). *The definition of blended learning.* Retrieved May 10, 2019 from https://www.teachthought.com/learning/the-definition-of-blended-learning/

Tsai, C.-W., Shen, P.-D. & Chiang, I.-C. (2018). Investigating the effects of ubiquitous self-organized learning and learners-as-designers to improve students' learning performance, academic motivation, and engagement in a cloud course. *Universal Access in the Information,* 1-16. doi:10.100710209-018-0614-8

Vargo, J. (2017). *Six examples of what personalized learning looks like.* Retrieved April 5, 2019 from https://www.edelements.com/blog/six-examples-of-what-personalized-learning-looks-like

Virtanen, M., Kääriäinen, M., Liikanen, E., & Haavisto, E. (2017). The comparison of students' satisfaction between ubiquitous and web-based learning environments in clinical histotechnology studies. *Education and Information Technologies, 22,* 2565–2581. doi:10.100710639-016-9561-2

Vo, H. M., Zhu, C., & Diep, N. A. (2017). The effect of blended learning on student performance at course-level in higher education: A meta-analysis. *Studies in Educational Evaluation, 53,* 17–28. doi:10.1016/j.stueduc.2017.01.002

Wang, H.-Y., Lin, V., Hwang, G.-J., & Liu, G.-Z. (2018). Context-aware language-learning application in the green technology building: Which group can benefit the most? *Journal of Computer Assisted Learning, 2018,* 1–19. doi:10.1111/jcal.12336

Wang, H. Y., Liu, G. Z., & Hwang, G. J. (2017). Integrating socio-cultural contexts and location-based systems for ubiquitous language learning in museums: A state of the art review of 2009–2014. *British Journal of Educational Technology, 48*(2), 653–671. doi:10.1111/bjet.12424

Weiser, M. (1991). The computer of the 21st century. *Scientific American, 265*(3), 66–75. doi:10.1038 cientificamerican0991-94 PMID:1754874

Wu, P. H., Hwang, G. J., & Tsai, W. H. (2013). An expert system-based context-aware ubiquitous learning approach for conducting science learning activities. *Journal of Educational Technology & Society, 16*(4), 217–230.

Yamada, M., Okubo, F., Oi, M., Shimada, A., Kojima, K., & Ogata, H. (2016). Learning Analytics in Ubiquitous Learning Environments: Self-Regulated Learning Perspective. In *ICCE 2016 - 24th International Conference on Computers in Education: Think Global Act Local - Main Conference Proceedings* (pp. 306-314). Asia-Pacific Society for Computers in Education.

Yang, H.-C., & Chang, W.-C. (2017). Ubiquitous smartphone platform for K-7 students learning geography in Taiwan. *Multimedia Tools and Applications, 76*(9), 11651–11668. doi:10.100711042-016-3325-2

Zarghami-Hamrah, S., & de Vries, M. J. (2018). Ubiquitous learning and massive communication in MOOCs: Revisiting the role of teaching as a praxis. *Ethics and Education, 13*(3), 370–384. doi:10.1080/17449642.2018.1509189

Zhang, J. P. (2008). Hybrid learning and ubiquitous learning. *Hybrid Learning and Education, 5169*, 250–258. doi:10.1007/978-3-540-85170-7_22

Zhu, Z.-T., Yu, M.-H., & Riezebos, P. (2016). A research framework of smart education. *Smart Learning Environments, 3*(4), 1–17. doi:10.118640561-016-0026-2

ADDITIONAL READING

Alexander, B., Ashford-Rowe, K., Barajas-Murphy, N., Dobbin, G., Knott, J., McCormack, M., ... Weber, N. (2019). *EDUCAUSE Horizon Report: 2019 Higher Education Edition*. Louisville, CO: EDUCAUSE.

Chia-Chen, C., & Tien-Chi, H. (2012). Learning in a u-Museum: Developing a context-aware ubiquitous learning environment. *Computers & Education, 59*(3), 873–883. doi:10.1016/j.compedu.2012.04.003

Dziuban, C., Graham, C. R., Moskal, P., Norberg, A., & Sicilia, N. (2018). Blended learning: The new normal and emerging technologies. *International Journal of Educational Technology in Higher Education, 15*(3), 1–16. doi:10.118641239-017-0087-5

Ossiannilsson, E. (Ed.). (2018). *Ubiquitous Inclusive Learning in a Digital Era*. USA: IGI Global.

Sampson, D. G., Isaias, P., Ifenthaler, D., & Spector, J. M. (Eds.). (2013). *Ubiquitous and mobile learning in the digital age*. New York, NY: Springer. doi:10.1007/978-1-4614-3329-3

Wang, C., & Wu, F. (2018). An Expert System Approach to Support Blended Learning in Context-Aware Environment. In S. Cheung, L. Kwok, K. Kubota, L. K. Lee, & J. Tokito (Eds.), Lecture Notes in Computer Science: Vol. 10949. *Blended Learning. Enhancing Learning Success. ICBL 2018*. Cham: Springer. doi:10.1007/978-3-319-94505-7_3

Yen, J. C., & Lee, C. Y. (2011). Exploring problem solving patterns and their impact on learning achievement in a blended learning environment. *Computers & Education, 56*(1), 138–145. doi:10.1016/j.compedu.2010.08.012

Yu, S., Ally, M., & Tsinakos, A. (Eds.). (2018). *Mobile and ubiquitous learning: An international handbook*. Singapore: Springer. doi:10.1007/978-981-10-6144-8

KEY TERMS AND DEFINITIONS

Blended Learning: An instructional design approach which integrates on-line and/or virtual learning with face-to-face learning by decreasing seat-time in class and increasing out-door learning activities to facilitate learning from not just the teacher but from on-line learning communities as well.

Flexible Learning: An approach which suggests instructional designers to provide learning facilities which gives learners choices for time and/or place for learning in a customized way.

Mobile Learning: An approach which facilitates mobile devices such as laptops, tablets, smartphones, etc. for learning and teaching purposes.

Outdoor Learning: An approach which offers experiential learning activities outside the class to ensure learners different learning experiences.

Personalized Learning: An approach which considers individual learning needs, learning styles and background in an instructional design.

Seamless Learning: An approach which suggests connecting private and personal lives of learners to continue learning outside the class as well.

Ubiquitous Blended Learning: An instructional design approach which integrates ubiquitous technologies involved on-line and/or virtual learning with face-to-face learning by decreasing seat-time in class and increasing outdoor learning activities to facilitate learning from not just the teacher but from on-line learning communities as well.

Chapter 12
The Challenges and Opportunities of Partnership in Establishing Online Postgraduate Provision

Faye Taylor
Nottingham Trent University, UK

ABSTRACT

This chapter shares some of the 'lessons learned' from the author's perspective of adopting a higher education services provider as partner for the design, development, and delivery of online postgraduate provision. Ultimately, partnering with a higher education services provider for the development of online learning offers distinct benefits in terms of marketing support, project management, and instructional design but the key to ensuring the partnership works effectively and impacts positively upon student experience, is to ensure a clear delineation of roles and responsibilities from the outset, avoid unnecessary shifts in personnel, and have a system of monitoring and control in place from the university's perspective to ensure that roles and responsibilities within the partnership are being upheld.

DOI: 10.4018/978-1-5225-9779-7.ch012

INTRODUCTION

Nottingham Trent University and specifically Nottingham Business School are increasingly regarded at the forefront of innovation within academia (The Times and Sunday Times Good University Guide, 2018). This being ratified by a number of recent accolades and accreditations to include EQUIS and AACSB (The Guardian, 2018; Financial Times, 2018), and, most recently, The Guardian's University of the Year 2019. The University's strategic intent focuses upon 'creating the University of the future'. Two of the principles of this strategy seek to 'create opportunity' and 'connect globally'. A resultant action of pursuing these goals may be seen in the recent expansion of online learning, underpinned by a new structure which incorporates Flexible and Online Learning, viewed through the University's strategic 'Digital Lens'.

Over the numerous options available to an educational provider intending to establish online provision, the University selected to partner with a Higher Education Services provider, in order to contribute certain services to the partnership, to include; marketing, recruitment, project management and instructional design. The pilot programmes for this venture included three postgraduate programmes from three different academic Schools; an MBA, an Msc in Construction Project Management and MA in International Relations. There are some notable implications of this decision, both positively and negatively; with the key concern being the impact upon student experience.

Subsequently, this chapter considers the value of the relationship and shares experiences, particularly with regard to student experience. To do this, a qualitative, interpretivist approach was taken in which the author (who is also a programme leader) will draw upon in depth interviews with key stakeholders of the project in addition to various forms of student evaluation. It is hoped that by sharing these experiences, it will enable other academics and institutions, in a similar position, to make an informed choice regarding the benefits of partnership and collaboration for online learning development. To date, whilst there is a growing body of research from a pedogogical perspective that concerns the characteristics of online learning (Arbaugh, 2018), its challenges and its design (Arkorful & Abaidoo, 2015; Porter, 2015; Porter, Graham, Spring & Welch, 2014; Richey & Klein, 2014); there is an apparent lack of attention to the modes through which online learning can be established. Something that this research seeks to remedy.

BACKGROUND

Universities have been traditionally independent, and competitive (Hawkins, 2003). Whereas, distance learning institutions have traditionally been more cooperative and accommodating with partner institutions. Interestingly, Rubin (2003) has noted that "traditional universities are becoming more like distance learning universities and not the opposite" (p. 59). With this shift, more institutions are creating partnerships with other colleges, universities, companies, and other kinds of institutions to share technology and to produce and deliver courses (Carnevale, 2000c; Dunn, 2000; Cheney, 2002). However, partnerships present "obstacles as well as benefits. Winning accreditation, providing student services, setting tuition, figuring out finances, and transferring course credits are among the thorny issues that administrators find themselves struggling to face collectively" (Carnevale, 2000b, p. 2).

The Challenges and Opportunities of Partnership in Establishing Online

With the online market becoming increasingly competitive and traditional universities wanting to increase their global footprint, it is clear to see why online, blended and flexible learning may be viewed as a way to access new markets and have a significant impact upon students around the globe. This being particularly important in Nottingham Trent University whose strategic intent is to communicate a 'connecting globally' focus of a quality that would mirror the existing on-campus provision that has won the University such high rankings and accolades.

New entrants to the online market have a variety of options concerning how they will approach the development of flexible and online provision. Clearly, to retain the locus of control internally, the development can be resourced using existing infrastructure. However, another option is to partner with a Higher Education Academic Services provider. There are a number of competitors within this field; offering a similar range of services dependent upon the contractual details agreed, but to include; marketing and recruitment support, instructional design services, project management, technical helpdesk and administrative services. In the case of Nottingham Trent University, this second option was favoured and adopted.

The project constituted a pilot in respect of the development of online and flexible provision, at scale, across the University. Three Schools were involved in the pilot and, from this, three postgraduate programmes were agreed upon and subsequently validation was sought. This represented the University's first systematic phase to get involved in real distance learning.

The initial rationale for using a partner for this venture was rooted in expertise. It was anticipated that the necessary infrastructure to support 100% online learning, at scale, was not yet present within the University's capacity. From this pilot, the stakeholders would take learning concerning the digital tools, pedagogies, methods, and skills set required to update the University's infrastructure to offer high quality, online and flexible provision, at scale. Over time the rationale for the partnership has crept further towards a testing of established infrastructure, policies and processes that would ensure that when blended, flexible or online learning is rolled out at scale within the University, it could be assured any initial teething problems or inefficiencies in working had been previously ironed out.

CONSIDERING THE VALUE OF PARTNERSHIP

In considering the value of the partnership, a number of different data sources are used. Firstly, the author's own emic insight of the project, since appointment as programme leader for the MBA (Online) in April 2016, has immersed her in the lived experience of the development, design and delivery of an online postgraduate programme using a partner. Inevitably personal observation and that of the multiple stakeholders involved in the project is a valuable data source. The University has a strong system of governance surrounding these programmes (as any other programme) and therefore the author has been present at and contributed to discussions and reflection on the partnership at a Governance, Steering and Operational level, as well as working closely with the course leaders of the other postgraduate programmes involved in the pilot.

Secondly, the ongoing monitoring and dialogue with project stakeholders has heightened awareness of the benefits and challenges of the partnership in all areas, to include, module design and authorship, student recruitment, technical support and administrative activity. Finally, in preparation for this chapter, the views of key internal stakeholders involved in the project were sought via qualitative survey using Qualtrics. These views were drawn from Module Authors (who are academics belonging to the School), Academic Mentors, Module Tutors, Library Staff, and Subject Administration. Dominant themes emerging from these collective data sources are discussed below.

Primarily, the research interest, in this case, is the benefit that partnering offers the academic institution, as the chapter is intended to aid the evaluation process of academic institutions seeking to enter the online market. Clearly an extension of this work would be to canvas views of the entire stakeholder group of the project, inclusive of the academic partner.

Benefits of Partnership

Experience and Best Practice

Academic partnering was selected on the promise of providing expertise that wasn't, at that time, available (or at least in the volume required) within the existing University structure. Certainly, this is one of the greatest benefits realised, although in the author's opinion, it was not the expertise that was lacking per se; just the manner in which that expertise was structured as a discrete project team to support such a project. The expertise required for such a project includes:

- Discipline knowledge of the modules to be authored
- Project management
- Instructional design
- Marketing
- Admissions
- Technical support
- Administrative support
- Library services
- Student support services

Certainly, the feeling is that the partnership has worked well in fusing together the expertise of module authors, who are largely University staff regarded as experts in their particular field, with the project management and instructional design services offered by the partner. This has permitted both parties to focus upon their core expertise, and thus work more efficiently. As one module author found, they really valued the, "Division of labour, distinct responsibilities playing to strengths of each organisation - being able to concentrate on own responsibilities and having distinct areas of responsibility." Concerns associated with how the module would 'look' online did not therefore detract from the author's ability to focus upon the message that needed to be conveyed. "The interactive nature of online platforms like this is beyond my academics skills (and many other academics from what I understand from colleagues across HE) and the support of a provider is helpful in enabling more engaging interactive content, structure and flow".

Instructional design was not the only aspect of specialist support and guidance that the University has benefited from through the partnership. There is a strong system of support that surrounds the student experience to include student facing subject administration, a University facing technical support team,

The Challenges and Opportunities of Partnership in Establishing Online

and, importantly 365 day a year technical support hotline that the students can access. Clearly this is of great value to students who are studying across a variety of time zones at whatever time suits them, and in the event that they encounter difficulties, they want somebody to speak to there and then. At present the University working practices mirror a traditional working week, with the exception of library services, but no doubt this would cause frustrations to students who predominantly would want to be completing their work on the course at times when they were not undertaking their day job. The ability to access effective support at a time that students require it, is instrumental in driving student satisfaction and therefore the ability to be able to email or pick up the phone and speak to someone who may be able to help them resolve the problem or at least signpost them elsewhere, is of real benefit. There is a cultural shift required, one would argue across the entire HE sector, to change working practices and make them suitable for the needs of the online learner, if there is a true commitment to offer this study format.

Another area of expertise that was presented as valuable to the partnership is in the guidance and training for faculty staff who would become online tutors and also those who were recruited as bespoke online tutors. This is in recognition that the nature of online tuition differs in a number of ways to that of traditional face-to-face delivery and appropriate development training was therefore necessary. The key tenets of the learning design pedagogy used within these programs is based upon the community of enquiry model (Garrison, 2007) which places emphasis upon the three-dimensional framework of cognitive presence, community and social presence and teaching presence. The goal of effective tutor induction is therefore for tutors to appreciate the role that they would play within the learning community and maintaining strong connections with the subject matter (addressing cognitive presence) in a context whereby themselves they may not have developed the module; encouraging a sense of community and interaction with peers via the use of discussion boards and assessed discussion as a valuable tool designed into each module. Finally, their own teaching presence in maintaining motivation and interest, driving discussions forward, managing engagements and providing constructive, personalised and developmental feedback. This shift is not necessarily such a challenge for experienced online tutors but even the most experienced lecturers and academic staff were surprised at the comparable intensity of the working pattern of an online tutor and challenge of maintaining engagement when the student was not in front of you.

The partner was therefore able to offer an online teaching strategies course, that was of some value in clarifying the pedagogical approach, demonstrating the virtual learning environment and enabling tutors to witness and also practice effective skills of online tuition in a simulated environment. This four-week online course held a thematic bank of online material that was worked through in sequence, but was also supported by an online tutor. The extent to which the online tutor themselves demonstrated effective online tutoring practice was however questionable and, at the time this training was offered, one would argue that a far more valuable form of training would be targeted at module developers, giving them instruction in effective online learning design.

Ongoing, recognising that not every staff member would be in a position to engage in a four-week online course there was agreement that the partner would develop a set of briefer materials in the form of an online tutor handbook importantly with extracts of exemplars and effective tutoring practice as well as talking heads and video diaries from strong tutors. The idea being that this would be a resource that could be shared as part of the induction process and referred back to any point in the future. This work is still under development as the main course development waterfall has taken priority.

Superior Virtual Learning Environment

Within this pilot a different Virtual Learning Environment (VLE) to that of the University centrally is used. This VLE is based upon a Moodle platform, whilst the University's own VLE is sourced from Desire2learn

"The e-learning and 'developer' input to the web platform is more sophisticated than general Moodle or other based HEI platforms – it appears more 'polished' than others I have seen, and user friendly"

One aspect of the partner's offer is the provision of the virtual learning environment, which differs from the one used by the University for other programs. This virtual learning environment is based upon the Moodle platform, and in appearance has a slick, web-based presentation. It receives mixed feedback from staff and students alike, and ultimately the feeling is the preference of VLE is an entirely personal choice however largely the sentiment is that the VLE is superior to that of the University's, and the perception is that it both appears and functions better. Other University stakeholders may counter that to argue that NOW offers entirely comparable functions. Ultimately, as University staff are not creating content using the VLE, more so demonstrating content and accessing content using the VLE, then the tools of the VLE and their compatibility to NOW tools may not be so prominent. Feedback is suggestive that it is more the visual appearance of the partner's VLE that is dominant in stakeholders' minds or as a factor of superiority then other factors.

Project Management

The key responsibility of the partner is managing the project; both in respect of development and delivery. This involves liaison with all stakeholders, including course leaders, module authors, module leaders and online tutors, to establish both a waterfall of development for the initial delivery of the program, but then also a waterfall of redevelopment on an annual and three-year cycle to address minor and major updates, as required. The lead instructional designer is responsible for managing the waterfall and allocating instructional design resources to both the initial model development and redevelopment. The development phase spans a period of 24 weeks and therefore, in managing the project, will need to ensure that effective reporting mechanisms are in place to report back to key stakeholders on the success and progress of developments. Whilst undoubtedly, University stakeholders were grateful and appreciative of project oversight being in somebody else's hands on account of existing workloads, the method of reporting used by the partner has caused discontent at times, because it was felt that the modus operandi of the partner was not necessarily mindful of the academic working pattern and there was not suitable for flex built-in to appreciate peaks and troughs in on-campus academic activity.

Relationship Management

The partnership affords a dedicated marketing team who are responsible for establishing core marketing messages, identifying appropriate channels, and targeting marketing activity. This also ensures that leads gained via the various channels are followed up and the relationship with the enquirer is managed right through to the point of (hopeful) enrolment. As the partner is a specialist in the online learning market, it is anticipated that this affords superior insight into the most appropriate markets to target and methods to adopt. In addition, it also affords experience in light of the partner having worked with various other HEIs domestically and internationally on similar projects.

What is notable is that, on account of the time devoted by the partner to managing the relationship with prospective students, students arrive at the point of Induction very well informed about features and characteristics of the programme. They have been furnished with a realistic and insightful impression of what studying the MBA will involve. This provides a seamless transition into induction and benefits student experience as expectations are effectively managed.

One must be mindful that there is inevitably a cost associated with this activity, but it is felt that this perhaps is one of the most significant benefits of the relationship, on account of the approach taken by the partner in tirelessly pursuing leads and fostering relationships with enquiries, sometimes that spanned over six months to a year. In dialogue with all new entrants to the program, without exception they report positively and thankfully regarding the recruitment process and the level of attention given by the partner's admissions team, the level of knowledge shown, the value of the promotional webinars that are offered, in collaboration with University staff, ultimately impacting upon a feeling of preparedness for the program. Again, as they aren't University staff, one might be concerned that the University, School, or program are not being represented in the manner in which one would intend. However, in this case, it is certainly not the case. Having sat in on a number of sales calls, the course leader can confirm that the knowledge demonstrated by the admissions team was excellent.

Challenges of Partnership

Delineation of Responsibility

"Where there are grey areas in terms of responsibility it can be very hard to make progress, and where processes have not yet been agreed and we are deciding on procedure for the first time it has been time consuming and sometimes frustrating" (Programme Leader of one of the Postgraduate pilots)

At the outset of the project, at the time of appointment of the partner there was a bespoke role in existence at the University which focused upon the development of online learning. On account of internal changes within the University, this role ceased to exist but then was absorbed by another department to act as the conduit between the partner and the respective Schools, playing a key part in establishing shared working practices and policy. Before long, these roles were redeployed elsewhere and a link didn't exist; therefore communication occurred directly between the partner and course leaders as well as other stakeholders in the project. This situation, of having no one with the day-to-day University oversight of the project in a strategic and operational format, essentially with insight into the detail of the partnership contract, at times presented challenges. Coupled with fluctuating roles and personnel both institutionally and within the partner, this left many grey areas of how responsibility would be delineated and the governance of such responsibility. One such area was in the development of the tutoring induction materials, which ultimately caused the delay in the production of the materials and a lower quality of initial tutor induction. Thankfully, in recent years the situation has been resolved through the appointment of a University-wide Head of flexible and online learning manager who is instrumental in monitoring roles and responsibilities within the partnership in ensuring that these roles are effectively fulfilled.

Communication Complexity

On account of the nature of the partnership, the stakeholders involved in the project become increasingly complex as do monitoring changes in roles and responsibilities and therefore importantly who to contact for what and for the quickest resolution to any issues that might arise. Essentially, as the partner's employees are not University staff there is a duplication of some of the roles and responsibilities which creates not one but two additional layers of communication, which, at times, causes delays in information being received and inaccuracies in information sometimes as this respondent states requests can get lost in translation "Communication sometimes harder or has to go through more people to get to students". Within any business there is jargon and accepted terminology and this is not always translated effectively to the partner which hinders a timely and accurate response "sometimes requests can get lost in translation or partners at xxxx don't understand our terminology/vice-versa". For example, in initial reporting of marketing activity, reports would cite "booked applicants", but this would be of no significance to the University staff who are more familiar with the terminology of offer status, such as "unconditional offer confirmed" et cetera this created confusion and lack of clarity concerning the effectiveness of marketing campaigns.

A particularly challenging aspect of communication is that of monitoring student engagement. Despite being an incredibly beneficial aspect of the online MBA's design, the added role of the Academic Mentor may create even further complexities in communication. It has taken some time, and one would argue that we are still not there yet, to encourage the partner and their employees to ensure that in communicating about a student's position on the course, they share this information with the appropriate people, which includes the current module tutor and their Academic Mentor. Closing this communication loop is particularly important in providing the wraparound support that we pride ourselves on as a Business School. In the early days, quite often, Academic Mentors would be left out of communications when, arguably they are the ones that have a greater insight into the students' current position and therefore are best able to share information about the students' engagement and course intentions.

Lack of Autonomy

Whilst some stakeholders express a satisfaction that the technical aspects of the course delivery and their role can be referred on to a specialist, for others it creates a sense of frustration. There is a notable feeling of a lack of autonomy to make, for example small changes to the module contents if, for example, one spots an error. As one module tutor commented, "If there is a problem with a link or a resource, as a tutor you do have to act as a messenger between students and XXXX and wait for resolution rather than having the ability to fix it yourself".

The agreed process is that this always has to be referred back to the lead instructional designer who will then allocate the work to one of their team. Whilst this is often actioned extremely quickly, it adds a layer of complexity that, at times, causes delays and therefore frustrations for staff and students alike. Some academic staff who worked as module authors have extensive experience in online learning design and communicated even higher levels of frustration that they couldn't simply access the virtual learning environment to make changes themselves.

Consistency and Quality

A project of this nature is not a short-term undertaking and therefore, inevitably it is to be expected that there will be shifts and changes within the team structure. Sometimes this may bring about positive changes, as new skills and expertise are introduced and new, maybe more effective ways of working may be experienced. Certainly, this relationship is benefited from that. However, as the partner organisation grows and recruits new partners off the back of the success of our project, their existing resource has become squeezed and personnel are allocated to areas whereby they are deemed best able to make a contribution by the partner organisation. A shared sentiment amongst professional services stakeholders is that "I don't think they are delivering the level of support that was offered at the start of the work".

This has caused fluctuations and variations in working practice that have, at times, caused instability in terms of what we, as an institution, can expect from our partner and ultimately our fundamental concern being the potential risk to student experience and the wider reputation of the organisation for the quality of our provision. As one module developer stated, "a lack of expertise of the provider on the content/topics may create more of a risk in terms of something being positioned or structured inappropriately".

Whilst the University's project team have established and maintain a very positive relationship with all of the stakeholders within the partner organisation, it is felt that sometimes the quality of what is offered by the partner is affected by frequent changes in roles and responsibilities. Another aspect of this is in consistency. The partner uses a team of instructional designers and have a lead instructional designer overseeing activity. Managing the different personalities and approaches of the instructional design team, especially when some are not employed by the partner is challenging and on numerous occasions requests to proactively ensure that changes resulting from the previous round of module delivery had been implemented, were found to have not been actioned. Again, whilst when issues are picked up, they are resolved swiftly, it is felt that a high-volume of these could've been avoided, and therefore the polished appearance of the modules to the students could have been maintained.

SOLUTIONS AND RECOMMENDATIONS

One must note that the discussion within this chapter is highly personalised and subjective, being influenced by the unique nature of the partners, and therefore partnership in question. The themes that are emerging from this relationship may well be unique to this University, these programmes and this partnership.

But the discussion is rather more intended as a guide for those considering partnership as strategic option for developing online provision. A pre-cursor to deciding whether partnership is the right option for the institution, and from that, who the right partner might be. The experiences here are inevitably framed within the context of the precise nature of the partnership agreement and contract. Ultimately, it depends upon the details related to cost of the partnership, and what is included or excluded for that cost, what the expectations are and therefore whether one might judge the partnership to be of value or not.

Irrespective of the cost of the partnership, below is some of the key advice the author would offer in light of their experience. This advice is most applicable at the stage whereby to partner (or not) is being evaluated, and in selecting the right partner.

- Roles and responsibilities within the partnership should be clarified and understood by all stakeholders and monitored regularly
- Ensure that instructional designers have experience of the discipline as well as the process of instructional design
- Evaluate the characteristics of the VLE as part of the evaluation and partner selection process
- Assess any proven track record carefully. Is the experience in the same geographical region/ market?
- Communication policies must be developed and agreed at the outset
- Obtain academic editing rights – but train first!
- There should be a substantial acclimatisation/ knowledge sharing period for both parties

FUTURE RESEARCH DIRECTIONS

It is hoped that by sharing these experiences it will enable other academics and institutions, in a similar position, to make an informed choice regarding the benefits of partnership and collaboration for online learning development. Personally, the author wishes to develop this work into a framework for partnership in online learning development. However, this is by no means to say that the challenges and opportunities encountered in this particular relationship are typical of these kind of partnerships. Collaborative research could shed light on this although commercial sensitivities may prohibit this.

CONCLUSION

In conclusion, the partnership, and to partner for this type of endeavour certainly does have its benefits. These may be cited in what the partner can bring to the relationship, which, in this context, is likely to be rooted in expertise and the opportunity to outsource activity that might not, at that time, be viable within the existing infrastructure.

The key areas of risk to impact negatively upon the student experience sit within the realms of the communication complexity that is created through a partnership, which can, at times cause delays in flows of essential communication and errors in communication being shared. The other area that seems to impact significantly upon the student experience and satisfaction is with regard to consistency and quality and in the differential styles to module set up being employed by different instructional designers. Ultimately, with any new endeavour there are teething problems and systems and processes take time to establish and to refine. With the introduction of the role of Head of flexible on online learning, which is a cross-University role and with the supporting infrastructure of flexible and online learning, many of these issues are now mitigated through the close monitoring of both partner's activity.

REFERENCES

Arbaugh, J. B. (2014). System, scholar or students? Which most influences online MBA course effectiveness? *Journal of Computer Assisted Learning, 30*(4), 349–362. doi:10.1111/jcal.12048

Arkorful, V., & Abaidoo, N. (2015). The role of e-learning, advantages and disadvantages of its adoption in higher education. *International Journal of Instructional Technology and Distance Learning, 12*(1), 29–42.

Garrison, D. R. (2007). Online community of inquiry review: Social, cognitive, and teaching presence issues. *Journal of Asynchronous Learning Networks, 11*(1), 61–72.

Howell, S. L., Williams, P. B., & Lindsay, N. K. (2003). Thirty-two trends affecting distance education: An informed foundation for strategic planning. *Online Journal of Distance Learning Administration, 6*(3), 1–18.

Porter, S. (2015). *To MOOC or Not to MOOC: how can online learning help to build the future of higher education?* Chandos Publishing.

Porter, W. W., Graham, C. R., Spring, K. A., & Welch, K. R. (2014). Blended learning in higher education: Institutional adoption and implementation. *Computers & Education, 75*, 185–195. doi:10.1016/j.compedu.2014.02.011

Richey, R. C., & Klein, J. D. (2014). *Design and development research: Methods, strategies, and issues.* Routledge. doi:10.4324/9780203826034

Chapter 13
A Framework for Developing Open Distance E-Learning Curriculum for Library and Information Science (LIS) Programme in Eswatini

Vusi W. Tsabedze
University of South Africa, South Africa

ABSTRACT

The dependency by foreign countries institutions such as South Africa, Botswana, and Namibia for library and information science (LIS) training and development of staff members, to acquire higher education, has become expensive and complex for Eswatini government to handle. The expensive nature and complex situation of sending employees out of the country for training has paralysed most of the organisation due to their absence from operations in the office. This study therefore seeks to investigate, developing open distance e-learning curriculum for LIS programme in Eswatini. The University of Eswatini (UNESWA), which is one among other institution of higher learning in the country, does not offer any programme in LIS. Considering this situation in Eswatini, this chapter proposes a framework for developing the ODeL curriculum for LIS. Such a programme could be offered through the UNESWA to accommodate students within and outside the country. Thus, ensuring Eswatini becomes a player in LIS space within the African continent.

DOI: 10.4018/978-1-5225-9779-7.ch013

INTRODUCTION AND BACKGROUND

The advent and rapid development in Information and Communication Technologies (ICTs), brought about fundamental and dramatic shifts in the global educational landscape. The reason was that the advent and transformation witnessed in ICTs ushered in recent technological, devices now used in the education sector globally. The purpose of applying ICTs in the educational sector was based on its effectiveness and efficiency in fostering service delivery. The increasing use of the Internet worldwide as one of the components of ICTs is now a new phenomenon in open distance e-learning (ODeL). ODeL has created new opportunities for lifelong learning characterised by costless high-quality education beyond the limitations of time zones and physical boundaries (Sonwalkar, 2013). According to Edegbo (2011), the adaptation of ICT in higher education has changed the way and manner through which education is conducted. Edegbo (2011) asserts that, apart from the provision of opportunities in ODeL and collaboration, ICTs has paved the way for a new pedagogical approach characterised for independent learning. Students can communicate, create and share presentations in multimedia format. The interaction between students and teachers is enhanced through technology.

The Library and Information Science (LIS) field of study, has become more vibrant and dynamic due to the emergence and application of ICTs. The application of ICTs in the profession results in novelty concepts of a digital library, metadata, and many more, being topical in the twenty-first century. The rapid changes experienced in LIS spurred educators to continually recommend a revision to course content and program directions in line with the global trends. Such initiatives have seen some LIS institutions introducing new degrees with new nomenclature.

The International Federation of Library Associations and Institutions (IFLA) have recommended that the LIS curriculum should consist of the following core modules:

- The information environment, information policy and ethics, the history of information science;
- Information generation, communication and use;
- Assessing information needs and designing responsive services;
- The information transfer process;
- The organization, retrieval, preservation and conservation of information;
- Research, analysis and interpretation of information;
- Applications of information and communication technologies;
- Library and information products and services;
- Information resource management and knowledge management;
- Management of information agencies; and
- Quantitative and qualitative evaluation of the outcomes of information and library use (IFLA, 2009).

In affirmation of IFLA mandate on how LIS curriculum should consist of, Wilson (2001) made similar remarks on the same note, to include:

- Information content (the traditional function of library and information centres);
- Information systems (human/systems interaction and organizational systems);
- Information users and providers (information use and information seeking behaviour);

- Information organizations (information producers, libraries, information centres and their operations, etc.).
- Supplemental knowledge skills not included in any of the above (such as subject bases, e.g., philosophy, history, etc.) and
- Practicum (prescribed practical experience as a programme of study) (Wilson, 2001).

Drawing from the analogy above, the Kellogg-ALISE Information Professions and Education Reform Project (2000), it was emphasised that most LIS institutions are undergoing a vibrant, dynamic and significant change, even though the areas targeted for such changes varied from institution to institution, and some LIS institutions are in periods of greater flux than others. Related to the changes within the LIS education, six trends were identified by the KALIPER report as follows:

- LIS curricula were addressing broad-based information environments and information problems;
- Incorporating perspectives from other disciplines, and the emergence of a distinct core that is predominantly user-centred;
- Increasing investment and infusion of IT into their curricula;
- Experimenting with the structure of specialization within the curriculum;
- Providing instruction in different formats;
- LIS institutions were expanding curricula through offering related degrees at the undergraduate, masters, and doctoral levels.

The LIS profession over the years has witnessed a series of transformation, and changes, particularly, in relation to ICTs. Such a transformation is believed to influence how LIS professionals are trained (Chu, 2010). Similarly, Rehman (2012) notes that changes which occur in the LIS profession should also reflect in academic policies, procedures and curriculum. The issues pertaining to the direction of LIS programmes, rooted in their curriculum could change the subjects being taught. The essence is to make sure LIS graduate possess the knowledge and skills to function better after they graduate. This has been widely discussed in several kinds of literature based on its importance (Xu, 2003). According to Mammo (2007), the nature of the curricula in LIS education has changed drastically due to the application of technology and the advent of the technology has equally affected the information needs of the society. The curriculum content of any programme keeps pace with the demands of the profession and societal needs (Edzan and Abrizah, 2003). In time past, most of the educational training had are in the conventional institution but recently some of the LIS institutions in Sub-Saharan Africa have embraced the provision of training through the ODeL platform. For instance, the University of South Africa (UNISA), and Zimbabwe Open University (ZOU) have begun offering some of their programmes online. LIS institutions offering Library and Information Science programmes have been changing the course contents of their curriculum and as well, renaming the departments, to attract more students into the programmes and offerings (Jamaludin, Hussin & Wan Mokhtar, 2006; Ameen, 2007; Rehman, 2003). Recently, due to the changes that has evolved in LIS programmes, the institutions offering the course have introduced more recent new modules such as Bibliometric and other Metric tools – ORCID, Innovative library services – Mobile Apps, Web 2.0 to 4.0, Big data, Cloud Computing, Artificial Intelligence(AI),

A Framework for Developing Open Distance E-Learning Curriculum for Library

Internet of Things, Gamification, Talent acquisition tools and retention, Learning technologies such as e-learning Platforms, MOOC, LMS, Swayam, among many. In attribution to the above assertion, Islam et al. (2011) argued in an online survey conducted, which explore the global scenario of ODeL in LIS programmes. Findings from the study established that 370 LIS programmes were examined and it was revealed that 85 LIS programmes provide degrees and other related certificates that comprises of certificate courses, diplomas, Bachelors, Masters and Doctoral programmes. It was further revealed that Blackboard or Blackboard Vista was the most often used ODeL platform in LIS institutions. Chowdhury and Chowdhury (2006), who conducted a study to examine the situation of ODeL facilities and the support given to LIS institutions in the United Kingdom, indicates that all the concerned LIS institutions have adopted ICTs for providing ODeL. Besides, some of the institutions used virtual learning environments (VLEs) for ODeL; while others used an in-house system. The LIS programmes across the world are adopting ODeL to provide education services (Shiful Islam et-al, 2011). The provision of such services in ODeL bringing about courses that could transform the entire LIS programme online (through the Web), which results to the widely adopted mode of education today in ODeL (Chu, 2010).

The intervention by several institutions of higher learning, through the provision of LIS education and training in Eswatini, is still at the infancy stage. The LIS programme is not yet grounded in terms of curriculum development and review, adequate qualified lecturers, introduction and application of digital technology for teaching and learning, an affirmation of policy formulation and implementation within the institutions of higher learning in Eswatini. The Institute of Development Management (IDM) is the only institution that offers LIS programme at an undergraduate and Diploma level. The University of Eswatini (UNESWA), which is the largest institution of higher learning in the country with economies of scale does not offer any programme in LIS. As a result, organisations in Eswatini either send their LIS professionals to neighbouring countries such as South Africa, Botswana and Namibia for training. Sending employees out of the country for training is quite expensive for organisations and it also paralyses operations during the absence of these staff members. Considering this situation in Eswatini, this chapter proposes a framework for developing the ODeL curriculum for the LIS programme. Such a programme could be offered through the UNESWA to accommodate students within and outside the country and thus ensuring Eswatini becomes a player in LIS space within the African continent. It also takes into consideration the global requirements in ODeL in the digital age.

Contextual Background

On the 19 April 2018, King Mswati III announced that Swaziland would now be known as Eswatini. The name changed was driven by a desire to fully break from the country's colonial past, while ending international confusion between Swaziland and Switzerland. The change was part of the double celebration of fifty years of the country's independence and Kind Mswati III fiftieth birthday. Eswatini is a landlocked country in the eastern flank of South Africa, where it adjoins Mozambique. Around 70 per cent of Eswatini 1.1 million people are based in rural areas, with livelihoods predominantly dependent on subsistence agriculture. The Swazi economy is mainly driven by its membership of the South African Customs Union (SACU) and the Common Monetary Area (CMA) (UNICEF, 2018).

Education and training is regarded as the foundation of economic and social development in Eswatini; and the government's objective is to provide education and training that is affordable, accessible and relevant to all Swazis. The main levels of education and training are primary, secondary and tertiary (higher education). Eswatini's higher education sector consists of seven institutions of higher learning including a publicly funded university, publicly funded polytechnics and specialised colleges, and privately funded accredited universities and colleges. Eswatini universities teach research skills and inculcate a culture of research for personal, professional and social development. According to the 2019/20 budget speech, education and training consume a significant proportion of government expenditure was allocated (E3,543 billion) (Rijkenberg, 2019). Literacy (through basic reading and writing) in Eswatini is about 87.5per cent. Higher education in Eswatini is provided through the University of Eswatini (public university), private universities, colleges and training institutions.

ODeL FRAMEWORK

In the context of the study, the ODeL is premised on the assumption that students learning can be supported by electronic technologies and other digital facilities. ODeL students are expected to have access to modern electronic technologies to able to have access to their educational material and to interact with their lecturers without necessarily being required to make physical contact (Ngubane-Mokiwa and Letseka,2015). The interaction in ODeL leads to a reduction in the transactional distance between the lecturers and the students (Carswell, Thomas, Petre and Price (2000). Therefore, modern electronic technologies result in e-learning, online learning or digital learning using remote electronic communication. The ODeL is guided by learner-centred educational theories. According to Benson and Samarawickrema (2009), learning designers in ODeL should consider the effect of context on the student's learning journey. Laurillard (2002) also proposes that technology-based learning would be more effective if its design is based on the conversational framework. There are specific technologies that can be used to for teaching and learning in the ODeL platform, for example, video conferencing can be used to facilitate dialogue and discussions between the lecturers and the students, and amongst students at different places. Such dialogue and discussions allow students to analyse each other's views (peer-to-peer assessment) and also develop critical thinking skills. In some instance, lecturers might make use of electronic discussion forums to promote collaboration, synthesis and reflection. The three activities bridge the spatial distance that might exist between the lecturers and the students; the students and the learning content, and amongst the students themselves.

Some lecturers use blogs to conduct their lessons in an online setting. In a blogs tool, students and lecturers can able to reflect on the processes of teaching and learning. They provide a form of support that enables students to have asynchronous communication while also enabling support during learning (Ngubane-Mokiwa and Letseka,2015). On the other hand, the podcast tool is used frequently to facilitate ODeL because it facilitates the consolidation of knowledge acquired during learning. They could also be instrumental in providing students with illustrations or demonstrations of the element of the learning content.

CURRICULUM DEVELOPMENT

A curriculum is a key factor shaping the educational outcomes of a programme and that the way it is developed and delivered affects the learning experience of students in the programme (Lester, 2011). Furthermore, in any educational programme, the curriculum is the best barometer of its nature and content (Chu, 2010). Glatthorn, Boschee and Whitehead (2009), view curriculum as the plan developed to guide made for guiding learning in a learning environment, normally represented in retrievable documents of several levels of generality, and the actualization of those plans in the classroom, as experienced by the learners and as recorded by an observer; those experiences that normally take place in a learning environment that also manipulates what is learned.

Similarly, Tomkins and Case (2011), considered curriculum development as the systematic planning of what is taught and learnt in schools as mirrored in courses to be studied and school programmes. Curricula is embodied in official documents and made compulsory by provincial and territorial departments of education. Curriculum development, according to Lawal (2000), refers to the continuous review of course content and relationships undertaken as required: such as, when the employment market, or professional thoughts, or manpower forecast, or the trend of research interests dictate that change is expected.

From the above, curriculum development involves a series of activities that encompasses syllabus formation, determining programme aims and objectives, course contents, learning outcomes, methods of delivery of the educational programmes and monitoring and evaluation. In summary, curriculum development entails continuous development and review of course contents to ensure that they are relevant and adequate in meeting the demand of the ever-changing job market.

LIBRARY AND INFORMATION SCIENCE EDUCATION AND TRAINING IN ESWATINI

There are many challenges of LIS education and training, for example, the need to make LIS education relevant and effective. It is no secret that the circumstances affecting LIS education and training in Eswatini have changed for the last years. There are numerous issues in this change. Smith (1983) claims that advent and rapid of technological developments in the discipline of information creation and dissemination, which includes the increasing use of computers, microforms, word processing equipment, and the use of lasers and a wide range of developments in the field of communications, including satellites. This technological change has continued to pose a challenge to LIS discipline. There are many challenges facing the LIS education and training in Eswatini that includes lack of adequate education and training institutions. It is noted that Eswatini has a notable number of LIS professionals trained and educated at various levels (certificates, diploma, degrees, masters and doctorate) in LIS. Most are employed within the country by government, private sector and training institutions. Ever since LIS become a recognised and required profession in Eswatini, government and private sector have been sponsoring prospective professionals for LIS higher education in other countries because of lack of such education in the country. Scholarships for prospective students have been available for LIS institutions namely at the University of Botswana, University of Namibia, University South Africa, University of KwaZulu Natal and other universities outside Africa. The government, through the Ministry of Education and Training (MOET) and the Ministry of Public Service (MOPS), has been the main sponsor behind incumbent professionals who have been trained at postgraduate degree level. In Eswatini, the Institute of Development Management (IDM) is the only institution which offers LIS programme at the undergraduate level. The institution is still inadequate in terms of standard and quality to meet the high intake due to the high demand for higher education in Eswatini. The Eswatini Higher Educational Council, which is tertiary institution accrediting body in Eswatini, recently has requires all higher institutions of learning to have graduate and postgraduate librarian. IDM alone cannot meet the demand for the librarians with graduate qualification. Since the LIS programme was launched in 2012 nobody has graduated with a degree at IDM to help to fill the human resources gap. This is partly attributed to the fact that there is an institution in the country that offers which offer LIS at the degree level.

The general norm in Eswatini for pre-service training in LIS has been in service or attachment in the functioning and recognised library or information centre in order to gain hands-on experience and improve the candidate's appreciation for the profession before embarking on formal tertiary education. This is largely still the case, with most training professionals having previously served in registries and libraries first. The pre-training practice has ensured that many LIS professionals who complete their formal higher education in other countries have a secure job with their employer when they return to the country. However, some LIS professionals continue to search for better opportunities with other employers after formal higher education because of remuneration from the government.

The education and training of LIS professionals outside Eswatini have several benefits to the country. The country's populace has, for instance, the opportunity to educate in well-established and reputable LIS institutions while experiencing different social and cultural environments, which also contribute towards their personal development and growth (Ndlangamandla, 2012). They may also establish out of the country contacts and networks that are necessary for their continuous professional development (CPD). However, there are also some challenges. One challenge, as observed by Johnson (2007), is the relevance of the education and training received, which is often based on western programs and modelled on the needs of developed countries. Education and training outside the country may also increase dependence on the external environment and promote the notion that valuable training can only be obtained outside the country. Another challenge is that of cost, as education and training outside the country require a considerable amount of money, therefore limiting the number of LIS applicants that may access to education and training at a given time.

THE RATIONALE OF DEVELOPING AN ODEL CURRICULUM FOR LIS INSTITUTIONS IN ESWATINI

The development of an ODeL curriculum for LIS institutions in Eswatini is imperative in this era of the 4th industrial revolution. The implication of such development would incorporate new ideas and techniques and tools in the training and education of a prospective student who desires to enrol for LIS programmes. It would help LIS institutions in Eswatini to become compliant and embrace best practices of the LIS profession. The development of an ODeL curriculum for LIS institutions in Eswatini would unveil the accessibility of LIS programme to prospective students such that LIS professionals already working in the diverse sector in the country would deepen their knowledge and skills in LIS practices. Catherall (2005) pointed out that the practice of ODeL offers immense benefits to learners because of its convenience, flexibility, accessibility and cost-effectiveness. Kala (2009) also stated that the ODeL approach allows quick, easy and relatively cheap sharing of information and ideas with people across the world. Abu Bakar, Harande and Abubakar (2009) stated that ODeL has the potentials of providing quality education.

As earlier mentioned, the increase in demand for higher learning requires the need for the full implementation of vigorous ODeL curriculum, to cater to the diverse needs of LIS institutions in Eswatini. Furthermore, the ODeL platform provides opportunities for prospective LIS part-time students who may not have the chance to enroll in a formalised LIS programme in those LIS institutions. The ODeL can be regarded as an alternative to old-style instruction for students who want to pursue a part-time postgraduate LIS programme, but who are hindered because of job responsibilities and time factor.

Islam, Chowdhury, and Islam (2009) identified the benefits of ODeL to LIS professionals as outlined below:

- It offers new opportunities for LIS professionals to develop their knowledge and skills in a wide variety of areas;
- ODeL makes LIS professionals more confident and competent in ICT usage;
- Provides the LIS professionals with the opportunity to develop new roles and responsibilities both within and outside the LIS environment; and
- It also provides prospects for professional partnership in a wide variety of areas, because of its flexibility and cost-effectiveness.

Waterhouse (2005) presented a comprehensive range of ODeL benefits that include the following:

- ODeL enables learner-centred learning which ensures that learners are vigorously involved in learning, by encouraging activities such as online self-assessment, web-based research etc. Therefore, this reduces the need for detailed note-making.
- ODeL ensures simplicity in learning which is a situation whereby learners learn at their own convenience as compared to having to attend frequently planned instructional gatherings
- Facilitates learners contact with course content that is a situation whereby learners interact with course content through the web, that is normally created by the instructors.
  ODeL enables and promotes communication and partnership in that, it enables learners to engage in online discussion for communication and cooperation. This online discussion offers an exceptional approach for examining issues
- ODeL makes course administration easier and lessens the cost of delivering instruction. In this situation, the practice of ODeL saves the time of the lecturer, and the learner, unlike in an old-style mode. Moreover, it has the potential of lessening the total costs of delivery, and at the same time improves learner learning.

Abubakar and Hassan (2013) summaries the benefits of ODeL as follows:

- Flexibility;
- Cost-effectiveness;
- Convenience;
- Accessibility; and
- Opportunities for part-time learners.

A PROPOSED FRAMEWORK FOR ODEL CURRICULUM IN LIS PROGRAMME IN ESWATINI

A proposed framework for ODeL Curriculum in the LIS Programme in Eswatini becomes essential due to the identified gap identified in the country. It was observed that the LIS is at its infancy, thus requiring growth and development in diverse ways. Besides it was noticed that the programme is not grounded yet in terms of curriculum development and review, adequate qualified lecturers, introduction and application and use of recent digital technology for teaching and learning, an affirmation of policy formulation and implementation within the institutions of higher learning in Eswatini. These among other factors necessitate the author intended to propose a framework that could drive the ODeL curriculum in LIS programme in Eswatini

This framework would open new opportunities for prospective LIS students who wish to enroll with UNESWA for the programme. This could also foster a convenient approach for the varied lifestyles and busy schedules of individuals who desire to develop themselves. High school levels preparing for such opportunity could transitions into UNESWA by taking the online versions of university-level or advance placement courses that expected of first-year retention rates. This is other ways to attract top students from other parts of the country and outside Eswatini. Adult learners could also overcome geographical barriers to this higher education by enrolling in flexible LIS degree programmes that do not dislocate them from work and home. Prospective students could be rewarded with better access to the University's ODeL offerings and support services through a single point-of-presence portal. This virtual consolidation of ODeL services alleviates confusion about where faculty, staff and students and external users go for information and support. The campus community could also benefit from a realigned central to ODeL unit that offers better - coordinated and quality service and support to the students. The University benefits from using these resources more effectively, taking into cognizance the advantage of economies of scale of preference. In light of this, the study designed a framework for developing the ODeL Curriculum for LIS programme in Eswatini as shown in Figure 1.

Explanation of the Framework

This explanation is based on the author knowledge, experience and exposition to Eswantini LIS institutions. Developing a curriculum can be both exciting and challenging. This is, because, proper curriculum development exercise is time-consuming, and needs the involvement of all stakeholders. Similarly, the curriculum is expected to reflect the local situation, as well as the current global trends in a discipline.

The framework explains what the Eswatini Institutions of Higher learning should do in developing an ODeL curriculum for the LIS institutions, the following elements should be included:

A Framework for Developing Open Distance E-Learning Curriculum for Library

Figure 1. Framework for developing ODeL curriculum for LIS programme in Eswatini

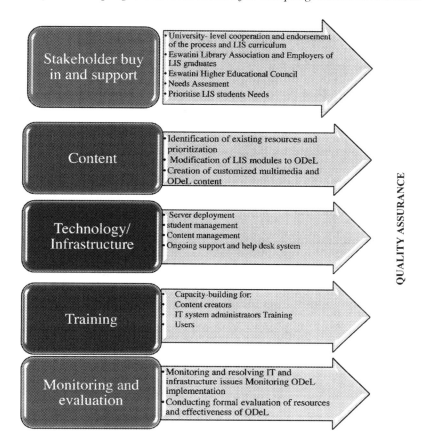

1. Stakeholder buy-in and support;
2. Content;
3. Technology/ infrastructure;
4. Training; and
5. Monitoring and evaluation.

Stakeholder Buy-In and Support

Before developing the curriculum, UNESWA should consider the current policy and regulatory environment in Eswatini. The following questions should be considered:

- What is the current policy on ODeL state?
- What are the regulatory requirements for creating and approving ODeL programmes for use in education or training?

The review of the existing national or institutional documents for guidance before embarking on ODeL. Ideally, stakeholders should be engaged such as Ministry of Education, Eswatini Higher education Council (EHEC), Eswatini Library association (EWALA), the employers of the LIS graduates. The participation of stakeholders in curriculum development is non-negotiable. Indeed, various professional associations like the IFLA, ALA, and ALIA have for long recommended for the participation of stakeholders in curriculum development.

It is important to ensure that the interests of the local condition of the respective countries in which the LIS institutions meticulously addressed in the curricular content. As in related to the above, LIS institutions in Eswatini should ensure conformity with the requirements of the established standards for ODeL programmes, such as the ones recommended by the IFLA, ALA, ALISE, and even beyond. This point was also raised by Panahon II (2007), who recommended for the benchmarking of the proposed ODeL curriculum in European Studies against established quality standards. The LIS institutions in Eswatini should, in addition, develop their own standard that will serve the interests of the Eswatini, from the existing standards. The concrete decision on the modalities of curriculum review and revision period should be clarified. In this regard, LIS institutions in Eswatini are expected to keep abreast of the latest developments in the LIS field, as well as in the ODeL world.

There is also a need for organised workshops by the LIS institutions in Eswatini to organise workshops that address and, at the same time identify the potential students, what they are expected to learn, the objectives of the ODeL programmes market demands, as well as how the programmes would be delivered. In addition, there is a need to determine the various levels of such programmes, the assessment methods, and the expected learning outcomes. These processes would ensure the establishment of sound and robust curriculum content for an ODeL programme. Govindasamy (2002) noted that for any ODeL implementation exercise to succeed, it must be rooted in effective teaching methods. LIS institutions in Eswatini should avoid overloading the ODeL curriculum with courses that are not directly relevant to the programme of study. There is the need to determine the level(s) of the LIS programmes and the courses to be offered in those level(s).

Task Force

The University of Eswatini should form a task force from the larger body of stakeholders who have sufficient authority, competency, and experience to define the goals and plans for implementing the ODeL programme. The task force should be created and led by the department of computer science, and its members should be partners in and key stakeholders of ODeL. The task force will provide high-level direction, identify and leverage available funding, and plan and support capacity development for ODeL. It can also help identify and recommend a technical working group to participate in providing technical support, reviewing and creating ODeL, and monitoring and evaluating progress.

Needs Assessment

The needs assessment should be conducted to identify infrastructure, personnel, and processes that need to be addressed to implement the LIS programme on ODeL. There is a need to also review the e-learning policy and other related policies or guidelines that might provide direction or guidance. The task force should identify key areas in LIS workforce development where ODeL can be implemented (i.e., in-service, pre-service, continuing professional development). The next step is to identify the best locations, partners, and institutions for the initial rollout plan for ODeL. The needs assessment should identify the following:

- IT infrastructure (supporting the use of computing devices);
- Availability of electricity; and
- Availability of internet access (for regular synchronization of results)

Technology/IT Infrastructure

For the curriculum to succeed, all the LIS institutions in Eswatini are expected to make adequate arrangements for the installation of state-of-the-art ODeL technologies, infrastructures, and all other necessary teaching aids. These ensure proper curricular implementation. ODeL requires an IT infrastructure for both implementation and user support. IT infrastructure refers not only to physical elements of technology, such as computers and software, but also to the systems, processes, and expertise that support the full functioning and productive use of those elements for the ODeL system. Determining the modes of delivery of the ODeL programmes. The ODeL can be delivered in one of the following two modes (Chowdhury & Chowdhury, 2006):

(i) Synchronous e-learning: this is a computer-assisted e-learning environment whereby the instructor and the participants are involved in the course, class or lesson at the same time, through Web conferencing. While;
(ii) Asynchronous ODeL, is a computer-assisted training where the instructor and the participants are involved in the course, class or lesson at different times. For example, through Web-based training (WBT), e-mail, blogs and electronic bulletin boards. This method allows participants to access training materials at any time. Therefore, LIS schools in the Muslim World need to choose from any of the two modes;

The IT staff at the Department of Information Science will support LIS students and lectures using the ODeL platform, importing the ODeL modules, synchronizing their data with the central server, and providing general troubleshooting and assistance.

Networking

Networking among the LIS institutions in Eswatini for cooperation. Further to this end, the networking among them would equally ensure consultation, and advice may be sought from each other regarding the experiences of the LIS institutions about the ODeL programmes. It is also expected that such networking would bring about an exchange of resources and technology in the LIS institutions.

Training

Another very crucial strategy is the need for training and re-training of the LIS faculty in the Eswatini, particularly, in relation to new ICTs and other emerging areas in the profession e.g. Bibliometric and other Metric tools – ORCID, Innovative library services – Mobile Apps, Web 2.0 to 4.0, Big data, Cloud Computing, Artificial Intelligence, Internet of Things, Learning technologies such as e-learning Platforms, MOOC, LMS, Swayam. Refreshing academic staff knowledge is a very critical factor in the success of ODeL programmes. A further strategy may involve the need for academic staff exchange programmes among LIS institutions in the Eswatini. This could bring cross-fertilization of ideas from the experiences of the academic staff in relations to the running of the ODeL programmes. The LIS institutions that are advanced technologically may be required to provide support to those that are not so incapacitated.

Monitoring and Evaluation

Evaluation plans and evaluation forms that analyzed the effectiveness of the learning design process and the ODeL system that supported pedagogy requirements must guide Monitoring and evaluation of the framework. A further assessment of the learner has to must be carried out to ascertain the relevance of design and development techniques, the quality of the learning provided, and method of instruction, layout, design and relevance of content. According to the development process, the learner's feedback must be analyzed, and subsequent changes referred to the development stage.

The review and improve stage proved functionally important at every step in the proposed pedagogical framework where systems were to be kept updated with:

- Learning trends, technology updates and research;
- Increased ODeL awareness of learners;
- Changes and developments in policy and curriculums;
- Technology and infrastructure changes; and
- Suggested improvements or enhancements based on objectives or stakeholder requirements

The reviews of the system and subsequent improvements took place from the foundation the dimension through the Curriculum stage in the proposed framework. The aim was to manage enhancements through the cyclic dimension in maintaining a structured approach. The role of the cyclic dimension was imperative and considered changes in stakeholder requirements, objectives and included comments and outcomes received through the assessment and feedback.

The proposed framework through the review and improve stage recommended that based on the complexity of the change, the request be addressed through the curriculum stage, maintaining structure in requested changes to the system.

IMPLEMENTATION OF THE LIS CURRICULUM

The implementation of the LIS programme requires proper planning (including the application for research), training, implementation testing, dissemination, formative evaluation, ongoing user support, and addressing any technical issues. The University should consider the following summary of steps.

Planning

In preparation for LIS programme implementation, it may be appropriate to develop a research plan and submit to local ethical review boards, to disseminate or present results of the LIS programme to a wider audience.

Training

The university must train everyone who will be involved in the implementation of the LIS programme, including IT staff, Lecturers, and users. Guidance must be provided on how to access the help desk, call line, and other IT support. Lecturers and students must be able to get their questions answered easily, get any technical problems solved, and receive support for their implementation.

Piloting

The LIS modules must be piloted with a small group to identify issues/problems. Adjust the curriculum as necessary. The piloting with a small user group and some lecturers to identify and solve any process or technical issues.

Dissemination

LIS course materials can include large files if they include video and multimedia. You might need to download and import the modules onto devices initially, while you train Lecturers or IT staff. The university must use stakeholder meetings, the Eswatini Library association (EWALA) meetings, media, and other forums both to disseminate LIS promotional materials and to share information about the LIS programme and how to access information or participate.

Ongoing Support

Ready support for Lecturers, students, and IT personnel is critical, especially in the early stages of the project. There must be dedicated contact in the form of telephone/ cellphone number, e-mail address, or access to live support to ensure that technical issues and other questions are addressed and answered. LIS lecturers should monitor on a regular basis, such as weekly, to determine how students are progressing with their modules and answer any questions. This includes managing the help desk or the support system established to document problems may arise and require redress.

CHALLENGES OF DEVELOPMENT OF AN ODEL CURRICULUM

Although the development of an ODeL curriculum for LIS programme will assist in enhancing teaching and learning in a flexible and cost-effective manner, they could be several challenges.

Abubakar and Hassan (2015) identified the challenges as follows:

Technology Challenges

Technology is a basic requirement for the development of any prospective ODeL programme, and this is due to the fast-changing nature of the technology that keeps on changing by the day. Therefore, to ensure the successful implementation of the ODeL programmes in the LIS institutions in Eswatini, there is a need for proper hardware and software must be provided, in addition to an adequate number of computers, Internet access, audio/video, as well as a robust LMS system.

Personnel Challenges

Another critical challenge is the need for highly qualified staff who continuously keep abreast of current skills and knowledge in ICTs area. ODeL programmes cannot successfully thrive if there is a lack of capacity in terms of human capital r. Therefore, there is a need for highly skilled personnel to manage ODEL programmes.

Administrative and Financial Challenges

The success of the implementation of the ODeL programme rests on the proper administrative and financial support, without which no meaningful progress can be achieved. The success of the ODeL programmes in the LIS institutions in Eswatini depends on a number of factors but not limited to adequate administrative and financial support by the respective parent bodies of the LIS institutions.

REFERENCES

Abu Bakar, A. B., Harande, Y. I., & Abubakar, B. M. (2009). *E-learning in Malaysia and Nigeria: A Bibliometric Study*. Paper presented at the 8th European Conference on E-Learning held at University, Bari, Italy.

Abubakar, B. M., & Hassan, B. B. (2013). Strategies for Developing an e-Learning Curriculum for Library and Information Science (LIS) Schools in the Muslim World: Meeting the Expectations in the Digital Age. *International Journal of Humanities and Social Science, 3*(1), 163–171.

Ameen, K. (2007). *Issues in Quality assurance in LIS higher education in Pakistan*. Paper presented at the IFLA General Conference and Council, Durban, South Africa. Available at http://www.ifla.org/IV/ifla73/index.htm

Benson, R., & Samarawickrema, G. (2009). Addressing the context of e-learning: Using transactional distance theory to inform design. *Distance Education, 30*(1), 5–21. doi:10.1080/01587910902845972

Carswell, L., Thomas, P., Petre, M., Price, B., & Richards, M. (2000). Distance education via the Internet: A report on students' experiences. *British Journal of Educational Technology, 31*(1), 29–46. doi:10.1111/1467-8535.00133

Catherall, P. (2005). *Delivering e-learning for information services in higher education*. Oxford, UK: Chandos. doi:10.1533/9781780630731

Chowdhury, G. G., & Chowdhury, S. (2006). *E-learning support for LIS education in the UK*. Available at: http://www.ics.heacademy.ac.uk/Events/HEADublin2006_V2/papers/Gobinda%20Chowdhury%2014.pdf

Chu, H. (2010). Library and information science education in the digital age. Advances in Librarianship, 32, 77-111. doi:10.1108/S0065-2830(2010)0000032007

Edegbo, W. O. (2011). Curriculum development in library and information science education in Nigeria: Issues and prospects. *Library Philosophy and Practice*. Available at: http: www.webpages.uidaho.edu/~mbolin/edegbo.pdf

Edzan, N. N., & Abdullah, A. (2003). Looking back: The Master of Library and Information Science programme at the University of Malaya, Malaysia. *Malaysian Journal of Library and Information Science, 8*(1), 1–8.

Glatthorn, A. A., Boschee, F., & Whitehead, B. M. (2009). *Curriculum leadership: Strategies for development and implementation (2nd ed.)*. Los Angeles, CA: Sage.

Govindasamy, T. (2002). Successful implementation of e-learning pedagogical considerations. *The Internet and Higher Education, 4*(3/4), 287–299.

IFLA. (2009). *Guidelines for professional library/informational educational programmes*. Available at: http://archive.ifla.org/VII/s23/bulletin/guidelines.htm

Islam, M. S., Chowdhury, S., & Islam, M. A. (2009). *LIS education in e-learning environment: Problems and proposal for Bangladesh.* Paper presented at the Asia-Pacific Conference on Library and Information Education and Practice held at the University, Tsukuba, Japan.

Islam, M. S., Kunifuji, S., Hayama, T., & Miura, M. (2011). Towards exploring a global Scenario of e-learning in library and information science schools. *The International Information & Library Review, 43*(1), 15–22. doi:10.1080/10572317.2011.10762876

Jamaludin, A., Hussin, N., & Mokhtar, W. N. H. W. (2006). Library and information career in Malaysia: Aspirations of educators and the reality of the industry. In Khoo, C., Singh, D. & Chaudry, A.S. (Eds.), *Proceedings of the Asia-Pacific Conference on Library & Information Education & Practice (A-LIEP),* (pp. 423-426). Academic Press.

Kala, S. (2009). *Development of an electronic learning programme for enhancing comprehensive midwifery competency among undergraduate Nursing students* (PhD Thesis). Prince Songkla University.

KALIPER. (2000). *Educating Library and Information Science Professionals for a New Century: The KALIPER Report.* Reston, VA: ALISE. Available at: http://durrance.people.si.umich.edu/TextDocs/KaliperFinalR.pdf

Lawal, O. O. (2000). *Professional education for librarianship: International perspectives. Calabar.* University of Calabar Press.

Lester, J. (2011). Use of adjunct faculty in the delivery of distance education in ALA-Accredited LIS Master's programmes in the U.S. and Canada. *Journal of Education for Library and Information Science, 52*(3), 212–237.

Mammo, W. (2007). Demise, renaissance or existence of LIS education in Ethiopia: Curriculum, Employers expectations and professionals dreams. *The International Information & Library Review, 39*(2), 145–157. doi:10.1016/j.iilr.2007.02.004

Ndlangamandla, K. C. (2011). Library and Information Education and Training in Swaziland: Are view of Opportunities and Challenges. *Mousaion, 29*(2), 158–172.

Ngubane-Mokiwa, S., & Letseka, M. (2015). *Shift from Open Distance Learning to Open Distance e-Learning.* New York: Nova Publishers.

Panahon, I. I. A. (2007). *Developing an e-learning curriculum in European studies: The Philippine experience.* Paper presented at the Workshop on the Future of European Studies in Asia, Manila, Philippines.

Rehman, S. (2003). Information studies curriculum based on competency definition. *Journal of Education for Library and Information Science, 44*(3-4), 276–295.

Rehman, S. (2012). Accreditation of library and information science programmes in the Gulf Cooperation Council nations. *Journal of Librarianship and Information Science, 44*(1), 65–72. doi:10.1177/0961000611427723

Rijkenberg, N. (2019). *Budget Speech 2019/ 2020 by Minister of Finance (Neil Rijkenberg) at the Official Opening of Parliament.* Available from http://www.gov.sz/images/PM/Budget_Estimates_2019.pdf

Sonwalkar, N. (2013). The First Adaptive MOOC: A Case Study on Pedagogy Framework and Scalable Cloud Architecture-Part I. In MOOCs Forum (Vol. 1, pp. 22-29). Academic Press.

Tomkins, G. S., & Case, R. (2011). Curriculum development. In *Canadian Encyclopedia*. Historica-Dominion. Available at: http://www.thecanadianencyclopedia.com /articles/curriculum-development

Waterhouse, S. (2005). *The power of e-learning: The essential guide for teaching in the digital age.* Boston: Pearson Education Inc.

Wilson, T. D. (2001). Mapping the curriculum in information studies. *New Library World*, *102*(11), 436–442. doi:10.1108/03074800110411875

Xu, H. (2003). Information technology courses and their relationship to faculty in different professional ranks in library and information science programmes. *Library & Information Science Research*, *25*(203), 207–222. doi:10.1016/S0740-8188(03)00007-0

Chapter 14
The Usability of Mobile Devices in Distance Learning

Fırat Sarsar
Ege University, Turkey

Tarık Kişla
Ege University, Turkey

Melih Karasu
https://orcid.org/0000-0002-5849-6278
Ege University, Turkey

Yüksel Deniz Arıkan
Ege University, Turkey

Murat Kılıç
Ege University, Turkey

ABSTRACT

Thanks to technological developments, distance education helped new techniques and strategies to emerge in the instruction field. However, these developments may cause problems about integration of the interaction between students and instructors. Communication is seen as one of the biggest problems. Instructors' online communications and their attitudes towards this process affect quality of teaching and learning processes. Other factors affecting this process are learning environment and its effective use. This study is designed to incorporate a mixed method with the aim of reflecting instructors' experiences about different communication techniques and learning environments. In scope of this research, the researchers planned a four-week process using the communication that the researchers have been establishing with Ege University Faculty of Education's instructors. The researchers will use different mobile devices and feedback methods for the process.

DOI: 10.4018/978-1-5225-9779-7.ch014

The Usability of Mobile Devices in Distance Learning

INTRODUCTION

Distance education, which is becoming widespread in Turkey as well as throughout the world, is a learning process. Distance education systems are linked to interactions created at different place and time periods by factors such as instructor, learner, material and resource (Özkul and Aydın, 2012). Distance education, which started with letters in Turkey, advanced itself with technological developments such as TV and radio's coming to the country, is undoubtedly intertwined with technology. There are significant similarities between using TV to reach and educate people when it was merely popular and using mobile devices these days along with technological developments in education. Devices such as TV and radio which are pioneers of "education in times of need, wherever and whenever you want" ideas lead to today's distance education understanding. With the technology constantly developing, the mobile devices gave an opportunity to support lifelong learning which is one of the most important benefits of distance education and initiated mobile learning. Academicians reached a consensus on the need for further research to understand mobile learning better (as cited in Crompton, 2013). There are different definitions of mobile learning in the literature, but an old definition may lose its validity with new research, because it is a field which consistently makes progress. This is why we should ask more questions to understand mobile learning better.

BACKGROUND

How Did Mobile Learning Emerge?

With population growth, the need for a new education method and an action grew as well. Topics such as equality and lifelong learning in education were affected positively by the advantages of mobile learning. After mobile learning emerged and people noticed its advantages, it became easier to enhance and spread mobile learning devices thanks to technological developments. With the advancements in mobile learning devices, indications for their use changed. Their wide spread usage makes them reasonable to use in education.

What Is Mobile Learning?

Mobile learning is one of the branches of distance education and it is directly affected from technological advancements. Due to the wide range of studies in mobile learning and its tools, different views emerged. Even though academicians have not reached a consensus about its definition, the existing definitions give an idea.

According to Quinn (2000), mobile learning is a subtopic of e-learning managed through portable digital devices, but to Shepherd (2001), mobile learning is not only electronic but also mobile. Looking at these definitions, we can see how science works cumulatively. First definition is focused on general terms but the latter emphasizes specific words.

To O'Malley (2003), mobile learning takes place when learners are not in a designated or adjusted setting and when learners benefit from mobile technologies' advantages and opportunities. This definition includes mobile learning tools, mobile environment and its advantages. It is more detailed than the previous definitions, which leads us to the idea that further explanations about mobile learning will be more detailed. Because technological developments and prevalence of technological device use create new findings. Academicians mention those findings in their definitions as new findings emerge.

Trifonova (2003) defines mobile learning as any learning occurring in a mobile environment or through a mobile device. On the other hand, Keegan (2005) explains mobile learning with mobile learning devices; he says "it is instructional preparations and studies through PDAs, palmtops, handheld computers, smart phones and mobile devices". General definitions may lack findings of the current era but may have similarities with older ones. PDA devices Keegan mentioned in his definition mostly lost their own popularity. That shows that definition of mobile learning has been changed every year. Some researchers prefer to use more general concepts and hence they make long-lasting definitions. According to Peters (2007), m-learning is a subset of e-learning and is a step towards tailoring the education process as just in time, just enough and just for the person. Peters also mentioned m-learning's advantages in this definition. The reason why he mentioned "just for person" in education process may be the studies made about autonomous learners until 2007. These definitions include information about what mobile learning is, which provides opportunities to ask more questions thanks to their content. When we search for what is m-learning we see "mobile tools, mobile devices, mobile equipment and mobile technologies" words frequently. This leads us to another question.

Prevalence of Mobile Learning Tools

Frequent use of mobile devices is a big reason to prefer them as learning and teaching tools. According to statista's data (https://www.statista.com/), there will be more than 5 billion people using cell phones in 2019. Mobile devices are not just cell phones or smart phones. When it can be considered other mobile devices like tablets, PDAs, Notebooks we come across to larger numbers. It can be assumed that more than half of the world population uses at least one mobile device. According to internetlivestats' statistics, as seen in Figure 1, more than 196 million smart phones and 21 million tablet pcs are sold in 2019 around the world (internetlivestats, 2019).

There is data on the number of people online and number of smart phones sold every second, which demonstrates how mobile devices are popular and will become even more popular.

What Are Mobile Learning Tools?

There are many different mobile devices, but some of them are more popular than others such as PDAs, smart phones, tablets and laptops. Those all are also the kind of tools used in m-learning (Connolly and Stansfield, 2006).

Figure 1. Smartphone and tablet PC sales amounts in 2019 (internetlivestats, 2019)

PDAs (Personal Digital Assistant)

They are known as pocket computers, and they work just like a computer. Similar to a cell phone, a PDA has a battery which needs to be charged. Usually PDAs have touch screens and we can call them the ancestors of today's smart phones.

Laptops

They are designed for making desktop computers portable and can be used easily without needing a desk. Basically, there is nothing you cannot do with a laptop that you can do with a desktop. Windows and Linux which are among the most common operating systems are highly preferred for laptops. The biggest differences they have besides their size, are the battery and charging device. Their screen sizes are very similar to the desktops. Depends on the preference, you can choose 15, 17 or a 19+ inch screen. You can change your monitor size preference after you buy a desktop via changing the monitor, unfortunately, that feature does not apply to laptops because screen is not separate from the body.

Smart Phones

Usually they have Android or IOS operating systems. They can be called as the next generation of PDA devices. Today they are preferred by a huge population of users thanks to their fast internet connection, high resolution photograph, durable screen and high-quality image features. Portability in a pocket is a very proper feature for mobile learning. The battery life changes according to use but the average is one day. Apart from PDAs, they have diverse application markets. Since they are easier to carry and are used more frequently, some applications do not have a computer version.

Additionally, there are smart phones with a tablet size. They are known as "phablet" which is derived from the words "phone" and "tablet". Common features of these tools are portability and internet connection but this does not mean a person cannot benefit from mobile learning tools when there is no internet connection. Mobile learning tools can be used both online and offline. Today it is known that use of mobile learning tools in education is increased. To be aware of its reasons we have new questions to ask. Why do we need mobile learning tools? How did they come out? Why did this need emerge? What are their benefits?

Advantages of Mobile Learning

Mobile learning provides a great convenience for both learners and teachers. Mobile learning came out as a technological tool to address the needs. Exponential growth of knowledge began with quicker access to information and more attention to scientific research. Access to more information provided people not only more learning opportunities but also more time to learn. Distance education aims to remove the time and place limitations by extending the distance between learners and teachers. Audio and image transfer followed the process where only writing was transferred. People benefited from TV and radio in this process. After instruction was carried to homes, by benefiting from advanced technology, education opportunities were carried to pockets and bags; which meant learning through portable devices (mobile learning) emerged. Mobile learning provides people the opportunity to learn through portable devices wherever they want without being in a school building or without a predetermined time as it supports lifelong learning (Nordin, Embi, Yunus 2010).

Mobile learning provides interaction between two people in different places and delivers the same information to people who are available at different times (El-Hussein and Cronje, 2010). It creates an alternative way for disabled people going to school. It can reach people in different health conditions, with different levels of intelligence, age, interest, income and position by presenting contents prepared according to their needs and interests. It provides more materials and resources by presenting multimedia learning opportunity. Additionally, thanks to m-learning students can use their free time and time they spend in school more effectively and can get feedback immediately (Bozkurt, 2015).

Motivation is one of the most important factors in education. Letting a person to choose where and when to learn is an important factor in learner motivation (as cited in Kilis, 2013), which can reflect on productivity. M-learning contributes to out of school time and it can be adjusted for different people. Its feedback time, easier and faster communication and student-centred education increase the effectiveness of the time spent in school (Ergüney, 2017). Student centred education is highly preferred in modern education, which not only focuses on student's needs but also changes teacher's role. According to the student-centred education perspective, teachers are guides and not information providers. Leaving rote-learning behind, student-centered education aims to achieve higher learning objectives. There are more advantages to add but these are enough to give us a perspective on what contributions mobile learning and its tools made to education. Is it possible to create an instruction method with no disadvantages or limitations? Does m-learning also have disadvantages?

Disadvantages of Mobile Learning

M-learning is not just a title contributing to education. Even though it has a lot of advantages, it does not change the fact that it has disadvantages as well. Problems related to mobile learning tools' screen size are the first ones to think of when it comes to m-learning.

"Small screen size means low resolution in the course materials presented" is a common belief. Even though this problem was mentioned in a lot of articles, with technology developing we cannot say small screen size affects resolution too much anymore. However, there are still other disadvantages of m-learning protecting their validities strongly (Bridgeman, Lennon and Jackenthal, 2003).

Battery life, storage space and usability bring limitations to learning (as cited in Alonso, 2014, p.. 10-19). Battery life of m-learning tools may affect portability. If your battery dies and you don't have the opportunity to charge it, having a portable device may be meaningless in terms of educational purposes. In addition to this, m-learning tools such as music player, smart phone and PDA usually have limited storage and this can create a problem for resources desired to be stocked.

M-learning tools preferred by students will differ from each other because of the variety and price levels. This may cause a student to use a less efficient m-learning tool. Considering its advantages and disadvantages, we may need to ask another question. What kind of studies should we make to benefit from m-learning?

There are projects about m-learning in Turkey and other countries. We can learn in what kind of projects m-learning is used and have ideas about future of m-learning by analysing them.

IOS vs. Android

There are two main operating systems for mobile devices: IOS and Android. There are quitly different than each other. While IOS is a limited system, Android gives more interaction opportunities with outside. IOS has a better protection against malicious software since it is a closed system. Android has more weaknesses about security but since it is an open system, file transfer is easier, and it makes downloading educational materials easier. Notwithstanding, Android is more complex than IOS.

IOS' performance is better than Android at multitasking processes due to its closed system. Android's performance is worse because of the open system and widget system it uses. IOS had the first application store experience and maintained its success and now presents better opportunities for applications than Android. That is why we can see that applications are first designed for IOS and then they are designed for Android. Even though IOS seems to have a lot of comparative advantages, it has a lot of limitations, which makes Android a better choice for most people. Android almost has no limitations. It allows you to control CPU speed, storage, special software and different modes. When you connect it to a computer, it works as a USB driver and makes file transfer possible. IOS does not allow those features and file transfer is also limited. Despite the fact that this limitation is positive in terms of security, it may not be good for an easy and comfortable use for IOS.

Android is preferred by more manufacturer firms, as it can be used on different models manufactured by different firms. It shows us that Android has a wide user profile. On the other hand IOS is manufactured by a single firm and it does not allow its users to use another brand. This is why its user profile is limited. The factors above should be compared before deciding on "which operating system is better for whom". Using conditions and features needed affect the answer of "which device should be preferred". Another big factor affecting people's choice is the screen size.

Screen Sizes on Mobile Devices

"Inch" is the unit used for describing screen sizes. Its symbol is " " ". An inch is approximately 2.5 centimetres. To show it with a symbol, 1" = 2.5 cm. Smart phone screens are sized from approximately 4-5 inches to 6.5 inches while tablets can have 10 inches screens. PDAs are not very popular nowadays but they are pocket computers with smart phone sizes. On the other hand laptops can go up to 19 inches. Screen sizes of smart phones are illustrated in Figure 2.

Students using PDAs, became more successful than students using cell phones (Thornton and Gaukin, 2005). In this research, the PDAs' screen sizes were bigger than cell phones' screen sizes. Even though

Figure 2. Screen sizes of smart phones
("Which Screen Size", 2016)

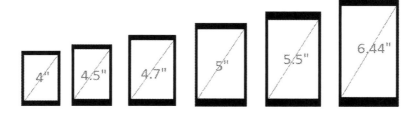

it was mentioned that bigger screens have better resolution quality, this does not apply today. In addition, 69% of the students participating in this study told that small screen sizes do not create a problem. Small screen makes learners scroll too much when they are reading (Nulden and Lundin, 2003). M-learning tools with big screens may be more beneficial for reading long texts.

Maniar, Bennett, Hand and Allan (2008) analysed relationship between m-learning tools with small-medium-big screen sizes and learning in their study. Small screen size was 1.65 inches, medium size was 2.38 inches and big screen size was 3.78 inches in this study. People whose age between 24-58 were asked to watch a 5-minute video in a busy cafe. After the video, they were asked to fill a scale with 9 items, where 1=strongly disagree, 2=disagree, 3= not sure, 4= agree, and 5 was determined as strongly agree. Participants who had big screens marked their responses close to 5 for the items related to quality of the video, screen brightness and carrying a mobile phone. After that, participants were evaluated with a video teaching how to measure blood pressure. Results show that screen size affects learning and small screen is a limitation for learning. These studies were carried out in 2008. There are big differences between today's mobile devices and 2008's. 3.78 inches were determined as a big screen size in the study, but today 3.78 inches can only be accepted as a small screen. With high quality screens and increase of mobile device use, it is possible to say that problems such as low resolution and sizing a video according to the screen are left behind. Today basic questions related to the quality of a video are "which device recorded the video, in which resolution the video is (480p, 720p...) and if it is watched online, how fast was the internet? etc.".

When we analyse results of the mentioned studies, we see that m- learning is defined by academicians with its features, such as having no time and place limitation, and devices' portability. These features are listed as the advantages of m-learning. These features demonstrate that m-learning increases learner motivation. On the other hand, battery life, storage and screen size act as disadvantages.

THE USABILITY OF MOBILE DEVICES: A CASE STUDY

This section covers the model, working group, data collection tools and application process of the research, which was conducted to determine the usability of mobile devices in distance education, as well as the analysis results of data obtained in the data collection process.

The research model was planned as a mixed design. Both qualitative and quantitative data were collected in the research process. The research was conducted in three courses: two undergraduate levels and one graduate level. The data for the research were collected from three faculty members (one assistant professor and two doctors) and an expert who provides technical support to courses.

Six different mobile devices were used in the research. The mobile devices used were chosen to have two separate operating systems and 3 different screen sizes in each operating system (Table 1).

One of the most important criteria in the selection of mobile devices is the operating systems of these mobile devices. Operating systems are an important criterion since they ensure that technical features run actively according to the compatibility of the devices used and that applications speak the same language with the device in a meaningful way. Users can prefer operating systems because they offer different user interfaces and functions. Mobile devices with IOS and Android operating systems were used in the research.

The Usability of Mobile Devices in Distance Learning

Table 1. Screen size and operating system features of mobile devices used

Device No	Screen Size	Operating System
1	9 inches and above (Large)	Android
2	9 inches and above (Large)	IOS
3	Between 6 inches and 8 inches (Medium)	Android
4	Between 6 inches and 8 inches (Medium)	IOS
5	5.5 inches and below (Small)	Android
6	5.5 inches and below (Small)	IOS

The other criterion employed in the selection of mobile devices is the screen sizes of the devices. The researchers categorized the screen sizes into three; namely small, medium and large. Mobile devices with a screen size of 5.5 inches and below were selected as small screen size. Available mobile devices with a screen size of 6 to 9 inches were selected when determining the medium screen size. Available mobile devices with a screen size of 9 inches and above were selected when determining the large screen size.

During the research process, the participants were asked to use a mobile device for at least 4 hours in their distance education courses. Each participant used 6 mobile devices in total. After teaching the course, the faculty members filled the data collection tools on the basis of their experience with the mobile device.

Due to the limited number of studies in the literature and the inapplicability of previously-used data collection tools to the research purposes, all data collection tools used in the research were developed by the researchers. In this context, (i) Mobile Device Effectiveness Evaluation Questionnaire and (ii) Mobile Device Evaluation Questions were prepared in line with expert opinions. In addition, researchers also kept (iii) research logs in order to report the situations that were deemed important during the distance education activities.

1. **Mobile Device Effectiveness Evaluation Questionnaire**: Prepared by experts and researchers, this questionnaire is based on scoring. Efficiency scores were determined in defined subcategories and headings.
2. **Mobile Device Evaluation Questions**: The open-ended questions prepared by experts and researchers were answered by the faculty members after each course.
3. **Research Logs**: Research logs are the diaries kept by the faculty member and attending researcher during and after the course.

Research Findings

This heading covers the findings in consequence of analysis of data obtained by data collection tools.

Opinion of the Experts

The results of the researchers' evaluation of "Screen Features", "Operating System", "Application", "Audio and Video", "Course Duration", "After the Course" and "Ergonomy" categories of the mobile devices used will be given under this heading.

Table 2 presents the average scores given by experts in this sub-problem, where screen features of mobile devices were studied in terms of "Size", "Image Quality", "Touch Sensitivity" and "Resolution". The experts rated each feature for all devices.

It is seen in Table 2 that the highest average score for "Size" feature was given to the Android device of 9 inches and above. The lowest score is found to be devices of 5.5 inches or below. From this point of view, it is concluded that using mobile devices with large screen size in distance education would have better results. In terms of "Image Quality", it is observed that IOS devices have higher scores. Similarly, in terms of "Touch Sensitivity", it can be said that average scores of IOS devices are higher than those of Android devices. Finally, in terms of "resolution" feature, it is seen that all devices were scored above 9 points. When Table 2 is reviewed considering all screen features, it is seen that Android device of 9 inches and above had the highest score (9.63).

In the research, experts evaluated the effect of some features regarding the mobile devices' operating system during distance education. Sub-elements such as "Speed", "Running with Application", "Direction (horizontal and vertical)" and "Virtual keyboard (practicality)" were evaluated within this scope. Data obtained from experts are presented in Table 3. The experts rated each feature for all devices.

It is seen in Table 3 that the highest average score for "Speed" feature was given to the device with IOS operating system and a screen size of 9 inches and above, while the lowest score was given to the Android device of 5.5 inches and below. According to the results of another question where experts evaluated the operating system's "running compatibly with application", the highest score (9.5) was given to IOS devices of 6 to 8 inches and of 9 inches and above. When the scores in this section are reviewed, it is seen that IOS devices get higher scores than Android devices in general. The experts were asked

Table 2. Average scores given by experts for screen features

Device Type	Screen Size	Size	Image Quality	Touch Sensitivity	Resolution	Average
IOS	5.5 inc and below	3,5	9,5	9,5	9,75	8,06
	Between 6-8 inc	7,5	9,75	9,75	9	9,00
	9 inc and above	9,25	9,5	9,75	9,75	9,56
Android	5.5 inc and below	3,5	7	9	9,25	7,19
	Between 6-8 inc	7	8	9,25	9,25	8,38
	9 inc and above	9,5	9,5	9,5	10	9,63

Table 3. Average scores given by experts for operating system

Device Type	Screen Size	Speed	Working with Application	Virtual Keyboard (Usability)	Average
IOS	5.5 inc and below	9	9	3	5,25
	Between 6-8 inc	9,5	9,5	4	5,75
	9 inc and above	9,75	9,5	5	6,06
Android	5.5 inc and below	8	4,75	3	3,94
	Between 6-8 inc	8,75	7	4,25	5,00
	9 inc and above	9,25	5,75	4	4,75

The Usability of Mobile Devices in Distance Learning

the device's "Direction (horizontal-vertical)" in the next question. This feature was not scored by the experts because the mobile application only runs horizontally. In the question for evaluating the "virtual keyboard practicality" feature of devices, the experts gave the highest score to IOS devices of 9 inches and above, while the lowest score was given to devices of 5.5 inch and below. It can be concluded that the small size of devices affects the virtual keyboard usage negatively. Looking at the total scores obtained in this section, it is seen that the highest average score was given to IOS devices of 9 inches and above.

Table 4 presents the data for this section where experts evaluate the mobile version of online course application used in distance education. The application used was evaluated in terms of "Compatibility", "Functions" and "Feedback and Pedagogical".

It is seen in Table 4 that the highest average scores for "compatibility" feature was given to IOS devices of 9 inches and above, while the lowest score was given to Android devices of 5.5 inch and below. In the next question where the "functions" of the application are evaluated, the highest score was given to Android devices of 6 to 8 inches, while the lowest score was given to Android devices of 9 inches and above. In this question, the scores of iOS devices were very close to each other. Again, for "feedback and pedagogical" features, the highest score was given to Android devices of 6 to 8 inches, while the lowest score was given to Android devices of 9 inches and above. When the average scores for this feature are reviewed, it is seen that iOS devices of 6 inches and above have the highest average score.

Audio and video features of mobile devices used in the distance education process are analyzed in this section. Table 5 presents data, for which experts evaluated three elements in total; namely, "Audio Quality (Input-Output)", "Video Quality (Camera resolution)" and "Audio-Video Synchronization."

According to Table 5, devices of 9 inches and above have the highest average scores for "Audio Quality" feature. It is seen that all devices have scores of 9.5 and above in terms of audio quality. From this point of view, it can be said that all devices have good sound quality. In terms of "audio quality", it is seen that devices of 6 inches to 8 inches have lower averages; however, devices of 5.5 inches and below and devices of 9 inches and above have at least 9 points. In terms of "audio-video synchronization," the last feature in this section, it is seen that the scores of all devices except Android devices of 6 to 8 inches are 9 points and above. When the average scores are reviewed in general, it is seen that Android devices of 9 inches and above have the highest scores, while devices of 6 to 8 inches have lower scores than others.

Table 6 presents scores obtained upon experts' evaluation of some features of mobile devices used during distance education, such as "Interaction", "Student Video" and "Student Audio".

According to the data presented in Table 6, it can be said that the devices were given low scores in terms of "interaction" feature during the course. In this section, the highest score was given to Android

Table 4. Average scores given by experts for online course mobile application

Device Type	Screen Size	Compatibility	Functions	Feedback and Pedagogical	Average
IOS	5.5 inc and below	6	7	8,75	7,25
	Between 6-8 inc	6,5	7,5	9	7,67
	9 inc and above	6,75	7,25	9	7,67
Android	5.5 inc and below	4	7,5	9,25	6,92
	Between 6-8 inc	3,5	8,5	9,5	7,17
	9 inc and above	4,5	6	8,5	6,33

Table 5. Average scores given by experts for audio and video qualities of mobile devices

Device Type	Screen Size	Audio Quaility Input/Output	Video Quality (Camera Resolution)	Audio - Video Synchronisation	Average
IOS	5.5 inc and below	9,5	9	9,5	9,33
	Between 6-8 inc	9,75	5,25	9	8,00
	9 inc and above	10	9	9,75	9,58
Android	5.5 inc and below	9,5	9,25	9,5	9,42
	Between 6-8 inc	9,75	6	4	6,58
	9 inc and above	10	10	9,75	9,92

Table 6. Average scores given by experts for "interaction", "student video" and "student audio"

Device Type	Screen Size	Interaction	Student Video	Student Audio	Average
IOS	5.5 inc and below	4	4,75	9	5,92
	Between 6-8 inc	4	6	9,5	6,50
	9 inc and above	4,5	6,25	9,5	6,75
Android	5.5 inc and below	3,5	5,25	9,75	6,17
	Between 6-8 inc	4,5	6,25	4,25	5,00
	9 inc and above	5,25	6,75	9,5	7,17

devices of 9 inches and above, while the lowest scores were given to Android devices of 5.5 inches and below. In terms of "student video", experts gave the highest score to devices of 9 inches and above, and the lowest scores to Android devices of 5.5 inches and below. "Student audio", the last feature in this section, was found to be considerably high for devices except Android devices of 6 to 8 inches. When the features are examined in general, it is seen that the highest average score belongs to Android devices of 9 inch and above.

The records taken during distance education were displayed on the mobile device after the course, and evaluated by experts in terms of features such as "Video Recording" and "Audio Recording" etc. Table 7 presents data on the evaluation by the experts.

According to Table 7 presenting the experts' answers to questions on redisplaying the recorded course on the mobile device, it is seen that the highest score in terms of "Video recording" belongs to Android devices of 9 inch and above with a great difference compared to others. Scores of other devices are very close to each other. In terms "Audio recording", it is seen that the scores given to all devices by experts were very close to each other. When all features in this section are examined, it is seen that the highest score (8.75 points) belongs to Android devices of 9 inches and above.

Table 8 presents data on the evaluation of experts regarding ergonomic features of mobile devices. Sub-elements such as "Grip", "Weight", "Screen Usage", "Pen Usage" and "Button Usage" were evaluated within this scope.

The Usability of Mobile Devices in Distance Learning

Table 7. Average scores given by experts for video and audio features of course records

Device Type	Screen Size	Video Recording	Audio Recording	Average
IOS	5.5 inc and below	6,00	7,75	6,88
	Between 6-8 inc	6,00	8,50	7,25
	9 inc and above	7,00	8,25	7,63
Android	5.5 inc and below	5,75	7,50	6,63
	Between 6-8 inc	6,25	8,00	7,13
	9 inc and above	9,50	8,00	8,75

Table 8. Average scores given by experts for ergonomy of mobile devices

Device Type	Screen Size	Grip	Weight	Screen Usage	Pen Usage	Button Usage	Average
IOS	5.5 inc and below	3,50	5,50	6,75	0,00	9,00	4,95
	Between 6-8 inc	4,75	4,75	9,25	0,00	9,25	5,60
	9 inc and above	4,75	4,75	9,25	0,00	9,50	5,65
Android	5.5 inc and below	3,75	3,75	5,25	5,25	7,00	5,00
	Between 6-8 inc	4,00	3,25	9,25	0,75	9,50	5,35
	9 inc and above	3,75	2,75	9,00	1,00	9,50	5,20

In this section, where questions on the ergonomy of devices were answered, experts gave low scores to all devices in terms of "grip" and "weight" features. It is seen that Android devices have relatively lower scores than IOS devices for these two features. In terms of "screen usage", devices of 6 inch and above have scores of 9 and above. IOS devices could not be given any points in terms of "pen usage", because no pens were used during application. As Android devices of 5.5 inches and below have pen (stylus) features, they were given the highest scores in this section. In terms of "button usage", all devices except Android devices of 5.5 inches and below were given 9 points and above. When the general averages were reviewed, IOS devices of 9 inches and above were given the highest scores.

General Evaluation of Expert Opinions

Table 9 presents the average scores obtained for devices with different features and screen sizes used in the research, all features of which were evaluated by experts.

Table 9. Average scores given by experts for devices of different sizes

	IOS			Android		
Screen Size	5.5 inch and below	Between 6-8 inch	9 inch and above	5.5 inch and below	Between 6-8 inch	9 inch and above
General Avarage	6,69	7,00	7,42	6,26	6,28	7,14

Table 10. Opinions of faculty members

Variables	Views of Faculty Members
Size	• As the screen size gets larger, the ease of using the distance education media increases • As the screen size gets larger, it becomes easier to use the screen horizontally • Keyboard usage leads to restrictions independently from screen size • As the screen size gets larger, ergonomy and ease of carrying decrease • Support (table stand) is needed according to screen sizes, which has an effect on the use of this facilitative tool • There is no multi-image support in mobile devices used Screen image quality
Operating Systems	• Fast operating systems are more effective • Although application usage in IOS operating system is not significantly different from Android, the experts stated it to be more efficient. Android operating system is widely used, which provides ease of access
General Technical Issues	• Keyboard usage leads to restrictions • Touch screen pen (stylus) is an easy-to-use and necessary tool • Uploading and sharing files • Sharing audio, video, and screen with users Lack of multi-process

When the table was examined, the highest average score (7.42) was given to IOS devices of 9 inch and above, while the second highest score (7.14) to Android devices of 9 inch and above. The lowest two scores were given to Android devices of 5.5 inches and below and Android devices of 6 to 8 inches. In general, it can be said that the scores of IOS devices are relatively higher than Android devices.

Opinions of Faculty Members to Interview Questions

In this section, the findings of analysis results of faculty members' opinions were presented in tables.

The opinions of faculty members were examined, and it was deemed appropriate to classify the opinions in three main categories; namely (i) Screen Size, (ii) Operating Systems and (iii) General Technical İssues. In this context, after content analyzes were made, opinions of the faculty members were stated in an explanatory manner as in Table 17. Although faculty members found screen size to be a positive element in distance education, they indicated some restrictions. Screen size was emphasized as a problem for carrying or holding in hand, while continuity of learning process at any place and time was described as positive. They also stated that the direct proportion of screen size with video quality helped the course materials look more effective and quality.

Faculty members also indicated that the operating system in mobile devices was an element that would affect the distance education process. It was stated that the speed of the operating system affects video quality and connection time to the distance learning environment. In this context, the faculty members that participated in courses with mobile devices observed that IOS operating system was connected faster than Android operating system. However, the faculty members expressed their opinion that Android operating system might be more preferable due to the higher number of Android phone users.

Faculty members who teach by distance education emphasized that, in addition to the operating system and screen size, there were some technical problems affecting the learning process. They stated that, the availability or unavailability of some functions in addition to screen sizes affected active participation to

The Usability of Mobile Devices in Distance Learning

distance education. Within this scope, they underlined that keyboard application on mobile devices, which does not open during the course or overlays the most part of the screen, negatively affects the interaction in the learning environment. Moreover, lack of effective file and image sharing during distance education is one of the important technical problems emphasized by the faculty members. The faculty members offered their suggestions on the importance and necessity of touch screen pens (stylus) in order to use touch screens more effectively in their courses. It was stated that, regardless of screen sizes, audio and video sharing is limited and multi-processes cannot be conducted very effectively.

Research Log

This section presents analyses of research logs, where the experiences of faculty members and experts during and after the course were reflected. In the light of the researchers' notes, it was observed that the students stated some opinions frequently throughout the process. When these notes were analyzed, it was observed that student expectations were grouped under three main headings (Table 11).

Students who participated in the course with their mobile devices stated as a positive situation to connect to the course independently at any place and time, while limited internet quotas and occasional disconnection of internet were emphasized as negative situations in research logs. In the light of the same notes, students emphasized that connecting to the course with mobile devices was a freedom, while they stated that technical problems caused negative situations. Important items specified in research logs throughout the process include the facts that connecting to the course with mobile devices ensured ease of access and that the process was more pleasant and practical. They also emphasized the screen size as a negative situation. According to the researchers' notes, students prefer to use laptops.

Table 11. Student opinions and expectations according to research logs

Status	Student Opinions and Expectations	
	Code	Frequency (n=50)
Positive	Independence from Space	20
	Independence from Time	20
	Flexible	18
	Accessibility	17
	Freedom	12
	Pleasant	10
	Practical	10
Negative	Internet Quota	12
	Connection	11
	Screen Size	11
	Technical Problems	11
	File Sharing	8
Neutral	Laptop usage	14

CONCLUSION

As a result, screen sizes are a decisive and significant feature for mobile devices to be used in distance education. As the screen size gets larger, the image quality of learning materials in distance education increases. As the screen size gets smaller, visibility of images decreases. There are two elements regarding operating systems, one of which is speed and the other is common use. It was observed that IOS operating system is faster than Android, although not very significantly. However, as Android operating system is more commonly used, it is expected that the distance education system will be designed accordingly. In addition to screen size and operating system, there are some elements that affect the distance learning process, the most important of which is touch screen pen (stylus). Keyboard use, camera opening problems, ergonomic problems, internet and quota problems are stated as other factors affecting the distance education process.

ACKNOWLEDGMENT

This research was supported by the Scientific Research Project Coordinator of Ege University with project number 15EGF003.

REFERENCES

Alonso de Castro, M. (2014). Educational projects based on mobile learning. *Teoría de la Educación. Educación y Cultura en la Sociedad de la Información, 15*(1).

Bozkurt, B. (2015). Mobil öğrenme: Her zaman, her yerde kesintisiz öğrenme deneyimi. *Açıköğretim Uygulamaları ve Araştırmaları Dergisi, 1*(2), 65–81.

Bridgeman, B., Lennon, M. L., & Jackenthal, A. (2003). Effects of screen size, screen resolution, and display rate on computer-based test performance. *Applied Measurement in Education, 16*(3), 191–205. doi:10.1207/S15324818AME1603_2

Connolly, T., & Stansfield, M. (2006). Using Games-Based eLearning Technologiesin Overcoming Difficulties in Teaching Information Systems. *Journal of Information Technology Education Research, 5*, 459–476.

Crompton, H. (2013). A historical overview of mobile learning: Toward learner-centered education. Handbook of Mobile Learning, 3-14.

El-Hussein, M. O. M., & Cronje, J. C. (2010). Defining mobile learning in the higher education landscape. *Journal of Educational Technology & Society, 13*(3), 12–21.

Ergüney, M. (2017). Uzaktan Eğitimde Mobil Öğrenme Teknolojilerinin Rolü. *Ulakbilge, 5*(13), 1009–1021. doi:10.7816/ulakbilge-05-13-02

Internetlivestats. (2019, 17 February). Retrieved from http://www.internetlivestats.com/

Keegan, D. (2005, October). The incorporation of mobile learning into mainstream education and training. In *World Conference on Mobile Learning, Cape Town* (p. 11). Academic Press.

Kilis, S. (2013). Impacts of Mobile Learning in Motivation, Engagement and Achievement of Learners: Review of Literature. *Gaziantep University Journal of Social Sciences, 12*(2).

Lundin, J., & Nulden, U. (2003). Mobile scenarios: Supporting collaborative learning among mobile workers. *Educating Managers with Tomorrow's Technologies*, 173-190.

Maniar, N., Bennett, E., Hand, S., & Allan, G. (2008). The effect of mobile phone screen size on video based learning. *JSW, 3*(4), 51–61. doi:10.4304/jsw.3.4.51-61

Nordin, N., Embi, M. A., & Yunus, M. M. (2010). Mobile learning framework for lifelong learning. *Procedia: Social and Behavioral Sciences, 7*, 130–138. doi:10.1016/j.sbspro.2010.10.019

O'Malley, C., Vavoula, G., Glew, J. P., Taylor, J., Sharples, M., Lefrere, P., ... Waycott, J. (2005). *Guidelines for learning/teaching/tutoring in a mobile environment*. Academic Press.

Özkul, A. E., & Aydın, C. H. (2012). Öğrenci adaylarının açık ve uzaktan öğrenmeye yönelik görüşleri. In *Akademik Bilişim Konferansı*. Uşak: Uşak Üniversitesi. Retrieved from http://ab.org.tr/ab12/bildiri/42.pdf

Peters, K. (2007). m-Learning: Positioning educators for a mobile, connected future. *The International Review of Research in Open and Distributed Learning, 8*(2). doi:10.19173/irrodl.v8i2.350

Quinn, C. (2000). *mLearning: Mobile, wireless, in-your-pocket learning.* LiNE Zine.

Shepherd, M. (2001). *M is for Maybe. Tactix: Training and communication technology in context.* Retrieved from http://www.fastrak-consulting.co.uk/tactix/features/mlearning.htm

Trifonova, A. (2003). *Mobile learning-review of the literature.* University of Trento.

Chapter 15
Ubiquitous Learning and Heutagogy in Teacher Education

Beril Ceylan
Ege University, Turkey

ABSTRACT

The learning and teaching horizon is changing nowadays. Learner-centered learning is preferable to teacher-centered learning. Teachers and learners prefer mobility and flexibility in education. Ubiquitous learning provides the flexibility and connection with mobility. Due to advantages of technology use, ubiquitous learning is preferred for individual and public learning. Heutagogy emphasizes the capability of learners' self-regulation process. Heutagogical learning occurs at two levels. The first level is competencies. The second level is deeper learning. In heutogogy, learners design their learning situation in a non-linear learning approach in a flexible way. In this chapter, heutagogy and ubiquitous learning connection will be discussed in the light of literature in the context of education and teacher education. A heutagogical ubiquitous learning interaction will be offered.

DOI: 10.4018/978-1-5225-9779-7.ch015

INTRODUCTION

Learners of 21st century, take an active role in achieving competency on their learning goals. They develop strategies, methods and skills for learning and gaining useful information. Each person has different characteristics and use different learning strategies. Several studies emphasis transformation of learning and learning environments. Governments, foundations, societies, experts, and academicians make statements for education standards on different communication channels. These groups make meetings, symposiums and conferences to announce the revealed standards. One of the most important society on Educational development is International Society for Teaching in Education (ISTE). ISTE, studies on educational standards for educators, students, leaders, coaches and computer science educators. ISTE announced new learner standards in 2016 and new educator standards in 2017. Most of the countries read these reports to empower and redesign their educational systems. Education faculties are responsible for to educate 21st century teacher candidates. These standards transform teacher candidates into heutagogical and ubiquitous learners. For ISTE (2017) As a learner, an educator continues learning from others to improve his/her teaching practice and technology knowledge. It is important to for educators to set professional goals, reach technological pedagogical success and reflect the effectiveness of the goals. Teachers take the advantage of ubiquitous environments to enrich their profession in local or global learning areas. Teachers investigate the ways for supporting their learning and teaching process in order to be novel and heutagogical individuals. As a leader, an educator supports students' empowerment and achievement in learning process. Digitalization makes teachers fell comfortable in accessing ubiquitous environments with heutagogical approaches. Educators take the advantage of technology, digital content and resources. Furthermore, they become models to their colleagues on using digital environments for presentation, evaluation and identification. As an analyst, an educator use technology to reflect students' competencies and give feedbacks. Technological assessment tools guiding students to being self-determined and ubiquitous learners.

As it seen at previous paragraph, educators' professional development perception is changing with ubiquitous approaches. Educator needs technological support to use ubiquitous learning environments, materials and technological tools. Ubiquitous learning (U-learning) is supported by mobile, embedded and network systems for everyday life (Ogata, Matsuka, El-Bishouty & Yano, 2009). It supports flexibility like independence of time, location, content, and environment. Chen, Chiang, Jiang & Yu (2016) proposed a teacher-training model in a ubiquitous learning environment. This ubiquitous learning environment includes QR codes for physical resources, wireless network and a learning system. The model supports teacher's teaching abilities on subject specific content. For their research, teaching ability was positively affected by novel training fields, materials and experience. For Camilleri & Camilleri (2017) teachers' professional development is engaged with digital learning sources and ubiquitous technologies for adapt educational methodologies to today's perspective. Nowadays, teacher education and professional development paradigms shift from pedagogy (instructed directed learning approach) and andragogy (learner directed learning approach) to heutagogy (learner determined learning approach).

Agonacs and Matos (2019) describe that heutagogy is extended form of andragogy. However, heutagogy is an extension and supply from different learning approaches; it does not mean that heutagogy is the alternative of pedagogy and andragogy (Kenyon & Hase, 2013). In heutagogical approach learners take the role of assistant, guide and facilitator of their own education process (Hase & Kenyon, 2000; Kenyon & Hase, 2013). Learning occurs with learner centered learning and as result of personal experiences. Abraham and Komattil (2017) claims that heutagogy is important reform that empower learners to reflect their learning process. They become self-directed and life-long learners. Learners develop their individual abilities, values, and assumptions in the process of flexible, critical, and meaningful learning experiences (Tiwari, 2017). Hase and Kenyon (2007) state that learning experiences and competencies repeated and adapted to unfamiliar and unexpected situations. 21st century learning and teaching process offers connectivity and new learning spaces shifting technology to alternative encouraging systems.

Heutagogy, includes learner's individual effort and scaffold. This effort is supported with ubiquitous environments. Individuals who want to improve their professional development, technology use and ability prefer ubiquitous environments and its learning advantages.

In this chapter an overview of ubiquitous learning and heutagogy are presented. First, the definition and background and its characteristics of ubiquitous learning are explained than the heutagogy, it is principles, and educational use are explained. Then the chapter continuous with recommendation and solutions solution part, that gives information about their combination over educational perspective. Finally, the conclusion part is explained for the future researchers. This review study aims to explain the educational structure foregrounding the basis of U-learning and heutagogical design along with literature. The questions "How can be combine U-learning and Heutagogy?" and "What are the possible the suggestions of heutagogical U-learning?" will be discussed.

BACKGROUND

The two main situations became popular on higher education between the years 1990s and mid-2000s. These situations are implementation of learning management systems (e.g. Canvas, Moodle, Blackboard) and pilot projects having large- scale funding. These situations improve the digitalization at universities (Heidkamp & Kergel, 2018). There was an innovation increase in higher education after the discussions of possibilities and limitations of digitally supported learning environments.

Due to technological innovations and learning management systems a critical component, internet, convert to mobile forms. With the help of ubiquity, nature of mobile learning in education allows human beings to personalize their learning process obtaining knowledge for maintaining their daily life, for solving real world problems, for collaborating with other people and for creating new connectomes with the help of its ubiquity component. Ubiquitous systems track learner behaviors and offer students to personalize their curriculums.

Before the definition of Ubiquitous learning (U-learning), it would be better to explain mobile learning. Mobile learning is a part of e-learning and supported by educational technologies. Mobile learning enables an educational structure including learning activities, learning process, outcomes, strategies, curriculum, collaboration and etc. Mobile learning is an individual or a dominant technology that delivers educational content to learners in an accessible way (Traxler, 2005; 2009). Mobile learning and e-learning includes ubiquity and also mobility. If mobility increases and embeddedness decreases than the environment is transformed to "mobile learning". If mobility and embeddedness increases, the learning environment is transformed to "ubiquitous" form. (Lyytinen & Yoo, 2002; Ogata & Yano, 2004; Ogata et al, 2009).

The Definition and Characteristics of Ubiquitous Learning

Ubiquitous term defined as "seem to be everywhere" and "has the ability to be everywhere" and "everywhere at the same time" (Collins Dictionary, 2019). According to Shih, Chu, Hwang & Kinshuk (2011) ubiquitous means that being available anywhere and anytime. U-learning means accessing the learning environment and contents anytime or anywhere for to support students' learning during to educational process with the aid of mobile tools and wireless internet. For Hwang, Tsai & Yang (2008), U-learning is anywhere and anytime learning, where the learning environment allows students to access content at any location and any time, no matter whether wireless communications or mobile devices are employed or not. These definitions show that U-learning includes mobile learning and e-learning philosophies beyond the ability to learn rich content everywhere and every time (Burbules, 2009; Daily- Hebert and Dennis, 2015). While specifying the characteristic of u-learning, researchers take the advantage of mobile learning too. The historical presentation of the u- learning characteristics is in the following part.

Ubiquitous Learning Characteristics

Curtis, Luchini, Bobrowsky, Quintana and Soloway (2002) claim that permanency, accessibility and immediacy are the three key of U-learning. At that moment Chen, Kao, Sheu and Chiang (2002) were identifying mobile learning characteristics. These two categorization merged and adapted to u-learning characteristics. At literature, this adaptation is very popular. This adaptation concerns six characteristics: permanency, accessibility, immediacy, interactivity of learning process, integration of instructional content and situating of instructional activities. On the other hand, Cheng, Sun, Kansen, Hosokawa, Huang and He (2006) works on the four characteristics of U-learning. These characteristics are termed as pervasive, cooperative, context-aware and seamless. Also Chiu, Kuo, Huang &Chen (2008) emphasis context-awareness, learning community, self-regulated learning as a characteristic of U-learning. As a result, context-awareness is the most adopted characteristics into U-learning.

Recently, Wang, Lui & Hwang (2017) make a comparison between the adapted the factors from Chin & Chen (2013), Hwang et al. (2008) and Lui & Hwang (2010) investigations. According to the statements on U-learning common characteristics four similarities permanency, accessibility, immediacy and interactivity is important. Additionally, context-awareness is an important characteristic. Yahya, Ahmad and Jalil (2010) announced that permanency, accessibility, immediacy, interactivity, and context-awareness are the five characteristics of U-learning. This specification is the most adopted and explained one at literature. In this chapter, these specifications are explained in detail to comprehend the intersection of heutagogy and ubiquitous learning at solutions and recommendation part.

- **Permanency**: Learners perform and manage their learning process benefit and purpose. Learning process backs up every day with all the components unless learners decide to remove the learned information.
- **Accessibility**: Learners want to access the data, text, documents, voices and videos anywhere or any time. The learning process is managed by learners and is formed on their needs.
- **Immediacy**: Learners compose and organize the information immediately. Learner gain knowledge, solve problems, find a creative way to answer the questions. The learning is embedded into life and transform to experiences.

- **Interactivity**: Learners can interact with materials, teachers, mentors, peers and collaborative systems. In other words, search and access the right knowledge, information or data is easier and teachers, mentors and peers are more reachable with the help of internet.
- **Context-Awareness**: Abowd & Dey (1999) clarify the synonyms of context-awareness are "adaptive, reactive, responsive, situated, context-sensitive and environment directed". They use this term to emphasize context. According to them, context-awareness is a system depending on user's task using context to provide relevant information. In other words, this environment provides learners' adaptation into real situation get adequate information.

These characteristics are help researchers to comprehend learning process. Tahir, Haron & Singh (2018) emphasis that these characteristics must be major characteristic of ubiquitous learning in the context of learner behavior and instructional activities. These characteristics are studied both empirical and theoretical context. The Researches and reviews about these characteristics present the whole picture on U-learning. The following part includes the reviews of U-learning.

The Reviews of Ubiquitous Learning

Empirical studies on U-learning have wide coverage at literature. Pimmer, Mateescu & Gröhbiel (2016) analyzed 36 empirical mobile learning and ubiquitous learning articles. They investigated these articles on the categories of instructionism, situated action and contextual scaffolding, constructionist and collaborative learning and hybrids of constructionist and collaborative design. They claim that mixed research on learning is significant and provide compared knowledge for the researchers. The learning occurs at outside of the class is helped learners to personalize their learning.

Another review is about ubiquitous language learning and museums. The review was done during the 2009-2014 for to investigate the socio-cultural context. The sample was composed of 12 article from WOS. These articles evaluated into three categories; system usefulness, activity usefulness and activity playfulness in museum learning. As a result, museum education transformed from m-learning to u-learning. Learners prefer to interact with u-materials that tracked by a system than instead of reading or listening material in traditional museums (Wang et. al, 2017).

Cardenas-Robledo & Pena-Ayala (2018) made a systematic review analysis on U-learning. Their research was aimed to assert conceptual insights, perspectives, approaches, highlights, labor traits, outcome patterns, and field tendencies. The sample was composed of 176 article from different journals between the years 2010-2017. The articles were put into nine categories: Physical settings, learning sceneries, functionality, domain knowledge, learning paradigms, effects, academic level, devices and technology. These categories split into several subcategories and topics. Functionality and effects categories were mostly investigated but Learning sceneries and academic level categories were less investigated ones. It would be said that investigations about education must be in increased.

All these reviews show that u-learning is greatly worked on empirically or theoretically. And also it shows that u-learning is an increasing field at recent years. Learning tending to u-learning be influenced by mobile tools, flexible environments, learner interaction, system accessibility and content diversity. Learners choose accessibility and flexible environments supports. It couldn't be wrong to say that learners want to be individual and manage their learning process. This situation is in a relation with heutagogy. Now the other term heutagogy will be explained at previous part.

The Definition, Background and Principles of Heutagogy

Ackoff and Greenberg (2008) state that "the objective of education is learning not teaching". Teaching transformed to a powerful learning in two ways. One is explaining something with your own aspects, especially gain an understanding. The other is explaining something in a deeper enriched view. It could be said that Heutagogy is encompassed and established on this belief (Blaschke, 2016).

Heutagogy is encouraged by several philosophies, theories and approaches. Human motivation (Maslow, 1943) constructivism (Vygotsky, 1978), transformational learning (Mezirow & Associates, 1990; Mezirow, 1991) are some of them (Blaschke, 2018). On the other hand, humanistic philosophies like student- centered learning (Rogers, 1969) that was adopted from Rogers' client-centred approach1 (Rogers, 1946; 2003) is important for this term. Heutagogy also influenced by phenomenological systems and self-determination (Deci & Ryan, 2002; Ryan & Deci, 2000) theory (Blaschke, 2012; 2016; 2018).

Self-determined learning theory deals with human motivation, psychological and personal development and autonomy concerning to act at healthy and effective ways. It focusses on intrinsic resources like become a well-being person, social and cultural personality development and behavioral self-regulation. In other words, this theory highlights behaviors and social and cultural conditions like self-management and self-monitoring. It suggests that human beings engage or avoid relationships, roles or activities to promote basic needs (Canning, 2010; Canning & Callan, 2010; La Guardia, 2009; Deci and Ryan, 2002; Hase & Kenyon, 2007; Ryan & Deci, 2000; Ryan, Kuhl & Deci, 1997).

Heutagogy in other words self-determined learning was first announced in 2000 by Steward Hase and Chris Kenyon. They were working a postgraduate program for Royal Australian Air Force. The theory and practice of Heutagogy was first developed for working with postgraduate learners. (Hase, 2016). Heutagogy term comes from the Greek verb "Heureskein". It is defined as discover learning methods of students about themselves (Parslow, 2010).

Heutagogical learning occurs at two levels. The first level is competencies. Competency includes knowledge and skills. Learning experiences are effected by motivation, learning environments and dependence. Only learner solves this complex situation. The role of the learner is enhance their competencies to drive their learning process (Hase and Kenyon, 2000; Hase, 2009). The second level is deeper learning. This phase includes learner's curiosity, motivation, confusion and creativeness. The learning experiences increased with enjoyment and excitement (Hase, 2009). Heutagogic learners have the potential of continuing their learning towards the interaction of environment and own life (Leone, 2013). Learners have the capacity to make choices and take decisions than act attitudes. Learners connect knowledge, prior knowledge and previous experiences in terms of meaningfull and active way into their ability and behaviors (Hase & Kenyon 2000; Hase, 2011).

As shown previous paragraphs, heutagogy is inspired from many approaches, theory, concept or insights. This complete structure has some properties. The common principles are explained into four main area. These are (a) human agency (learner-centeredness), (b) capability, (c) self-reflection and metacognition (Double-loop learning) and (d) Non-linear teaching and learning (Blashke, 2013; Hase & Kenyon, 2000). Now, these principles are explained in detail.

Principles of Heutagogy

Human agency (learner-centeredness): The heutagogical learning process includes competency and capability (Hase, 2009). Competencies is an action of problem solving. If a learner has a competency this means that, he or she has the ability on acquiring knowledge skills (Blashke, 2012; Gardner, Hase, Gardner, Dunn, Carryer, 2008). Human agency term is related with this situation. It means that learners driver their learning and have the ability of decision making (Blaschke, 2016). Learners take the responsibilities of their learning process. They select what they want to learn and which way they want to use. (Deci and Ryan, 2002). This shows that learners are in the center of learning process including self-motivation, responsibility, and autonomy. In other words, human agency affected by student-centered learning (learner-centered learning), system thinking techniques, learner-generated contexts and project based learning (Booth, Blaschke & Hase, 2017).

Capability: In learning process, learners are responsible for their learning. At that moment, the key point is "capability". Capability is a definitive attribute dealing with know how to learn. (Hase and Kenyon, 2007). In other words, capability is the capacity of the learners' problem solving and confidence. Learners gain capacity using their competencies in uncertain situations (Stumberg & Farmer, 2009). Hase and Davis (1999) postulate that competency measures previous performance whereas capability focuses on the unknown future, on change and unfamiliar circumstances. As a result, capability means one's own competencies concerning familiar and unfamiliar situations, values and communication alternatives.

Capability concerns the situations about post-truth competency movements. It is affected by changing contexts, educational standards, sense of learning and teaching and transformation of student tasks. In heutagogy, learner sets the learning course, design and develop the map of learning from curriculum to assessment (Hase, 2009). Gardner at all (2008) claims that capable people work with others to achieve outcomes and have the abilities of independent action, competency and high-level self-efficacy for metacognitive and personal attributes. In other words, capable human beings have the specialties like self-efficacy, communication and cooperative skills, creativity and positive values and reflects them to their learning process (Blashke, 2012; Kenyon & Hase, 2010).

Self-reflection and metacognition (Double-loop learning): Double-loop learning means that test someone's learning process in terms of his/her values and assumptions, problem solving ability, result action and outcome (Hase, 2009). Hence, it involves self-reflection on learning process (learner's knowledge, perceptions, actions, outcomes, problem, belief, solutions.. etc) (Blashke, 2012; 2013; Hase and Kenyon, 2000). Double-loop learning involves individual learning. With the aid of Web 2.0 environment reflective tools support learners to connect the knowledge and experiences to occur the learning. Learners make individual or group projects using multiple resources to answer, reflect or discuss the problems. Learners use arguments to provide suggestions, arguments or critics. At that moment, teachers present several different kind of resources, support individual or group works and leads learners.

Non-linear teaching and learning: Hetutagogy is focus on learners' life-long learning skills and proactive learning process. Learners take the responsibility of their learning situations. Their personal experiences become major factor on their learning process (Hase and Kenyon, 2007; Narayan and Herrington, 2014). In other words, heutagogical learning occurs because of learners' life experiences, practices, beliefs and reflections. Blashke (2012) claims that learners conclude what to learn and how to learn. Non-linear design gives learner the flexibility to define their learning paths independence of knowledge, time, place, person or technology. They discover the world except form a structured conceptual construct.

This principle is directly related with ubiquitous learning. Individuals especially adult learners like teacher and teacher candidates manage their professional development process. It can be said that these four principles transform learning from being objective, common and gathered to subjective, singular and indigenous. Blashke (2016) claims that heutagogical learning is take place any time on individuals learning life from early childhood to old age. But there is not any the educational researches with early childhood, primary students and secondary students yet. All the researches about heutagogy are done with higher education students, professionals and post-graduate students. The following part is give examples of these researches.

Heutagogy in Education

Heutagogy is first occurred as an adult learning approach. It can use on teacher education for implementing the different perspective on learning and teaching process. (Hase and Kenyon, 2007; Narayan and Herrington, 2014). Heutagogical thinking includes some key points to explain the learning process. These are in the following: (Hase & Kenyon, 2007).

- A living curriculum is significant. Because aims, inputs, outputs and learning processes are formed for learner's needs. As a result, the curriculum transformed a flexible, modifiable and renewable structure. Learners collaboratively co-create the curriculum for the skills they needed. This learner directed situation prepare learners to U-learning (Herie, 2013).
- Learners are the key component for heutagogical curriculum. Learners are sophisticated. They drive their learning activities, process, tasks, and opportunities and find solutions on their learning process problems. They are responsible for their learning.
- Teachers are bridges in the learning process. They guide learners. They are leaders, mentors, coaches or a person who support the learners' motivation. They are not responsible for learners performing; they are responsible for supporting and encouraging.
- Knowledge and skill acquisition uses educational methods and is different from learning. Knowledge construction is non-linear. Learners reflects real world solutions with the aid of knowledge and skill acquisition.
- Learners' experiences gain by action learning methods and investigated by action research methods. Their view, insights, opinions, practices are important to picturize the learning experiences.

In a heutagogical learning design, students are self-determined learners. Teachers empower students learning and provide various learning resources. The content is meaningful and relevant to learners' needs. Also supports independent and collaborative learning. Furthermore, technology use to facilitate exploration, collaboration and self-development. A heutagogical learner is explorer, creator, sharer, collaborator, connecter, reflector human being. A heutagogical teacher is learning facilitator, scaffolder, self-management supporter. Blashke (2012) claims that teachers have the role of supporting learners to get their ownership of their learning path and process.

At literature, there are few empirical studies about heutagogoy (Blashke, 2014; Cochrane and Narayan, 2013). Hase (2016) claims that the researches about heutagogy are related with lifelong learning; higher education; e-learning, digital technologies and distance education; school education; teaching practices;

and workplace and professional education. Clinical learning like nursing has practice based- educational components. Heutagogical approach in this area provides different point of view between practice and pre-registration frameworks (Bhoyrub, Hurley, Neilson, Ramsay and Smith, 2010). Herie (2013) emphasis that developing capabilities in a learner-directed, non-linear and process-oriented way is explain today's digital generation. Heutagogy is highlight digital literacy and global citizenship. Eachempati, Kumar KS, K. Komattil and Ismail (2017) explain a case study including Facebook use of dental students grounded on heutagogy principles. The shift of pedagogy to andragogy and heutagogy is presented. While learner maturity and autonomy is increasing on heutagogical learning, Instructional control is decreasing. In the study final year dental students divided into four group. There are 18-19 students in each group. The Facebook groups were designed as closed group; only members saw the contents and posted comments and two facilitators monitored the group discussions. On the other hand, a common discussion room created for all 74 students. The students interacted with each other. The students use these groups for five weeks. Their comments were analyzed for qualitative analysis methods, a thematic analysis process carried out. The themes were (a) independent learning and autonomy, (b) flexibility in learning, capability, teamwork and respect for others, (c) effective discussions and instant feedback, (d) Facebook as a tool for learning and (e) miscellaneous. The group was get an innovative and a novel experience. They find that learner autonomy has an important role for successfully implementing heutagogical approaches. The role of the teacher is being a navigator and doing limited movements, deploy scaffolding to accomplish the learner's capabilities. Narayan, Herrington and Cochrane (2019) designed a course for journalism students on heutagogical approach using mobile and social media tools. This was a design based research and takes over two years. Data were collected two times during 12 weeks over two years. Students and teachers collaborate with each other to set design principles with regard to literature. The draft design implemented for one year and evaluated with different students for two years. As a result, mobile devices and social media environments are used for capability to guide practitioners and designing and facilitating student-determined learning.

The researches common points are heutagogical studies must be long term and carefully designed. Learner- centeredness is surrounded by today's social, digital and technological tools that embedded into learning environments. These studies aim to develop learner's capability, autonomy and self-determined learning.

SOLUTIONS AND RECOMMENDATIONS

Learning occurs everywhere with the aid of digital platforms and technology. Educational contents delivered to learners with internet use. Learners has the flexibility and ubiquity for accessing the digital contents Learners want to be individual. Individualism includes self-development, self-efficacy, self-management, self-monitoring, self-motivation, self-reflection and self-determination. Individual learners reflect own knowledge on their life, and gain experiences to make them permanent. At that moment heutagogy approach come to help all the period of our lives. At literature, the heutagogy be examined with lifelong learning, web 2.0 technologies and mobile learning, open learning etc. But there isn't any researches that combines ubiquitous learning and heutagogy together.

According to this review, ubiquitous learning and heutagogy intersect together on the basis of their principles and specifications. The ubiquitous learning environments support learners to manage their learning process, gain knowledge, solve problems, access all forms of information, interact with learning components and self- adaptation. Heutagogy supports learners' learner-centeredness, capability, self-reflection and flexibility.

Heutagogical U-learning can be defined as learners drive their own attention on accessible information and reflect experiences to the learning process interacting with flexible environments. The internalized information is independent from time and place and develops learner self-determination.

- The possible suggestions on effective design for this proposal can be like that:
- An open and flexible environment is appropriate for design heutagogical U-learning programs.
- Learning environment provides collaboration, group work and individualism.
- Learning environment includes all type of information that provides interaction with learners.
- Learners are self-motivated and self-reflected.
- Learners have the capacity and competency to gain deeper learning adapt it into their life.

CONCLUSION

Heutagogy conducts a holistic framework for formal and informal learning to organize self-learning and teaching into ubiquitous pattern (Blashke & Hase, 2016). Therefore, this transition can be applied to mobile and flexible learning environments especially U-learning environments. Chin, Lee, Chen (2018) investigate an interactive U-learning system (IULS) in cultural heritage course with 96 university student. They integrate context-aware technologies to provide personalized learning to improve students teaching practices. This system is facilitating students' knowledge, improve motivation, and provide authentic learning experiences. The result shows that there is a significant difference between control and experimental groups' posttest scores of learning performance. Second result is gender is not a significant factor both experimental and control group on the basis of learning performance. This means that IULS group learning performance is higher than control group but gender is not affect this situation. The other result shows that there is not a significant effect between cognitive-styles and learning performance on the group factor. But motivation on instructional materials survey shows that, students had high motivation on using IULS, positive feelings on using system.

This review shows that digital technologies, learner motivation and performance is important for using systems. Digital technologies support heutagogical learning on the issue of gaining skills of learning and teaching. Heutagogy emphasis connectivity, creativity and being digital citizen with the answers of what and how to learn. It highlights global citizenship and collaboration with web environments (Blaschke, 2013).

Canter (2012) suggests a structure e-heutagogy for lifelong e-learning. A small experiment with students was designed. First, the participants learning styles determined. Than all of them choose a subject, they interested in, then the subjects were presented to entire group and was argued in the class. As a result, there was a relation defined between the subject choice and students learning styles. The self-determined theory, educational software, learning styles an e-learning being together to adopt an e-heutagogical approach. It can be determined that E-heutagogy has three-column: self-determination theory, e-learning and complex e-learning adaptive systems.

Ubiquitous Learning and Heutagogy in Teacher Education

Narayan & Herrington (2014) design a mobile heutagógy framework. The relationship between heutagogy, mobile learning and pedagogy 2.0 is discussed. They suggested a model including the isteraction of these structures. On the middle of the model, learning and teaching (intersection of heutagogy, mobile learning and pegogy 2.0) is take part in. The other structures are participation (intersection of heutagogy and pedagogy 2.0), personalization (intersection of heutagogy and mobile learning) and productivity (intersection of mobile learning and pedagogy 2.0). They offered that this model has the potential to transform pedagogy practices into ubiquitous technologies for the education of 21st century learning system.

Another e-learning example is describe heutagogy-based MOOCs (Massive Online Open Courses). For Agonacs & Matos (2017) MOOCs are metacognitive work and critical reflection on cognitive and behavioral change for successful learning in an open, barely structured and self-organized environment. In that project, the two MOOCs: xMOOCs and cMOOCs were combined for a new structure. The combination of these two model provides learners to be more motivational, more effective and more self-organizer. The heutagogical based MOOC model includes multimedia use, communication with each other, collaboration, high amount of reflection and autonomy. Based on these classifications, this model emphasis critical reflection (double and triple loop learning) for gaining knowledge and capability and self-determined learning for developing skill and competency. They suggest an empirical study to examine this model for future researches. This chapter offers heutagogical U-learning and like heutagogy-based MOOCs, it could be better to examine it with empirical researches.

Marcut & Chişiu (2018) designed a mixed design research with 59 teacher candidates (post-graduate students who wants to be teacher) to explore their heutagogy and mobile devices using ability. There was a course module includes psychology- pedagogoy disiplines focuses on self-determined learning model. The research results were shown that heutagogic framework support students motivation, material design and Internet and mobile device use. They claim that a heutagogy is an appropriate framework to prepare teachers to be a future creative, collobrative, reflective teachers.

This given literature is concerning the examples to connect heutagogy and ubiquitous learning. The characteristics of both heutagogy and ubiquitous learning take strength from each other. Both these structures emphasize individualism and accessibility. In my opinion heutagogical learning theoretical background and practices could be engage with ubiquitous learning empirical practices using technological tools and systems. The heutagogical ubiquitous learning systems will be frequently announce in the future, but today they are upgrading, ongoing and continuous structures.

REFERENCES

Abowd, G. D., & Dey, A. K. (1999, September). Towards a better understanding of context and context-awareness. In *International symposium on handheld and ubiquitous computing* (pp. 304-307). Springer. Retrieved from https://link.springer.com/chapter/10.1007/3-540-48157-5_29

Abraham, R. R., & Komattil, R. (2017). Heutagogic approach to developing capable learners. *Medical Teacher, 39*(3), 295–299. doi:10.1080/0142159X.2017.1270433 PMID:28019131

Ackoff, R. L., & Greenberg, D. (2008). *Turning Learning Right Side Up: Putting Education Back on Track*. Pearson Education, Wharton School Publishing.

Agonacs, N., & Matos, J. F. (2017). *Towards a Heutagogy-Based MOOC Design Framework*. In Work in Progress Papers of the Experience and Research Tracks and Position Papers of the Policy Track, EMOOCs Proceedings, University of Lisbon (pp. 22–26). Lisbon, Portugal: Mayıs.

Agonacs, N., & Matos, J. F. (2019). Heutagogy and self-determined learning: a review of the published literature on the application and implementation of the theory. *Open Learning: The Journal of Open, Distance and e-Learning*, 1-19.

Bhoyrub, J., Hurley, J., Neilson, G. R., Ramsay, M., & Smith, M. (2010). Heutagogy: An alternative practice based learning approach. *Nurse Education in Practice, 10*(6), 322–326. doi:10.1016/j.nepr.2010.05.001 PMID:20554249

Blaschke, L. M. (2012). Heutagogy and lifelong learning: A review of heutagogical practice and self-determined learning. *The International Review of Research in Open and Distributed Learning, 13*(1), 56–71. doi:10.19173/irrodl.v13i1.1076

Blaschke, L. M. (2013). Self-determined Learning (Heutagogy) and Digital Media Creating integrated Educational Environments for Developing Lifelong Learning Skills. In S. Hase & C. Kenyon (Eds.), *Self-determined learning: Heutagogy in action* (pp. 55–67). London, UK: Bloomsbury Academic.

Blaschke, L. M. (2014). Moving students forward in the PAH continuum: Maximizing the power of the social web. In L. M. Blaschke, C. Kenyon, & S. Hase (Eds.), Experiences in self-determined learning (pp.56-67). Amazon.com Publishing.

Blaschke, L. M. (2016). Heutagogy and lifelong learning: A review of heutagogical practice and self-determined learning. *The International Review of Research in Open and Distributed Learning, 13*(1), 56–71. doi:10.19173/irrodl.v13i1.1076

Blaschke, L. M. (2018). Self-determined Learning (Heutagogy) and Digital Media Creating integrated Educational Environments for Developing Lifelong Learning Skills. In D. Kergel, B. Heidkamp, P. Kjaersdam Telleus, T. Rachwal, & S. Nowakowski (Eds.), *The digital turn in Higher education: International Perspectives on Learning and Teaching in a Changing World* (pp. 129–137). Wiesbaden, Germany: Springer. doi:10.1007/978-3-658-19925-8_10

Blaschke, L. M., & Hase, S. (2016). Heutagogy: A holistic framework for creating 21st century self-determined learners. In *The future of ubiquitous learning: Learning designs for emerging pedagogies* (pp. 25–40). Heidelberg, Germany: Springer-Vergel. doi:10.1007/978-3-662-47724-3_2

Booth, M., Blaschke, L. M., & Hase, S. (2017). Practicing the Practice: The Heutagogy Community of Practice. In J. McDonald & A. Cater-Steel (Eds.), Implementing Communities of Practice in Higher Education (pp. 549-572). Springer.

Burbules, N. C. (2009). Meanings of ubiquitous learning. In B. Cope & M. Kalantzis (Eds.), *Ubiquitous learning* (pp. 15–20). Champaign, IL: University of Illinois Press.

Camilleri, M. A., & Camilleri, A. C. (2017). Digital Learning Resources and Ubiquitous Technologies in Education. *Technology. Knowledge and Learning*, 22(1), 65–82. doi:10.100710758-016-9287-7

Canning, N. (2010). Playing with heutagogy: Exploring strategies to empower mature learners in higher education. *Journal of Further and Higher Education*, 34(1), 59–71. doi:10.1080/03098770903477102

Canning, N., & Callan, S. (2010). Heutagogy: Spirals of reflection to empower learners in higher education. *Reflective Practice*, 11(1), 71–82. doi:10.1080/14623940903500069

Canter, M. (2012). E-heutagogy for lifelong e-learning. *Proceedings of INSODE Procedia Technology*, 1, 129-131. 10.1016/j.protcy.2012.02.025

Cardenas-Robledo, L. A., & Pena-Ayala, A. (2018). Ubiquitous learning: A systematic review. *Telematics and Informatics*, 35(5), 1097–1132. doi:10.1016/j.tele.2018.01.009

Chen, M., Chiang, F. K., Jiang, N., & Yu, Q. (2017). A context-adaptive teacher training model in a ubiquitous learning environment. *Interactive Learning Environments*, 25(1), 113–126. doi:10.1080/10494820.2016.1143845

Chen, Y. S., Kao, T. C., Sheu, J. P., & Chiang, C. Y. (2002). A Mobile Scaffolding-Aid-Based Bird-Watching Learning System. *Proceedings of IEEE International Workshop on Wireless and Mobile Technologies in Education*, 15-22. 10.1109/WMTE.2002.1039216

Cheng, Z., Han, Q., Sun, S., Kansen, M., Hosokawa, T., Huang, T., & He, A. (2006, April). A proposal on a learner's context-aware personalized education support method based on principles of behavior science. *20th International Conference on Advanced Information Networking and Applications (AINA'06)*, 1, 1-5. 10.1109/AINA.2006.50

Chin, K. Y., & Chen, Y. L. (2013). A mobile learning support system for ubiquitous learning environments. *Procedia: Social and Behavioral Sciences*, 73, 14–21. doi:10.1016/j.sbspro.2013.02.013

Chin, K. Y., Lee, K. F., & Chen, Y. L. (2018). Using an interactive ubiquitous learning system to enhance authentic learning experiences in a cultural heritage course. *Interactive Learning Environments*, 26(4), 444–459. doi:10.1080/10494820.2017.1341939

Chiu, P. S., Kuo, Y., Huang, Y., & Chen, T. (2008). A Meaningful Learning based u-Learning Evaluation Model. *Eighth IEEE International Conference on Advanced Learning Technologies*, 77-81. 10.1109/ICALT.2008.100

Cochrane, T., & Narayan, V. (2013). Redesigning professional development: Reconceptualising teaching using social learning technologies. *Research in Learning Technology*, *21*, 1–19. doi:10.3402/rlt.v21i0.19226

Collins Dictionary. (2019). *Definition of ubiquitous*. Retrieved from https://www.collinsdictionary.com/dictionary/english/ubiquitous

Curtis, M., Luchini, K., Bobrowsky, W., Quintana, C., & Soloway, E. (2002). Handheld Use in K-12: A Descriptive Account. *Proceedings of IEEE International Workshop on Wireless and Mobile Technologies in Education (WMTE'02)*, 23-30. 10.1109/WMTE.2002.1039217

Dailey-Hebert, A., & Dennis, K. S. (2015). Introduction: New Opportunities for Development? In A. Dailey-Hebert & D. Kergel (Eds.), *Transformative Perspectives and Processes in Higher Education* (pp. 1–12). Cham: Springer. doi:10.1007/978-3-319-09247-8_1

Deci, E. L., & Ryan, R. M. (2002). *The handbook of self-determination research*. Rochester, NY: The University of Rochester Press.

Eachempati, P., Ks, K. K., Komattil, R., & Ismail, A. R. H. (2017). Heutagogy through Facebook for the Millennial learners. *MedEdPublish*, *6*(4), 25. doi:10.15694/mep.2017.000194

Gardner, A., Hase, S., Gardner, G., Dunn, S. V., & Carryer, J. (2008). From competence to capability: A study of nurse practitioners in clinical practice. *Journal of Clinical Nursing*, *17*(2), 250–258. PMID:17419787

Hase, S. (2009). Heutagogy and e-learning in the workplace: Some challenges and opportunities. *Impact: Journal of Applied Research in Workplace E-learning*, *1*(1), 43–52.

Hase, S. (2011). Learner defined curriculum: heutagogy and action learning in vocational training. *Southern Institute of Technology Journal of Applied Research*. Retrieved from https://www.sit.ac.nz/Portals/0/upload/documents/sitjar/SITJAR%20AR%20edition%20A.pdf 25.04.2019

Hase, S. (2016). Self-determined learning (heutagogy) - Where have we come since 2000? *Southern Institute of Technology Journal of Applied Research (SITJAR)*. Retrieved from https://www.sit.ac.nz/Portals/0/upload/documents/sitjar/Heutagogy - One.pdf

Hase, S., & Davis, L. (1999). Developing capable employees: The work activity briefing. *Journal of Workplace Learning*, *11*(8), 298–303. doi:10.1108/13665629910300432

Hase, S., & Kenyon, C. (2000). *From andragogy to heutagogy*. Retrieved from: http://pandora.nla.gov.au/nph-wb/20010220130000/http://ultibase.rmit.edu.au/Articles/dec00/hase2.htm 12.02.2019

Hase, S., & Kenyon, C. (2007). Heutagogy: A child of complexity theory. *Complicity: An International Journal of Complexity and Education, 4*(1), 111–119. doi:10.29173/cmplct8766

Hase, S., & Kenyon, C. (2013). The Nature of Learning. In S. Hase & C. Kenyon (Eds.), Self-Determined Learning: Heutagogy in Action (pp. 19-35). London, UK: Bloomsbury Publishing.

Heidkamp, B., & Kergel, D. (2018). From e-learning to eBlogna in an Augmented Reality The past and Future of E-Learning in German Higher Education. In D. Kergel, B. Heidkamp, P. Kjaersdam Telleus, T. Rachwal, & Nowakowski (Eds.), The digital turn in Higher education: International Perspectives on Learning and Teaching in a Changing World (pp. 37-45). Wiesbaden, Germany: Springer.

Herie, M. (2013). Andragogy 2.0? Teaching and Learning in the Global Classroom: Heutagogy and Paragogy. *Global Citizen Digest, 2*(2), 8–14.

Hwang, G. J., Tsai, C. C., & Yang, S. J. H. (2008). Criteria, strategies and research issues of context-aware ubiquitous learning. *Journal of Educational Technology & Society, 11*(2), 81–91.

ISTE. (2017). *ISTE Standards for Educators*. Retrieved form https://www.iste.org/standards/for-educators

Kenyon, C., & Hase, S. (2010). Andragogy and heutagogy in postgraduate work. In T. Kerry (Ed.), *Meeting the challenges of change in postgraduate education* (pp. 165–187). London: Continuum Press.

Kenyon, C., & Hase, S. (2013). Heutagogy Fundamentals. In S. Hase & C. Kenyon (Eds.), Self-Determined Learning: Heutagogy in Action (pp. 7-17). London, UK: Bloomsbury Publishing.

LaGuardia, J. G. (2009). Developing Who I Am: A Self-Determination Theory Approach to the Establishment of Healthy Identities. *Educational Psychologist, 44*(2), 90–104. doi:10.1080/00461520902832350

Leone, S. (2013). Characterisation of a personal learning environment as a lifelong learning tool. New York: Springer Science+ Business Media. doi:10.1007/978-1-4614-6274-3

Liu, G., & Hwang, G. (2010). A key step to understanding paradigm shifts in e-learning. *British Journal of Educational Technology, 41*(2), E1–E9. doi:10.1111/j.1467-8535.2009.00976.x

Lyytinen, K., & Yoo, Y. (2002). Issues and challenges in ubiquitous computing. *Communications of the ACM, 45*(12), 63–65.

Maslow, A. H. (1943). A Theory of Human Motivation. *Psychological Review, 50*(4), 370–396. doi:10.1037/h0054346

Mezirow, J., & ... (1990). *Fostering critical reflection in adulthood: A guide to transformative and emancipatory learning*. San Francisco, CA: Jossey-Bass Publishers.

Mezirow, J. (1991). *Transformative Dimensions of Adult Learning*. San Francisco, CA: Jossey-Bass Publishers.

Narayan, V., & Herrington, J. (2014) Towards a theoretical mobile heutagogy framework. In ASCILITE 2014: Rhetoric and Reality, Dunedin, New Zealand.

Narayan, V., Herrington, J., & Cochrane, T. (2019). Design principles for heutagogical learning: Implementing student-determined learning with mobile and social media tools. *Australasian Journal of Educational Technology*, *35*(3), 86–101.

Ogata, H., Matsuka, Y., El-Bishouty, M. M., & Yano, Y. (2009). LORAMS: Linking physical objects and videos for capturing and sharing learning experiences towards ubiquitous learning. *International Journal of Mobile Learning and Organisation*, *3*(4), 337–350. doi:10.1504/IJMLO.2009.027452

Ogata, H., & Yano, Y. (2004). Context-aware support for computer-supported ubiquitous learning. *Proceedings of the 2nd IEEE International Workshop on Wireless and Mobile Technologies in Education*, 27-34.

Parslow, G. R. (2010). Multimedia in Biochemistry and Molecular Biology Education Commentary: Heutagogy, the practice of self-learning. *Biochemistry and Molecular Biology Education*, *38*(2), 121–121. doi:10.1002/bmb.20394 PMID:21567809

Pimmer, C., Mateescu, M., & Gröhbiel, U. (2016). Mobile and ubiquitous learning in higher education settings. A systematic review of empirical studies. Computers in human. *Behaviour*, *63*, 490–501.

Rogers, C. R. (1946). Significant aspects of client-centered therapy. *The American Psychologist*, *1*(10), 415–422. doi:10.1037/h0060866 PMID:20280375

Rogers, C. R. (1969). *Freedom to Learn*. Columbus, OH: Merill.

Rogers, C. R. (2003). *Client-Centered Therapy*. Constable & Robinson Ltd.

Ryan, R. M., & Deci, E. L. (2000). Self-determination theory and the facilitation of intrinsic motivation, social development, and well-being. *The American Psychologist*, *55*(1), 68–78. doi:10.1037/0003-066X.55.1.68 PMID:11392867

Ryan, R. M., Kuhl, J., & Deci, E. L. (1997). Nature and autonomy: An organizational view of social and neurobiological aspects of self-regulation in behavior and development. *Development and Psychopathology*, *9*(4), 701–728. doi:10.1017/S0954579497001405 PMID:9449002

Shih, J.-L., Chu, H., Hwang, G.-J., & Kinshuk. (2011). An investigation of attitudes of students and teachers about participating in a context-aware ubiquitous learning activity. *British Journal of Educational Technology*, *42*(3), 373–394. doi:10.1111/j.1467-8535.2009.01020.x

Sturmberg, J. P., & Farmer, L. (2009). Educating capable doctors-a portfolio approach. Linking learning and assessment. *Medical Teacher*, *31*(3), 85–89. doi:10.1080/01421590802512912 PMID:19089726

Tahir, Z. M., Haron, H., & Singh, J. K. G. (2018). Evoluton of Learning Environmnt: A review of Ubiquitous Learning Paradigm Characteristics. *Indonesian Journal of Electirical Engineering and Computer Science*, *11*(1), 175–181. doi:10.11591/ijeecs.v11.i1.pp175-181

Tiwari, D. (2017). Paradigm Shifts in the Pedagogical Approaches. *Business Education and Ethics: Concepts, Methodologies, Tools, and Applications: Concepts, Methodologies, Tools, and Applications*, 343.

Traxler, J. (2005). Defining mobile learning. *IADIS International Conference Mobile Learning Conference*, 261-266.

Traxler, J. (2009). Current state of mobile learning. In M. Ally (Ed.), *Mobile learning: Transforming the delivery of education and training* (pp. 9–24). Edmonton: AU Press, Athabasca University.

Vygotsky, L. S. (1978). *Mind in society: The development of higher psychological processes.* Cambridge, MA: Harvard University Press.

Wang, H. Y., Lui, G. Z., & Hwang, G. J. (2017). Integrating socio-cultural contexts and location-based systems for ubiquitous language learning in museums: A state of the art review of 2009–2014. *British Journal of Educational Technology, 48*(2), 653–671. doi:10.1111/bjet.12424

Yahya, S., Ahmad, E. A., & Jalil, K. A. (2010). The definition and characteristics of ubiquitous learning: A discussion. *International Journal of Education and Development Using Information and Communication Technology, 1*(6), 117–127.

KEY TERMS AND DEFINITIONS

Context-Awareness: A system includes tasks for learners to get solutions on real life problems.
Heutagogy: An approach that provides learners self-motivation and capability.
Mobility: A specialty that provides human beings flexibility, accessibility.
Self-Determined Learning: A theory that explains that learners have the capacity to make choices and act.
Teacher Education Standards: A guide that give suggestions to be a successful educator.
Technology: An environment that help educators and learners.
Ubiquitous Learning: A combination of m-learning and e-learning.

ENDNOTE

[1] The client-centered theory is first announced in 1951 into education (Hase & Kenyon, 2013).

Chapter 16
Transition From E-Learning to U-Learning:
Basic Characteristics, Media, and Researches

Alaattin Parlakkılıç
Ufuk University, Turkey

ABSTRACT

E-learning systems have increased the prevalence of information and computer technologies in education. U-learning is a modern teaching system based on the use of computer technologies (ubiquitous computing technology) everywhere in the environment of existing wired, wireless, mobile, and sensor systems. The interaction between information, object/device, and user/learner/student is formed at any time, anywhere, and form in the communication environment called u-environment. In u-learning, the presence of information in objects (embeded) and mobility is the highest. Training services are among mobile systems and sensors that can move independently in the environment. The status of the learners is followed due to the characteristics of the server systems and objects. Researches on u-learning are ongoing. Especially u-learning system theory and application methods are being investigated. Most of the researches are about u-learning applications rather than u-learning framework. This chapter focuses on basic features, media, and research in the transition from e-learning to u-learning.

DOI: 10.4018/978-1-5225-9779-7.ch016

INTRODUCTION

With the increasing use of computer technologies in all areas of society, lifelong learning and universal education became indispensable needs of societies. Nowadays, the functions of devices and computers that use mobile technologies continue to increase. Individuals in need of learning are trying to meet their learning needs at any time, anywhere and in accordance with their own learning situations by using the means of communication technologies. Learning activities can be carried out with wireless, mobile and sensor systems that are available everywhere using Ubiquitous Learning (U-learning), which is accepted as an advance of e-learning and spreading rapidly (Yumei, 2010).

OVERVIEW OF U-LEARNING

Many e-learning systems have been developed from the past to the present and the studies are still continuing. Most of these systems work on a client-server architecture structure or on a central server logic. In this environment, the learner is dependent on the system and the teacher and often uses the specific resources provided to him or her (Sung, 2009).

E-learning can be defined as the distribution and use of information in the network environment in education and training. The system in this structure is sometimes called distributed learning, online learning, virtual learning, and web based learning. In fact, these terms do not adequately describe the e-learning system. E-learning covers all of these and is conducted online, offline, synchronously and asynchronously with networked wired devices and systems (Naido, 2006). As an extension of e-learning, m-learning is used today, but m-learning is considered a new level of development as a subset of e-learning. M-learning is a wireless and internet-based e-learning system and requires a permanent commitment to the physically existing network. The advantages of m-learning over e-learning are elasticity, cost, ease of use and use in time-dependent applications. The devices used in the m-learning system are PDA, mobile phones, laptop, notebook and tablet computer devices (Sung, 2009).

The idea behind the u-learning covers all kinds of electronic systems, space and time. Learning is considered as part of the activity being performed and includes feeling, touching and accessing all possible communication beyond text-based instruction and auditory-processed courses. U-learning can be defined as the realization of learning through uninterrupted access to information and learning resources at any time (Junqi and Yumei, 2010).

E-learning reduces the limitations of traditional education, but u-learning offers more opportunities by reducing it further. U-learning is a system based on the concept of Ubiquitous Computing Technology. Ubiquitous Computing Technology allows the learning environment to be used anywhere and in any form, and any time the learner wants.

With the development of wireless and mobile technologies, e-learning will begin to give way to u-learning over time. The aim of U-learning is to provide learning services in the right place and time. For a better understanding u-learning, e-learning, u-learning, pervasive plearning (p-learning) methods are shown in Figure 1 for mobility and embedding. Here, mobility and ease of transport and computer systems in large information are shown in storage space and memory. While e-learning shows the lowest burden and mobility, u-learning shows the highest level of mobility. In this case, u-learning provides more benefits to learners (Boyinbode and Akintola, 2009).

Figure 1. Comparison of e-learning with u-learning

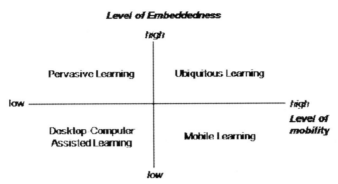

BASIC CHARACTERISTICS AND ADVANTAGES OF U-LEARNING

While U-learning carries the basic features of the e-learning system, it focuses on technologies that are more flexible, dependence on computer which use other mobile and sensor systems. It provides integration of human, physical resources and information objects in U-learning communication environment (Boyinbode and Akintola, 2009).

Formulated as U-learning = {U-environment, U-content, U-behavior, U-interface, U-service};

U-media includes invisible, embedded computers and plug-in devices,
U-content includes interpreted information, common knowledge and embedded information,
U-behavior includes learning process elements such as gestures, behavior, speech
U-interface includes welcome screens between learner and u-environment,
U-service is a support function that provides pedagogical, psychological and social situation and supports activities such as cognition, technology, analysis and inquiry.

When we look at the characteristics of U-learning, we see continuity, accessibility, memory, interaction, situationality and adaptability of teaching activities (Jones and Jo, 2005). We can explain these as follows:

- **Continuity**: The learners do not lose learning results unless they themselves want. All learning processes are continuously recorded.
- **Accessibility**: Learners can obtain documents, information and videos, and use them in a personal process according to their needs wherever and whenever they want.
- **Instant**: The whereabouts of the learners are no problem, they can immediately access the information. Thus, learners can easily solve problems or take notes and then find answers.
- **Interaction**: Learners interact with teachers, experts and other friends. Access to experts is used more effectively as the most accessed source.

- **Situationality of Learning Activities**: Learning may be integrated with the daily life of the learner. Problems and other necessary information can be presented in a natural and effective way. Thus, learners can spend their attention on more problematic situations.
- **Adaptation**: U-learning provides information and learning support at any time, anywhere, at the desired time, and easily (Jones and Jo, 2005).

There have been many benefits regarding u-learning in the studies. The important ones are as follows:

- The learning environment is contextually conscious. The place and environment parameters of the learner are perceived by the learning system.
- The interaction between the system and the learner is individual. In the learning process, the system provides support to the learner.
- The learning process is continuous. The learner is constantly guided from one place to another, and continuous communication is maintained (Boyinbode and Akintola, 2009).

Looking at these advantages, the e-learning system and the e-learning system can be shown as in Table 1.

U-LEARNING ENVIRONMENT

Internet and its functionalities have affected and transformed our life more than anything else in the digital millennium. Digital transformation with the Internet has added plenty of things to human life such as The Internet of Things (IoT) which connects things, extracts data, stores, processes and analyzes in various data platforms (Sadeep, 2017).

Ubiquitous computing Ubiquitous computing is crucial in environments in which computing is seamlessly integrated and embedded in the background. Teachers can exploit it in education coupled with innovative pedagogies, like constructionism and 'learning-bydoing', in order to augment the learning experience and showcase how programmable, mobile and personal devices can impact people's lives. C. Internet of Things Internet of Things (IoT) is a relatively new technology that leverages the ubiquity of the Internet by integrating physical objects for interaction via embedded systems. This type of inter-

Table 1. Advantages of u-learning compared to e-learning

	U-learning	E-learning
	The system detects the environment of the learner.	The system cannot detect the environment of the learner. The environment is not contextual conscious.
	The system is contextually conscious.	Learners may lose their work.
	Learners do not lose their work.	There is no continuity.
	There is continuity in studies.	Learners can only access information in certain places.
	Learners can access information from anywhere.	Learners cannot access information immediately.
	Learners can access their information immediately.	The learner's interaction is limited.

actions lead to a highly distributed network of devices communicating with humans and other devices (Xia t al., 2012).

The ubiquitous computing (UbiComp) is considered as an extension of the computational capabilities of the physical environment, allowing the computational structure to be present everywhere in the form of small, robust, networked processing devices distributed at all scales through everyday life and generally turned to distinctly common place ends. There are various research challenges regarding the design and use of instructional design tools in complex learning contexts such as Ubiquitous Computing, Mobile learning (m-learning) and Internet of Things (IoT), the technologies defined as UMI Technologies (Fragou, Kameas & Zaharakis, 2017).

U-learning environment is a set of learning processes in which the learners interact in. In the U-learning environment as understood from the description (Jones and Jo, 2005):

Ubiquitous = Places that are common everywhere, always located;
Learning = Educational, educational, didactic and pedagogical,
Environment = Environment, set, condition, atmosphere is revealed with the help of concepts.

As understood from the above statements, the u-learning environment is a common educational environment and situation. Education occurs in every environment of learners, but the learner may not be aware of it. The information is embedded in various objects and the student acquires them. In the U-learning environment, physical objects are in microprocessors, wireless and mobile technological devices and sensors. There is potentially service delivery from a device to multiple learners in the environment. That is, when a student interacts with an object in a network environment, other devices and objects in the environment know it. The connection of each learner works singly and independently, does not interrupt other connections, and work continues (Jones and Jo, 2005).

Components of U-learning

In the u-learning environment, certain components are used in the formation of the u-learning model and the information is reached. These components are described below.

- **Microprocessors**: Memory microprocessors are embedded in the object or device. The information in the microprocessor is related to the device and when the learner approaches, the sensor detects and sends the information to the personal digital assistant (PDA) of the learner.
- **U-Learning Server Module:** This server consists of the Training Strategy Unit database. This server manages the network. The Training Strategy Unit provides learners interactivity and feedback. Interaction information about the device and users is kept in the database.
- **Wireless Technologies:** These technologies are made of WIFI, Bluetooth and mobile technologies. While Bluetooth performs relatively short distances and little data transmission, WIFI and mobile technologies are characterized by greater range and data transfer rates. Most access points and client devices are WiFi and mobile technology compatible.
- **Sensors**: Detects changes in the environment and recognizes learners and devices. They are sensitive to light, approach, and movement (Jones and Jo, 2005).

In the U-learning environment, education and training services are basically found. The training environment consists mainly of resource libraries, personal terminals (such as PDAs and notebooks), communication infrastructure and communication protocols. Educational services consist of smart education services, distance education services, educational resource provisioning services and websites. The interaction status for U-learning is shown in Figure 2 (ZhangAiHua, 2010).

In the U-learning environment, interaction takes place between the learner and the object / devices that make up the system. The learner interacts when approaching the object in the environment, the object also detects the learner and sends information to the learner and receives his / her responses. The information is then transmitted to all objects in the u-learning environment. In the U-learning center, each student carries a wireless or mobile device. The U-learning server module monitors and detects every student in u-space with sensors. When a learner approaches the object, the sensor reaches the internal network and the u-server via wireless communication and transfers information about the object. Then the information is sent from any object in the u-learning center to the learner's handheld computer (Jones and Jo, 2005).

Continuous Communication Between Learner and Device

Figure 3 shows the interaction between a learner and the system. Here he approaches and observes the learning object. Nearby sensors detect the student's presence and send information about the object to the learner's PDA (a1). It can be sent to the learner in pictures, text, sound or other formats (a2). At the same time, the object will access the u-learning server module (b1) to request information about the object.

Figure 2. U-learning environment interaction model

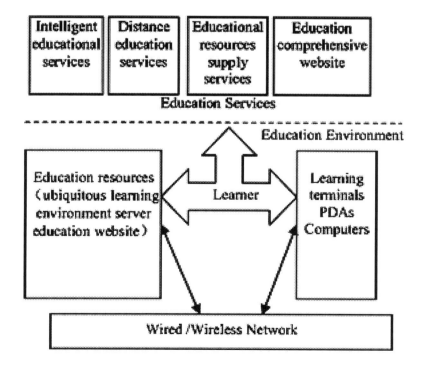

Figure 3. Communication between the learner and the device

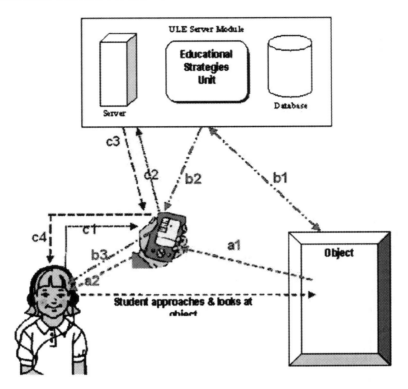

In spite of the network and independent working environment, the object can work alone and send data. It is sent by the u-learning server module to which the learner has previously reached this information and which format is more suitable for the learner. This information is also sent if the learner has given correct answers to visual and audio information.

A short quiz and educational game can be sent to the learner's handbook about the subjects (b2 and b3). The student will send it back to the u-learning server module (c1 and c2) and the results will be analyzed by the Education Strategy unit. If the student requires additional information and further clarification, the learners' handheld computer is sent for these requests (c3 and c4). Information about the subject is kept in the U-learning module while the information about the object is kept on the object itself and in the u-learning server module (Jones and Jo, 2005).

Communication Between Devices / Objects

Figure 4 shows the communication between the devices. The learner learns and observes Object1. In this case, the item, such as text, image and sound related to Object1 is sent to the learner's handheld. If the system receives a response from the learner, it reviews the transmitted information and tests whether the learner understands it. After this operation, Object1 is distributed to other objects such as Object2 and Object3. This allows the u-server module and other objects to download information about the learners. The specified process is shown in the following steps.

Transition From E-Learning to U-Learning

Figure 4. Communication between objects / devices

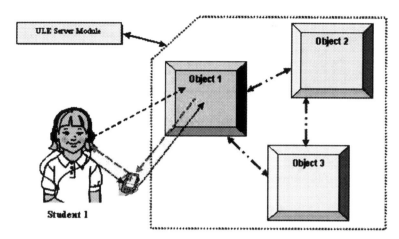

1. Learning 1 approaches Object1.
2. Information is sent to the learner.
3. Analyze the answers of the learner and understand the subject.
4. This information is sent to the objects in the media. For example, "Learner1 understands 6/10 of this issue.

When the learner approaches the next object, the object is aware of what the learner knows and will try to explain the remaining 4/10 of 6/10. The U-training module is accessed by objects only when necessary. On the next visit of the learner, the server is now aware of the learner's cumulative knowledge and adds information as constructive. In this way, the learning experience of the learner is supported and deep learning is provided.

The content suitable for teaching in the U-server environment covers knowledge-based disciplines such as History, Geography, Science, information transfer, reflection and active participation. Learners are encouraged to create their own knowledge by communicating with devices and objects as they move through the u-space, making use of their environment. Constructive theory is used for what the learners see, what they hear, what they read and what they perceive (Jones & Jo, 2005).

Teaching Architecture of U-learning

While determining the U-learning structure, some general thoughts are acted upon. Content developers cannot create different websites for different desktop and mobile systems. All site or course information presentation interfaces are designed in a common structure. This common structure can be implemented with XML files or a standard database. The applications respond to the browser's request and work according to the features of the device. In the application architecture of U-learning, filtering is done both technically and educationally. For example, a technically positive activity may not be considered useful as a training and activity filtering for mobile devices may be performed. Given the basic learning needs, the education architecture of u-learning can be determined as follows (Casey, 2008):

- **Learning Objects**: Media objects that cover the content of learning modules, such as text, graphics, sound, video, and other media.
- **Presentation of Learning**: To present the content of the learners in relation to the content by means of reading materials or methods of monitoring or listening.
- **Learning Tasks**: Learning the content of the learner, taking personal notes, participating in discussions, doing exercises, and performing tasks.
- **Learning Communication:** The learner-teacher is the method used for communication between the learner and the learner. These can be text-based systems, real-time audio, video and animated sessions broadcast on the Internet.
- **Administrative Functions:** These are the applications required for the management and evaluation of various administrative tasks in relation to teaching.

The U-learning architecture includes communication and administrative functions together with all objects, tasks, presentations, with a common warehouse space. These objects and tasks are displayed in browsers embedded in HTML as text, image, sound, images. Objects in architecture need to be filtered from common storage according to certain filtering criteria. Criteria include whether the object is technically good for personal computers or mobile devices, and whether it is educationally useful or on a desktop. For example, as a criterion, it should be implemented by determining that large files will not be suitable for mobile devices, but that sound files will be more useful and useful. Educationally, the use of audio files in lessons can be shaped as a criterion where m-learning is appropriate (Casey, 2008).

U-LEARNING FRAMEWORK PROPOSED

Ubiquity of Internet and proliferation of social networking, as well as the ever-growing computer literacy of personnel encourages utilization of information technologies in order to provide a very efficient, easy-to-use and cost-effective medium of sharing information among nations.

The key to wide acceptance is simplicity, familiarity and intuitive functionality; users will respond very positively to this new approach, if the required computer and social interactions bear a striking similarity to their professional or -even better- leisure activities, such as Internet browsing, chat e.t.c. Most people should be intimately familiar with the described functionality herein. Another aspect of this proposal is to foster cooperation, raise interest and social activity in the website. Furthermore, realization of this proposal will have negligible impact on the technical requirements of the website and operation costs. The services rendered by the website can be expanded to include the following:

- Sharing of medical views on general or specific topics in a more informal but direct and scientific valid way.
- Presenting specific cases, that provides valuable insight on the diagnosis or treatment of patients.
- Exchange of medical opinions on specific cases, colloquially known as "second opinion".
- International collaboration, especially among junior personnel (or trainees) for their specialty training or thesis.
- Groups sharing common interests based on specialty, country or even ad-hoc groups.

Usable Emerging Technologies

The information portal for exchange information provides a robust and user friendly repository of knowledge and media. The portal uses modern content management tools that enable proper indexing, tagging and retrieval of information. Another very important functionality of the portal is to integrate social networking functions, as well as provide robust and flexible means of communication, both asynchronous (e-mail) and synchronous (Instant Messaging, Video conference). Finally, forums allow for conversations in the form of posted messages.

Functionalites and Tools

The the home page should provide a plethora of navigations choices, grouped together in logical entities called menus.

- **Articles**: Allows the user to browse the article entries, usually provided users.
- **Forum**: Navigates the user to the forum area, where he can read and post in one or more conversations (threads) about specific topics.
- **Gallery**: Allows the user to browse the image repository of the site.
- **Video**: Allows the user to browse the video repository of the site.
- **Events**: Provides access to a calendar populated with all scheduled events.
- **Conferencing**: Provides access to the conferencing functions of the site.
- **Users**: Enables the user to participate in ad-hoc groups .
- **Profile**: Provides access to the user's public profile.

Articles

Articles are usually submitted by users and published under specific categories of medical speciality. Apart from text, an article may include images as well as hyperlinks to other articles. The title and the author of each article is presented at the top, as well as the publish date.

Interaction is a very important aspect of the site. Since this site is a community driven initiative, such actions can enhance and tighten the cooperation between nations and colleagues. Users can provide feedback through comments. The "Leave a comment" frame provides a straightforward and easy-to-use function to add a comment. Comments are displayed in chronological order. Finally, standard social network interactions are provided such as Like, Tweet and Share. An example of remark use is shown in the next picture.

Under the basic article information, further functionality is provided in the form of tab windows interface, as follows:

- **Content**: Allows user to compose the article's body by adding, editing and formatting text by use of a WYSIWYG (an acronym for What You See Is What You Get) editor. The term is used to describe content-editing tools that let you view your text formatting as you work.
- **Image**: Allows user to add a main image to the article. Such images are shown in the beginning of the article. Images can also be added in the body by use of editor commands.

- **Gallery**: Allows user to add or remove images in an article gallery. This option is used, if a lot of images need to be attached to an article. Work in progress.
- **Media**: Allows user to add a main image to the article. Such images are shown in the beginning of the article. Images can also be added in the body by use of editor commands.
- Image: Allows user to add videos to the article.
- **Attachments**: Allows user to add or remove files relevant to the article. This option is used, if a PDF document or MS Word form needs to be attached to an article.

Video

The video is represented by a thumbnail. The user can click the thumbnail to view the video. Users can rate and comment on media. Various sorting options are provided for convenience, such as latest entries, popularity and rating.

Events

The Ievent calendar can be reached by use of the top menu. In the calendar scheduled events are marked. The user can change the view by week, by month or even by year. Users can add events in order to inform the community about upcoming activities. All users can be notified also by e-mail about the new events.

Groups

Groups are collection of users which have a common interest, such as members of a medical speciality. Users can be members of one or more groups. A group manager can be assigned to supervise the group, invite other users to the group and organize activities. By using the Users entry, a user can browse existing groups. The groups are presented alphabetically. Alternative, search options are available.

Mail

A standard web mail service is provided. The functionality is almost similar to most web mail services (such as hotmail and gmail). Users can see the contents of their inbox directly by using the "Inbox" function in the user menu or compose a new message by using the "New message" function.

Conferencing

The web portal provides teleconference and e-learning capabilities. Specifically, the system provides VoIP communications (like Skype) in a conference or class environment, as well as other services such as desktop and file sharing as well as chat, whiteboard and presentation facilities. All communications are handled by a streaming server, seamlessly integrated in the website. Each user can attend meetings, which in this case are virtual "rooms", each one assigned to a particular topic. In most rooms are dedicated to specialties, however there are no restrictions and more rooms can be added. Meetings are

Transition From E-Learning to U-Learning

usually prearranged events. An e-mail to potential attendees is sent beforehand, usually with the "room" and the date of the meeting. For sensitive discussions, a special password can be included. The Group functionality supplements very well event arrangements; group managers can post relevant information in the bulletin or e-mail all users automatically with meeting arrangements. The users enter their name, which is shown to other attendees, as well as a password. By using the "join" button, the user can enter the selected conference room.

Desktop Sharing

By using the desktop icon, a user has the capability to broadcast what he sees and does in his computer to the audience. This capability is very helpful, if a tutor wishes to show a step-by-step example or execute an ad-hoc training (freeform presentation without slides but by using a hands-on approach). The feature requires a JAVA Virtual machine installed in the system. The system will notify the user and request permission to download and install the appropriate software, in order to be activated. Before the "share desktop" feature is activated, the user can select to broadcast an area (such as a window) instead of the whole screen. The system will take snapshots of the selected area and present them to the users. Because this desktop sharing feature is computationally and bandwidth demanding, the user is advices to:

- Reduce the screen size to a lower resolution (1024x768)
- Display only a region (the appropriate window).

Otherwise, it is highly recommended to (temporarily) replace any desktop background image with a solid color (this also helps the user distinguish the cursor or other desktop elements).

Chat

The chat panel allows users to discuss, comment and ask questions without interrupting the presentation flow, or provide feedback and fruitful conversation after the presentation. Also, allows active participation for users with limited bandwidth. In the chat panel, user input is added in chronological order. The user name and time of entry is also shown. The user can post an entry by using the textbox at the bottom and pressing the "Send" button. The message is then posted in the main common area. Also a distinct color can be selected to highlight or distinguish an entry. However, very bright colors can be offensive to the eye, so this feature must be handled in an organized prearranged color scheme to be effective: for example the presenter uses blue and the attendees black.

U-LEARNING RESEARCHES

Through the development of portable and ubiquitous computer systems, social interaction has contributed to the implementation of activities regardless of time and place. Nowadays, improved wireless communication skills, open networks, extended use of computer battery power, and the introduction of technological and flexible software have increased the use of computers everywhere. By using these technologies, the integration of individual learning environment into daily real life has been ensured. He has also focused on computer-aided collaborative learning environments, social knowledge formation and sharing, socio-cognitive processes with u-learning.

To date, some research on m-learning and u-learning has been conducted. Some of them used the resource definition standards of e-learning for u-learning studies but they did not get enough results. This is evident in the Taiwan project açıkça Pocket Scormé Bu. Some of the others have developed e-learning standard definitions for u-learning. This feature can be seen in the British Tony Chan's göre M-learning metadata 'and the Chinese LOM project conducted by Yang Zongaki. While the studies for meta knowledge of U-learning resource definitions continue, the definitions are insufficient to meet the needs. There are deficiencies in meaning and knowledge management (Su L and Ma1, 2009).

Currently, research on u-learning continues. Especially u-learning system theory and application methods are being investigated. Theoretically, research on u-learning proceeds in the following ways:

- U-pedagogy,
- Class-centered u-learning method,
- Special curriculum-based u-learning method,
- U-learning applications for faculty training,
- Development standards for U-learning resources,
- U-learning is a teaching management system development.

Nowadays, the transition from mobile learning to u-learning is observed. Most of the research is about u-learning rather than u-learning framework. Other important u-learning projects are (Zhang, 2008):

- In Active campus, active class GPS project at UCSD University, mobile (GPS) navigation service and in-class collaborative studies were conducted with mobile devices.
- RFID mobile device navigation, lecture note distribution and homework assignments were carried out with mobil Ubi-campus. Project at Hannover University (Germany) and UTT (Fillandiya) universities.
- Tokoshima University (Japan) "learning service and exchange of information between users ılar with mobile devices with the TANGO project.
- Smart laboratory studies with AR, image-based sensors, RFID and interfaces were carried out with 2008 Oxygen akıllı project at MIT University (Zhang, 2008).

CONCLUSION

U-learning is a modern teaching system based on the use of computer technologies (Ubiquitous Computing Tehnology) everywhere in the environment of existing wired, wireless, mobile and sensor systems nowadays called IoT. The interaction is ubiquitous. The information in objects (embeded) and mobility is the highest. U-learning have continuity, accessibility, memory, interaction, educational status and adaptation. Training services are among mobile systems and sensors that can move independently in the IoT. The architecture of U-learning is based on the distribution and dissemination of information in u-environement. U-learning system theory and application methods are being investigated. Nowadays, the transition from mobile learning to u-learning is observed. Most of the researches are about u-learning applications and effective use of IoT.

REFERENCES

Boyinbode, O. K., & Akintola, K. G. (2009). *Effecting E-Learning with U-Learning Technology in Nigerian Educational System. The Pacific Journal of Science and Technology.*

Bruce, B. C. (2008). *Ubiquitous learning, ubiquitous computing, and lived experience, Graduate School of Library and Information Science.* University of Illinois at Urbana-Champaign.

Casey, D. (2008). U-learning:Educational Models and System architectures. Handbook of Research on Instructional Systems and Technology.

Fragou, O., Kameas, A., & Zaharakis, I. D. (2017). An instructional design process for creating a U-learning ecology. *2017 IEEE Global Engineering Education Conference (EDUCON)*, 1817-1823. 10.1109/EDUCON.2017.7943097

Jones, V., & Jo, J. H. (2005). *Ubiquitous learning environment: An adaptive teaching system using ubiquitous technology.* School of Information Technology Griffith University.

Junqi, W., & Yumei, L. (2010). Study of Instructional design in Ubiquitous Learning. *2010 Second International Workshop on Education Technology and Computer Science.* 10.1109/ETCS.2010.522

Naido, S. (2006). *E-learning:a gude book of Principles, Procedures and Practices.* Commonwealth Educational Media Center for Asia.

Sandeep, R. (2017). *Internet of (Medical) things in Healthcare.* IoT Central.

Su, L., & Ma1, J. (Eds.). (2009). Semantic-oriented Ubiquitous Learning Object Model. National Research Project named Resources mService Architecture and Key Technology Study on Ubiquitous Learning.

Sung, J.S. (2009). U-Learning Model Design Based on Ubiquitous Environment. *International Journal of Advanced Science and Technology, 13.*

Xia, F. L. T., Yang, L., Wang, L., & Vinel, A. (2017). Internet of things. *International Journal of Communication Systems, 25*(9), 1101–1102. doi:10.1002/dac.2417

Zhang. (2010). *Study of Ubiquitous Learning Environment Based on Ubiquitous Computing.* Tianjin University of Science and Technology, Department of Computer Science and Information.

Zhang, J. (2008). *Hybrid Learning and Ubiquitous Learning.* East China Normal University. doi:10.1007/978-3-540-85170-7_22

KEY TERMS AND DEFINITIONS

Internet of Things (IoT): The internet of things, or IoT, is a system of interrelated computing devices, mechanical and digital machines, objects, animals or people that are provided with unique identifiers (UIDs) and the ability to transfer data over a network without requiring human-to-human or human-to-computer interaction.

Ubiquitous Computing Tehnology: Ubiquitous computing is a paradigm in which the processing of information is linked with each activity or object as encountered. It involves connecting electronic devices, including embedding microprocessors to communicate information.

Ubiquitous Learning (U-Learning): Ubiquitous learning, an amalgam of e-learning and m-learning, allowing learning to take place independantly of time and place.

Compilation of References

Abowd, G. D., & Dey, A. K. (1999, September). Towards a better understanding of context and context-awareness. In *International symposium on handheld and ubiquitous computing* (pp. 304-307). Springer. Retrieved from https://link.springer.com/chapter/10.1007/3-540-48157-5_29

Abraham, R. R., & Komattil, R. (2017). Heutagogic approach to developing capable learners. *Medical Teacher, 39*(3), 295–299. doi:10.1080/0142159X.2017.1270433 PMID:28019131

Abu Bakar, A. B., Harande, Y. I., & Abubakar, B. M. (2009). *E-learning in Malaysia and Nigeria: A Bibliometric Study.* Paper presented at the 8th European Conference on E-Learning held at University, Bari, Italy.

Abubakar, B. M., & Hassan, B. B. (2013). Strategies for Developing an e-Learning Curriculum for Library and Information Science (LIS) Schools in the Muslim World: Meeting the Expectations in the Digital Age. *International Journal of Humanities and Social Science, 3*(1), 163–171.

Açıkgöz, K. Ü. (2003). *Etkili Öğrenme ve Öğretme.* İzmir: Eğitim Dünyası Yayınları.

Ackoff, R. L., & Greenberg, D. (2008). *Turning Learning Right Side Up: Putting Education Back on Track.* Pearson Education, Wharton School Publishing.

Adams Becker, S., Cummins, M., Davis, A., Freeman, A., Hall Giesinger, C., & Ananthanarayanan, V. (2017). *NMC Horizon Report: 2017 Higher Education Edition.* Austin, TX: The New Media Consortium.

Adams, C., & Van Manen, M. (2008). Phenomenology. In L. M. Given (Ed.), *The Sage Encyclopedia of Qualitative Research Methods* (pp. 614–619). Thousand Oaks, CA: Sage.

Adler, M., & Ziglio, E. (1996). *Gazing into the oracle.* Bristol, PA: Jessica Kingsley Publishers.

Agarwal, S., & Nath, A. (2011). Some Challenges in Designing and Implementing Learning Material for Ubiquitous E-learning Environment. *Journal of Global Research in Computer Science Journal of Global Research in Computer Science, 2*(2), 29–32.

Agonacs, N., & Matos, J. F. (2019). Heutagogy and self-determined learning: a review of the published literature on the application and implementation of the theory. *Open Learning: The Journal of Open, Distance and e-Learning,* 1-19.

Agonacs, N., & Matos, J. F. (2017). *Towards a Heutagogy-Based MOOC Design Framework. In Work in Progress Papers of the Experience and Research Tracks and Position Papers of the Policy Track, EMOOCs Proceedings, University of Lisbon* (pp. 22–26). Lisbon, Portugal: Mayıs.

Akcaoglu, M., & Lee, E. (2016). Increasing social presence in online learning through small group discussions. *International Review of Research in Open and Distributed Learning, 17*(3), 1–17. doi:10.19173/irrodl.v17i3.2293

Akyol, Z., & Garrison, D. R. (2008). The development of a Community of Inquiry over time in an online course: Understanding the progression and integration of social, cognitive and teaching presence. *Journal of Asynchronous Learning Networks*, *12*(3–4), 3–22.

Alabay, A. (2015). *Ortaöğretim öğretmenlerinin ve öğrencilerinin EBA (eğitimde bilişim ağı) kullanımına ilişkin görüşleri üzerine bir araştırma* (Unpublished master's thesis). İstanbul Aydın University, İstanbul, Turkey.

Alhassan, R. (2016). Mobile Learning as a Method of Ubiquitous Learning: Students' Attitudes, Readiness, and Possible Barriers to Implementation in Higher Education. *Journal of Education and Learning*, *5*(1), 176–189. doi:10.5539/jel.v5n1p176

Aliponga, J. (2013). Reading Journal : Its Benefits for Extensive Reading. *International Journal of Humanities and Social Science*, *3*(12), 73–80.

Alonso de Castro, M. (2014). Educational projects based on mobile learning. *Teoría de la Educación. Educación y Cultura en la Sociedad de la Información*, *15*(1).

Altınışık, H. Z., & Adıgüzel, T. (2016). A brief review of ubiquitous learning. *Ardahan Üniversitesi İktisadi ve İdari Bilimler Fakültesi Dergisi*, *2*(3), 121–130.

Amann, W., Kruckeberg, K., & Green, M. (Eds.). (2011). *Leadership and personal development: a toolbox for the 21st century professional*. IAP.

Ameen, K. (2007). *Issues in Quality assurance in LIS higher education in Pakistan*. Paper presented at the IFLA General Conference and Council, Durban, South Africa. Available at http://www.ifla.org/IV/ifla73/index.htm

American Psychological Association Dictionary. (n.d.a). *Career Counseling*. Retrieved May 20, 2019, from https://dictionary.apa.org/career-counseling

American Psychological Association Dictionary. (n.d.b). *Counseling Psychology*. Retrieved May 20, 2019, from https://dictionary.apa.org/counseling-psychology

Anderson, T., Rourke, L., Garrison, D. R., & Archer, W. (2001). Assessing teaching presence in a computer conference context. *Journal of Asynchronous Learning Networks*, *5*(2).

Andersson, P., Fejes, A., & Sandberg, F. (2013). Introducing research on recognition of prior learning. *International Journal of Lifelong Education*, *32*(4), 405–411. doi:10.1080/02601370.2013.778069

Aragon, S. R. (2003). Creating social presence in online environments. *New Directions for Adult and Continuing Education*, *100*(100), 57–68. doi:10.1002/ace.119

Arbaugh, J. B. (2014). System, scholar or students? Which most influences online MBA course effectiveness? *Journal of Computer Assisted Learning*, *30*(4), 349–362. doi:10.1111/jcal.12048

Arkorful, V., & Abaidoo, N. (2015). The role of e-learning, advantages and disadvantages of its adoption in higher education. *International Journal of Instructional Technology and Distance Learning*, *12*(1), 29–42.

Arkün, S., & Aşkar, P. (2010). Çevreleyen Öğrenme: Kavramsal Çerçeve Ambient Learning: Conceptual Framework. In *Uluslararası Öğretmen Yetiştirme Politikaları ve Sorunları Sempozyumu II*. Hacettepe University.

Armstrong, M. (2012). *Armstrong's handbook of management and leadership: developing effective people skills for better leadership and management* (3rd ed.). Kogan Page Publishers.

Compilation of References

Aronson, J. (1995). A pragmatic view of thematic analysis. *Qualitative Report, 2*(1), 1–3.

Asiimwe, E. N., & Khan, S. Z. (2013, October). *Ubiquitous computing in education: A SWOT analysis by students and teachers.* Paper presented at the 12th World Conference on Mobile and Contextual Learning (mLearn 2013), College of the North Atlantic, Qatar. 10.5339/qproc.2013.mlearn.18

Association of College & Research Libraries (ACRL). (2015). *Framework for information literacy for higher education.* Retrieved from http://www.ala.org/acrl/standards/ilframework

Aydın, İ. (2011). *Kamu ve özel sektörde hizmet içi eğitim el kitabı.* Ankana: Pegem Akademi.

Aydın, H. C. (2011). *Açık ve uzaktan öğrenme: Öğrenci adaylarının bakış açısı* [Open and distance learning: The perspective of prospective learners]. Ankara: Pegem.

Baich, T. (2015). Open access: Help or hindrance to resource sharing? *Interlending & Document Supply, 43*(2), 68–75. doi:10.1108/ILDS-01-2015-0003

Baldwin, T. T., & Ford, J. K. (1988). Transfer of learning: A review and directions for future research. *Personnel Psychology, 4*(1), 63–105. doi:10.1111/j.1744-6570.1988.tb00632.x

Bandura, A. (1971). *Social learning theory.* New York, NY: General Learning Press.

Bandura, A. (1986). *Social foundations of thought and action: A social cognitive theory.* Englewood Cliffs, N.J: Prentice-Hall.

Banks, J. A. (1993). Multicultural education: Characteristics and goals. In J. A. Banks & C. A. M. Banks (Eds.), *Multicultural education: Issues and perspectives* (2nd ed.; pp. 3–28). Boston: Allyn & Bacon.

Barak, A. (1999). Psychological applications on the internet: A discipline on the threshold of a new millennium. *Applied & Preventive Psychology, 8*(4), 231–245. doi:10.1016/S0962-1849(05)80038-1

Barbosa, J., Barbosa, D., & Rabello, S. (2016). A collaborative model for ubiquitous learning environments. *International Journal on E-Learning: Corporate, Government, Healthcare, and Higher Education, 15*(1), 5–25.

Barron, A. (1999). *A Teacher's Guide to Distance learning.* Florida Center for Instructional Technology, College of Education, University of South Florida. Retrieved May 20, 2019, from https://fcit.usf.edu/distance/

Bates, A. W. (2015). *Teaching in a Digital Age.* BC Open Textbooks. Retrieved from https://opentextbc.ca/teachinginadigitalage/

Bates, T. (2014). *Teaching in a digital age.* Open Textbook.

Baturay, M. H. (2015). An overview of the world of MOOCs. *Procedia: Social and Behavioral Sciences, 174*, 427–433. doi:10.1016/j.sbspro.2015.01.685

Beall, J. (2012). *Predatory publishers and opportunities for scholarly societies.* Retrieved from http://eprints.rclis.org/18044/

Beel, N. & Court, J.H. (2000). Ethical issues in counselling over the internet: an examination of the risks and benefits. *Ethical Issues in Internet Counselling, 4*(2), 35-42.

Beilin, I. (2015). Beyond the threshold: Conformity, resistance, and the ACRL Information Literacy Framework for Higher Education. *In the Library with the Lead Pipe.* Retrieved from http://www.inthelibrarywiththeleadpipe.org/2015/beyond-the-threshold-conformity-resistance-and-the-aclr-information-literacy-framework-for-higher-education/

Bell, F. (2011). Connectivism: Its place in theory-informed research and innovation in technology-enabled learning. *International Review of Research in Open and Distance Learning, 12*(3), 98. doi:10.19173/irrodl.v12i3.902

Bennett, L. (2012). *The potential effect of making journals free after a six-month embargo: A report for the Association of Learned, Professional and Society Publishers [ALPSP] and The Publishers Association*. Retrieved from https://www.recolecta.fecyt.es/sites/default/files/contenido/documentos/ALPSPPApotentialresultsofsixmonthembargofv.pdf

Benson, R., & Samarawickrema, G. (2009). Addressing the context of e-learning: Using transactional distance theory to inform design. *Distance Education, 30*(1), 5–21. doi:10.1080/01587910902845972

Benson, V., & Morgan, S. (2013). Student Experience and Ubiquitous Learning in Higher Education: Impact of Wireless and Cloud Applications. *Creative Education, 04*(08), 1–5. doi:10.4236/ce.2013.48A001

Bergamin, P. B., Ziska, S., & Groner, R. (2012). The relationship between flexible and self-regulated learning in open and distance universities. *International Review of Research in Open and Distributed Learning, 13*(2), 102–123. doi:10.19173/irrodl.v13i2.1124

Berge, Z. L. (1995). Facilitating Computer Conferencing: Recommendations From the Field. *Educational Technology, 15*(1), 22–30.

Bernard, R. M., Borokhovski, E., Schmid, R. F., Tamim, R. M., & Abrami, P. C. (2014). A meta-analysis of blended learning and technology use in higher education: From the general to the applied. *Journal of Computing in Higher Education, 26*(1), 87–102. doi:10.100712528-013-9077-3

Bhaskar, N. U., Naidu, P. P., Babu, S. R. C., & Govindarajulu, P. (2011). Principles of good screen design in websites. *International Journal of Human-Computer Interaction, 2*(2), 48–57.

Bhoyrub, J., Hurley, J., Neilson, G. R., Ramsay, M., & Smith, M. (2010). Heutagogy: An alternative practice based learning approach. *Nurse Education in Practice, 10*(6), 322–326. doi:10.1016/j.nepr.2010.05.001 PMID:20554249

Bill & Melinda Gates Foundation. (2017). *Bill & Melinda Gates Foundation open access policy*. Retrieved from http://www.gatesfoundation.org/How-We-Work/General-Information/Open-Access-Policy

Bischoff, R. J. (2004). Considerations in the use of telecommunications as a primary treatment medium: The application of behavioral telehealth to marriage and family therapy. *The American Journal of Family Therapy, 32*(3), 173–187. doi:10.1080/01926180490437376

Blaschke, L. M. (2014). Moving students forward in the PAH continuum: Maximizing the power of the social web. In L. M. Blaschke, C. Kenyon, & S. Hase (Eds.), Experiences in self-determined learning (pp.56-67). Amazon.com Publishing.

Blaschke, L. M. (2012). Heutagogy and lifelong learning: A review of heutagogical practice and self-determined learning. *The International Review of Research in Open and Distributed Learning, 13*(1), 56–71. doi:10.19173/irrodl.v13i1.1076

Blaschke, L. M. (2013). Self-determined Learning (Heutagogy) and Digital Media Creating integrated Educational Environments for Developing Lifelong Learning Skills. In S. Hase & C. Kenyon (Eds.), *Self-determined learning: Heutagogy in action* (pp. 55–67). London, UK: Bloomsbury Academic.

Blaschke, L. M. (2018). Self-determined Learning (Heutagogy) and Digital Media Creating integrated Educational Environments for Developing Lifelong Learning Skills. In D. Kergel, B. Heidkamp, P. Kjaersdam Telleus, T. Rachwal, & S. Nowakowski (Eds.), *The digital turn in Higher education: International Perspectives on Learning and Teaching in a Changing World* (pp. 129–137). Wiesbaden, Germany: Springer. doi:10.1007/978-3-658-19925-8_10

Compilation of References

Blaschke, L. M., & Hase, S. (2016). Heutagogy: A Holistic Framework for Creating Twenty-First-Century Self-determined Learners. In K. Begoña & M. Maina (Eds.), *The Future of Ubiquitous Learning. Gros* (pp. 25–41). Berlin: Springer. doi:10.1007/978-3-662-47724-3_2

Boer, P. M. (2001). *Career counseling over the internet: An emerging model for trusting and responding to online clients.* Mahwah, NJ: Lawrence Erlbaum Associates Publishers.

Bohl, O., Schellhase, J., Sengler, R., & Winand, U. (2002). The Sharable Content Object Reference Model (SCORM) – A Critical Review. In *Proceedings of the International Conference on Computers in Education (ICCE02)* (pp. 950-951). Auckland, New Zealand: Academic Press.

Boishwarelo, B. (2011). Proposing an integrated research framework for connectivism: Utilizing theoretical synergies. *International Review of Research in Open and Distance Learning, 12*(3). Retrieved from http://www.irrodl.org/index.php/irrodl/article/view/881

Bomsdorf, B. (2005). Adaptation of learning spaces: Supporting ubiquitous learning in higher distance education. In *Dagstuhl Seminar Proceedings*. Schloss Dagstuhl-Leibniz-Zentrum fr Informatik.

Bomsdorf, B. (2005). *Adaptation of learning spaces: Supporting ubiquitous learning in higher distance education.* Paper presented at the meeting of Mobile Computing and Ambient Intelligence: The Challenge of Multimedia, Schloss Dagstuhl, Germany.

Bonn, M. (2015). Maximizing the benefits of open access: Strategies for enhancing the discovery of open access content. *College & Research Libraries News, 76*(9), 491–494. doi:10.5860/crln.76.9.9381

Booth, M., Blaschke, L. M., & Hase, S. (2017). Practicing the Practice: The Heutagogy Community of Practice. In J. McDonald & A. Cater-Steel (Eds.), Implementing Communities of Practice in Higher Education (pp. 549-572). Springer.

Booth, S. (2011). *Cultivating knowledge sharing and trust in online communities for educators: A multiple case study* (Unpublished doctoral dissertation). North Carolina State University, Raleigh, NC.

Bosch, S., & Henderson, K. (2016). Fracking the ecosystem: Periodicals price survey 2016. *Library Journal, 141*(7), 32–38. Retrieved from http://lj.libraryjournal.com/2016/04/publishing/fracking-the-ecosystem-periodicals-price-survey-2016/#_

Boyinbode, O. K., & Akintola, K. G. (2009). *Effecting E-Learning with U-Learning Technology in Nigerian Educational System. The Pacific Journal of Science and Technology.*

Bozkurt, A. (2013). Mega üniversitelerde öğrenci destek hizmetleri [Support services in mega universities]. In *Proceedings of the Academic Informatics Conference* (pp. 395-401). Antalya: Akdeniz University. Retrieved October, 15, 2017, from https://www.academia.edu/2536907/Mega_%C3%9Cniversitelerde_%C3%96%C4%9Frenci_Destek_Hizmetleri

Bozkurt, A. (2013). *Açık ve uzaktan öğrenmeye yönelik etkileşimli e-kitap değerlendirme kriterlerinin belirlenmesi.* Eskişehir: Anadolu Üniversitesi, Sosyal Bilimler Enstitüsü, Uzaktan Eğitim Anabilim Dalı.

Bozkurt, A. (2016). Öğrenme analitiği: E-öğrenme, büyük veri ve bireyselleştirilmiş öğrenme. *Açık Öğretim Uygulamaları ve Araştırmaları Dergisi, 2*(4), 55–81.

Bozkurt, A., & Uçar, H. (2018). E-Öğrenme ve e-sınavlar: Çevrimiçi ölçme değerlendirme süreçlerinde kimlik doğrulama yöntemlerine ilişkin öğrenen görüşlerinin incelenmesi. *Mersin Üniversitesi Eğitim Fakültesi Dergisi, 14*(2), 745–755. doi:10.17860/mersinefd.357339

Bozkurt, A., Yazıcı, M., & Erdem Aydın, İ. (2018). Cultural diversity and its implications in online networked learning spaces. In E. Toprak (Ed.), *Supporting Multiculturalism in Open and Distance Learning Spaces* (pp. 56–81). Hershey, PA: IGI Global. doi:10.4018/978-1-5225-3076-3.ch004

Bozkurt, B. (2015). Mobil öğrenme: Her zaman, her yerde kesintisiz öğrenme deneyimi. *Açıköğretim Uygulamaları ve Araştırmaları Dergisi*, *1*(2), 65–81.

Branch, R. M. (2009). *Instructional design: The ADDIE approach*. New York, NY: Springer. doi:10.1007/978-0-387-09506-6

Bridgeman, B., Lennon, M. L., & Jackenthal, A. (2003). Effects of screen size, screen resolution, and display rate on computer-based test performance. *Applied Measurement in Education*, *16*(3), 191–205. doi:10.1207/S15324818AME1603_2

Brindley, E. J., Walti, C., & Zavachki-Richter, O. (2004). The current context of learner support in open, distance and online learning: An introduction. In J. E. Brindley, C. Walti, & O. Zawacki-Richter (Eds.), *Learner support in open, distance and online learning environments* (pp. 9–27). Oldenburg: BIS-Verlag der Carl von Ossietzky Universität Oldenburg.

Briz-Ponce, L., Pereira, A., Carvalho, L., Juanes-Méndez, J. A., & García-Peñalvo, F. J. (2017). Learning with mobile technologies–Students' behavior. *Computers in Human Behavior*, *72*, 612–620. doi:10.1016/j.chb.2016.05.027

Brooks, C., & Gibson, S. (2012). Professional Learning in a Digital Age. *Canadian Journal of Learning and Technology*, *38*(2), n2. doi:10.21432/T2HS3Q

Brown, J. S. (2002). *Growing Up Digital: How the Web Changes Work, Education, and the Ways People Learn*. United States Distance Learning Association. Retrieved from http://www.usdla.org/html/journal/FEB02_Issue/article01.html

Brown, J. S., & Duguid, P. (1991). Organizational learning and communities-of-practice: Toward a unified view of working, learning, and innovation. *Organization Science*, *2*(1), 40–57.

Bruce, B. C. (2008). *Ubiquitous learning, ubiquitous computing, and lived experience, Graduate School of Library and Information Science*. University of Illinois at Urbana-Champaign.

Budapest Open Access Initiative. (2002). Retrieved from http://www.budapestopenaccessinitiative.org/read

Bulock, C., Hosburgh, N., & Mann, S. (2015). OA in the library collection: The challenges of identifying and maintaining open access resources. *The Serials Librarian*, *68*(1-4), 79–86. doi:10.1080/0361526X.2015.1023690

Burbules, N. C. (2009). Meanings of ubiquitous learning. In B. Cope & M. Kalantzis (Eds.), *Ubiquitous learning* (pp. 15–20). Champaign, IL: University of Illinois Press.

Burgstahler, S. (2002a). Universal design of distance learning. *Information Technology and Disabilities E-Journal*, *8*(1). Retrieved December 17, 2017, from http://itd.athenpro.org/volume8/number1/burgstah.html

Burgstahler, S. (2002b). Distance learning: Universal design, universal access. *AACE Journal*, *10*(1), 32–61.

Calhoun, J. C. (1996). *The student learning imperative: implications for student affairs*. Washington, D.C.: American College Personnel Association. Retrieved from http://www.housing.berkeley.edu/student/ACPA_student_learning_imperative.pdf

Calimag, J. N. V., Miguel, P. A. G., Conde, R. S., & Aquino, L. B. (2014). Ubiquitous Learning Environment Using Android Mobile Application. *International Journal of Research in Engineering & Technology*, *2*(2), 119–128. Retrieved from http://oaji.net/articles/2014/489-1393936203.pdf

Compilation of References

Camilleri, M. A., & Camilleri, A. C. (2017). Digital Learning Resources and Ubiquitous Technologies in Education. *Technology. Knowledge and Learning*, *22*(1), 65–82. doi:10.100710758-016-9287-7

Canning, N. (2010). Playing with heutagogy: Exploring strategies to empower mature learners in higher education. *Journal of Further and Higher Education*, *34*(1), 59–71. doi:10.1080/03098770903477102

Canning, N., & Callan, S. (2010). Heutagogy: Spirals of reflection to empower learners in higher education. *Reflective Practice*, *11*(1), 71–82. doi:10.1080/14623940903500069

Canter, M. (2012). E-heutagogy for lifelong e-learning. *Proceedings of INSODE Procedia Technology*, 1, 129-131. 10.1016/j.protcy.2012.02.025

Cárdenas-Robledo, L. A., & Peña-Ayala, A. (2018). Ubiquitous learning: A systematic review. *Telematics and Informatics*, *35*(5), 1097–1132. doi:10.1016/j.tele.2018.01.009

Carswell, L., Thomas, P., Petre, M., Price, B., & Richards, M. (2000). Distance education via the Internet: A report on students' experiences. *British Journal of Educational Technology*, *31*(1), 29–46. doi:10.1111/1467-8535.00133

Casey, D. (2008). U-learning:Educational Models and System architectures. Handbook of Research on Instructional Systems and Technology.

Caswell, T., Henson, S., Jensen, M., & Wiley, D. (2014). February – 2008 Open Educational Resources : Enabling universal education. *International Review of Research in Open and Distance Learning*, *9*(1), 1–7.

Catherall, P. (2005). *Delivering e-learning for information services in higher education*. Oxford, UK: Chandos. doi:10.1533/9781780630731

Chan, T. W., Roschelle, J., Hsi, S., Kinshuk, Sharples, M., Brown, ... Hoppe, U. (2006). One-to-one technology-enhanced learning: An opportunity for global research collaboration. *Research and Practice in Technology Enhanced Learning*, *1*(1), 3–29. doi:10.1142/S1793206806000032

Chen, C. C., & Huang, T. C. (2012). Learning in a u-Museum: Developing a context-aware ubiquitous learning environment. *Computers & Education*, *59*(3), 873–883. doi:10.1016/j.compedu.2012.04.003

Chen, C. M., & Li, Y. L. (2010). Personalised context-aware ubiquitous learning system for supporting effective English vocabulary learning. *Interactive Learning Environments*, *18*(4), 341–364. doi:10.1080/10494820802602329

Cheng, Z., Han, Q., Sun, S., Kansen, M., Hosokawa, T., Huang, T., & He, A. (2006, April). A proposal on a learner's context-aware personalized education support method based on principles of behavior science. *20th International Conference on Advanced Information Networking and Applications (AINA'06)*, 1, 1-5. 10.1109/AINA.2006.50

Cheng, Z., Sun, S., Kansen, M., Huang, T., & He, A. (2005). A personalized ubiquitous education support environment by comparing learning instructional requirement with learner's behavior. In *19th International Conference on Advanced Information Networking and Applications (AINA'05)* (Vol. 2, pp. 567-573). IEEE. 10.1109/AINA.2005.46

Chen, M., Chiang, F. K., Jiang, N., & Yu, Q. (2017). A context-adaptive teacher training model in a ubiquitous learning environment. *Interactive Learning Environments*, *25*(1), 113–126. doi:10.1080/10494820.2016.1143845

Chen, Y. S., Kao, T. C., Sheu, J. P., & Chiang, C. Y. (2002). A mobile scaffolding-aid-based bird-watching learning system. In *Proceedings. IEEE International Workshop on Wireless and Mobile Technologies in Education* (pp. 15-22). IEEE. 10.1109/WMTE.2002.1039216

Chen, Y., Chen, N. S., & Tsai, C. C. (2009). The use of online synchronous discussion for web-based professional development for teachers. *Computers & Education*, *53*(4), 1155–1166. doi:10.1016/j.compedu.2009.05.026

Cher-Ping, L., & Libing, W. (2017). *Blended learning for quality higher education: Selected case studies on implementation from Asia-Pacific*. United Nations Educational, Scientific and Cultural Organization.

Chester, A., & Glass, C. A. (2006). Online counselling: A descriptive analysis of therapy services on the internet. *British Journal of Guidance & Counselling*, *34*(2), 145–160. doi:10.1080/03069880600583170

Chin, K. Y., Lee, K. F., & Chen, Y. L. (2018). Using an interactive ubiquitous learning system to enhance authentic learning experiences in a cultural heritage course. *Interactive Learning Environments*, *26*(4), 444–459. doi:10.1080/10494820.2017.1341939

Chin, K.-Y., & Chen, Y.-L. (2013). A Mobile Learning Support System for Ubiquitous Learning Environments. *Procedia: Social and Behavioral Sciences*, *73*, 14–21. doi:10.1016/j.sbspro.2013.02.013

Chiou, C. K., Tseng, J. C. R., Hwang, G. J., & Heller, S. (2010). An adaptive navigation support system for conducting context-aware ubiquitous learning in museums. *Computers & Education*, *55*(2), 834–845. doi:10.1016/j.compedu.2010.03.015

Chiu, C.-K., Tseng, J. C. R., & Hsu, T.-Y. (2017). Blended Context-Aware Ubiquitous Learning in Museums: Environment, Navigation Support and System Development. *Personal and Ubiquitous Computing*, *21*(2), 355–369. doi:10.100700779-016-0986-9

Chiu, P. S., Kuo, Y., Huang, Y., & Chen, T. (2008). A Meaningful Learning based u-Learning Evaluation Model. *Eighth IEEE International Conference on Advanced Learning Technologies*, 77–81. 10.1109/ICALT.2008.100

Choi, S. (2016). The flipside of ubiquitous connectivity enabled by smartphone-based social networking service: Social presence and privacy concern. *Computers in Human Behavior*, *65*, 325–333. doi:10.1016/j.chb.2016.08.039

Cho, V., Ro, J., & Littenberg-Tobias, J. (2013). What Twitter will and will not do: Theorizing about teachers' online professional communities. *Learning Landscapes*, *6*(2), 45–62.

Chowdhury, G. G., & Chowdhury, S. (2006). *E-learning support for LIS education in the UK*. Available at: http://www.ics.heacademy.ac.uk/Events/ HEADublin2006_V2/ papers/Gobinda%20Chowdhury%2014.pdf

Chu, H. (2010). Library and information science education in the digital age. Advances in Librarianship, 32, 77-111. doi:10.1108/S0065-2830(2010)0000032007

Chute, A., Thompson, M., & Hancock, B. (1999). *McGraw-Hill handbook of distance learning: An implementation guide for trainers and human resource professionals*. New York: McGraw-Hill.

Clancey, W. J. (1995). A tutorial on situated learning. In *Proceedings of the International Conference on Computers and Education (Taiwan)*. Charlottesville, VA: AACE.

Clayton Christensen Institute. (2019). *Models*. Retrieved May 9, 2019 from https://www.blendedlearning.org/models/

Cochrane, T., & Narayan, V. (2013). Redesigning professional development: Reconceptualising teaching using social learning technologies. *Research in Learning Technology*, *21*, 1–19. doi:10.3402/rlt.v21i0.19226

Cochran, S. W. (1983). The Delphi method: Formulating and refining group judgments. *Journal of Human Sciences*, *11*(2), 111–117.

Cohen, L., Manion, L., & Morrison, K. (2018). *Research methods in education*. New York, NY: Routledge.

Compilation of References

Collins Dictionary. (2019). *Definition of ubiquitous*. Retrieved from https://www.collinsdictionary.com/dictionary/english/ubiquitous

Collis, B., & Moonen, J. (2006). The contributing student: Learners as co-developers of learning resources for reuse in web environments. In D. Hung & M. S. Khine (Eds.), *Engaged learning with emerging technologies* (pp. 49–67). Dordrecht: Springer. doi:10.1007/1-4020-3669-8_3

Colvard, N. B., Watson, C. E., & Park, H. (2018). The impact of open educational resources on various student success metrics. *International Journal on Teaching and Learning in Higher Education*, *30*(2), 262–276. Retrieved from http://www.isetl.org/ijtlhe/

Connaway, L. S., White, D., Lanclos, D., & Le Cornu, A. (2014). Visitors and residents: What motivates engagement with the digital information environment? *Information Research, 18*(1). Retrieved from http://www.informationr.net/ir/18-1/paper556.html#.WNKwysDyu00

Connolly, T., & Stansfield, M. (2006). Using Games-Based eLearning Technologies in Overcoming Difficulties in Teaching Information Systems. *Journal of Information Technology Education Research*, *5*, 459–476.

Conole, G., Galley, R., & Culver, J. (2010). Frameworks for understanding the nature of interactions, networking, and community in a social networking site for academic practice. *The International Review Of Research In Open And Distributed Learning, 12*(3), 119-138. Retrieved from http://www.irrodl.org/index.php/irrodl/article/view/914/1666

Cormier, D. (2015). What was #rhizo15. *The Association for Learning Technology (ALT) Newsletter*. Retrieved from https://newsletter.alt.ac.uk/2015/07/what-was-rhizome15/

Couros, A. (2010). Developing Personal Learning Networks for Open and Social Learning. In G. Veletsianos (Ed.), *Emerging technologies in distance education*. Edmonton: Univ of British Columbia Pr.

Coursera. (2013). *Coursera blog*. Retrieved from http://coursera.tumblr.com/post/42486198362/five-courses-receive-college-credit

Coursera. (2018a). *Coursera | Online Courses Credentials by Top Educators*. Retrieved from https://www.coursera.org/

Coursera. (2018b). *Free courses*. Retrieved from https://www.coursera.org/courses?languages=en&query=free+courses

Coursera. (2019). *Partners | Coursera*. Retrieved from https://www.coursera.org/about/partners

Creswell, J. W., & Creswell, J. D. (2017). *Research design: Qualitative, quantitative, and mixed methods approaches*. Sage Publications.

Crompton, H. (2013). A historical overview of mobile learning: Toward learner-centered education. Handbook of Mobile Learning, 3-14.

Crompton, H., & Burke, D. (2018). The use of mobile learning in higher education: A systematic review. *Computers & Education*, *123*, 53–64. doi:10.1016/j.compedu.2018.04.007

Cross, J. (2007). *Informal learning: Rediscovering the natural pathways that inspire innovation and performance*. San Francisco, CA: Pfeiffer/John Wiley & Sons.

Crosslin, M. (2016). *Customizable Modality Pathway Learning Design: Exploring Personalized Learning Choices through a Lens of Self-Regulated Learning* (Doctoral dissertation). University of North Texas. Retrieved from https://digital.library.unt.edu/ark:/67531/metadc849703/

Cui, Y., & Bull, S. (2005). Context and learner modelling for the mobile foreign language learner. *System*, *33*(2), 353–367. doi:10.1016/j.system.2004.12.008

Curtis, M., Luchini, K., Bobrowsky, W., Quintana, C., & Soloway, E. (2002). Handheld use in K-12: A descriptive account. In *Proceedings. IEEE International Workshop on Wireless and Mobile Technologies in Education* (pp. 23-30). IEEE. 10.1109/WMTE.2002.1039217

Curzon, L. B., & Tummons, J. (2013). *Teaching in further education: An outline of principles and practice (7th ed.)*. Bloomsbury Academic.

Dabbagh, N., & Kitsantas, A. (2012). Personal learning environments, social media, and self-regulating learning: A natural formula for connecting formal and informal learning. *Internet and Higher Education*, *15*(1), 3–8. doi:10.1016/j.iheduc.2011.06.002

Dailey-Hebert, A., & Dennis, K. S. (2015). Introduction: New Opportunities for Development? In A. Dailey-Hebert & D. Kergel (Eds.), *Transformative Perspectives and Processes in Higher Education* (pp. 1–12). Cham: Springer. doi:10.1007/978-3-319-09247-8_1

Dalkey, N. C. (1972). The Delphi method: An experimental study of group opinion. In N. C. Dalkey, D. L. Rourke, R. Lewis, & D. Snyder (Eds.), Studies in the quality of life: Delphi and decision-making (pp. 13-54). Lexington, MA: Lexington Books.

Davies, R. S., Dean, D. L., & Ball, N. (2013). Flipping the classroom and instructional technology integration in a college-level information systems spreadsheet course. *Educational Technology Research and Development*, *61*(4), 563–580. doi:10.100711423-013-9305-6

Deci, E. L., & Ryan, R. M. (2002). *The handbook of self-determination research*. Rochester, NY: The University of Rochester Press.

DelCampo, R. G., Haggerty, L. A., & Haney, M. J. (2010). *Managing the multi-generational workforce: From the GI generation to the millennials*. Gower Publishing, Ltd.

Department of Disability Research and Statistical Turkey. (2006). *Türkiye özürlüler araştırması temel göstergeleri* [Main indicators of Turkey disability research]. Retrieved October 20, 2017, from http://www.engelsiz.hacettepe.edu.tr/belge/ozida.pdf

Diaz-Maggioli, G. (2004). *Teacher-centered professional development*. ASCD.

Dick, W., Carey, L., & Carey, J. O. (2009). *The systematic design of instruction*. Upper Saddle River, NJ: Merrill/Pearson.

Díez-Gutiérrez, E., & Díaz-Nafría, J. (2018). Ubiquitous learning ecologies for a critical cybercitizenship. *Comunicar*, (54), 49–58. doi:10.3916/C54-2018-05

Dillenbourg, P. (1999). *What do you mean by collaborative learning? Collaborative-learning: Cognitive and Computational Approaches*. Oxford, UK: Elsevier.

Dowling, M., & Rickwood, D. (2013). Online counseling and therapy for mental health problems: A systematic review of individual synchronous interventions using chat. *Journal of Technology in Human Services*, *31*(1), 1–21. doi:10.1080/15228835.2012.728508

Drage, K. (2010). Professional Development: Implications for Illinois Career and Technical Education Teachers. *Journal of Career and Technical Education*, *25*(2), 24–37. doi:10.21061/jcte.v25i2.477

Compilation of References

DuFour, R. (2004). What is a "professional learning community?". *Educational Leadership*, *61*(8), 6–11.

Dufour, R., & Eaker, R. (1998). *Professional learning communities at work: Best practices for enhancing student achievement*. Alexandria, VA: Association for Supervision and Curriculum Development.

Dunaway, M. (2011). Connectivism: Learning theory and pedagogical practice for networked information landscapes. *RSR. Reference Services Review*, *39*(4), 675–685. doi:10.1108/00907321111186686

Dunlap, J. C., & Lowenthal, P. R. (2009). Tweeting the night away: Using Twitter to enhance social presence. *Journal of Information Systems Education*, *20*(2).

Dunlap, J. C., & Lowenthal, P. R. (2014). The power of presence: Our quest for the right mix of social presence in online courses. In A. A. Piña & A. P. Mizell (Eds.), *Real life distance education: Case studies in practice* (pp. 41–66). Charlotte, NC: Information Age Publishing.

Dunlosky, J., Rawson, K. A., Marsh, E. J., Nathan, M. J., & Willingham, D. T. (2013). Improving Students' Learning With Effective Learning Techniques: Promising Directions From Cognitive and Educational Psychology. *Psychological Science in the Public Image*, *14*(1), 4–58. doi:10.1177/1529100612453266 PMID:26173288

Durak, G. (2017). Uzaktan eğitimde destek hizmetlerine genel bakış: Sorunlar ve eğilimler [A general outlook on the issue of support services in open and distance learning: trends and problems]. *Açıköğretim Uygulamaları ve Araştırmaları Dergisi*, *3*(4), 160–173.

Eachempati, P., Ks, K. K., Komattil, R., & Ismail, A. R. H. (2017). Heutagogy through Facebook for the Millennial learners. *MedEdPublish*, *6*(4), 25. doi:10.15694/mep.2017.000194

Edegbo, W. O. (2011). Curriculum development in library and information science education in Nigeria: Issues and prospects. *Library Philosophy and Practice*. Available at: http: www.webpages.uidaho.edu/~mbolin/edegbo.pdf

Edmonds, D. C. (2004). Providing access to students with disabilities in online distance education: Legal and technical concerns for higher education. *American Journal of Distance Education*, *18*(1), 51–62. doi:10.120715389286ajde1801_5

edX. (2014). *Schools and partners*. Retrieved from https://www.edx.org/schools-partners

edX. (2019). *edX Courses | View all online courses on edX.org*. Retrieved from https://www.edx.org/course

Edzan, N. N., & Abdullah, A. (2003). Looking back: The Master of Library and Information Science programme at the University of Malaya, Malaysia. *Malaysian Journal of Library and Information Science*, *8*(1), 1–8.

Efstathiou, G. (2009). Students' psychological web consulting: Function and outcome evaluation. *British Journal of Guidance & Counselling*, *37*(3), 243–255. doi:10.1080/03069880902956983

Egbert, J. (2009). *Supporting Learning with Technology: Essentials of Classroom Practice*. Upper Saddle River, NJ: Pearson Merrill Prentice Hall.

El-Hussein, M. O. M., & Cronje, J. C. (2010). Defining mobile learning in the higher education landscape. *Journal of Educational Technology & Society*, *13*(3), 12–21.

Elsafi, A. (2018). Formal and Informal Learning Using Mobile Technology. In S. Yu, M. Ally, & A. Tsinakos (Eds.), *Mobile and Ubiquitous Learning An International Handbook*. Singapore: Springer. doi:10.1007/978-981-10-6144-8_11

Erdoğdu, E., & Kesim, M. (2015). Ağ günlüklerinin kurumsal düzeyde kullanılması. *Açıköğretim Uygulamaları ve Araştırmaları Dergisi*, *1*(2), 8–23.

Ergüney, M. (2017). Uzaktan Eğitimde Mobil Öğrenme Teknolojilerinin Rolü. *Ulakbilge*, *5*(13), 1009–1021. doi:10.7816/ulakbilge-05-13-02

Erickson, A. S. G., Noonan, P. M., & McCall, Z. (2012). Effectiveness of online professional development for rural special educators. *Rural Special Education Quarterly*, *31*(1), 22–32. doi:10.1177/875687051203100104

Ezziane, Z. (2007). Information technology literacy: Implications on teaching and learning. *Journal of Educational Technology & Society*, *10*(3).

Fern, E. F., & Fern, E. E. (2001). Advanced focus group research. *Sage (Atlanta, Ga.)*.

Fiege, K. (2010). *Successful practices in supporting students in distributed learning; Meeting the needs of diverse students engaging in e-learning*. Calgary, Canada: Bow Walley.

Finfgeld, D. L. (1999). Psychotherapy in cyberspace. *Journal of the American Psychiatric Nurses Association*, *5*(4), 105–110. doi:10.1177/107839039900500401

Finn, J. (2002). MSW student perceptions of the efficacy and ethics of internet-based therapy. *Journal of Social Work Education*, *38*(3), 403–419. doi:10.1080/10437797.2002.10779107

Finn, J., & Banach, M. (2000). Victimization online: The down side of seeking human services for women on the internet. *Cyberpsychology & Behavior*, *3*(5), 243–254. doi:10.1089/109493100316102

Flior, E., & Kowalski, K. (2010, April). Continuous biometric user authentication in online examinations. In *Seventh International Conference on Information Technology (ITGN2010)* (pp. 488-492). Las Vegas, NV: Academic Press. 10.1109/ITNG.2010.250

Floyd, L. D., & Casey-Powell, D. (2004). New roles for student support services in distance learning. *New Directions for Community Colleges*, *2004*(128), 55–64. doi:10.1002/cc.175

Fons, T. (2016). Improving web visibility: Into the hands of readers. *Library Technology Reports*, *52*(5).

Fraenkel, J. R., & Wallen, N. E. (2011). *How to design and evaluate research in education*. New York: McGraw-Hill Humanities.

Fragou, O., Kameas, A., & Zaharakis, I. D. (2017). An instructional design process for creating a U-learning ecology. *2017 IEEE Global Engineering Education Conference (EDUCON)*, 1817-1823. 10.1109/EDUCON.2017.7943097

Frankland, J., & Ray, M. A. (2017). Traditional versus open access scholarly publishing: An economic perspective. *Journal of Scholarly Publishing*, *49*(1), 5–25. doi:10.3138/jsp.49.1.5

Freeland Fisher, J., & White, J. (2017). *From maverick to mainstream: Takeaways from the 2017 blended and personalized learning conference*. Retrieved June 5, 2019 from https://files.eric.ed.gov/fulltext/ED586384.pdf

Fry, H., Ketteridge, S., & Marshall, S. (2015). A Handbook for Teaching and Learning in Higher Education (4th ed.). Academic Press.

Fry, H., Ketteridge, S., & Marshall, S. (2009). Understanding student learning. In H. Fry, S. Ketteridge, & S. Marshall (Eds.), *A Handbook for Teaching and Learning in the Higher Education: Enhancing Academic Practice (3rd ed.)*. New York: Routledge.

Compilation of References

Gaebel, M. (2013). *MOOCs – Massive Open Online Courses*. Retrieved from http://www.leru.org/files/meetings/A3_EUA_Occasional_papers_MOOCs.pdf%5Cnhttp://www.leru.org/index.php/private/communities/vice-rectors-for-learning-and-teaching/

Gagné, R. M., Wager, W. W., Goals, K., & Keller, J. (2005). *Principles of instructional design*. Belmont, CA: Wadsworth.

Galbraith, M. W. (2017). Philosophy and the instructional process. *Adult Learning, 11*(2), 11–13. doi:10.1177/104515959901100204

García-Sánchez, S. (2016). Ubiquitous interaction for ESP distance and blended learners. *Journal of Applied Research in Higher Education, 8*(4), 489–503. doi:10.1108/JARHE-04-2014-0052

Gardner, A., Hase, S., Gardner, G., Dunn, S. V., & Carryer, J. (2008). From competence to capability: A study of nurse practitioners in clinical practice. *Journal of Clinical Nursing, 17*(2), 250–258. PMID:17419787

Garrison, D. R. (2007). Online community of inquiry review: Social, cognitive, and teaching presence issues. *Journal of Asynchronous Learning Networks, 11*(1), 61–72.

Garrison, D. R., Anderson, T., & Archer, W. (2000). Critical inquiry in a text-based environment: Computer conferencing in higher education. *The Internet and Higher Education, 2*(2-3), 87–105. doi:10.1016/S1096-7516(00)00016-6

Garrison, D. R., Anderson, T., & Archer, W. (2001). Critical thinking, cognitive presence, and computer conferencing in distance education. *American Journal of Distance Education, 15*(1), 7–23. doi:10.1080/08923640109527071

Garrison, D. R., & Vaughan, N. D. (2008). *Blended learning in higher education: Framework, principles, and guidelines*. Wiley.

Gatti, F. M., Brivio, E., & Calciano, S. (2016). Hello! I know you help people here, right? A qualitative study of young people's acted motivations in text-based counseling. *Children and Youth Services Review, 71*, 27–35. doi:10.1016/j.childyouth.2016.10.029

Georgas, H. (2015). Google vs. the library (part III): Assessing the quality of sources found by undergraduates. *Libraries & The Academy, 15*(1), 131–161. doi:10.1353/pla.2015.0012

Gerber, L. (2013). *What is the difference between Open Distance Learning and Distance Learning*. Pretoria: University of South Africa. Retrieved from https://www.careersportal.co.za/education/universities/what-is-the-difference-between-open-distance-learning-and-distance-learning

Gerhart, N. (2017). Technology Addiction: How Social Network Sites Impact Our Lives. *Informing Science, 20*.

Giannarou, L., & Zervas, E. (2014). Using Delphi technique to build consensus in practice. *International Journal of Business Science and Applied Management, 9*(2), 65–82.

Gillett-Swan, J. (2017). The Challenges of Online Learning Supporting and Engaging the Isolated Learner. *Journal of Learning Design, 10*(1), 20–30. doi:10.5204/jld.v9i3.293

Gill, P., Stewart, K., Treasure, E., & Chadwick, B. (2008). Methods of data collection in qualitative research: Interviews and focus groups. *British Dental Journal, 204*(6), 291–295. doi:10.1038/bdj.2008.192 PMID:18356873

Giorgi, A., & Giorgi, B. (2009). Phenomenology. In J. A. Smith (Ed.), *Qualitative psychology: A practical guide to research methods* (pp. 26–52). Los Angeles, CA: Sage.

Gkiosos, I., Mavroeidis, I., & Koutsoumpa, M. (2008). Η έρευνα στην από απόσταση εκπαίδευση: Ανασκόπηση και προοπτικές [Distance education research: Review and prospects]. *Open Education-The Journal for Open and Distance Education and Educational Technology, 4*(1), 49–60.

Glatthorn, A. A., Boschee, F., & Whitehead, B. M. (2009). *Curriculum leadership: Strategies for development and implementation (2nd ed.).* Los Angeles, CA: Sage.

Godwin-Jones, R. (2018). *Six models of blended learning: Part 2.* Retrieved June 10, 2019 from https://blog.softchalk.com/six-models-of-blended-learning-part-2

Google Scholar. (n.d.). *Inclusion guidelines for webmasters.* Retrieved from https://scholar.google.com/intl/en/scholar/inclusion.html

Govindasamy, T. (2002). Successful implementation of e-learning pedagogical considerations. *The Internet and Higher Education, 4*(3/4), 287–299.

Graf, S. (2008). Adaptivity and personalization in ubiquitous learning systems. In *Symposium of the Austrian HCI and Usability Engineering Group* (pp. 331-338). Springer. 10.1007/978-3-540-89350-9_23

Graham, C. R., Borup, J., Short, C. R., & Archambault, L. (2019). *K-12 Blended Teaching: A Guide to Personalized Learning and Online Integration.* Ed Tech Books. Teacher Edition Version 1.0. Retrieved May 5, 2019 from https://drive.google.com/file/d/1P-2nftugd8ALWddD50tsXxrpZpkDvucT/view

Graham, C. R. (2006). Blended learning systems: Definition, current trends, and future directions. In C. J. Bonk & C. R. Graham (Eds.), *Handbook of blended learning: Global perspectives, local designs.* San Francisco: Pfeiffer Publishing.

Grant, J. (2002). Learning needs assessment: Assessing the need. *BMJ (Clinical Research Ed.), 324*(7330), 156–159. doi:10.1136/bmj.324.7330.156 PMID:11799035

Gravani, M. N., Hatzinikita, V., & Zarifis, G. K. (2012). Factors influencing adult distance teaching and learning processes: The case of the Open University. *International Journal of Learning, 18*(5), 307–319.

Greene, J. C., Caracelli, V. J., & Graham, W. F. (1989). Toward a conceptual framework for mixed-method evaluation designs. *Educational Evaluation and Policy Analysis, 11*(3), 255–274. doi:10.3102/01623737011003255

Green, R. A. (2014). The Delphi technique in educational research. *SAGE Open, 4*(2), 1–8. doi:10.1177/2158244014529773

Gros, B. K., & Maina, M. (Eds.). (2016). The future of ubiquitous learning. Berlin: Springer.

Grose, M. (2011). *XYZ: The new rules of generational warfare.* Random House Australia.

Groves, R. M., Fowler, F. J. Jr, Couper, M. P., Lepkowski, J. M., Singer, E., & Tourangeau, R. (2011). *Survey Methodology.* John Wiley & Sons.

Gülbahar, Y., Kalelioğlu, F., & Madran, O. (2010). Sosyal ağların eğitim amaçlı kullanımı. *XV. Türkiye'de İnternet Konferansı.* İstanbul Teknik Üniversitesi.

Gunawardena, C. N., Hermans, M. B., Sanchez, D., Richmond, C., Bohley, M., & Tuttle, R. (2009). A theoretical framework for building online communities of practice with social networking tools. *Educational Media International, 46*(1), 3–16. doi:10.1080/09523980802588626

Gunawardena, C. N., & McIsaac, M. S. (2004). Distance education. In D. H. Jonassen (Ed.), *Handbook of research on educational communications and technology.* London: Lawrence Erlbaum Associates Publishers.

Compilation of References

Gunawardena, C. N., & Zittle, F. J. (1997). Social presence as a predictor of satisfaction within a computer-mediated conferencing environment. *American Journal of Distance Education, 11*(3), 8–26. doi:10.1080/08923649709526970

Haberstroh, S., Parr, G., Bradley, L., Morgan-Fleming, B., & Gee, R. (2008). Facilitating online counseling: Perspectives from counselors in training. *Journal of Counseling and Development, 86*(4), 460–470. doi:10.1002/j.1556-6678.2008.tb00534.x

Hahn, S. E., & Wyatt, A. (2014). Business faculty's attitudes: Open access, disciplinary repositories, and institutional repositories. *Journal of Business & Finance Librarianship, 19*(2), 93–113. doi:10.1080/08963568.2014.883875

Hammersley, M., & Atkinson, P. (2007). *Ethnography: Principles in practice*. Routledge. doi:10.4324/9780203944769

Hartnett, M. (2016). *Motivation in Online Education*. Singapore: Springer; doi:10.1007/978-981-10-0700-2

Hartnett, M., George, A. S., & Zealand, N. (2011). Examining Motivation in Online Distance Learning Environments : Complex, Multifaceted, and Situation-Dependent. *International Review of Research in Open and Distance Learning, 12*(6), 20–38. doi:10.19173/irrodl.v12i6.1030

Harzing, A., & Adler, N. J. (2016). Disseminating knowledge: From potential to reality– New open-access journals collide with convention. *Academy of Management Learning & Education, 15*(1), 140–156. doi:10.5465/amle.2013.0373

Hase, S. (2011). Learner defined curriculum: heutagogy and action learning in vocational training. *Southern Institute of Technology Journal of Applied Research*. Retrieved from https://www.sit.ac.nz/Portals/0/upload/documents/sitjar/SITJAR%20AR%20edition%20A.pdf 25.04.2019

Hase, S. (2016). Self-determined learning (heutagogy) - Where have we come since 2000? *Southern Institute of Technology Journal of Applied Research (SITJAR)*. Retrieved from https://www.sit.ac.nz/Portals/0/upload/documents/sitjar/Heutagogy - One.pdf

Hase, S., & Kenyon, C. (2000). *From andragogy to heutagogy*. Retrieved from: http://pandora.nla.gov.au/nph-wb/20010220130000/http://ultibase.rmit.edu.au/Articles/dec00/hase2.htm 12.02.2019

Hase, S., & Kenyon, C. (2013). The Nature of Learning. In S. Hase & C. Kenyon (Eds.), Self-Determined Learning: Heutagogy in Action (pp. 19-35). London, UK: Bloomsburry Publishing.

Hase, S. (2009). Heutagogy and e-learning in the workplace: Some challenges and opportunities. *Impact: Journal of Applied Research in Workplace E-learning, 1*(1), 43–52.

Hase, S., & Davis, L. (1999). Developing capable employees: The work activity briefing. *Journal of Workplace Learning, 11*(8), 298–303. doi:10.1108/13665629910300432

Hase, S., & Kenyon, C. (2007). Heutagogy: A child of complexity theory. *Complicity: An International Journal of Complexity and Education, 4*(1), 111–119. doi:10.29173/cmplct8766

Heidkamp, B., & Kergel, D. (2018). From e-learning to eBlogna in an Augmented Reality The past and Future of E-Learning in German Higher Education. In D. Kergel, B. Heidkamp, P. Kjaersdam Telleus, T. Rachwal, & Nowakowski (Eds.), The digital turn in Higher education: International Perspectives on Learning and Teaching in a Changing World (pp. 37-45). Wiesbaden, Germany: Springer.

Helmer, O. (1977). Problems in futures research: Delphi and causal cross-impact analysis. *Futures, 9*(1), 17–31. doi:10.1016/0016-3287(77)90049-0

Herie, M. (2013). Andragogy 2.0? Teaching and Learning in the Global Classroom: Heutagogy and Paragogy. *Global Citizen Digest, 2*(2), 8–14.

Hill, M., Sharma, M. D., & Johnston, H. (2015). How online learning modules can improve the representational fluency and conceptual understanding of university physics students. *European Journal of Physics, 36*(4), 1–20. doi:10.1088/0143-0807/36/4/045019

Hodkinson, P., Colley, H., & Malcolm, J. (2003). The interrelationships between informal and formal learning. *Journal of Workplace Learning, 15*(7/8), 313–318. doi:10.1108/13665620310504783

Holmberg, B. (1995). *Theory and practice of distance education* (2nd ed.). London: Routledge.

Hord, S. M. (1997). *Professional learning communities: Communities of continuous inquiry and improvement.* Austin, TX: Southwest Educational Development Laboratory.

Hord, S. M. (2004). Professional learning communities: An overview. In S. Hord (Ed.), *Learning together, leading together: Changing schools through professional learning communities* (pp. 5–14). New York: Teacher College Press.

Howell, S. L., Williams, P. B., & Lindsay, N. K. (2003). Thirty-two trends affecting distance education: An informed foundation for strategic planning. *Online Journal of Distance Learning Administration, 6*(3), 1–18.

Hrynaszkiewicz, I., & Cockerill, M. J. (2012). Open by default: A proposed copyright license and waiver agreement for open access research and data in peer-reviewed journals. *BMC Research Notes, 5*(1), 494–505. doi:10.1186/1756-0500-5-494 PMID:22958225

Huang, Y. M., Chiu, P. S., Liu, T. C., & Chen, T. S. (2011). The design and implementation of a meaningful learning-based evaluation method for ubiquitous learning. *Computers & Education, 57*(4), 2291–2302. doi:10.1016/j.compedu.2011.05.023

Hung, J.-L., & Zhang, K. (2012). Examining Mobile Learning Trends 2003-2008: A Categorical Meta-Trend Analysis Using Text Mining. *Journal of Computing in Higher Education, 24*(1), 1–17. doi:10.100712528-011-9044-9

Hung, P.-H., Hwang, G.-J., Lee, Y.-H., Wu, T.-H., Vogel, B., Milrad, M., & Johansson, E. (2014). A Problem-based Ubiquitous Learning Approach to Improving the Questioning Abilities of Elementary School Students. *Journal of Educational Technology & Society, 17*(4), 316–334.

Hwang, G. J., Tsai, C. C., & Yang, S. J. H. (2008). Criteria, strategies and research issues of context-aware ubiquitous learning. *Journal of Educational Technology & Society, 11*(2), 81–91.

Hwang, G. J., Yang, T. C., Tsai, C. C., & Yang, S. J. H. (2009). A context-aware ubiquitous learning environment for conducting complex science experiments. *Computers & Education, 53*(2), 402–413. doi:10.1016/j.compedu.2009.02.016

Hwang, G.-J., Wu, C.-H., Tseng, J. C. R., & Huang, I. (2011). Development of a ubiquitous learning platform based on a real-time help-seeking mechanism. *British Journal of Educational Technology, 42*(6), 992–1002. doi:10.1111/j.1467-8535.2010.01123.x

Hwang, G.-J., & Wu, P.-H. (2014). Applications, impacts and trends of mobile technology-enhanced learning: A review of 2008-2012 publications in selected SSCI journals. *Int. J. of Mobile Learning and Organisation, 8*(2), 83–95. doi:10.1504/IJMLO.2014.062346

Hwang, G.-J., Wu, P.-H., & Ke, H.-R. (2011). An interactive concept map approach to supporting mobile learning activities for natural science courses. *Computers & Education, 57*(4), 2272–2280. doi:10.1016/j.compedu.2011.06.011

Compilation of References

Hysong, S. J. (2008). The role of technical skill in perceptions of managerial performance. *Journal of Management Development, 27*(3), 275–290. doi:10.1108/02621710810858605

IFLA. (2009). *Guidelines for professional library/informational educational programmes.* Available at: http://archive.ifla.org/VII/s23/bulletin/guidelines.htm

Ilgaz, H., & Aşkar, P. (2009). Çevrimiçi uzaktan eğitim ortamında topluluk hissi ölçeği geliştirme çalışması. *Turkish Journal of Computer and Mathematics Education, 1*(1), 27–34.

Illich, I. (2006). *Okulsuz toplum.* İstanbul: Oda Yayınları.

Ilomäki, L., Kantosalo, A., & Lakkala, M. (2011). *What is digital competence? 2. Digital competence is an evolving concept.* Retrieved from https://tuhat.helsinki.fi/portal/files/48681684/Ilom_ki_etal_2011_What_is_digital_competence.pdf

Internet Society. (2017). *Internet Access and education: Key considerations for policy makers.* Retrieved from https://cdn.prod.internetsociety.org/wp-content/uploads/2017/11/Internet-Access-Education_2017120.pdf

Internetlivestats. (2019, 17 February). Retrieved from http://www.internetlivestats.com/

Islam, M. S., Chowdhury, S., & Islam, M. A. (2009). *LIS education in e-learning environment: Problems and proposal for Bangladesh.* Paper presented at the Asia-Pacific Conference on Library and Information Education and Practice held at the University, Tsukuba, Japan.

Islam, M. S., Kunifuji, S., Hayama, T., & Miura, M. (2011). Towards exploring a global Scenario of e-learning in library and information science schools. *The International Information & Library Review, 43*(1), 15–22. doi:10.1080/10572317.2011.10762876

ISTE. (2017). *ISTE Standards for Educators.* Retrieved form https://www.iste.org/standards/for-educators

Izmirli, S. (2017). Can we use Facebook groups to establish social presence in online courses? *World Journal on Educational Technology: Current Issues, 9*(4), 173–182.

Jack, J. (2017). Free-to-publish, free-to-read, or both? Cost, equality of access, and integrity in science publishing. *Journal of the Association for Information Science and Technology, 68*(6), 1584–1589. doi:10.1002/asi.23757

Jackson, N. J. (n.d.) Lifewide learning and education in universities & colleges: Concepts and conceptual Aids. In N. Jackson & J. Willis (Eds.), *Lifewide learning and education in universities & colleges* (pp. 1-27). Academic Press. Retrieved May 20, 2019, from http://www.learninglives.co.uk/uploads/1/0/8/4/10842717/chapter_a1.pdf

Jackson, S. L. (2011). Research methods and Statistics: a critical approach. *Cengage Learning, 17.*

Jamaludin, A., Hussin, N., & Mokhtar, W. N. H. W. (2006). Library and information career in Malaysia: Aspirations of educators and the reality of the industry. In Khoo, C., Singh, D. & Chaudry, A.S. (Eds.), *Proceedings of the Asia-Pacific Conference on Library & Information Education & Practice (A-LIEP),* (pp. 423-426). Academic Press.

Jansen, B. J., & Spink, A. (2006). How are we searching the World Wide Web? A comparison of nine search engine transaction logs. *Information Processing & Management, 42*(1), 248–263. doi:10.1016/j.ipm.2004.10.007

Johnson, L., Smith, R., Willis, H., Levine, A., & Haywood, K. (2011). *The 2011 Horizon Report.* Austin, TX: The New Media Consortium.

Johnson, R. B., & Onwuegbuzie, A. J. (2004). Mixed methods research: A research paradigm whose time has come. *Educational Researcher, 33*(7), 14–26. doi:10.3102/0013189X033007014

Johnson, R. D., Hornik, S., & Salas, E. (2008). An empirical examination of factors contributing to the creation of successful e-learning environments. *International Journal of Human-Computer Studies*, *66*(5), 356–369. doi:10.1016/j.ijhcs.2007.11.003

Jomah, O., Masoud, A. K., Kishore, X. P., & Aurelia, S. (2016). Micro learning: A modernized education system. BRAIN. *Broad Research in Artificial Intelligence and Neuroscience*, *7*(1), 103–110.

Jones, V., & Jo, J. H. (2004). Ubiquitous learning environment: An adaptive teaching system using ubiquitous technology [Ambiente de aprendizaje ubicuo: Un sistema de enseñanza adaptativa utilizando tecnología ubicua]. *Beyond the Comfort Zone: Proceedings of the 21st ASCILITE Conference*, 468–474.

Jones-Roberts, C. A. (2018). Increasing social presence online: Five strategies for instructors. *FDLA Journal*, *3*.

Jones, V., & Jo, J. H. (2005). *Ubiquitous learning environment: An adaptive teaching system using ubiquitous technology*. School of Information Technology Griffith University.

Joordens, S. (2019). *Introduction to Psychology - Home | Coursera*. Retrieved from https://www.coursera.org/learn/introduction-psych/home/welcome

Jung, H.-J. (2014). Ubiquitous Learning: Determinants Impacting Learners' Satisfaction and Performance With Smartphones. *Language Learning & Technology*, *18*(3), 97–119. doi:10.21614/chirurgia.111.5.379

Junqi, W., & Yumei, L. (2010). Study of Instructional design in Ubiquitous Learning. *2010 Second International Workshop on Education Technology and Computer Science*. 10.1109/ETCS.2010.522

Kala, S. (2009). *Development of an electronic learning programme for enhancing comprehensive midwifery competency among undergraduate Nursing students* (PhD Thesis). Prince Songkla University.

Kalaivani, R., & Sivakumar, R. (2017). A Survey on context-aware ubiquitous learning systems. *International Journal of Control Theory and Applications*, *10*(23), 111–124.

KALIPER. (2000). *Educating Library and Information Science Professionals for a New Century: The KALIPER Report*. Reston, VA: ALISE. Available at: http://durrance.people.si.umich.edu/TextDocs/KaliperFinalR.pdf

Karavakou, V. (2011). Το φάσμα και η πρό(σ)κληση της δια βίου μάθησης [The spectrum and call/challenge for lifelong learning]. In V. Karavakou (Ed.), *Lifelong learning: Interdisciplinary approaches* (pp. 1–32). Thessaloniki, Greece: University of Macedonia Press.

Kargın, T. (2007). Eğitsel değerlendirme ve bireyselleştirilmiş eğitim programı hazırlama süreci. *Ankara Üniversitesi Eğitim Bilimleri Fakültesi Özel Eğitim Dergisi*, *8*(1), 1-16.

Karimi, S. (2016). Do learners' characteristics matter? An exploration of mobile-learning adoption in self-directed learning. *Computers in Human Behavior*, *63*, 769–776. doi:10.1016/j.chb.2016.06.014

Keast, A. D. (1997). Toward an effective model for implementing distance education programs. *American Journal of Distance Education*, *11*(2), 39–55. doi:10.1080/08923649709526960

Kebritchi, M., Lipschuetz, A., & Santiague, L. (2017). Issues and Challenges for Teaching Successful Online Courses in Higher Education. *Journal of Educational Technology Systems*, *46*(1), 4–29. doi:10.1177/0047239516661713

Keegan, D. (2003). Introduction. In H. Fritsch (Ed.), The role of student services in e-learning systems (pp. 1-6). ZIFF.

Compilation of References

Keegan, D. (2005, October). The incorporation of mobile learning into mainstream education and training. In *World Conference on Mobile Learning, Cape Town* (p. 11). Academic Press.

Keegan, D. J. (1980). On defining distance education. *Distance Education, 1*(1), 13–36. doi:10.1080/0158791800010102

Kentnor, H. (2015). Distance education and the evolution of online learning in the United States. *Curriculum and Teaching Dialogue, 17*(1 &2), 21–34.

Kenyon, C., & Hase, S. (2013). Heutagogy Fundamentals. In S. Hase & C. Kenyon (Eds.), Self-Determined Learning: Heutagogy in Action (pp. 7-17). London, UK: Bloomsburry Publishing.

Kenyon, C., & Hase, S. (2010). Andragogy and heutagogy in postgraduate work. In T. Kerry (Ed.), *Meeting the challenges of change in postgraduate education* (pp. 165–187). London: Continuum Press.

Kidd, J. M. (2006). *Understanding career counselling: Theory, research and practice*. London: Sage Publications.

Kilis, S. (2013). Impacts of Mobile Learning in Motivation, Engagement and Achievement of Learners: Review of Literature. *Gaziantep University Journal of Social Sciences, 12*(2).

Kim, B. (2013). Responsive web design, discoverability and mobile challenge. *Library Technology Reports, 49*(6), 29–39.

Kimbrough, J. L., & Gasaway, L. N. (2016). Publication of government-funded research, open access, and the public interest. *Vanderbilt Journal of Entertainment & Technology Law, 18*(2), 267–302. Retrieved from http://www.jetlaw.org/wp-content/uploads/2016/03/KimbroughGasaway_SPE_7-FINAL.pdf

Kim, D., Ruecker, D., & Kim, D.-J. (2017). Mobile Assisted Language Learning Experiences. *International Journal of Mobile and Blended Learning, 9*(1), 49–66. doi:10.4018/IJMBL.2017010104

Kim, I., Jung, G., Jung, H., Ko, M., & Lee, U. (2017). Let's FOCUS: Mitigating Mobile Phone Use in College Classrooms. *Proceedings of the ACM on Interactive, Mobile, Wearable and Ubiquitous Technologies, 1*(3), 63. 10.1145/3130928

Kim, J. A. (2000). *Community Building on the Web: Secret strategies for successful online communities*. Berkeley, CA: Peachpit Press.

Kinshuk & Huang. (2015). Ubiquitous Learning Environments and Technologies. Berlin, Germany: Springer Berlin Heidelberg.

Kinshuk, & Graf, S. (2012). Ubiquitous Learning. In *Encyclopedia of the Sciences of Learning*. Springer.

Kirschner, P. A., & Van Merriënboer, J. J. G. (2008). Ten steps to complex learning: A new approach to instruction and instructional design. In T. L. Good (Ed.), 21st century education: A reference handbook (pp. 244-253). Thousand Oaks, CA: Sage. doi:10.4135/9781412964012.n26

Kitzinger, J. (1995). Qualitative research: Introducing focus groups. *British Medical Journal, 311*(7000), 299–302. doi:10.1136/bmj.311.7000.299 PMID:7633241

Kocken, G. J., & Wical, S. H. (2013). "I've never heard of it before": Awareness of open access at a small liberal arts university. *Behavioral & Social Sciences Librarian, 32*(3), 140–154. doi:10.1080/01639269.2013.817876

Kolomvatsos, K. (2007). Ubiquitous Computing Applications in Education. In *Ubiquitous and Pervasive Knowledge and Learning Management: Semantics, Social Networking and New Media to Their Full Potential* (pp. 94–117). London: IGI Global.

Kop, R., & Hill, A. (2008). Connectivism: Learning theory of the future or vestige of the past? *International Review of Research in Open and Distance Learning, 9*(3). doi:10.19173/irrodl.v9i3.523

Kreijns, K., Kirschner, P. A., Jochems, W., & Van Buuren, H. (2007). Measuring perceived sociability of computer-supported collaborative learning environments. *Computers & Education, 49*(2), 176–192. doi:10.1016/j.compedu.2005.05.004

Krueger, R. A., & Casey, M. A. (2014). *Focus groups: A practical guide for applied research*. Sage publications.

Kuh, G. D. (1996). Guiding principles for creating seamless learning environments for undergraduates. *Journal of College Student Development, 37*(2), 135–148.

Kukulska-Hulme, A., & Shield, L. (2007). An overview of Mobile Assisted Language Learning: Can mobile devices support collaborative practice in speaking and listening. *EuroCALL, 2007*, 1–20. doi:10.1017/S0958344008000335

Kukulska-Hulme, A., & Viberg, O. (2018). Mobile collaborative language learning: State of the art. *British Journal of Educational Technology, 49*(2), 207–218. doi:10.1111/bjet.12580

Kurşun, E. (2016). Açık eğitim kaynaklari. In *Öğretim Teknolojilerinin Temelleri Teoriler, Araştırmalar* (pp. 667–682). Eğilimler.

Kwon, S. (2011). Technical, educational issues and challenges in ubiquitous learning. In *2011 International Conference on Pattern Analysis and Intelligent Robotics (ICPAIR 2011)*. Putrajaya, Malaysia, *20110628* (p. 183). IEEE. 10.1109/ICPAIR.2011.5976940

La Guardia, J. G. (2009). Developing Who I Am: A Self-Determination Theory Approach to the Establishment of Healthy Identities. *Educational Psychologist, 44*(2), 90–104. doi:10.1080/00461520902832350

Laisema, S., & Wannapiroon, P. (2013). Development of a Collaborative Learning with Creative Problem-Solving Process Model in Ubiquitous Learning Environment. *International Journal of e-Education, e-Business, e- Management Learning, 3*(2), 102–106.

Lalonde, C. (2011). *The Twitter experience: The role of Twitter in the formation and maintenance of personal learning networks* (Doctoral dissertation). Royal Roads University.

Lapadula, M. (2003). Comprehensive look at online student support services for distance learners. *American Journal of Distance Education, 17*(2), 119–128. doi:10.1207/S15389286AJDE1702_4

Lave, J. (1991). Situating learning in communities of practice. *Perspectives on Socially Shared Cognition, 2*, 63-82.

Lave, J., & Wenger, E. (1991). *Situated Learning: Legitimate peripheral participation*. New York: Cambridge University Press. doi:10.1017/CBO9780511815355

Lawal, O. O. (2000). *Professional education for librarianship: International perspectives. Calabar*. University of Calabar Press.

Lawrence, C. N., & Lester, J. A. (2018). Evaluating the effectiveness of adopting open educational resources in an introductory American Government course. *Journal of Political Science Education, 14*(4), 555–566. doi:10.1080/15512169.2017.1422739

Lee, H. J. (2005). Developing a Professional Development Program Model Based on Teachers' Needs. *Professional Educator, 27*, 39–49.

Compilation of References

Lee, Y. J. (2012). Developing an efficient computational method that estimates the ability of students in a Web-based learning environment. *Computers & Education*, *58*(1), 579–589. doi:10.1016/j.compedu.2011.09.008

Leone, S. (2013). Characterisation of a personal learning environment as a lifelong learning tool. New York: Springer Science+ Business Media. doi:10.1007/978-1-4614-6274-3

Leone, S., & Leo, T. (2011). The synergy of paper-based and digital material for ubiquitous foreign language learners. *Knowledge Management & E-Learning: An International Journal*, *3*(3), 319–341.

Lester, J. (2011). Use of adjunct faculty in the delivery of distance education in ALA-Accredited LIS Master's programmes in the U.S. and Canada. *Journal of Education for Library and Information Science*, *52*(3), 212–237.

Letseka, M., Letseka, M., & Pitsoe, V. (2018). The challenges of e-Learning in South Africa. In M. Sinecen (Ed.), *Trends in e-Learning*. London: IntechOpen. doi:10.5772/intechopen.74843

Lewis, B., & Rush, D. (2013). Experience of developing Twitter-based communities of practice in higher education. *Research in Learning Technology*, *21*.

Li, L., Zheng, Y., Ogata, H., & Yano, Y. (2005). A Conceptual framework of computer-supported Ubiquitous Learning Environment. In *4th IASTED International Conference on Web-Based Education, WBE 2005* (pp. 243-248). Academic Press. 10.2316/Journal.208.2005.4.208-0861

Linguistic Society of America (LSA). (2013). *Changes to LSA publications (2013)*. Retrieved from http://www.linguisticsociety.org/content/update-status-lsa-publications

Lin, H. C. (2002). Current research in organizational systems: Higher education. *Futurics*, *26*(1-2), 11–19.

Lin, N. (1976). *Foundations of social research*. McGraw-Hill Companies.

Liu, S., Ogata, H., & Mouri, K. (2015). Accelerate location-based context learning for second language learning using ubiquitous learning log. In Emerging issues in smart learning. Springer. doi:10.1007/978-3-662-44188-6_7

Liu, G., & Hwang, G. (2010). A key step to understanding paradigm shifts in e-learning. *British Journal of Educational Technology*, *41*(2), E1–E9. doi:10.1111/j.1467-8535.2009.00976.x

Liu, Q., Peng, W., Zhang, F., Hu, R., Li, Y., & Yan, W. (2016). The effectiveness of blended learning in health professions: Systematic review and metaanalysis. *Journal of Medical Internet Research*, *18*(1), e2. doi:10.2196/jmir.4807 PMID:26729058

Lombardi, M. M. (2007). *Authentic learning for the 21st century: an overview*. Retrieved June 18, 2019 from https://net.educause.edu/ir/library/pdf/ELI3009.pdf

Looi, C. K., So, H. J., Chen, W., Zhang, B., Wong, L. H., & Seow, P. (2012). Seamless Learning. In N. M. Seel (Ed.), *Encyclopedia of the Sciences of Learning*. Boston, MA: Springer. doi:10.1007/978-1-4419-1428-6_251

Looi, C. K., Zhang, B., Chen, W., Seow, P., Chia, G., Norris, C., & Soloway, E. (2011). 1: 1 mobile inquiry learning experience for primary science students: A study of learning effectiveness. *Journal of Computer Assisted Learning*, *27*(3), 269–287. doi:10.1111/j.1365-2729.2010.00390.x

Looi, C., & Peter, S. (2010). Leveraging mobile technology for sustainable seamless learning: A research agenda. *British Journal of Educational Technology*, *41*(2), 154–169. doi:10.1111/j.1467-8535.2008.00912.x

Lowenthal, P. R., & Dunlap, J. C. (2018). Investigating students' perceptions of instructional strategies to establish social presence. *Distance Education*, *39*(3), 281–298. doi:10.1080/01587919.2018.1476844

Lundin, J., & Nulden, U. (2003). Mobile scenarios: Supporting collaborative learning among mobile workers. *Educating Managers with Tomorrow's Technologies*, 173-190.

Lyytinen, K., & Yoo, Y. (2002). Issues and challenges in ubiquitous computing. *Communications of the ACM*, *45*(12), 63–65.

Lyytinen, K., & Yoo, Y. (2002). Research Commentary: Issues and challenges in ubiquitous computing. *Communications of the ACM*, *45*(12), 62–65.

Mackness, J., & Tschofen, C. (2012). Connectivism and dimensions of individual experience. *International Review of Research in Open and Distance Learning*, *13*(1). Retrieved from http://www.irrodl.org/index.php/irrodl/article/view/1143

MacMillan, D., & MacMillan, R. (2018). Google exposed user data, feared repercussions of disclosing to public. *The Wall Street Journal*. Retrieved May 20, 2019, from https://www.wsj.com/articles/google-exposed-user-data-feared-repercussions-of-disclosing-to-public-1539017194

Mallen, M. J., & Vogel, D. L. (2005). Introduction to the major contribution: Counseling psychology and Online Counseling. *The Counseling Psychologist*, *33*(6), 761–775. doi:10.1177/0011000005278623

Mallen, M. J., Vogel, D. L., & Rochlen, A. B. (2005). The practical aspects of online counselling: Ethics, training, technology and competency. *The Counseling Psychologist*, *33*(6), 776–818. doi:10.1177/0011000005278625

Mammo, W. (2007). Demise, renaissance or existence of LIS education in Ethiopia: Curriculum, Employers expectations and professionals dreams. *The International Information & Library Review*, *39*(2), 145–157. doi:10.1016/j.iilr.2007.02.004

Maniar, N., Bennett, E., Hand, S., & Allan, G. (2008). The effect of mobile phone screen size on video based learning. *JSW*, *3*(4), 51–61. doi:10.4304/jsw.3.4.51-61

Manuel, P.-M., Aparicio Martinez, P., & Maria, D. R.-M., MP, D., Pinzi, S., & Pilar, M.-J.M. (2019). Characterization of biodiesel using virtual laboratories integrating social networks and web app following a ubiquitous- and blended-learning. *Journal of Cleaner Production*, *215*, 399–409. doi:10.1016/j.jclepro.2019.01.098

Manzo, K. K. (2009). Twitter lessons in 140 characters or less. *Education Week*, *29*(8), 1–14.

Maples, M. F., & Han, S. (2008). Cybercounseling in the United States and South Korea: Implications for counseling college students of the millennial generation and the networked generation. *Journal of Counseling and Development*, *86*(2), 178–183. doi:10.1002/j.1556-6678.2008.tb00495.x

Marinagi, C., Skourlas, C., & Belsis, P. (2013). Employing ubiquitous computing devices and technologies in the higher education classroom of the future. *Procedia: Social and Behavioral Sciences*, *73*, 487–494. doi:10.1016/j.sbspro.2013.02.081

Marks, J., & Janke, R. (2009). The future of academic publishing: A view from the top. *Journal of Library Administration*, *49*(4), 439–458. doi:10.1080/01930820902832579

Martinez, M. (2001). Key design considerations for personalized learning on the web. *Journal of Educational Technology & Society*, *4*(1), 26–40.

Martin, R. A. (2010). Finding free and open access resources: A value-added service for patrons. *Journal of Interlibrary Loan. Document Delivery & Electronic Reserves*, *20*(3), 189–200. doi:10.1080/1072303X.2010.491022

Compilation of References

Maslow, A. H. (1943). A Theory of Human Motivation. *Psychological Review*, *50*(4), 370–396. doi:10.1037/h0054346

Maternowsky, K. (2009). *Who profits from for-profit journals?* Retrieved from Inside Higher Ed website: https://www.insidehighered.com/news/2009/06/12/journals

Mayer, R. E. (1997). Multimedia learning: Are we asking the right questions? *Educational Psychologist*, *32*(1), 1–19. doi:10.120715326985ep3201_1

Mayer, R. E. (2001). *Multimedia learning*. New York: Cambridge University Press. doi:10.1017/CBO9781139164603

Mayring, P. (2000). Qualitative content analysis [28 paragraphs]. *Forum Qualitative Sozialforschung/Forum: Qualitative. Social Research*, *1*(2), 20. Retrieved from http://nbn-resolving.de/urn:nbn:de:0114-fqs0002204

McCrindle, M., & Wolfinger, E. (2009). *The ABC of XYZ: Understanding the global generations*. The ABC of XYZ.

McCrindle, M. (2008). *The ABC of XYZ: Generational diversity at work*. McCrindle Research Pty Ltd.

McGrath, M. (2014). Viewpoint: Open access–a nail in the coffin of ILL? *Interlending & Document Supply*, *42*(4), 196–198. doi:10.1108/ILDS-07-2014-0035

McGrath, M. (2015). A review of changes in the delivery of information to users. *The Bottom Line (New York, N.Y.)*, *28*(1/2), 70–76. doi:10.1108/BL-12-2014-0031

McLeod, B., & Allen-Craig, S. (2007). What outcomes are we trying to achieve in our outdoor education programs? *Australian Journal of Outdoor Education*, *11*(2), 41–49. doi:10.1007/BF03400856

McMillan, J. (2004). *Educational research fundamentals for the consumer* (4th ed.). Hershey, PA: Pearson Education.

Means, B., Toyama, Y., Murphy, R. F., & Baki, M. (2013). The effectiveness of online and blended learning: A meta-analysis of the empirical literature. *Teachers College Record*, *115*(3), 1–47. Retrieved from http://www.tcrecord.org/library/content.asp?contentid=16882

Meriläinen, M., & Piispanen, M. (2017). Ubiquitous learning in appropriate learning environments. *International Journal of Technology and Inclusive Education*, *7*(1), 1215–1223.

Merrill, M. D. (2002). First principles of instruction. *Educational Technology Research and Development*, *50*(3), 43–59. doi:10.1007/BF02505024

Merrill, M. D. (2007). First principles of instruction: a synthesis. In R. A. Reiser & J. V. Dempsey (Eds.), *Trends and issues in instructional design and technology* (pp. 62–71). Upper Saddle River, NJ: Pearson.

Merrill, M. D. (2009). First principles of instruction. In C. M. Reigeluth & A. Carr (Eds.), *Instructional design theories and models: Building a common knowledge base* (Vol. 3). New York, NY: Routledge Publishers.

Mezirow, J., & ... (1990). *Fostering critical reflection in adulthood: A guide to transformative and emancipatory learning*. San Francisco, CA: Jossey-Bass Publishers.

Mezirow, J. (1991). *Transformative Dimensions of Adult Learning*. San Francisco, CA: Jossey-Bass Publishers.

Mikelloydtech. (2013). *Internet of Learning-Things*. Retrieved from https://clwb.org/2013/06/10/what-is-ubiquitous-learning/

Milrad, M., Wong, L.-H., Sharples, M., Hwang, G.-J., Looi, C.-K., & Ogata, H. (2013). Seamless learning: an international perspective on next-generation technology enhanced learning. In Z. L. Berge & L. Y. Muilenburg (Eds.), Handbook of Mobile Learning (pp. 95-108). New York: Routledge.

Ministry of National Education Turkey. (2006). *Özel eğitim hizmetleri yönetmeliği* [Special education services regulation]. Author.

Misko, J. (2008). *Combining formal, non-formal and informal learning for workforce development.* Adelaide: National Council for Vocational Education Research.

Mouri, K., Uosaki, N., & Ogata, H. (2018). Learning analytics for Supporting Seamless Language Learning using E-book with Ubiquitous Learning System. *Journal of Educational Technology & Society, 21*(2), 150–163.

Moustakas, C. (1994). *Phenomenological research methods.* Thousand Oaks, CA: Sage. doi:10.4135/9781412995658

Muilenburg, L. Y., & Berge, Z. L. (2005). Students Barriers to Online Learning: A factor analytic study. *Distance Education, 26*(1), 29–48. doi:10.1080/01587910500081269

Mullen, P. M. (2003). Delphi: Myths and reality. *Journal of Health Organization and Management, 17*(1), 37–52. doi:10.1108/14777260310469319 PMID:12800279

Murillo, E. (2008). Searching usenet for virtual communities of practice: using mixed methods to identify the constructs of Wenger's theory. *Information Research, 13*(4). Available at: http://InformationR.net/ir/13-4/paper386.html

Murphy, A. (2012). Benchmarking OER use and assessment in higher education. *29th Annual Conference of the Australasian Society for Computers in Learning in Tertiary Education,* (1), 675–677.

Murray, C. (2008). Schools and social networking: Fear or education. *Synergy Perspectives: Local, 6*(1), 8–12.

Nadler, L. (1965). *Employee Training in Japan.* Education and Training Consultants.

Naido, S. (2006). *E-learning:a gude book of Principles, Procedures and Practices.* Commonwealth Educational Media Center for Asia.

Narayan, V., & Herrington, J. (2014) Towards a theoretical mobile heutagogy framework. In ASCILITE 2014: Rhetoric and Reality, Dunedin, New Zealand.

Narayan, V., Herrington, J., & Cochrane, T. (2019). Design principles for heutagogical learning: Implementing student-determined learning with mobile and social media tools. *Australasian Journal of Educational Technology, 35*(3), 86–101.

Nations, U. (1948). Universal Decleration. *Human Rights (Chicago, Ill.).*

Ndlangamandla, K. C. (2011). Library and Information Education and Training in Swaziland: Are view of Opportunities and Challenges. *Mousaion, 29*(2), 158–172.

Nejad, B. A., Abbaszadeh, M. M. S., Hassani, M., & Bernousi, I. (2012). Study of the entrepreneurship in universities as learning organization based on Senge model. *International Education Studies, 5*(1).

Ngubane-Mokiwa, S., & Letseka, M. (2015). *Shift from Open Distance Learning to Open Distance e-Learning.* Academic Press.

Ngubane-Mokiwa, S., & Letseka, M. (2015). *Shift from Open Distance Learning to Open Distance e-Learning.* New York: Nova Publishers.

Compilation of References

Ng, W., Nicholas, H., Loke, S., & Torabi, T. (2010). Designing effective pedagogical systems for teaching and learning with mobile and ubiquitous devices. In T. T. Goh (Ed.), *Multiplatform e-learning systems and technologies: Mobile devices for ubiquitous ICT-based education* (pp. 42–56). New York: IGI Global. doi:10.4018/978-1-60566-703-4.ch003

Nicholas, H., & Ng, W. (2009). Ubiquitous Learning and Handhelds. In P. Rogers, G. Berg, J. Boettcher, C. Howard, L. Justice, & K. Schenk (Eds.), *Encyclopedia of Distance Learning* (2nd ed.; pp. 2171–2176). Hershey, PA: IGI Global. doi:10.4018/978-1-60566-198-8.ch321

Nir-Gal, O. (2002). Distance Learning: The Role of the Teacher in a Virtual Learning Environment. *Ma'of u-Ma'aseh, 8*, 23–50.

Norberg, A., Dziuban, C. D., & Moskal, P. D. (2011). A time-based blended learning model. *On the Horizon, 19*(3), 207–216. doi:10.1108/10748121111163913

Nordin, N., Embi, M. A., & Yunus, M. M. (2010). Mobile learning framework for lifelong learning. *Procedia: Social and Behavioral Sciences, 7*, 130–138. doi:10.1016/j.sbspro.2010.10.019

Oblinger, D. (2003). Boomers gen-xers millennials. *EDUCAUSE Review, 500*(4), 37–47.

OECD. (2009). *Creating Effective Teaching and Learning Environments First Results from TALIS*. Retrieved 30.03.2019 from http://www.oecd.org/education/school/43023606.pdf

OECD. (2010). *Teachers' Professional Development: Europe in international comparison*. Retrieved 30.03.2019 from http://www.dgeec.mec.pt/np4/105/%7B$clientServletPath%7D/?newsId=157&fileName=Teachers__Professional_Development.pdf

Ogata, H., & Yano, Y. (2004). Context-aware support for computer-supported ubiquitous learning. In *The 2nd IEEE International Workshop on Wireless and Mobile Technologies in Education, 2004. Proceedings.* (pp. 27-34). IEEE. 10.1109/WMTE.2004.1281330

Ogata, H., Li, M., Hou, B., Uosaki, N., El-bishouty, M. M., & Yano, Y. (2011). SCROLL: Supporting to share and reuse ubiquitous learning log in the context of language learning. *Research and Practice in Technology Enhanced Learning, 6*(2), 69–82. Retrieved from http://apsce.net/RPTEL/RPTEL2011JulIssue-Article1_pp69-82.pdf

Ogata, H., Akamatsu, R., Mitsuhara, H., Yano, Y., Matsuura, K., Kanenishi, K., ... Morikawa, T. (2004). TANGO: supporting vocabulary learning with RFID tags. *Proc. Int. Workshop Series on RFID*.

Ogata, H., Matsuka, Y., El-Bishouty, M. M., & Yano, Y. (2009). LORAMS: Linking physical objects and videos for capturing and sharing learning experiences towards ubiquitous learning. *International Journal of Mobile Learning and Organisation, 3*(4), 337–350. doi:10.1504/IJMLO.2009.027452

Ogata, H., & Yano, Y. (2004). Context-aware support for computer-supported ubiquitous learning. *Proceedings of the 2nd IEEE International Workshop on Wireless and Mobile Technologies in Education*, 27-34.

Okur, R. M. (2012). *Açık ve uzaktan öğrenmede öğretim elemanlarına yönelik çevrimiçi destek sistemi tasarımı* [Designing online faculty support system for open and distance learning] (Unpublished doctoral dissertation). Anadolu University.

Oliveira, P. R. d., Oesterreich, S. A., & Almeida, V. L. d. (2017). School dropout in graduate distance education: Evidence from a study in the interior of Brazil. *Educação e Pesquisa, 44*, 1–20.

O'Malley, C., Vavoula, G., Glew, J. P., Taylor, J., Sharples, M., Lefrere, P., ... Waycott, J. (2005). *Guidelines for learning/teaching/tutoring in a mobile environment*. Academic Press.

Ommerborn, R. (1998). *Distance study for the disabled: National and international experience and perspectives.* Hagen, Germany: FernUniversität.

Ono, T., Iida, K., & Yamazaki, S. (2017). Achieving sustainable development goals (SDGs) through ICT services. *Fujitsu Scientific and Technical Journal, 53*(6), 17–22.

Organisation for Economic Co-operation and Development & European Commission. (2004). *Career guidance: A handbook for policy makers.* Retrieved May 20, 2019, from http://www.oecd.org/education/innovation-education/34060761.pdf

Oyarzun, B., Barreto, D., & Conklin, S. (2018). Instructor social presence effects on learner social presence, achievement, and satisfaction. *TechTrends, 62*(6), 625–634. doi:10.100711528-018-0299-0

Özdamar-Keskin, N., & Kılınç, H. (2015). Mobil öğrenme uygulamalarına yönelik geliştirme platformlarının karşılaştırılması ve örnek uygulamalar. *Açıköğretim Uygulamaları ve Araştırmaları Dergisi, 1*(3), 68–90.

Özkul, A. E., & Aydın, C. H. (2012). Öğrenci adaylarının açık ve uzaktan öğrenmeye yönelik görüşleri. In *Akademik Bilişim Konferansı.* Uşak: Uşak Üniversitesi. Retrieved from http://ab. org. tr/ab12/bildiri/42. pdf

Palloff, M. R., & Pratt, K. (1999). *Building Learning Communities in Cyberspace.* San Francisco: Jossey-Bass.

Palloff, M. R., & Pratt, K. (2007). *Building online learning communities: effective strategies for the virtual classroom.* San Francisco, CA: Jossey-Bass.

Palloff, R. M., & Pratt, K. (2003). *The virtual student: A profile and guide to working with online learners.* San Francisco, CA: Jossey-Bass.

Panagiotakopoulos, C., Lionarakis, A., & Xenos, M. (2003). Open and distance learning: tools of information and communication technologies for effective learning. *Proceedings of the 6th Hellenic European Research on Computer Mathematics and its Applications Conference.*

Panahon, I. I. A. (2007). *Developing an e-learning curriculum in European studies: The Philippine experience.* Paper presented at the Workshop on the Future of European Studies in Asia, Manila, Philippines.

Pandelis, P., Agnes, P., Isabel, B., Carles, S., Nardine, O., Concha, M., & Emilio, L. (2017). OPRM: Challenges to including open peer review in open access repositories. *Code4lib Journal,* (35). Retrieved from http://journal.code4lib.org/articles/12171

Pappano, L. (2012). Massive open online courses are multiplying at a rapid pace. *The New York Times.* Retrieved from https://www.nytimes.com/2012/11/04/education/edlife/massive-open-online-courses-are-multiplying-at-a-rapid-pace.html

Park, Y. (2011). A pedagogical framework for mobile learning: Categorizing educational applications of mobile technologies into four types. *The International Review of Research in Open and Distributed Learning, 12*(2), 78–102. doi:10.19173/irrodl.v12i2.791

Parslow, G. R. (2010). Multimedia in Biochemistry and Molecular Biology Education Commentary: Heutagogy, the practice of self-learning. *Biochemistry and Molecular Biology Education, 38*(2), 121–121. doi:10.1002/bmb.20394 PMID:21567809

Patton, M. Q. (2002). *Qualitative research and evaluation methods.* Thousand Oaks: Sage.

Pelling, N. (2009). The use of email and the internet in counselling and psychological service: What practitioners need to know. *Counselling, Psychotherapy, and Health, 5*(1), 1–25.

Compilation of References

Peña-Ayala, A. & Cárdenas-Robledo, L. A. (2019). A cybernetic method to regulate learning through learning strategies: A proactive and reactive mechanism applied in U–Learning settings. *Computers in Human Behavior*. doi: .2019.03.036 doi:10.1016/j.chb

Pence, H. E., & Losoff, B. (2011). Going beyond the textbook: The need to integrate open access primary literature into the chemistry curriculum. *Chemistry Central Journal*, *5*(1), 18–21. doi:10.1186/1752-153X-5-18 PMID:21470429

Peters, K. (2007). m-Learning: Positioning educators for a mobile, connected future. *The International Review of Research in Open and Distributed Learning*, *8*(2). doi:10.19173/irrodl.v8i2.350

Pimmer, C., Mateescu, M., & Gröhbiel, U. (2016). Mobile and ubiquitous learning in higher education settings. A systematic review of empirical studies. *Computers in Human Behavior*, *63*, 490–501. doi:10.1016/j.chb.2016.05.057

Pimmer, C., Mateescu, M., & Gröhbiel, U. (2016). Mobile and ubiquitous learning in higher education settings. A systematic review of empirical studies. Computers in human. *Behaviour*, *63*, 490–501.

Piovesan, S. D., Passerino, L. M., & Medina, R. D. (2012). U-ALS : A Ubiquitous Learning Environment. In *IADIS International Conference on Cognition and Exploratory Learning in Digital Age (CELDA 2012)* (pp. 197–204). Academic Press.

Piovesan, S. D., Passerino, L. M., & Medina, R. D. (2012). U-ALS : A Ubiquitous Learning Environment. *IADIS International Conference on Cognition and Exploratory Learning in Digital Age (CELDA 2012)*, 197–204.

Porter, S. (2015). *To MOOC or Not to MOOC: how can online learning help to build the future of higher education?* Chandos Publishing.

Porter, W. W., Graham, C. R., Spring, K. A., & Welch, K. R. (2014). Blended learning in higher education: Institutional adoption and implementation. *Computers & Education*, *75*, 185–195. doi:10.1016/j.compedu.2014.02.011

Powell, C. (2003). The Delphi technique: Myths and realities. *Journal of Advanced Nursing*, *41*(4), 376–382. doi:10.1046/j.1365-2648.2003.02537.x PMID:12581103

Pozdnyakova, O., & Pozdnyakov, A. (2017). Adult Students' Problems in the Distance Learning. Procedia Engineering, 178, 243–248. doi:10.1016/j.proeng.2017.01.105

Prabha, C. (2007). Shifting from print to electronic journals in ARL university libraries. *Serials Review*, *33*(1), 4–13. doi:10.1080/00987913.2007.10765086

Premlatha, K. R., & Geetha, T. V. (2015). Learning content design and learner adaptation for adaptive e-learning environment: A survey. *Artificial Intelligence Review*, *44*(4), 443–465. doi:10.100710462-015-9432-z

Prinsloo, P., & Slade, S. (2014). Educational triage in open distance learning: Walking a moral tightrope. *International Review of Research in Open and Distributed Learning*, *15*(4). doi:10.19173/irrodl.v15i4.1881

Quinn, C. (2000). *mLearning: Mobile, wireless, in-your-pocket learning.* LiNE Zine.

Ravenscroft, A. (2011). Dialogue and connectivism: A new approach to understanding and promoting dialogue-rich networked learning. *International Review of Research in Open and Distance Learning*, *12*(3), 139. doi:10.19173/irrodl.v12i3.934

Rehman, S. (2003). Information studies curriculum based on competency definition. *Journal of Education for Library and Information Science*, *44*(3-4), 276–295.

Rehman, S. (2012). Accreditation of library and information science programmes in the Gulf Cooperation Council nations. *Journal of Librarianship and Information Science*, *44*(1), 65–72. doi:10.1177/0961000611427723

Rekkedal, T., & Qvist-Eriksen, S. (2003). Internet based e-learning, pedagogy an support systems. In H. Fritsch (Ed.), The role of student services in e-learning systems (pp. 8-32). ZIFF.

Richards, D., & Vigano, N. (2013). Online counseling: A narrative and critical review of the literature. *Journal of Clinical Psychology*, *69*(9), 994–1011. doi:10.1002/jclp.21974 PMID:23630010

Richardson, J. C., & Swan, K. (2003). Examining social presence in online courses in relation to students' perceived learning and satisfaction. *Journal of Asynchronous Learning Networks*, *7*(1), 68–88.

Richardson, W., & Mancabelli, R. (2011). *Personal learning networks: using the power of connections to transform education*. Solution Tree Press.

Richey, R. C., & Klein, J. D. (2014). *Design and development research: Methods, strategies, and issues*. Routledge. doi:10.4324/9780203826034

Rienties, B., Brouwer, N., & Lygo-Baker, S. (2013). The effects of online professional development on higher education teachers' beliefs and intentions towards learning facilitation and technology. *Teaching and Teacher Education*, *29*, 122–131. doi:10.1016/j.tate.2012.09.002

Rijkenberg, N. (2019). *Budget Speech 2019/ 2020 by Minister of Finance (Neil Rijkenberg) at the Official Opening of Parliament*. Available from http://www.gov.sz/images/PM/Budget_Estimates_2019.pdf

Rodriguez, C. O. (2012). MOOCs and the AI-Stanford like courses: Two successful and distinct courses formats for massive open online courses. *European Journal of Open Distance and E-Learning*, *2*, 1–13.

Rogers, C. R. (1946). Significant aspects of client-centered therapy. *The American Psychologist*, *1*(10), 415–422. doi:10.1037/h0060866 PMID:20280375

Rogers, C. R. (1969). *Freedom to Learn*. Columbus, OH: Merill.

Rogers, C. R. (2003). *Client-Centered Therapy*. Constable & Robinson Ltd.

Rosen, L. D., Carrier, L. M., Pedroza, J. A., Elias, S., O'Brien, K. M., Lozano, J., & Ruiz, A. (2018). The role of executive functioning and technological anxiety (FOMO) in college course performance as mediated by technology usage and multitasking habits. *Educational Psychology*, *24*(1), 14–25.

Roubides, P. (2018). Emergent technologies shaping instructional design. In *Innovative Applications of Online Pedagogy and Course Design* (pp. 1–24). IGI Global. doi:10.4018/978-1-5225-5466-0.ch001

Rourke, L., Anderson, T., Garrison, D. R., & Archer, W. (1999). Assessing social presence in asynchronous text-based computer conferencing. *Journal of Distance Education*, *14*(2), 50–71.

Rowley, J., Johnson, F., Sbaffi, L., Frass, W., & Devine, E. (2017). Academics' behaviors and attitudes towards open access publishing in scholarly journals. *Journal of the Association for Information Science and Technology*, *68*(5), 1201–1211. doi:10.1002/asi.23710

Rubin, H. J., & Rubin, I. S. (2012). *Qualitative interviewing: The art of hearing data*. Thousand Oaks, CA: Sage Publications.

Compilation of References

Rumble, G. (2000). Student support in distance education in the 21st century: Learning from service management. *Distance Education*, *21*(2), 216–235. doi:10.1080/0158791000210202

Ryan, R. M., & Deci, E. L. (2000). Self-determination theory and the facilitation of intrinsic motivation, social development, and well-being. *The American Psychologist*, *55*(1), 68–78. doi:10.1037/0003-066X.55.1.68 PMID:11392867

Ryan, R. M., Kuhl, J., & Deci, E. L. (1997). Nature and autonomy: An organizational view of social and neurobiological aspects of self-regulation in behavior and development. *Development and Psychopathology*, *9*(4), 701–728. doi:10.1017/S0954579497001405 PMID:9449002

Saban, A. (2002). *Öğrenme Öğretme Süreci*. Ankara: Nobel Yayın Dağıtım.

Saccol, A. Z., Kich, M., Schlemmer, E., Reinhard, N., Barbosa, J. L., & Hahn, R. (2009, January). A framework for the design of ubiquitous learning applications. In *2009 42nd Hawaii International Conference on System Sciences* (pp. 1-10). IEEE.

Saccol, A. Z., Reinhard, N., Kich, M., Barbosa, J. L. V., Schlemmer, E., & Hahn, R. (2009). A framework for the design of ubiquitous learning applications. *Proceedings of the 42nd Annual Hawaii International Conference on System Sciences, HICSS*, 1–10. 10.1109/HICSS.2009.13

Şahin, A. E. (2001). Eğitim araştırmalarında Delphi tekniği ve kullanımı. *Hacettepe Üniversitesi Eğitim Fakültesi Dergisi*, *20*, 215–220.

Sahrir, M. S., Yahaya, M. F., Nasir, M. S., & Hamid, M. F. A. (2018). Design and Development of Mobile EZ-Arabic. Net for Ubiquitous Learning Among Malaysian Primary School Learners from Experts' Perspective. In *Mobile and Ubiquitous Learning* (pp. 341–361). Singapore: Springer. doi:10.1007/978-981-10-6144-8_20

Saint-Onge, H., & Wallace, D. (2012). Leveraging communities of practice for strategic advantage. Boston: Routledge. doi:10.4324/9780080496085

Saint-Onge, H., & Wallace, D. (2003). *Leveraging communities of practice for strategic advantage*. Boston: Butterworth-Heinemann.

Sakamura, K., & Koshizuka, N. (2005). Ubiquitous computing technologies for ubiquitous learning. In *Proceedings - IEEE International Workshop on Wireless and Mobile Technologies in Education, WMTE 2005* (Vol. 2005, pp. 11–18). IEEE. 10.1109/WMTE.2005.67

Salleh, A., Hamzah, R., Nordin, N., Ghavifekr, S., & Joorabchi, T. N. (2015). Online counseling using email: A qualitative study. *Asia Pacific Education Review*, *16*(4), 549–563. doi:10.100712564-015-9393-6

Sandeep, R. (2017). *Internet of (Medical) things in Healthcare*. IoT Central.

Scheer, B. S., & Lockee, B. B. (2003). Addressing the wellness needs of online distance learners. *Open Learning: The Journal of Open, Distance and eLearning*, *18*(2), 177-196.

Scott, D., & Morrison, M. (2005). *Key ideas in educational research*. A&C Black.

Seemiller, C., & Grace, M. (2016). *Generation Z goes to college*. John Wiley & Sons.

Senge, P. M. (1990). *The fifth discipline: The art and practice of the learning organization*. New York: Doubleday/Currency.

Seow, P., Hui, Z. B., Hyo-jeong, S., Chee-kit, L., Wenli, C., & Seow, P. Chen, W. (2008). Towards a framework for seamless learning environments 3Rs – A Primary Environment Education Project. *8th International Conference of the Learning Sciences (ICLS)*, *2*, 327–334.

Seow, P., Zhang, B., So, H. J., Looi, C. K., & Chen, W. (2008). Towards a framework for seamless learning environments. In *Proceedings of the 8th international conference on International conference for the learning sciences. International Society of the Learning Sciences*, (pp. 327-334). Utrecht, The Netherlands: Academic Press.

Sergiovanni, J. T. (1994). *Building community in schools*. San Francisco, CA: Jossey-Bass.

Sewart, D. (1993). Student support systems in distance education. *Open Learning*, *8*(3), 3–12. doi:10.1080/0268051930080302

Sezer, A., & Tokcan, H. (2003). İş birliğine dayalı öğrenmenin coğrafya dersinde akademik başarı üzerine etkisi. *Gazi Üniversitesi Gazi Eğitim Fakültesi Dergisi*, *23*(3), 227–242.

Sezgin, S., Bozkurt, A., Yılmaz, E. A., & van der Linden, N. (2018). Oyunlaştırma, eğitim ve kuramsal yaklaşımlar: Öğrenme süreçlerinde motivasyon, adanmışlık ve sürdürülebilirlik. *Mehmet Akif Ersoy Üniversitesi Eğitim Fakültesi Dergisi*, *45*, 169–189. doi:10.21764/maeuefd.339909

Shah, D. (2017). *Massive list of MOOC providers around the world*. Retrieved from https://www.class-central.com/report/mooc-providers-list/

Shah, D. (2018). *A product at every price: A review of MOOC stats and trends in 2017*. Retrieved from https://www.class-central.com/report/moocs-stats-and-trends-2017/

Shamseer, L., Moher, D., Maduekwe, O., Turner, L., Barbour, V., Burch, R., ... Shea, B. J. (2017). Potential predatory and legitimate biomedical journals: Can you tell the difference? A cross-sectional comparison. *BMC Medicine*, *15*(28), 1–14. doi:10.118612916-017-0785-9 PMID:28298236

Sharples, M. (2015). Seamless learning despite context. In Seamless learning in the age of mobile connectivity (pp. 41-55). Springer Singapore. doi:10.1007/978-981-287-113-8_2

Sharples, M. (2000). The design of personal mobile technologies for lifelong learning. *Computers & Education*, *34*(3-4), 177–193. doi:10.1016/S0360-1315(99)00044-5

Sharples, M., McAndrew, P., Weller, M., Ferguson, R., FitzGerald, E., Hirst, T., ... Whitelock, D. (2012). *Innovating Pedagogy 2012: Open University Innovation Report 1*. Milton Keynes, UK: The Open University.

Shearer, R. (2003). Instructional design in distance education: An overview. In M. G. Moore & W. G. Anderson (Eds.), *Handbook of Distance Education* (pp. 275–286). Mahwah, NJ: Lawrence Erlbaum Associates.

Shepherd, M. (2001). *M is for Maybe. Tactix: Training and communication technology in context*. Retrieved from http://www.fastrak-consulting.co.uk/tactix/features/mlearning.htm

Shih, J.-L., Chu, H., Hwang, G.-J., & Kinshuk. (2011). An investigation of attitudes of students and teachers about participating in a context-aware ubiquitous learning activity. *British Journal of Educational Technology*, *42*(3), 373–394. doi:10.1111/j.1467-8535.2009.01020.x

Short, J., Williams, E., & Christie, B. (1976). *The social psychology of telecommunications*. New York: Wiley.

Shotsberger, P. G., & Vetter, R. (2000). The Handheld Web: How Mobile Wireless Technologies Will Change Web-based Instruction and Training. *Educational Technology*, *40*(5), 49–52. doi:10.2307/44428613

Compilation of References

Siddiqui, S., Waqas, A., Soomrani, M. A. R., Qureshi, F., Gul, M., & Memon, I. (2018, July). *U-learning: A modern paradigm shift of learning from higher education students' perspective*. Paper presented at the 2018 International Conference on Information and Communication Technology for the Muslim World (ICT4M), Kuala Lumpur, Malaysia. 10.1109/ICT4M.2018.00043

Siemens, G. (2004). *Connectivism: A Learning Theory for the Digital Age*. Elearnspace. Retrieved January 8, 2014, from http://www.elearnspace.org/Articles/connectivism.htm

Siemens, G. (2004). *Connectivism: A learning theory for the digital age*. Retrieved from http://www.elearnspace.org/Articles/connectivism.htm

Siemens, G. (2005). Connectivism: A learning theory for the digital age. *International Journal of Instructional Technology and Distance Learning*, *2*(1), 3–10.

Siemens, G., & Gasevic, D. (2012). Guest editorial–Learning and knowledge analytics. *Journal of Educational Technology & Society*, *15*(3), 1–2.

Simonson, M., Smaldino, S., Albright, M., & Zvacek, S. (2014). *Teaching and learning at a distance: Foundations of distance education*. Charlotte, NC: IAP–Information Age Publishing, Inc.

Simpson, O. (2002). *Supporting students in online open and distance learning*. London: Kogan Page.

Simpson, O. (2012). *Supporting students for success in online and distance education*. New York: Routledge.

Skikos, N., Louka, V., Zwgopoulos, E., & Moschoudi, A. (2010). Η μεθοδολογία εκπαίδευσης ενηλίκων στην εξ αποστάσεως επιμόρφωση εκπαιδευτικών [Adult education methodology in distance learning teachers' training]. *Proceedings of the 2ndPanhellenic Educational Conference of Imathia "Digital and Online Applications in Education"*.

Skinner, A., & Zack, J. S. (2004). Counseling and the internet. *The American Behavioral Scientist*, *48*(4), 434–446. doi:10.1177/0002764204270280

Skolverket. (2000). *Lifelong learning and lifewide learning*. Retrieved May 20, 2019, from https://moodle.fct.unl.pt/pluginfile.php/32501/mod_glossary/attachment/10340/lifelong_and_lifewide.pdf

Smith, P. L., & Ragan, T. J. (2005). *Instructional design*. New York, NY: John Wiley & Sons, Inc.

Snape, D., & Spencer, L. (2003). The foundations of qualitative research. In J. Ritchie & J. Lewis (Eds.), *Qualitative Research Practice: a guide for social science students and researchers* (pp. 1–23). Thousand Oaks: Sage.

Solomon, D. J., & Björk, B. (2012). Publication fees in open access publishing: Sources of funding and factors influencing choice of journal. *Journal of the American Society for Information Science and Technology*, *63*(1), 98–107. doi:10.1002/asi.21660

Sonwalkar, N. (2013). The First Adaptive MOOC: A Case Study on Pedagogy Framework and Scalable Cloud Architecture-Part I. In MOOCs Forum (Vol. 1, pp. 22-29). Academic Press.

Specht, M. (2015). Connecting Learning Contexts with Ambient Information Channels. In *Seamless Learning in the Age of Mobile Connectivity* (pp. 121–140). Singapore: Springer. doi:10.1007/978-981-287-113-8_7

Srichanyachon, N. (2014). The barriers and needs of online learners. *Turkish Online Journal of Distance Education*, *15*(3), 50–59. doi:10.17718/tojde.08799

Ströhlein, G. (2003). On the use of information and telecommunication technology to support learning. In H. Fritsch (Ed.), The role of student services in e-learning systems (pp. 62-76). ZIFF.

Sturmberg, J. P., & Farmer, L. (2009). Educating capable doctors-a portfolio approach. Linking learning and assessment. *Medical Teacher*, *31*(3), 85–89. doi:10.1080/01421590802512912 PMID:19089726

Su, L., & Ma1, J. (Eds.). (2009). Semantic-oriented Ubiquitous Learning Object Model. National Research Project named Resources mService Architecture and Key Technology Study on Ubiquitous Learning.

Suler, J. (2000). Psychotherapy in cyberspace: A 5-dimensional model of online and computer-mediated psychotherapy. *Cyberpsychology & Behavior*, *3*(2), 151–159. doi:10.1089/109493100315996

Suler, J. (2011). The psychology of text relationships. In R. Kraus, G. Stricker, & C. Speyer (Eds.), *Online counseling: A handbook for mental health professionals* (pp. 21–53). San Diego, CA: Academic Press. doi:10.1016/B978-0-12-378596-1.00002-2

Sung, J.S. (2009). U-Learning Model Design Based on Ubiquitous Environment. *International Journal of Advanced Science and Technology, 13*.

Sun, P., Tsai, R., Finger, G., Chen, Y., & Yeh, D. (2008). What drives a successful e-learning? An empirical investigation of the critical factors influencing learner satisfaction. *Computers & Education*, *50*(4), 1183–1202. doi:10.1016/j.compedu.2006.11.007

Sussman, R. J. (2004). Counseling over the internet: Benefits and challenges in the use of new technologies. In G. R. Waltz & C. Kirkman (Eds.), *Cyberbytes: Highlighting compelling uses of technology in counseling* (pp. 17–20). Greensboro, NC: ERIC Clearinghouse on Counseling and Student Services.

Swan, K. (2003). Developing social presence in online discussions. In S. Naidu (Ed.), Learning and teaching with technology: Principles and practices (pp. 147-164). London: Kogan.

Swan, K., Garrison, D. R., & Richardson, J. C. (2009). A constructivist approach to online learning: the Community of Inquiry framework. In C. R. Payne (Ed.), *Information Technology and Constructivism in Higher Education: Progressive Learning Frameworks* (pp. 43–57). Hershey, PA: IGI Global. doi:10.4018/978-1-60566-654-9.ch004

Tahir, Z. M., Haron, H., & Singh, J. K. G. (2018). Evoluton of Learning Environmnt: A review of Ubiquitous Learning Paradigm Characteristics. *Indonesian Journal of Electirical Engineering and Computer Science*, *11*(1), 175–181. doi:10.11591/ijeecs.v11.i1.pp175-181

Tait, A. (2000). Planning student support for open and distance learning. *Open Learning*, *15*(3), 287–299. doi:10.1080/713688410

Tan, T. H., Liu, T. Y., & Chang, C. C. (2007). Development and evaluation of an RFID-based ubiquitous learning environment for outdoor learning. *Interactive Learning Environments*, *15*(3), 253–269. doi:10.1080/10494820701281431

Tan, T.-H., & Liu, T.-Y. (2004). The MObile-Based Interactive Learning Environment (MOBILE) and A Case Study for Assisting Elementary School English Learning 2. The MObile-Based Interactive Learning. In *Proceedings of the IEEE* (pp. 4–8). IEEE.

Tashakkori, A., & Teddlie, C. (Eds.). (2010). *Sage handbook of mixed methods in social & behavioral research*. Sage Publications. doi:10.4135/9781506335193

Taymaz, H. (1997). *Hizmetiçi Eğitim*. Ankara: Tokav Tapu ve Kadastro Vakfı Matbaası.

Compilation of References

TeachThought Staff. (2018). *The definition of blended learning*. Retrieved May 10, 2019 from https://www.teachthought.com/learning/the-definition-of-blended-learning/

Thomas, D., & Brown, J. S. (2011). *A new culture of learning: Cultivating the imagination for a world of constant change* (Vol. 219). Lexington, KY: CreateSpace.

Thomas, M. (Ed.). (2011). *Deconstructing digital natives: Young people, technology, and the new literacies*. Taylor & Francis. doi:10.4324/9780203818848

Thomas, R. M. (1998). *Conducting educational research: A comparative view*. Greenwood Publishing Group.

Thompson, A. D., Chuang, H. H., & Sahin, I. (Eds.). (2007). *Faculty mentoring: The power of students in developing technology expertise*. Charlotte, NC: Information Age.

Thorpe, M. (2003). Collaborative on-line learning: transforming learner support and course design. In A. Tait & R. Mills (Eds.), *Rethinking learner support in distance education* (pp. 198–210). London: Routledge.

Tindell, D. R., & Bohlander, R. W. (2012). The Use and Abuse of Cell Phones and Text Messaging in the Classroom: A Survey of College Students. *College Teaching*, *60*(1), 1–9. doi:10.1080/87567555.2011.604802

Tiwari, D. (2017). Paradigm Shifts in the Pedagogical Approaches. *Business Education and Ethics: Concepts, Methodologies, Tools, and Applications: Concepts, Methodologies, Tools, and Applications*, 343.

Tomkins, G. S., & Case, R. (2011). Curriculum development. In *Canadian Encyclopedia*. Historica-Dominion. Available at: http://www.thecanadianencyclopedia.com /articles/curriculum-development

Traxler, J. (2005). Defining mobile learning. *IADIS International Conference Mobile Learning Conference*, 261-266.

Traxler, J. (2009). Current state of mobile learning. In M. Ally (Ed.), *Mobile learning: Transforming the delivery of education and training* (pp. 9–24). Edmonton: AU Press, Athabasca University.

Trifonova, A. (2003). *Mobile learning-review of the literature*. University of Trento.

Trust, T. (2012). Professional learning networks designed for teacher learning. *Journal of Digital Learning in Teacher Education*, *28*(4), 133–138. doi:10.1080/21532974.2012.10784693

Tsai, C.-W., Shen, P.-D. & Chiang, I.-C. (2018). Investigating the effects of ubiquitous self-organized learning and learners-as-designers to improve students' learning performance, academic motivation, and engagement in a cloud course. *Universal Access in the Information,* 1-16. doi:10.100710209-018-0614-8

Turkish Statistical Institute. (2010). *Özürlülerin sorun ve beklentileri araştırması* [The problems and expactations of people with disability research]. Retrieved 10 December 2017, from http://www.tuik.gov.tr/PreTablo.do?alt_id=1017

Tyler, M. J., & Guth, L. J. (2003). Understanding online counseling services through a review of definitions and elements necessary for change. In J. W. Bloom & G. R. Walz (Eds.), Cybercounseling and cyberlearning: An encore. ERIC Document Reproduction Service No. ED 481146.

Uçar, H., & Kumtepe, A. T. (2018). Integrating Motivational Strategies into Massive Open Online Courses (MOOCs): The Application and Administration of the Motivation Design Model. In K. Buyuk, S. Kocdar, & A. Bozkurt (Eds.), *Administrative Leadership in Open and Distance Learning Programs* (pp. 213–235). Hershey, PA: IGI Global. doi:10.4018/978-1-5225-2645-2.ch009

University of California Office of Scholarly Communication and the California Digital Library eScholarship Program. (2007). *Faculty attitudes and behaviors regarding scholarly communication: Survey findings from the University of California.* Retrieved from http://osc.universityofcalifornia.edu/2007/08/report-onfaculty-attitudes-and-behaviors-regarding-scholarly-communication/

Valentine, D. (2002). Distance Learning: Promises, Problems, and Possibilities. *Online Journal of Distance Learning Administration, 5*(3). Retrieved from https://www.westga.edu/~distance/ojdla/fall53/valentine53.html

Van Merriënboer, J. J. G., Clark, R. E., & de Croock, M. B. M. (2002). Blueprints for complex learning: The 4C/ID-model. *Educational Technology Research and Development, 50*(2), 39–64. doi:10.1007/BF02504993

Van Merriënboer, J. J. G., & Stoyanov, S. (2008). Learners in a changing learning landscape: Reflections from an instructional design perspective. In J. Visser & M. Visser-Valfrey (Eds.), *Learners in a changing learning landscape: Reflections from a dialogue on new roles and expectations.* Dordrecht: Springer. doi:10.1007/978-1-4020-8299-3_4

Vargo, J. (2017). *Six examples of what personalized learning looks like.* Retrieved April 5, 2019 from https://www.edelements.com/blog/six-examples-of-what-personalized-learning-looks-like

Veletsianos, G. (2011). Higher education scholars' participation and practices on Twitter. *Journal of Computer Assisted Learning, 28*(4), 336–349. doi:10.1111/j.1365-2729.2011.00449.x

Verschraegen, G., & Schiltz, M. (2007). Knowledge as a global public good: The role and importance of open access. *Societies Without Borders, 2*(2), 157–174. doi:10.1163/187219107X203540

Virtanen, M. A., Haavisto, E., Liikanen, E., & Kääriäinen, M. (2018). Ubiquitous learning environments in higher education: A scoping literature review. *Education and Information Technologies, 23*(2), 985–998. doi:10.100710639-017-9646-6

Virtanen, M., Kääriäinen, M., Liikanen, E., & Haavisto, E. (2017). The comparison of students' satisfaction between ubiquitous and web-based learning environments in clinical histotechnology studies. *Education and Information Technologies, 22*, 2565–2581. doi:10.100710639-016-9561-2

Visser, R. D., Evering, L. C., & Barrett, D. E. (2014). #TwitterforTeachers: The implications of Twitter as a self-directed professional development tool for K–12 teachers. *Journal of Research on Technology in Education, 46*(4), 396–413. doi:10.1080/15391523.2014.925694

Vo, H. M., Zhu, C., & Diep, N. A. (2017). The effect of blended learning on student performance at course-level in higher education: A meta-analysis. *Studies in Educational Evaluation, 53*, 17–28. doi:10.1016/j.stueduc.2017.01.002

Vrasidas, C., & Glass, G. V. (Eds.). (2004). *Online Professional Development for Teachers.* Greenwich, CT: Information Age Publishing.

Vural, A. R., & Ceylan, V. K. (2014). *Fatih Projesi Eğitimde Teknoloji Kullanım Kursunun Öğretmen Görüşlerine Göre Değerlendirilmesi. 19. Türkiye'de İnternet Konferansı.* İzmir: Yaşar University.

Vygotsky, L. S. (1978). *Mind in society: The development of higher psychological processes.* Cambridge, MA: Harvard University Press.

Wang, H. Y., Liu, G. Z., & Hwang, G. J. (2017). Integrating socio-cultural contexts and location-based systems for ubiquitous language learning in museums: A state of the art review of 2009–2014. *British Journal of Educational Technology, 48*(2), 653–671. doi:10.1111/bjet.12424

Compilation of References

Wang, H.-Y., Lin, V., Hwang, G.-J., & Liu, G.-Z. (2018). Context-aware language-learning application in the green technology building: Which group can benefit the most? *Journal of Computer Assisted Learning, 2018*, 1–19. doi:10.1111/jcal.12336

Wang, R., Wiesemes, R., & Gibbons, C. (2012). Developing digital fluency through ubiquitous mobile devices: Findings from a small-scale study. *Computers & Education, 58*(1), 570–578. doi:10.1016/j.compedu.2011.04.013

Wang, W., & Wang, Z. (2008). Leveraging on u-learning to nurture a society of learning. *China Educational Technique & Equipment, 22*, 33–35.

Warlick, D. (2009). Grow Your Personal Learning Network: New Technologies Can Keep You Connected and Help You Manage Information Overload. *Learning and Leading with Technology, 36*(6), 12–16.

Wasko, M. M., Teigland, R., & Faraj, S. (2009). The provision of online public goods: Examining social structure in an electronic network of practice. *Decision Support Systems, 47*(3), 254–265. doi:10.1016/j.dss.2009.02.012

Waterhouse, S. (2005). *The power of e-learning: The essential guide for teaching in the digital age*. Boston: Pearson Education Inc.

Watson, J. (2018). The new world of republishing in open access: A view from the author's side. *Journal of Scholarly Publishing, 49*(2), 231–247. doi:10.3138/jsp.49.2.231

Wedemeyer, C. A. (1981). *Learning at the back door: Reflections on the non-traditional learning in the lifespan*. Madison, WI: University of Wisconsin Press.

Wei, C. W., Chen, N. S., & Kinshuk. (2012). A model for social presence in online classrooms. *Educational Technology Research and Development, 60*(3), 529–545. doi:10.100711423-012-9234-9

Weiser, M. (1991). The Computer for the 21st Century. *Scientific American, 265*(3), 94–105. doi:10.1038cientificamerican0991-94 PMID:1675486

Weiser, M. (1993). *Ubiquitous computing*. Computer.

Weller, M. (2011). *The Digital Scholar: How Technology is Transforming Scholarly Practice*. Bloomsbury Academic. doi:10.5040/9781849666275

Welsh Government. (2016). *Digital Competence Framework*. Cathays Park. Retrieved from http://learning.gov.wales/docs/learningwales/publications/160831-dcf-guidance-en-v2.pdf

Wenger, E. (2011). *Communities of practice a brief introduction*. Retrieved from http://wenger-trayner.com/wp-content/uploads/2013/10/06-Brief-introduction-to-communities-of-practice.pdf

Wenger, E. (1999). Communities of practice: The structure of knowledge stewarding. In C. Despres & D. Chauvel (Eds.), *Knowledge horizons: The present and the promise of knowledge management* (pp. 205–225). Boston, MA: Butterworth – Heinemann.

Wenger, E., McDermott, R., & Snyder, W. (2002). *Cultivating communities of practice*. Boston: Harvard Business School Press.

Wenzler, J. (2017). Scholarly communication and the dilemma of collective action: Why academic journals cost too much. *College & Research Libraries, 78*(2), 183–200. doi:10.5860/crl.78.2.183

Wesely, P. M. (2013). Investigating the community of practice of world language educators on Twitter. *Journal of Teacher Education*, *64*(4), 305–318. doi:10.1177/0022487113489032

Wexler, E. (2015). What a mass exodus at a linguistics journal means for scholarly publishing. *The Chronicle of Higher Education*. Retrieved from http://www.chronicle.com/article/What-a-Mass-Exodus-at-a/234066

Wicherts, J. M. (2016). Peer review quality and transparency of the peer review process in open access and subscription journals. *PLoS One*, *11*(1), 1–19. doi:10.1371/journal.pone.0147913 PMID:26824759

Wiebe, T. (2012). Books and websites, e-journals or print: If the source fits, use it. *College & Undergraduate Libraries*, *19*(1), 108–113. doi:10.1080/10691316.2012.652554

Wiley, D., & Hilton, J. III. (2009). Openness, dynamic specialization, and the disaggregated future of higher education. *The International Review of Research in Open and Distributed Learning*, *10*(5).

Wilson, E. K., & Humphrey, J. (2017). Successfully transitioning the world's largest chemistry subscription journal to a gold open access publication. Insights. *The UKSG Journal*, *30*(1), 38–46. doi:10.1629/uksg.343

Wilson, T. D. (2001). Mapping the curriculum in information studies. *New Library World*, *102*(11), 436–442. doi:10.1108/03074800110411875

Winitzky-Stephens, J. R., & Pickavance, J. (2017). Open educational resources and student course outcomes: A multilevel analysis. *The International Review of Research in Open and Distributed Learning*, *18*(4). doi:10.19173/irrodl.v18i4.3118

Wong, L. H. (2013a). Analysis of students' after-school mobile-assisted artifact creation processes in a seamless language learning environment. *Journal of Educational Technology & Society*, *16*(2), 198–211.

Wong, L. H. (2013b). Enculturating self-directed learners through a facilitated seamless learning process framework. *Technology, Pedagogy and Education*, *22*(3), 319–338. doi:10.1080/1475939X.2013.778447

Wong, L. H., & Looi, C. K. (2010). Vocabulary learning by mobile-assisted authentic content creation and social meaning-making: Two case studies. *Journal of Computer Assisted Learning*, *26*(5), 421–433. doi:10.1111/j.1365-2729.2010.00357.x

Wong, L. H., & Looi, C. K. (2011). What seams do we remove in mobile-assisted seamless learning? A critical review of the literature. *Computers & Education*, *57*(4), 2364–2381. doi:10.1016/j.compedu.2011.06.007

Wong, L.-H. (2012). A learner-centric view of mobile seamless learning. *British Journal of Educational Technology*, *43*(1), E19–E23. doi:10.1111/j.1467-8535.2011.01245.x

Wright, J. (2002). Online counselling: Learning from writing therapy. *British Journal of Guidance & Counselling*, *30*(3), 285–298. doi:10.1080/030698802100002326

Wu, H. K. (2003). Linking the microscopic view of chemistry to real-life experiences: Intertextuality in a high-school science classroom. *Science education*, *87*(6), 868–891. doi:10.1002ce.10090

Wu, P. H., Hwang, G. J., & Tsai, W. H. (2013). An expert system-based context-aware ubiquitous learning approach for conducting science learning activities. *Journal of Educational Technology & Society*, *16*(4), 217–230.

Xia, F., Yang, L. T., Wang, L., & Vinel, A. (2012). Internet of things. *International Journal of Communication Systems*, *25*(9), 1101–1102. doi:10.1002/dac.2417

Xia, J. (2010). A longitudinal study of scholars' attitudes and behaviors toward open-access journal publishing. *Journal of the American Society for Information Science and Technology*, *61*(3), 615–624. doi:10.1002/asi.21283

Compilation of References

Xu, H. (2003). Information technology courses and their relationship to faculty in different professional ranks in library and information science programmes. *Library & Information Science Research, 25*(203), 207–222. doi:10.1016/S0740-8188(03)00007-0

Yahya, S., Ahmad, E., & Jalil, K. A. (2010). The definition and characteristics of ubiquitous learning: A discussion. *International Journal of Education and Development Using ICT, 6*(1).

Yahya, S., Ahmad, E. A., & Jalil, K. A. (2010). The definition and characteristics of ubiquitous learning: A discussion [La definición y características del aprendizaje ubicuo: Un debate]. *International Journal of Education and Development Using Information and Communication Technology, 6*(1), 117–127.

Yahya, S., Ahmad, E. A., & Jalil, K. A. (2010). The definition and characteristics of ubiquitous learning: A discussion. *International Journal of Education and Development Using Information and Communication Technology, 6*(1), 117–127.

Yamada, M., Okubo, F., Oi, M., Shimada, A., Kojima, K., & Ogata, H. (2016). Learning Analytics in Ubiquitous Learning Environments: Self-Regulated Learning Perspective. In *ICCE 2016 - 24th International Conference on Computers in Education: Think Global Act Local - Main Conference Proceedings* (pp. 306-314). Asia-Pacific Society for Computers in Education.

Yang, H.-C., & Chang, W.-C. (2017). Ubiquitous smartphone platform for K-7 students learning geography in Taiwan. *Multimedia Tools and Applications, 76*(9), 11651–11668. doi:10.100711042-016-3325-2

Yang, S. J. H. (2006). Context aware ubiquitous learning environments for peer-to-peer collaborative learning. *Journal of Educational Technology & Society, 9*(1), 188–201.

Yang, Z. Y., & Li, Y. (2015). University faculty awareness and attitudes towards open access publishing and the institutional repository: A case study. *Journal of Librarianship and Scholarly Communication, 3*(1), 1–29. doi:10.7710/2162-3309.1210

Yen, C., Bozkurt, A., Tu, C., Sujo-Montes, L., Rodas, C., Harati, H., & Lockwood, A. (2018). A predictive study of students' self-regulated learning skills and their roles in the social network interaction of online discussion board. *Journal of Educational Technology Development and Exchange, 11*(1). doi:10.18785/jetde.0901.03

Yetik, E., & Keskin, N. Ö. (2016). Açık ve uzaktan eğitimde kesintisiz öğrenmenin kullanımı. *Journal of Research in Education and Teaching, 5*(1), 98–103.

Younghusband, D. (2005). Electronic journals and link resolver implementation. *Serials, 18*(1), 64–69. Retrieved from http://serials.uksg.org/articles/abstract/10.1629/1864/

Young, K. S. (2005). An empirical examination of client attitudes towards online counseling. *Cyberpsychology & Behavior, 8*(2), 172–177. doi:10.1089/cpb.2005.8.172 PMID:15938657

Zahrani, M. S. (2010). The benefits and potential of innovative ubiquitous learning environments to enhance higher education infrastructure and student experiences in Saudi Arabia. *Journal of Applied Sciences (Faisalabad), 10*(20), 2358–2368. doi:10.3923/jas.2010.2358.2368

Zamani, Z. A., Nasir, R., & Yusooff, F. (2010). Perceptions towards online counseling among counselors in Malaysia. *Procedia: Social and Behavioral Sciences, 5*, 585–589. doi:10.1016/j.sbspro.2010.07.146

Zarghami-Hamrah, S., & de Vries, M. J. (2018). Ubiquitous learning and massive communication in MOOCs: Revisiting the role of teaching as a praxis. *Ethics and Education, 13*(3), 370–384. doi:10.1080/17449642.2018.1509189

Zhang. (2010). *Study of Ubiquitous Learning Environment Based on Ubiquitous Computing*. Tianjin University of Science and Technology, Department of Computer Science and Information.

Zhang, J. P. (2008). Hybrid learning and ubiquitous learning. In *International Conference on Hybrid Learning and Education* (pp. 250-258). Springer. 10.1007/978-3-540-85170-7_22

Zhang, J., Zhang, L., & Liu, B. (2013). A Design of Ubiquitous Learning Environment with the Support of Pervasive Computing. *Applied Mechanics and Materials*, *397–400*, 2483–2486. doi:10.4028/www.scientific.net/AMM.397-400.2483

Zhu, Z.-T., Yu, M.-H., & Riezebos, P. (2016). A research framework of smart education. *Smart Learning Environments*, *3*(4), 1–17. doi:10.118640561-016-0026-2

About the Contributors

Serkan Çankaya completed his Ph.D. education in Anadolu University, Turkey. His areas of interest are educational technology, social learning networks, technology education, and coding education. He gives courses such as web design, operating systems, computer networks, and programming in Computer Education and Instructional Technology Department in Balikesir University, Turkey.

* * *

Yüksel Arıkan graduated Curriculum and Instruction field in 2002, his PhD in 2007 from Dokuz Eylül University (Izmir, Turkey) was received. Dr. Arikan currently teaches Project Development and Management, Measurement and Evaluation, School Experience and Teaching Practice at Computer Education and Instructional Technologies at Ege University (Izmir, Turkey). Dr. Arikan teaches New Trends in Instructional Technologies and E-learning Design at graduate level. Dr. Arikan also teaches Instructional Technologies and Material Design in other programs. Dr. Arikan in recent years, has been conducting academic studies in the areas of new learning environments and coding teaching.

Alev Ateş-Çobanoğlu received her MS in Computer Education and Instructional Technology (CEIT) from the Dokuz Eylul University in 2005 and her PhD in Curriculum and Instruction from Ege University in 2013. She worked as an ICT teacher at a high school of MoNE and is currently an Assistant Professor at CEIT program of Faculty of Education, Ege University. She studies blended learning, ICT integration in education, instructional technology and instructional design.

Aras Bozkurt is a researcher in the Department of Distance Education at Anadolu University, Turkey. He holds MA and Ph.D. degrees in distance education. He conducts empirical studies on online learning through resorting to critical theories including connectivism, rhizomatic learning, and heutagogy. He is interested in emerging research paradigms including social network analysis, sentiment analysis, and data mining.

Gökhan Çalışkan received B.A. and M.S. degrees in Computer Education and Instructional Technology from the Çanakkale Onsekiz Mart University. His research interests include: Online Learning, Technology Integration, Diffusion of Innovations, Teacher Training.

Beril Ceylan is a Dr. at Ege University, College of Education, Department of Computer Education and Instructional Technology in Turkey. She completed her PhD in 2015 at Anadolu University, Graduate School of Educational Sciences in Turkey. Among her research interests are technology integration, educational material design and instructional design. She has many book chapters, articles and presentations at these fields.

Veysel Demirer is an associate professor in Faculty of Education, Department of Computer Education and Instructional Technologies, Süleyman Demirel University where he lectures on educational science, educational technology, technology integration and teacher education. He specializes in educational technology, psycho-social aspects of technology use and Internet addiction.

Ibrahim Deryal is a Master graduate Student in Education Faculty of Suleyman Demirel University.

Sarah Felber is a Professor of writing at University of Maryland Global Campus and co-editor of the Journal of College Reading and Learning. She holds a Master of Distance Education and E-Learning degree from University of Maryland Global Campus and a Ph.D. in Linguistics from the University of Connecticut. Her research interests include academic literacy and online learning at the post-secondary level.

Hakan Genç currently works as an English teacher at the Ministry of National Education (MONE) in Turkey. He holds a bachelor's degree in education also a master's degree in distance education. He is a phd student at the department of distance education in Anadolu University. His research interests are lifelong learning, open and distance learning, learner support in open and distance learning.

Serkan Izmirli is an associate professor in the department of Computer Education & Instructional Technology at Canakkale Onsekiz Mart University in Turkey. He received his PhD in the same department at Anadolu University, Turkey. He is interested in multimedia learning, distance education, online learning, and instructional design.

Melih Karasu is phd student in department of Computer Education and Instructional Technologies (CEIT). He has also both bachelor's degree and master degree in department of CEIT. He is interested in research areas which are distance education, mobile learning, mobile programming and use of technology in education.

Whitney Kilgore has an extensive background in educational leadership, educational technology, strategic planning, learning management systems, professional service delivery, and organizational change. She holds a Master's in Curriculum and Instruction and a Ph.D. in Learning Technologies. Her primary areas of focus are faculty/teacher professional development, humanizing online instruction, and increasing learner engagement. She is currently the Co-founder & Chief Academic Officer for iDesign, a higher education service provider.

Murat Kılıç completed his undergraduate education in 2014 at Muğla Sıtkı Koçman University Department of English Language Teaching. He is currently pursuing his MA in Computer Education and Instructional Technology at Ege University.

About the Contributors

Tarik Kisla earned his BA degree in Mathematic department in 1998. Dr. Kisla graduate from International Computer Institute with his MS degree and Ph.D. in Information Technologies. He has another MS degree from Curriculum and Instruction at Ege University. Currently, Dr. Kisla is an Associate Professor at Ege University, Department of Computer Education and Instructional Technology in Turkey until 2002. His research interests are Distance Education, mobile Technologies and learning, mobile and web programming. Dr. Kisla teaches "web programming", "", Technology Integration in Education", "Mobile learning and programming", "Networks", "Operating Systems", "Object oriented Programing" courses in undergraduate and graduate levels in Ege University. He was in many projects related to information and communication technology and teacher education. He has presented in national and international conferences and published scholarly articles.

Serpil Kocdar works as an associate professor at the Open Education Faculty of Anadolu University, Turkey. She is a graduate of Economics and she has a master's degree in Distance Education. She worked in corporate banking sector as a vice manager from 1997 to 2002. She received her Ph.D. in Distance Education from Anadolu University in 2011. She worked at several departments of the Open Education Faculty such as the Assessment Department, R&D for Instructional Technologies Department and Quality Office. Currently, she works as a vice dean at the Open Education Faculty. Her research interests are quality assurance and accreditation, evaluation, e-assessment, instructional design and new learning technologies in open and distance learning.

Nikolaos Mouratoglou is graduate of the School of Philosophy and Education, Aristotle University of Thessaloniki. He holds an M.A. in Information Communication Technologies and an M.A. in Adult Education and Lifelong Learning. In addition, he is certified in Career Counseling and Vocational Guidance. Currently, he is pursuing a PhD in the School of Philosophy and Education. He is professionally involved in Career Counseling and delivers lectures at training programs provided by the National and Kapodistrian University of Athens and the University of the Aegean. He is an active researcher and writer in Greek Linguistics, Information and Communication Technologies, Career Counseling and Adult Education.

Ramashego Shila Shorty Mphahlele is a Lecturer at the University of South Africa in the Early Childhood Education. She obtained the following qualifications DEd: Psychology of Education (UNISA), Med: Inclusive Education (UNISA). She is teaching Mathematics, Science and Technology. Her research interests are Information Communication Technologies, student support and barriers to teaching and learning.

Nilgun Ozdamar received her Ph.D. from the Department of Computer Education and Instructional Technologies of the Graduate School of Educational Sciences of Anadolu University in the year of 2011. She was a visiting scholar at the University of Central Florida from 2009 to 2010. She got the best paper award at m-Learn Conference 2011 in China. Her research interests are Massive Open Online Courses, Global Education, Lifelong Learning, Mobile Literacy, Online Learning, Mobile Learning, Open and Distance Education.

About the Contributors

Alaattin Parlakkılıç is a faculty in Management Information System Department in Ufuk University in Ankara. He had been a faculty in Medical Informatics Department in Gülhane Medical School between 2012 and 2016. After graduation from Army Academy he also completed his information systems education in Computer Engineering and Information Technology, Middle East Technical University/ Turkey. He received PhD in Computer and Instruction Technology in Ankara University. His research focus and teaching is in the area of information technology, health informatics, e-learning, information security, web programming, system and network administration and computer networks. He completed his post-doctoral education in University of Missouri-Kansas City from 2013 to 2014 in USA.

Heather Robinson has worked in the computer technology field for 20 years and is presently an online learning consultant and adjunct faculty at the University of North Texas. She holds a Master's in Information Science and a Ph.D. in Learning Technologies from the University of North Texas. Heather has presented and is published on her research on social-constructivist online learning, instructional design, and faculty experiences with online technology adoption.

Pascal Roubides has spent two decades in the field of higher education, technology, and business, and has a diverse academic and professional background in both STEM and Social Sciences areas. His contributions are similarly diverse, from computational continuum mechanics, to online curriculum and program development, as well learning and behavioral analytics. He has been nationally recognized for excellence in learning design and has always been a proponent and leader in technology and online education initiatives.

Ozden Sahin Izmirli is an associate professor at Canakkale Onsekiz Mart University in Turkey. She earned her doctorate degree in Educational Technology from Anadolu University. Her research interests include: computer-supported collaborative learning, motivation and educational technology.

Fırat Sarsar is an Assistant Professor at Ege University, Department of Computer Education and Instructional Technology in Turkey. He earned his BA and MS degrees in the Department of Computer Education and Instructional Technology in Turkey. Dr. Sarsar graduated from Georgia State University in USA with his Ph.D. in Instructional Technology as a Fulbright scholar in 2014. His PhD was fully funded by Fulbright Scholarship. He taught "Computer Skills for the Information Age" course for undergraduate students at Georgia State University for 3 years. He was in many project related to technology integration and teacher education. He holds the Association for Educational Communications and Technology (AECT) Cochran Intern Award in 2013 which is given for recognition of young leaders of the field. Currently, He teaches "Social Media and Web2.0 tools in Education", "Internet for Educator", Technology Integration in Education" and "e-Learning Design" courses in undergrad and graduate levels in Ege University. His research interests are motivation, online learning, mobile technologies, e-learning and online feedback strategies.

Faye Taylor-Gribby completed her PhD in 2012 which concerned the influence of political economy and interpretations of sustainability within the post-disaster tourism redevelopment of Koh Phi Phi Island., Thailand. Her historical research has focused upon the political economy of post disaster tourism

About the Contributors

re-development and interpretations of sustainability. Currently however, she is pursuing research in the field of tourism and leisure behaviour; more specifically in respect of travel and nightlife consumption, neo-tribalism and the non-conformist behaviours of the cognitively young. She maintains an interest in the ethics and sustainability of tourism development and is currently planning to pursue pedagogical research concerning personalised and experiential learning.

Erkan Yetik is a researcher at Eskişehir Osmangazi University, Turkey. He holds an MA degree at Distance Education and, currently, works at the center of Distance Education at Eskişehir Osmangazi University.

George K. Zarifis is Associate Professor of Continuing Education in the Faculty of Philosophy, Department of Education at the Aristotle University of Thessaloniki. His research interests focus on adult educators' training and professionalisation, university continuing education, and comparative examination of adult learning and vocational education policies and practices in Europe. He has been an elected member of the Steering Committee of the 'European Society for Research on the Education of Adults' (ESREA) from 2008-2016, and he is the convener of the ESREA's Research Network on Adult Educators, Trainers and their Professional Development (ReNAdET). He publishes, edits and co-authors in the area of adult and continuing education, and participates in a large number of national and European research projects in the same field.

Index

A

Accommodation for Learners With Special Needs 151
ACRL Framework 59, 61, 70
adult education 94, 101, 118, 221, 223
affective expression 206, 214
Aristotle University 153, 158
Artificial Intelligence 2, 18, 179, 246, 256
assessment 107-108, 118, 120-121, 131-132, 141, 152, 157-158, 162, 168, 174, 248, 254-256, 280, 285
assistive technology 139, 142, 145, 147, 151
authentic learning 7-8, 203, 216, 221, 288

B

barriers 3-8, 10-11, 13-14, 54, 78, 95, 127, 139, 152, 159-162, 174, 252
blended learning 215, 217-219, 221-226, 231-232

C

challenges 3-4, 7, 11, 13-14, 58, 121, 138-139, 162, 233-235, 239, 242, 249-250, 258, 300
communities of practice 8, 72-74, 158
community of inquiry 201-202, 205, 210, 214
Community of Practices (CoPs) 91
context-awareness 97, 203-204, 217, 282, 295
CoPs 72-75, 77, 80-82, 84, 86, 91
Course Designer 70
curriculum 1-2, 26, 46, 144, 153, 159, 175, 244-247, 249-258, 281, 285

D

Delphi technique 106, 109-110, 121, 126
design 4, 19-20, 22-23, 25-26, 29, 45-46, 52-53, 55, 57, 62-63, 73, 80, 106-108, 111-114, 116-122, 129, 132, 140, 142, 145-146, 152-153, 155, 174, 182, 201-205, 209, 215-217, 220-226, 231-238, 240-241, 248, 256, 268, 279, 281, 283, 285-287, 289, 300
digital information literacy 52-55, 58-59, 62, 65, 70
digital world 2, 7, 18, 26, 47, 108, 117
discovery 55, 58, 61, 70
distance education 55, 95-96, 109, 111, 126, 129-132, 135, 139-140, 148, 154, 167, 177, 262-263, 265, 268-272, 274-276, 286, 301
Distance Education (DE) 126, 154
distance learning 8, 18, 106-107, 109, 111-112, 122, 126, 128-129, 131, 135-136, 138, 140, 148, 151, 153-154, 167, 226, 234-235, 262, 274, 276

E

Electronic Learning (E-Learning) 8, 18, 53, 97, 99, 101, 107, 112, 114, 126-127, 146-147, 177-178, 202, 206-208, 216, 218-219, 222, 238, 244-245, 247-248, 254, 256, 263-264, 281-282, 286, 288-289, 295-299, 306, 308, 310
Eswatini 244, 247-258

F

flexible learning 24, 128, 159, 162, 174, 231, 235, 288
Formal Settings 51
fulfillment 58-59, 70-71, 152

G

generations 176-177, 179-180, 183
group cohesion 206, 214

H

heutagogy 216, 279-289, 295
higher education services provider 233-234
human agency 284-285

I

informal learning 23, 25-27, 29, 45, 47, 73, 77, 86, 108, 111-112, 120, 127, 154, 177-178, 218, 288
informal settings 29, 51, 217
information literacy 52-59, 62, 65, 70
instructional design 20, 23, 25, 55, 153, 155, 174, 215, 220-221, 223-225, 231-236, 238, 241, 300
Internet of Things 115, 247, 256, 299-300, 310

L

learner support services 128-132, 135-136, 142
LEARNERS' EXPECTATIONS 176, 182
learning styles 4, 9-10, 18, 95-96, 118, 154, 232, 288
Library and Information Science 244-246, 249
lifelong learning 59, 153-154, 174, 245, 263, 266, 286-287, 297
Lifewide Learning 154, 175

M

MBA 234-235, 239-240
Mobile Learning 11, 28, 97-98, 108-109, 113-114, 126, 168, 177, 202, 215-216, 223-224, 231, 263-266, 281-283, 287, 289, 300, 308-309
Mobile-Assisted Language Learning 11, 13, 18
mobility 25, 28, 30, 93, 156, 178, 202, 222, 279, 281, 295-297, 308
MOOCs 19-20, 31-33, 39, 41-48, 51, 77, 221, 226, 289

O

online career counseling 152-153, 156-162, 164, 166-168, 175
online community 74, 85, 152-153, 157-158, 161, 163, 175
open access 52-65, 71, 222
Open and Distance Learning 106-107, 109, 122, 126, 128-129, 135-136, 138, 140, 148, 151
open and distance learning (ODL) 106-107, 126, 128
open communication 206, 214
Open Distance and e-Learning 8, 18
open distance e-learning 244-245
Open Education 127, 145-146
outdoor learning 203, 215, 217, 223-224, 232

P

Pedagogical Resource 1, 18
personal branding tools 159-160, 164-165, 175
Personal Professional Development 92, 94, 98-99
personalized learning 10, 97, 118, 121, 216-219, 221, 224-225, 232, 288
Professional Learning Communities 72-73, 75, 80-83, 91
Professional Learning Networks 72-73, 77, 80-83, 91

Q

QR code 97, 203, 209, 220

R

Radio Frequency Identification 11, 18, 202
Repository 71, 305
RFID 11, 31, 97, 202-204, 215-216, 223

S

scholarly sources 54-56, 58-59, 65, 71
seamless learning 1, 19-31, 43-48, 51, 106-108, 111-122, 127, 217, 220, 232
seamless learning management system 19-20, 45, 51
Self-Determined Learning 216, 284, 287, 289, 295
social learning 28, 44-45, 47, 74, 86, 91, 108, 112, 120, 127, 158
social presence 148, 201-202, 205-210, 214, 237
social presence techniques 208-210

T

Teacher Education Standards 295
technology integration 92, 101
tertiary education 250
traditional classroom 9, 18
Twitter 72-73, 77-79, 82-84, 191-192, 209

U

ubiquitous blended learning 215, 219, 221-226, 232
ubiquitous computing 19-20, 30-31, 42-44, 46-48, 51, 96-97, 177, 203, 216, 221-222, 296-297, 299-300, 308, 310
Ubiquitous Computing Tehnology 308, 310
Ubiquitous Learning 1-10, 13-14, 19-20, 30-31, 44-48, 51, 53, 55, 60, 65, 92, 96-97, 99-100, 107-109, 113, 127, 129, 176-178, 182-183, 190, 193-197, 201-204, 207-208, 214-226, 279-283, 286-289, 295, 297, 310
u-learning 30, 44, 96-99, 101-102, 127, 202-204, 206-210, 219, 221-223, 225-226, 280-283, 288-289, 296-304, 307-310
usability 262, 266, 268

W

web accessibility 139-140, 142, 148, 151

Purchase Print, E-Book, or Print + E-Book

IGI Global's reference books are available in three unique pricing formats:
Print Only, E-Book Only, or Print + E-Book.
Shipping fees may apply.
www.igi-global.com

Recommended Reference Books

ISBN: 978-1-5225-9348-5
© 2019; 454 pp.
List Price: $255

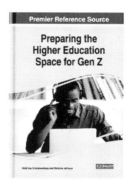

ISBN: 978-1-5225-7763-8
© 2019; 253 pp.
List Price: $175

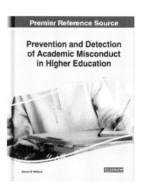

ISBN: 978-1-5225-7531-3
© 2019; 324 pp.
List Price: $185

ISBN: 978-1-5225-7802-4
© 2019; 423 pp.
List Price: $195

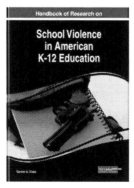

ISBN: 978-1-5225-6246-7
© 2019; 610 pp.
List Price: $275

ISBN: 978-1-5225-2998-9
© 2018; 352 pp.
List Price: $195

Do you want to stay current on the latest research trends, product announcements, news and special offers?
Join IGI Global's mailing list today and start enjoying exclusive perks sent only to IGI Global members.
Add your name to the list at **www.igi-global.com/newsletters**.

Publisher of Peer-Reviewed, Timely, and Innovative Academic Research

www.igi-global.com   Sign up at www.igi-global.com/newsletters   facebook.com/igiglobal   twitter.com/igiglobal   linkedin.com/igiglobal

Ensure Quality Research is Introduced to the Academic Community

Become an IGI Global Reviewer for Authored Book Projects

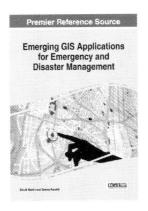
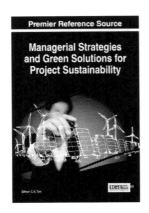

The overall success of an authored book project is dependent on quality and timely reviews.

In this competitive age of scholarly publishing, constructive and timely feedback significantly expedites the turnaround time of manuscripts from submission to acceptance, allowing the publication and discovery of forward-thinking research at a much more expeditious rate. Several IGI Global authored book projects are currently seeking highly-qualified experts in the field to fill vacancies on their respective editorial review boards:

Applications and Inquiries may be sent to:
development@igi-global.com

Applicants must have a doctorate (or an equivalent degree) as well as publishing and reviewing experience. Reviewers are asked to complete the open-ended evaluation questions with as much detail as possible in a timely, collegial, and constructive manner. All reviewers' tenures run for one-year terms on the editorial review boards and are expected to complete at least three reviews per term. Upon successful completion of this term, reviewers can be considered for an additional term.

If you have a colleague that may be interested in this opportunity,
we encourage you to share this information with them.

IGI Global Proudly Partners With eContent Pro International

Receive a 25% Discount on all Editorial Services

Editorial Services

IGI Global expects all final manuscripts submitted for publication to be in their final form. This means they must be reviewed, revised, and professionally copy edited prior to their final submission. Not only does this support with accelerating the publication process, but it also ensures that the highest quality scholarly work can be disseminated.

English Language Copy Editing

Let eContent Pro International's expert copy editors perform edits on your manuscript to resolve spelling, punctuaion, grammar, syntax, flow, formatting issues and more.

Scientific and Scholarly Editing

Allow colleagues in your research area to examine the content of your manuscript and provide you with valuable feedback and suggestions before submission.

Figure, Table, Chart & Equation Conversions

Do you have poor quality figures? Do you need visual elements in your manuscript created or converted? A design expert can help!

Translation

Need your documjent translated into English? eContent Pro International's expert translators are fluent in English and more than 40 different languages.

Hear What Your Colleagues are Saying About Editorial Services Supported by IGI Global

"The service was very fast, very thorough, and very helpful in ensuring our chapter meets the criteria and requirements of the book's editors. I was quite impressed and happy with your service."

– Prof. Tom Brinthaupt,
Middle Tennessee State University, USA

"I found the work actually spectacular. The editing, formatting, and other checks were very thorough. The turnaround time was great as well. I will definitely use eContent Pro in the future."

– Nickanor Amwata, Lecturer,
University of Kurdistan Hawler, Iraq

"I was impressed that it was done timely, and wherever the content was not clear for the reader, the paper was improved with better readability for the audience."

– Prof. James Chilembwe,
Mzuzu University, Malawi

Email: customerservice@econtentpro.com   www.igi-global.com/editorial-service-partners

www.igi-global.com

Celebrating Over 30 Years of Scholarly Knowledge Creation & Dissemination

InfoSci®-Books

A Database of Over 5,300+ Reference Books Containing Over 100,000+ Chapters Focusing on Emerging Research

GAIN ACCESS TO **THOUSANDS** OF REFERENCE BOOKS AT **A FRACTION** OF THEIR INDIVIDUAL LIST **PRICE**.

InfoSci®-Books Database

The **InfoSci®-Books** database is a collection of over 5,300+ IGI Global single and multi-volume reference books, handbooks of research, and encyclopedias, encompassing groundbreaking research from prominent experts worldwide that span over 350+ topics in 11 core subject areas including business, computer science, education, science and engineering, social sciences and more.

Open Access Fee Waiver (Offset Model) Initiative

For any library that invests in IGI Global's InfoSci-Journals and/or InfoSci-Books databases, IGI Global will match the library's investment with a fund of equal value to go toward **subsidizing the OA article processing charges (APCs) for their students, faculty, and staff** at that institution when their work is submitted and accepted under OA into an IGI Global journal.*

INFOSCI® PLATFORM FEATURES

- No DRM
- No Set-Up or Maintenance Fees
- A Guarantee of No More Than a 5% Annual Increase
- Full-Text HTML and PDF Viewing Options
- Downloadable MARC Records
- Unlimited Simultaneous Access
- COUNTER 5 Compliant Reports
- Formatted Citations With Ability to Export to RefWorks and EasyBib
- No Embargo of Content (Research is Available Months in Advance of the Print Release)

*The fund will be offered on an annual basis and expire at the end of the subscription period. The fund would renew as the subscription is renewed for each year thereafter. The open access fees will be waived after the student, faculty, or staff's paper has been vetted and accepted into an IGI Global journal and the fund can only be used toward publishing OA in an IGI Global journal. Libraries in developing countries will have the match on their investment doubled.

To Learn More or To Purchase This Database:
www.igi-global.com/infosci-books

eresources@igi-global.com • Toll Free: 1-866-342-6657 ext. 100 • Phone: 717-533-8845 x100

www.igi-global.com

Publisher of Peer-Reviewed, Timely, and Innovative Academic Research Since 1988

IGI Global's Transformative Open Access (OA) Model:
How to Turn Your University Library's Database Acquisitions Into a Source of OA Funding

In response to the OA movement and well in advance of Plan S, IGI Global, early last year, unveiled their OA Fee Waiver (Offset Model) Initiative.

Under this initiative, librarians who invest in IGI Global's InfoSci-Books (5,300+ reference books) and/or InfoSci-Journals (185+ scholarly journals) databases will be able to subsidize their patron's OA article processing charges (APC) when their work is submitted and accepted (after the peer review process) into an IGI Global journal.*

How Does it Work?

1. When a library subscribes or perpetually purchases IGI Global's InfoSci-Databases including InfoSci-Books (5,300+ e-books), InfoSci-Journals (185+ e-journals), and/or their discipline/subject-focused subsets, IGI Global will match the library's investment with a fund of equal value to go toward subsidizing the OA article processing charges (APCs) for their patrons.

   Researchers: Be sure to recommend the InfoSci-Books and InfoSci-Journals to take advantage of this initiative.

2. When a student, faculty, or staff member submits a paper and it is accepted (following the peer review) into one of IGI Global's 185+ scholarly journals, the author will have the option to have their paper published under a traditional publishing model or as OA.

3. When the author chooses to have their paper published under OA, IGI Global will notify them of the OA Fee Waiver (Offset Model) Initiative. If the author decides they would like to take advantage of this initiative, IGI Global will deduct the US$ 1,500 APC from the created fund.

4. This fund will be offered on an annual basis and will renew as the subscription is renewed for each year thereafter. IGI Global will manage the fund and award the APC waivers unless the librarian has a preference as to how the funds should be managed.

Hear From the Experts on This Initiative:

"I'm very happy to have been able to make one of my recent research contributions, 'Visualizing the Social Media Conversations of a National Information Technology Professional Association' featured in the *International Journal of Human Capital and Information Technology Professionals*, freely available along with having access to the valuable resources found within IGI Global's InfoSci-Journals database."

– **Prof. Stuart Palmer**,
Deakin University, Australia

For More Information, Visit: www.igi-global.com/publish/contributor-resources/open-access or contact IGI Global's Database Team at eresources@igi-global.com.

Are You Ready to Publish Your Research?

IGI Global offers book authorship and editorship opportunities across 11 subject areas, including business, computer science, education, science and engineering, social sciences, and more!

Benefits of Publishing with IGI Global:

- Free one-on-one editorial and promotional support.
- Expedited publishing timelines that can take your book from start to finish in less than one (1) year.
- Choose from a variety of formats including: Edited and Authored References, Handbooks of Research, Encyclopedias, and Research Insights.
- Utilize IGI Global's eEditorial Discovery® submission system in support of conducting the submission and blind review process.
- IGI Global maintains a strict adherence to ethical practices due in part to our full membership with the Committee on Publication Ethics (COPE).
- Indexing potential in prestigious indices such as Scopus®, Web of Science™, PsycINFO®, and ERIC – Education Resources Information Center.
- Ability to connect your ORCID iD to your IGI Global publications.
- Earn royalties on your publication as well as receive complimentary copies and exclusive discounts.

Get Started Today by Contacting the Acquisitions Department at:

acquisition@igi-global.com

www.igi-global.com/infosci-ondemand

InfoSci-OnDemand

Continuously updated with new material on a weekly basis, InfoSci®-OnDemand offers the ability to search through thousands of quality full-text research papers. Users can narrow each search by identifying key topic areas of interest, then display a complete listing of relevant papers, and purchase materials specific to their research needs.

Comprehensive Service
- Over 125,000+ journal articles, book chapters, and case studies.
- All content is downloadable in PDF and HTML format and can be stored locally for future use.

No Subscription Fees
- One time fee of $37.50 per PDF download.

Instant Access
- Receive a download link immediately after order completion!

"It really provides an excellent entry into the research literature of the field. It presents a manageable number of highly relevant sources on topics of interest to a wide range of researchers. The sources are scholarly, but also accessible to 'practitioners'."

– Lisa Stimatz, MLS, University of North Carolina at Chapel Hill, USA

"It is an excellent and well designed database which will facilitate research, publication, and teaching. It is a very useful tool to have."

– George Ditsa, PhD, University of Wollongong, Australia

"I have accessed the database and find it to be a valuable tool to the IT/IS community. I found valuable articles meeting my search criteria 95% of the time."

– Prof. Lynda Louis, Xavier University of Louisiana, USA

Recommended for use by researchers who wish to immediately download PDFs of individual chapters or articles.

www.igi-global.com/e-resources/infosci-ondemand

www.igi-global.com